SPARTA'S FIRST ATTIC WAR

The Grand Strategy of Classical Sparta,
478–446 B.C.

Paul A. Rahe

Yale UNIVERSITY PRESS

New Haven and London

Published with assistance from the Kingsley Trust Association Publication Fund
established by the Scroll and Key Society of Yale College.

Published with assistance from the foundation established in memory of
Amasa Stone Mather of the Class of 1907, Yale College.

Yale University Press books may be purchased in quantity for educational, business,
or promotional use. For information, please e-mail sales.press@yale.edu (U.S. office) or
sales@yaleup.co.uk (U.K. office).

Maps by Bill Nelson.

Set in Minion Roman and Trajan Pro types by Integrated Publishing Solutions.
Printed in the United States of America.

Library of Congress Control Number: 2018963646
ISBN 978-0-300-24261-4 (hardcover : alk. paper)

A catalogue record for this book is available from the British Library.

This paper meets the requirements of ANSI/NISO Z39.48-1992 (Permanence of Paper).

10 9 8 7 6 5 4 3 2 1

Laura T. Rahe

The Athenians are innovators, keen in forming plans, and quick to accomplish in deed what they have contrived in thought. You Spartans are intent on saving what you now possess; you are always indecisive, and you leave even what is needed undone. They are daring beyond their strength, they are risk-takers against all judgment, and in the midst of terrors they remain of good hope— while you accomplish less than is in your power, mistrust your judgment in matters most firm, and think not how to release yourselves from the terrors you face. In addition, they are unhesitant where you are inclined to delay, and they are always out and about in the larger world while you stay at home. For they think to acquire something by being away while you think that by proceeding abroad you will harm what lies ready to hand. In victory over the enemy, they sally farthest forth; in defeat, they give the least ground. For their city's sake, they use their bodies as if they were not their own; their intelligence they dedicate to political action on her behalf. And if they fail to accomplish what they have resolved to do, they suppose themselves deprived of that which is their own—while what they have accomplished and have now acquired they judge to be little in comparison with what they will do in the time to come. If they trip up in an endeavor, they are soon full of hope with regard to yet another goal. For they alone possess something at the moment at which they come to hope for it: so swiftly do they contrive to attempt what has been resolved. And on all these things they exert themselves in toil and danger through all the days of their lives, enjoying least of all what they already possess because they are ever intent on further acquisition. They look on a holiday as nothing but an opportunity to do what needs doing, and they regard peace and quiet free from political business as a greater misfortune than a laborious want of leisure. So that, if someone were to sum them up by saying that they are by nature capable neither of being at rest nor of allowing other human beings to be so, he would speak the truth.

THUCYDIDES' CORINTHIANS

Contents

Maps

Sparta's First Attic War

Introduction

From One War to the Next

IN his now neglected masterpiece *Marlborough: His Life and Times,* Winston Churchill once hazarded the following observation: "Battles are the principal milestones in secular history. Modern opinion resents this uninspiring truth, and historians often treat the decisions in the field as incidents in the dramas of politics and diplomacy. But great battles, won or lost, change the entire course of events, create new standards of values, new moods, new atmospheres, in armies and in nations, to which all must conform."[1] Though written with an eye to the duke of Marlborough's great victory in the battle of Oudenarde, Churchill's claim applies with no less and perhaps even greater force to the battle of Plataea.

Prior to Sparta's defeat of the Persian army captained by Mardonius on that occasion, there was every reason to suppose that the Greek resistance would collapse and that Hellas would soon fall under the sway of the Great King. When the dust had settled, however—after the Hellenes had capitalized on Sparta's victory by massacring the remains of Mardonius' army and after word came through that on the same day Hellenic marines had crushed the Achaemenid forces at Mycale on the coast of Asia Minor and had burned much of what remained after Salamis of the Great King's fleet—it gradually dawned on all concerned that affairs had undergone a decisive change; and everyone in and on the periphery of the Mediterranean world began to reassess.

Great victories provide an occasion for exultation. But when the celebration is over, the outcome can be sobering as well. This was especially true after

Plataea because the Hellenic victory had implications that were simply staggering. In absolute terms, Achaemenid Persia cannot now be judged the greatest power in human history. There were, in later ages, dominions that governed more individuals and a larger territory. Moreover, in modern times, technology has profoundly and repeatedly altered the strategic playing field. But if one were to assess the power of polities in relative terms, as perhaps one should, one would have to award this ancient Near Eastern kingdom the crown.

The empire ruled by Darius and his son Xerxes commanded a greater proportion of the world's population and of the world's resources than any dominion that preceded or followed it, and it dwarfed in size and population all conceivable rivals. The ancient world was lightly populated. The only regions of any size in which population density was considerable were the four great river valleys where irrigation made possible the production of grain or rice on a very grand scale. In the early fifth century, only one of these four—the Yellow River in China—lay outside Darius' and Xerxes' control. The Indus, the Nile, and the Tigris and Euphrates—over these mighty rivers, the fertile and well-watered valleys through which they ran, and the great civilizations to which they had given rise, the first two Achaemenid monarchs held sway; and the resources that this great empire afforded him Xerxes marshaled against the coalition of diminutive Greek cities that rallied behind Lacedaemon in 481, 480, and 479 B.C.

This, however, he did in vain. For the Greeks outfoxed him in 480, and they did the same in 479 to the commander Xerxes had left behind. To be precise, in 480, Themistocles of Athens lured the Great King's fleet into the narrows separating the island of Salamis from Attica—where, due to their numbers, the Persian triremes were apt to run afoul of one another and the much smaller, much less maneuverable Hellenic fleet could in familiar waters operate to best advantage; and there the Greek triremes wreaked such havoc on the Achaemenid force that it was left numerically and morally incapable of launching a second attack. In like fashion, in 479, Pausanias of Lacedaemon feigned a loss of nerve and staged an awkward, apparently desperate and disordered withdrawal from the southern bank of the Asopus River in Boeotia and lured Mardonius and the Persian infantry across that river onto terrain in the foothills of Mount Cithaeron where, he had good reason to believe, the Persian cavalry could not operate. There the badly outnumbered hoplites of Sparta and Tegea then formed up in a phalanx, shoved their way through the wall of wicker shields set up by the enemy, and relentlessly slaughtered without remorse the handful of dedicated spearmen bearing small shields and the multitude of shieldless archers doubling as spearmen whom Mardonius had deployed against them. That such a turn of events could take place—that a ragtag navy and militia, supplied by tiny communities hitherto best known for their mutual hostility, should annihilate an armada greater than any the world had ever known—this was then and remains today both a wonder and an occasion for rumination.

Was the war really over? Or would the Persians soon return? Was this victory an accident or an indication of a hitherto unsuspected strategic superiority on the part of the Hellenes? And if the war really was over, what was to come next? What in particular were the Greeks—and their Spartan leaders—going to do with this remarkable victory? Would they carry the war to Asia? Would they free from the Persian yoke the islanders of the eastern Aegean, the Greeks of Thrace and Asia Minor, as well as those of Cyprus? Or would they be satisfied with defending the Balkan peninsula and the nearby islands from Achaemenid domination?

These were the questions asked, and there were more—for the unity that the Hellenes had displayed to good effect in this war was unprecedented. Would they maintain the solidarity that they had achieved in 480 and 479? Or would they return to the petty squabbling among themselves that had occupied them in the past? Would the Spartans try to turn their hegemony into an empire? And what about the Athenians, who had demonstrated such remarkable prowess at Salamis?

These were among the concerns that preoccupied the handful of Greeks blessed with strategic vision and a broad, panoramic view—and none were more perplexing than those pertaining to Hellas proper. After all, wartime coalitions are fragile. Sentiment may well play a role in holding alliances together. But it is generally fear that occasions their formation and provides the requisite cement—and when, after a great victory, that fear gradually dissipates, as it will, coalitions tend slowly to dissolve and other antagonisms then emerge anew . . . or reappear.

There were a great many other questions asked as well. For each of the thirty-one cities participant in the victorious coalition had her own agenda; each had her own history and her own concerns; and the same can be said for the communities which had remained aloof—and also for those which had sided with the Mede. Moreover, most of the Greeks who lived in these divers cities and were possessed of a voice in the public assemblies that governed these tiny republics were not just parochial in their outlook. They were also profoundly confused, as well they might be. For they were on the threshold of an uncharted new world. The outcome of the contests at Plataea and Mycale had decisively altered not only the course of events. It had also opened up new vistas, and it had fired imaginations. In the process, it really had forged new standards of values, new moods, new atmospheres, in armies, in navies, and in cities, to which all in the foreseeable future would have to conform.

In *The Spartan Regime,* which was intended to serve as a prelude to a series of volumes on the evolution of Lacedaemonian foreign policy, I analyzed the character of the Spartan regime, traced its origins, and described the grand strategy it articulated before the Persians burst on the scene. In the early chapters of this volume's predecessor—*The Grand Strategy of Classical Sparta: The Persian Challenge*—I restated the conclusions reached in that prelude and explored in detail the manner in which the Lacedaemonians gradually adjusted that strategy to fit the new and unexpected challenge that suddenly loomed on the horizon when the Mede appeared. Then, in the last four chapters of the work, I described the fashion in which the Spartans organized and managed the alliance with which they confronted and defeated the invader bearing down on Hellas.

In this volume, I describe the manner in which the victorious Hellenes gradually and awkwardly worked out a postwar settlement that seemed to suit all concerned, and I pay particular attention, as in its predecessor, to a neglected aspect of the story—the grand strategy pursued by the Lacedaemonians, the logic underpinning it, and the principal challenge to which, in this period, it was exposed. Then, I consider the fragility of the postwar settlement; I trace its collapse, the manner in which Sparta and Athens came into conflict and then once again forged a modus vivendi; and I describe the character of the war they fought and explain its ultimate outcome. If I bring this volume to a close with the Thirty Years' Peace in 446, some thirty-three years after Mardonius' defeat in the battle of Plataea, it is not because I believe that this agreement settled anything. It is, rather, because Sparta's victory over Athens that year was a genuine achievement worthy of attention in its own right and because, in my judgment, Lacedaemon's Second Attic War deserves a separate treatment.

The series, of which this volume forms the second part, is meant to throw light not only on ancient Sparta; her first great adversary, Achaemenid Persia; and her initial chief ally and subsequent adversary, Athens. It is also intended as an invitation to reenvisage Greek history from a Spartan perspective, and I hope as well that these volumes will turn out to be a contribution to the study of politics, diplomacy, and war as such. As I have argued elsewhere and try in this volume and in its predecessors to demonstrate by way of my narrative, one cannot hope to understand the diplomatic and martial interaction of polities if one focuses narrowly on their struggle for power. Every polity seeks to preserve itself, to be sure; and in this crucial sense all polities really are akin. But there are also, I argue, moral imperatives peculiar to particular regimes; and, if one's aim is to understand, these cannot be dismissed and ostentatiously swept aside or simply ignored on specious "methodological" grounds. Indeed, if one abstracts entirely from regime imperatives—if one treats Sparta, Persia, Corinth, Argos, and Athens simply as "state actors," equivalent and interchangeable, in the manner advocated by the proponents of Realpolitik—one will miss much of what is going on.

Wearing blinders of such a sort can, in fact, be quite dangerous, as I suggested in the preceding volume. For, if policy makers were to operate in this fashion in analyzing politics among nations in their own time, they would all too often lack foresight—both with regard to the course likely to be taken by the country they serve and with regard to the paths likely to be followed by its rivals and allies. As I intimate time and again in this volume and in its predecessors, in contemplating foreign affairs and in thinking about diplomacy, intelligence, military strength, and its economic foundations, one must always acknowledge the primacy of domestic policy. This is the deeper meaning of Clausewitz' famous assertion that "war is the continuation of policy by other means."

It was with Clausewitz' dictum and this complex of concerns in mind that Julian Stafford Corbett first revived the term "grand strategy," reconfigured it, and deployed it both in the lectures he delivered at the Royal Naval War College between 1904 and 1906 and in the so-called Green Pamphlet that he prepared as a handout for his students.[2] And it was from this broad perspective that J. F. C. Fuller wrote when he introduced the concept to the general public in 1923. As he put it, "The first duty of the grand strategist is . . . to appreciate the commercial and financial position of his country; to discover what its resources and liabilities are. Secondly, he must understand the moral characteristics of his countrymen, their history, peculiarities, social customs and system of government, for all these quantities and qualities form the pillars of the military arch which it is his duty to construct." To this end, he added, the grand strategist must be "a student of the permanent characteristics and slowly changing institutions of the nation to which he belongs, and which he is called upon to secure against war and defeat. He must, in fact, be a learned historian and a far-seeing philosopher, as well as a skilful strategist and tactician."

With this in mind, Fuller drew a sharp distinction between strategy and grand strategy. The former is, he explained, "more particularly concerned with the movement of armed masses" while the latter, "including these movements, embraces the motive forces which lie behind them," whether they be "material" or "psychological." In short, "from the grand strategical point of view, it is just as important to realize the quality of the moral power of a nation, as the quantity of its man-power." To this end, the grand strategist must concern himself with establishing throughout his own nation and its fighting services "a common thought—the will to win"—and he must at the same time ponder how to deprive his country's rivals of that same will. If he is to outline for his own nation "a plan of action," he must come to know "the powers of all foreign countries and their influence on his own." Only then will he "be in a position, grand tactically, to direct the forces at his disposal along the economic and military lines of least resistance leading towards the moral reserve of his antagonist," which consists chiefly, he observed, in the morale of that nation's "civil population." In consequence, Fuller insisted, "the grand strategist" cannot restrict his purview to matters merely military. He cannot succeed unless he is also "a politician and a diplomatist."

Moreover, Fuller added, paradoxical though it may seem, "the resting time of the grand strategist is during war, for it is during peace that he works and labours."

> During peace time he not only calculates the resources in men, supplies and moral forces of all possible enemies, but, having weighed them, he, unsuspected by the enemy, undermines them by a plan. He attacks the enemy's man and weapon power by advising his government, (i.) to enter into alliance with other nations, (ii.) to limit his material resources by

gaining actual or fiscal control over commodities the enemy's country cannot produce; and, according to their ethics, his government attacks the enemy morally either by fostering sedition in his country or by winning over the approval of the world by the integrity of its actions.

It was Fuller's conviction that it is "manifestly impossible" for "one man to carry out the multifarious duties of the grand strategist," but he added that it is "manifestly absurd" for "more than one man to attempt to give direction to these duties, when combined in a plan of war."[3]

Some would argue that, in the absence of modern military education and something like a general staff, there can be no grand strategy; and there can be no doubt that in recent times institutions of this sort have proved invaluable. But, if having a general staff really were a necessity, we would have to reject the obvious: that the great statesmen of the past—such as Cardinal de Richelieu, Louis XIV, and the first duke of Marlborough; the elder William Pitt and George Washington; Alexander Hamilton and John Quincy Adams; Napoleon Bonaparte and the duke of Wellington; Otto von Bismarck; the Count of Cavour; and Woodrow Wilson—were all grand strategists. Moreover, as recent studies of the Roman, Byzantine, and Hapsburg empires strongly suggest, every political community of substance that manages to survive for an extended time is forced by the challenges it faces to work out—usually, by a process of trial and error—a grand strategy of sorts and to develop a strategic culture and an operational code compatible with that strategy.[4]

It is the burden of these volumes to show that in ancient Lacedaemon, Persia, Corinth, Argos, and Athens there were statesmen who approached the question of war and peace from a broad perspective of the very sort described by Fuller and that it is this that explains the consistency and coherence of these polities' conduct in the intercommunal arena. There is, I would suggest, nothing of lasting significance known by grand strategists today that figures such as Thucydides and the statesmen he most admired did not already understand.

When they alluded to Athens, Corinth, Megara, or Lacedaemon by name as a political community, and, strikingly, even when they spoke of one these *póleis* as their fatherland [*patrís*], the ancient Greeks employed nouns feminine in gender, personifying the community as a woman to whom they were devoted—which is why I with some frequency use the feminine pronoun to refer to Sparta and other Greek cities here.

Part I

YOKEFELLOWS

Many are the things that took place at that time in connection with that war that someone could mention with disguised malice while leveling an accusation against Hellas. For one would not be speaking correctly if one were to assert that Hellas defended itself. On the contrary, had the Athenians and the Lacedaemonians not made common cause in warding off the enslavement then on the march, all of the nations and peoples of Greece would in all likelihood be mixed up with one another, and there would be barbarians dispersed throughout Hellas and Greeks in barbarian lands, just like the peoples subject to Persia's tyranny who dwell in the present time carried from one place to another and herded about, miserably scattered in the manner of seeds.

PLATO

T HE battles of Plataea and Mycale are said to have taken place on the same day—27 or 28 August 479. When the dust settled, the supreme allied commander in each of the two theaters, a Spartan in each case, did what the immediate situation required.

In Boeotia, in the first ten days following the Greek massacre of Mardonius' Persian army, Pausanias son of Cleombrotus arranged for the burial of the dead and for the collection of booty. He made provision for the prisoners of war. He sacrificed to the gods; and, before distributing the booty, he set aside three-tenths of it for expenditure on dedications to Olympian Zeus, Poseidon, and Apollo. When a woman from the island of Cos, who had been the concubine of one of Xerxes' cousins, approached him as a suppliant, claiming to be the daughter of one of his guest-friends [*xénoi*], he treated her with kindness and apt consideration, sending her to Aegina in the Saronic Gulf, as she asked. When a leading figure from that island suggested that he mutilate the corpse of Mardonius as Xerxes had mutilated that of Leonidas after Thermopylae, Pausanias demurred. And when the Mantineians and Eleans appeared,

Figure 1. Marble torso of helmeted Spartan hoplite, fifth century B.C.
(Archaeological Museum of Sparta, Greece. Photographer: Ticinese, Wikimedia
Commons; Published 2019 under the following license: Creative Commons
Attribution-Share Alike 3.0 Unported).

weeks after the other Peloponnesians had joined the Hellenic forces and too
late to be of any use, he sent them back home in disgrace.[1]

At some point in this brief stretch of time—in the presence of all of the
allies within the Hellenic coalition—the Spartan regent formally returned to
the Plataeans, who resided in southwestern Boeotia, both their city and their
land. On this occasion, he solemnly acknowledged their right to reside there
and govern themselves by their own customs and laws, pledging in an oath to
which all subscribed that no one would be allowed to march against them
unjustly for the purpose of their enslavement, and promising that, if this happened, all of the allies then present would to the extent of their power come to
the Plataeans' defense.[2]

Once these pressing matters were settled, the son of Cleombrotus called
a formal meeting of the Greeks to consider what was to be done with the Thebans. It was September, and the normal campaigning season had come to an

end. Everyone involved was no doubt eager to return home. But something had to be done, nonetheless. They could not very well leave the Plataeans and the surviving Thespians undefended and at the mercy of the Medizers in charge of their openly hostile neighbor. Moreover, in the late 480s, when the Hellenic League was founded, its members had sworn to confiscate the lands of those communities which had joined the Persians without being compelled to do so, to sell their populations into slavery, and pay from the proceeds a tithe to Apollo at Delphi—and there is evidence suggesting that they may have reiterated this pledge in an oath taken not long before the recent battle.[3]

In the case of Thebes, however, there were reasons for hesitation. At that time, the city was not a democracy or even a broad-based oligarchy. She was governed by an exceedingly narrow clique. Moreover, although that clique had given earth and water when invited by Xerxes' emissaries to engage in that act of symbolic submission, it was an open question whether the city as such had medized willingly or only when compelled. After all, four hundred Thebans had volunteered to fight at Thermopylae; and, whatever its members' predilections may have been, the city's ruling order had not prevented them from showing up. The leading members of the Hellenic League were also, as it happened, members of an ancient body, called the Amphictyonic League, which was charged with looking after the temple of Apollo in Delphi and that of Artemis in Anthele near Thermopylae—and Thebes was a member as well. As such, they were pledged never to destroy another member or cut her off from fresh water, even in time of war.[4] It was up to the commanders conferring with Pausanias to judge how they should proceed.

In the event, in 479, Pausanias and his fellow commanders decided to demand of the Thebans only that they surrender those from among their compatriots who were most closely associated with the Mede. If the authorities at Thebes refused, they resolved to seize and destroy their city. To this end, on the eleventh day after the great battle, the Hellenes marched on Thebes and presented their demand. When it was rejected, they began ravaging the territory of the Thebans, and they initiated a siege. The terms on offer were generous, and the allied army was formidable. In fact, never in classical Greek history, before or after, was so great a host assembled. In time, the Thebans came to realize that their situation was dire and that resistance was futile. After twenty days, one of the principal Medizers suggested to his compatriots that

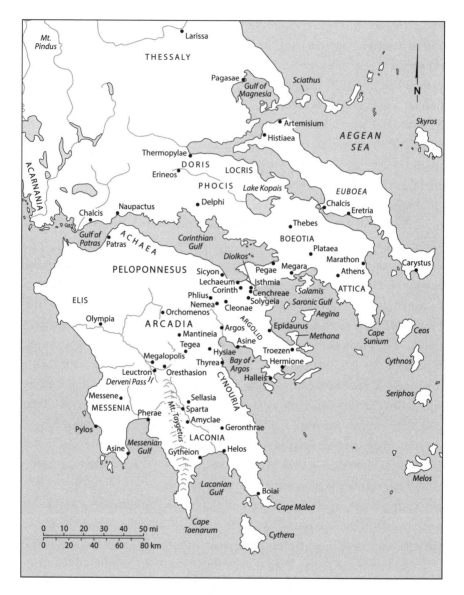

Map 1. Mainland Greece and the Islands Nearby

they offer the Hellenes as compensation a sum of money from the public treasury. If the Hellenes refused this as a settlement, he indicated a willingness to turn himself over for judgment and suggested that his colleagues do the same.

It was the latter course that was followed in the end. All of the leading Medizers—apart from the most prominent in their number, who managed to slip out of Thebes and effect an escape—handed themselves over to Pausanias. When it was learned that their chief had fled, his sons were seized and brought before the allied commander. But he deemed it an injustice to hold a man's offspring responsible for the misdeeds of their father, and so he ordered their release.

The Medizers were, we are told, confident that, if there was a trial, they could evade punishment by a resort to bribery. Pausanias anticipated this danger; and, after dismissing the allied army and sending everyone home, he carted his Theban captives off to Corinth and saw to their execution himself.[5] Though still in his twenties, the son of Cleombrotus proved to be judicious, and he handled himself throughout with dignity, magnanimity, grace, and dispatch.

If there was anything in the man's conduct at this time that might have seemed odd or in any way inappropriate, it was what he did after inspecting the tent of Xerxes, which had been left behind for Mardonius' use. For, on this occasion, Pausanias asked the Persian commander's cooks to prepare a meal of the sort that they customarily prepared for their master. And when they brought out the couches and tables of silver and gold with their expensive coverings and laid out for all to see a great and sumptuous feast, he asked his own servants to prepare a meal of the sort customarily consumed in Lacedaemon. Then, collapsing in laughter, he summoned the commanders of the various civic contingents within his army; and, pointing to the two meals, he said, "Men of Hellas, I have assembled you for this purpose—to show you the mindlessness of the Persian leader Mardonius, who, having a mode of living like this, came against us to deprive us of the dreary mode of living we possess."[6] Although one may doubt whether anyone at the time gave much thought to what these remarks revealed about the temptations to which Cleombrotus' young son was subject, in later years—for reasons that will soon become evident—there would be those who recognized in this event a portent of troubles to come.

Pausanias had been chosen to command the Lacedaemonians at Plataea as a consequence of his status as uncle of and regent for the boy-king Pleistarchus, the child to whom Gorgo, daughter of the Agiad king Cleomenes, had given birth not long after marrying her father's half-brother and heir Leonidas.[7] His success at Plataea had given Pausanias a measure of prestige that he would not otherwise have attained. But it did not alter the fact that he was not himself a king. He was, in fact, nothing more than a stand-in—destined to be superseded when Pleistarchus came of age—and everyone knew it, including, of course, Pausanias himself.

In exercising the powers associated with the kingship, Pausanias was not alone. Sparta was a constitutional monarchy of sorts; and, among other things, this polity was distinguished by the fact that in it there reigned not one, but two charismatic kings—both of whom traced back to the hero Heracles their lineage and their right to hold sway both in Messenia and in what we now call Laconia. To be precise, in addition to the Agiads, there was at Lacedaemon another royal family, that of the Eurypontids; and Leotychidas son of Menares, who held the Eurypontid kingship, had been dispatched in 479 to command the Hellenic fleet in the Aegean. His victory over the Persians at Mycale on the Anatolian coast brought to him as well both honor and renown. But it did not confer on him anything like the prestige that Pausanias had garnered—for Mycale was a sideshow in comparison with Plataea, and at Mycale the Spartans had played a secondary, supporting role. Nonetheless, the son of Menares was king in his own right, and this weighed heavily. In the Peloponnesus, as Dorians, the Spartans were recognized by all as interlopers. If, this fact notwithstanding, their dominion was considered meet and just, it was, as the Lacedaemonians readily acknowledged, solely because they were the followers of men who had inherited a rightful claim to Lacedaemon from Heracles, the laborious and long-suffering son of Zeus.[8]

After Plataea, it was for the most part obvious what Pausanias should do. There were major decisions to be thrashed out. But these required rumination; and, apart from the adjudication of matters regarding Thebes, they did not have to be made on the spot. In this particular, however, the situation in the Aegean in the immediate wake of the battle of Mycale was of a different character. Certain questions had to be confronted then and there, and their disposition had broad implications. In particular, Leotychidas and the other commanders, including Athens' admiral Xanthippus son of Ariphron, had to determine what should be done with the Aeolian and Ionian Greeks and their Dorian neighbors to the south—especially, the Hellenes residing on the large and fertile islands lying just off the Anatolian coast. For the Lacedaemonians and the vast majority of their Peloponnesian allies, this question posed a real dilemma.

Apart from the Corinthians, those within the Peloponnesus closely allied with Lacedaemon were landlubbers. They had learned the hard way an uncomfortable truth—that one could not prevent the Persians from launching assaults on mainland Greece if one left them in control of the sea. Ionia, however, they regarded as a land far away of which they knew little or nothing. The Samians, the Chians, and the citizens of Mytilene, Methymna, and the three other independent towns on the island of Lesbos were clamoring for admission into the Hellenic League. The Lacedaemonians were reluctant to make a permanent commitment to defend them against the Mede, and the same was almost certainly true for all or nearly all of their Peloponnesian allies. The war was over, and they had won. They all passionately wanted to go home and tend their farms—and none were more eager to bring the campaign to an end than the Spartans, who had peculiar reasons all their own for eschewing entangling alliances overseas.

Lacedaemonian Predilections

The citizens of Lacedaemon were all gentlemen of a sort. They did not work with their hands. They did not themselves farm. They relied, instead, on the labor of a servile population called helots. There was private property in land at Lacedaemon. Of this there can be no doubt. But we also have it on good authority that there was publicly held land and that an allotment carved out of this land and helots to work it were set aside for every member of the ruling order who was in good standing; and, though many scholars are incredulous, there is no good reason to reject the ancient reports. This system of provision left the Spartiates, who constituted Lacedaemon's juridically defined ruling order, free to devote their lives to exercise, to military training, to athletic contests, to music and the dance, to horseracing, hunting, dining together, and other gentlemanly pursuits.[9]

Theirs was a life of great privilege, which made them the envy of Greece. But with privilege, at Sparta, came heavy responsibilities—and danger besides. The helots greatly outnumbered their masters—perhaps by as much as a margin of seven to one, as the ancient literary evidence suggests; perhaps by a smaller ratio, as some modern scholars believe; but certainly by a lot. Those in Messenia—to the west across Mount Taygetus from the Eurotas valley, where the Spartans resided—regarded themselves and were regarded by outsiders as a people in bondage, and they sometimes rose up in revolt. Even in what we today call Laconia, it is fair to say, the helots lay in wait for a disaster to strike their masters. So, at least, we are informed by Aristotle.[10]

There appears to have been a helot revolt of some sort in 490 at about the time that the Persians had arrived at Marathon, and the Lacedaemonians, who lived in fear of another, were prepared to be extremely ruthless in their treatment of this servile class. Indeed, if Thucydides is to be believed, there was a time in which the Lacedaemonians, fearing the youthful vigor and the numerical superiority of the helots, issued a proclamation, inviting those in their number who regarded themselves as having demonstrated the greatest excellence in the city's wars to present themselves for judgment so that they could be freed. From among those who came forward, they then selected the two thousand they thought most likely to be formidable; and, after these men had celebrated their good fortune, they were made to disappear.

Thucydides does not specify the occasion, and many suggestions have been advanced by scholars. It is, however, tempting to suppose that, after the rebellion of 490 and the battle of Plataea in 479, the Spartans were especially nervous. And it is easy to imagine that they systematically culled from their helot population at this time the most manly of those who—as they marched from Lacedaemon through the Peloponnesus, the Megarid, and Attica into Boeotia; sojourned there for an extended period; and then marched back— had witnessed the freedom everywhere accorded their fellow Hellenes.[11]

In times of trouble, the Spartans could, of course, turn for help to their fellow Lacedaemonians—the *períoikoi* or "dwellers-about" who lived in villages or towns scattered about the margins of Laconia and Messenia. These Lacedaemonians, who may have been as numerous as were the Spartiates themselves, were not part of the ruling order at Lacedaemon. But, within their localities, they were self-governing, and at least some of them led a life of leisure and counted in their own right as gentlemen or *kaloì k'agathoí*, "men beautiful (or noble) and good (which is to say, brave)." Lacedaemon's *períoikoi* were loyal to the Spartiates, who provided them with protection and support. But they, too, harbored resentment; and, as the Spartans were reminded from time to time, they, too, were capable of revolt.[12]

At this time, Lacedaemon's rulers could also look to their allies within the Peloponnesus. The league that they had pieced together in the course of the sixth century was a real achievement. There had been wartime alliances in the past, but theirs was something new—a standing alliance system aimed solely at defense—and the circumstances in which it was forged deserve a glance, for they cast considerable light on the character of the league and on the role that it played in the calculations of the Spartans.

It was in the late eighth century that the Lacedaemonians first conquered the upper Pamisos valley in Messenia. There was a rebellion some two generations thereafter, and it was supported by the Arcadians, who lived to the north of Laconia and Messenia, as well as by the Argives, further afield in the northeast. With the latter, the Spartans had a long-standing dispute over the fertile district of Cynouria, which lay between Mount Parnon and the Aegean along the eastern coast of the Peloponnesus north-northeast of the Eurotas valley and directly south of the Argolid.

After putting down this seventh-century Messenian revolt and gradually extending their control to the entirety of Messenia, the Spartans fought a series of unsuccessful battles for the purpose of conquering the Arcadians. Then, at some point in the first half of the sixth century when the Argives and the Arcadians fell out and an opening presented itself, the Lacedaemonians did an about-face, abandoned the quest to extend their dominion, formed an alliance with the various cities in Arcadia, and ostentatiously associated themselves with the cause of liberty by toppling tyrannies throughout the Peloponnesus and replacing these populist regimes with broad-based oligarchies. To those who became their allies, the rulers of Lacedaemon offered protection, and in return they expected support should the helots of Messenia, those of Laconia, or both in tandem rise up in revolt. An elaborate system of carriage roads, built on a single gauge with an eye to linking the ancient political communities of that great peninsula, survives in fragments to this day as mute testimony to Lacedaemon's achievement as the hegemon of this alliance.[13]

The threat that the ruling order at Lacedaemon faced was formidable and permanent, and the grand strategy gradually worked out by the Spartans in response was all-encompassing. As I have argued in detail elsewhere, its dictates go a long way toward explaining the Spartans' aversion to commerce; their practice of infanticide; their provision to every citizen of an equal allotment of land and of servants to work it; the sumptuary laws they adopted; their sharing of slaves, horses, and hounds; their intense piety; the subjection of their male offspring to an elaborate system of education and indoctrination; their use of music and poetry to instill a civic spirit; their practice of pedagogic pederasty; the rigors and discipline to which they habitually subjected themselves;

and, of course, their constant preparation for war. It accounts as well for the articulation over time within Lacedaemon of a mixed regime graced with elaborate balances and checks. To sustain their dominion in Laconia and Messenia and to maintain the helots in bondage, the Spartans had to nourish within their ranks courage, discipline, determination, solidarity, and communal devotion. And to this end, they had to eschew faction; foster among themselves the same opinions, passions, and interests; and employ (above all, in times of great strain) procedures—recognized as fair and just and thought of as sanctioned by the gods—by which to reach a stable political consensus consistent with the dictates of prudence.[14]

At all costs, the Spartans also had to maintain the alliance system they had established within the Peloponnesus for the purpose of keeping the helots down, the Arcadians in, and the Argives out. In all other respects, however, Lacedaemon was what Otto von Bismarck would later call "a saturated power." All that she needed or wanted for the protection of her dominion and way of life was security for her hegemony within the Peloponnesus. If she erred with respect to matters in the world outside that great peninsular redoubt, she nearly always erred on the side of caution. This was her natural bias, for the Spartans had everything to lose and little to gain from risky adventures abroad. Prior to Xerxes' invasion of Greece, as I have demonstrated in this volume's predecessor, they watched and waited and did what they could do—unobtrusively without great risk of provocation—to delay, fend off, and otherwise thwart Persia's approach. In 481, however, the time for attempting to appear as inoffensive as possible came to an abrupt end; and, when the Great King announced his intentions regarding Hellas by demanding earth and water from all and sundry, the Lacedaemonians pulled together an alliance and girded their loins for the struggle to come. The *kaloì k'agathoí* of Sparta were not about to allow their well-being to become dependent on the whims of a Near Eastern despot.[15]

Leotychidas and the Greeks of the East

This did not, however, mean that the Spartans were eager to take to the sea permanently and extend their dominion to the shores of Anatolia. It was one thing to follow up on the Hellenic victory at Salamis, destroy the remnants of the Great King's fleet, and drive his navy out of the Aegean, as the forces commanded by Leotychidas had done. It was another for Lacedaemon

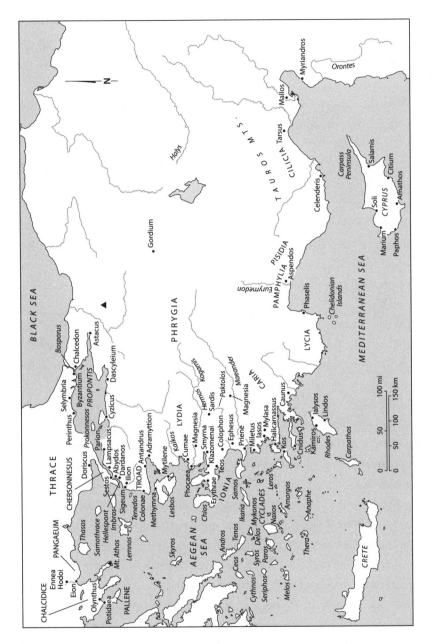

Map 2. Anatolia, the Aegean, and Cyprus

to become a full-fledged maritime power, sustain her wartime hegemony of the Hellenes, and extend her sway to Thrace and the shores of Asia Minor, to the approaches to the Black Sea, and even perhaps to Cyprus opposite the Levantine coast.

When the Samians, the Chians, and the citizens of the five *póleis* on the island of Lesbos came calling, Lacedaemon's Eurypontid king was not entirely pleased. He owed his office to the Agiad king Cleomenes, who was prepared to assert Spartan hegemony outside the Peloponnesus in places such as Aegina, Attica, and central Greece but who had repeatedly refused to countenance Spartan intervention overseas;[16] and he clearly shared the predilections of his late patron—as did most, but by no means all, of their compatriots. So, when approached by the Samians, the Chians, and the Lesbians, he and the other Peloponnesian leaders ventured a suggestion—that they be evacuated from the eastern Aegean and resettled on the lands of those who had medized in mainland Greece.

This was a canny proposal. It was consistent with the oath of vengeance taken by Athens, Sparta, Corinth, and the other cities that had joined the Hellenic League. It capitalized on the deep resentment directed both at the Argives, who had remained neutral in such a manner as to indicate that they favored the Mede, and at the Thebans and Thessalians who had—some with enthusiasm—embraced the cause of the Great King. If adopted, moreover, it promised to turn the Argeia, Boeotia, and Thessaly in central Greece into reliable dependencies of the eastern Greeks' prospective Lacedaemonian patrons. But, of course, it was not at all welcome to the Ionians, who were peoples of the sea—possessed of a great fondness for the islands on which they lived and for the region thereabout. And it should not have been welcome to any of the Hellenes—for the evacuation of these islands would have had as its consequence a surrender to the Mede of the eastern Aegean—which he could, in time, have employed as a staging ground for yet another invasion of Greece.

Leotychidas' suggestion was also not to the liking of the Athenians, who supplied more than half of the ships in his fleet and who had done most of the hard fighting at Mycale. They had no interest in making the Lacedaemonians masters of the Argeia within the Peloponnesus and of Boeotia and Thessaly to their north. In the waning years of the sixth century, the Spartans under the leadership of Leotychidas' patron Cleomenes had intervened in Athenian affairs on four occasions—twice, at the invitation of Athens' aristocratic Alcmeonid clan, to expel the offspring of the tyrant Peisistratus; again, to place in charge a narrow oligarchy made up of their clients; and a fourth time, in a vain and embarrassing attempt to restore Peisistratid rule.[17] The Athenians had not fought the Persians for the purpose of strengthening Sparta's hegemony within the Peloponnesus, of extending it to central Greece, and of subjecting themselves thereby to Lacedaemon.

Moreover, the Ionians were related to the Athenians—or, at least, thought they were. The Chians, the Samians, the Milesians, and their nearest neighbors spoke a dialect similar to Attic. They employed calendars almost identical to the one used at Athens. Their religious festivals were alike, and the Ionians traced their ancestry back to Attica. In antiquity, ethnicity may not have trumped all other concerns, but it nonetheless mattered a great deal.[18] It would not have been honorable for the Athenians to acquiesce in a surrender of the homelands of those everyone supposed their kin.

The Athenians had another reason for concern as well. Already at this time, Athens appears to have been dependent on imported grain; and, for this commodity, her citizens looked chiefly to the Milesian colonies in Crimea and scattered elsewhere about the Black Sea.[19] In consequence, they were eager to establish Hellenic control over the trade route running to the Euxine through the Hellespont, the Propontis, and the Bosporus; and they were intent on seeing that this route remained open. The Hellenic victory at Salamis, in which the Athenians and their commander Themistocles had played so prominent a role, was still fresh in their minds. They were not afraid of Persia's Great King. They had massacred his infantry at Marathon and Mycale. They had annihilated his navy at Salamis, and they saw no reason why they should not sweep his ships from the seas, defeat his soldiers again on land, and liberate the Greeks of the east from subjection.

Speaking on behalf of his compatriots, Xanthippus urged that the islanders be admitted to the Hellenic League, and he carried the day. Then, with Leotychidas in the lead, the Hellenes rowed up to the Hellespont to tear down the bridges built to enable Xerxes to lead his army from Asia to Europe, which they supposed then still intact. When they discovered that these bridges had been swept away by a storm, the Peloponnesians sailed home, which made good sense. It was September—a time of year when the weather is apt to be bad and certain to get much, much worse.

Xanthippus and the Athenians stayed on, nonetheless. For they were in-

tent on recovering for Athens the fertile farmland in the Thracian Chersonnesus, where Miltiades and his predecessors in the Philaid clan had long held
sway, and on securing for the Hellenes dominion over the Hellespont. They
even wintered there in order to join with the islanders of Ionia and the Greek
communities along the Hellespont that had already shaken off Persian rule in
besieging and capturing from the Mede that strategic peninsula's principal town
Sestos, which commanded the narrows where Xerxes' minions had bridged
the Hellespont. In time, at Athens, Sestos would come to be known proverbially as "the dinner table of the Peiraeus," which was by then the Athenians'
principal port.[20]

CHAPTER 1

The Postwar Settlement

If you were to overcome us and to take up an empire, you would swiftly lose all the goodwill which you have secured because of the fear we inspire—that is, if you hold to the pattern of conduct that you evidenced in the brief span when you were the leaders against the Mede. You have institutions, customs, and laws that do not mix well with those of others; and, in addition, when one of you goes abroad he follows neither his own customs and laws nor those employed in the rest of Hellas.

THUCYDIDES' ATHENIANS

IN late September or very early October 479, when the Thebans had surrendered their leaders and matters of immediate import had been sorted out at Plataea, the Hellenic army disbanded, and the various civic contingents marched home. It was time for the farmers of the Peloponnesus and the others who had gathered to fight the Mede to begin thinking about planting their crops in time for the winter rains.

The Plataeans, for the most part, remained where they were. Of course, some journeyed to the Peloponnesus, where their families had found refuge. But bringing them back did not take long, and all soon began rebuilding their homes and the walls of the town in which they resided. The Athenians were in a similar plight. Their families had been evacuated to Troezen, Aegina, and Salamis; and they had to be ferried home. Only then could they deal with the destruction wrought in Attica by the Mede.

Xerxes' stated aim had been to punish the Athenians for the damage that they had helped the rebellious Ionians inflict at Sardis in 498, and what he and the men under his command had failed to do when they briefly occupied Attica in 480 Mardonius and the soldiers whom Xerxes had left behind under his command did when they reoccupied Attica for a more extended period in the spring of 479. The city of Athens they left a shambles. The walls had for the most part been torn down and the temples leveled. Many of the houses had been destroyed.[1] Once the Athenians had retrieved their families, there was much for them to do.

The Persians were gone, and they were not apt to return any time soon. The Hellenes' control of the sea precluded that. To make it possible for his army to march from Sardis in Anatolia to and across the Hellespont, then through Thrace and Macedonia to Thessaly in Hellas and points south within the Balkan peninsula, Xerxes had had to ship foodstuffs in massive quantities well in advance by sea to depots established at regular intervals along the Aegean coast of Thrace and Macedonia. He had also had to send a great fleet and a host of merchant ships to accompany his army. He could not ignore the logistical imperatives. A second invasion of Greece by land he could not even begin to contemplate until he had first regained the maritime dominance Persia had once possessed.

One might then suppose that the Athenians could afford, at least for a time, to relax their guard and concentrate on rebuilding their homes and sowing their crops. They were not, however, a trusting lot; and so, with an eye to the danger that might be posed by their Hellenic neighbors and allies, they began right away to rebuild their city's walls.

Walls for Athens

Some of the Hellenes who lived in *póleis* nearby took fright. Initially, as long as the Persians were a presence in Greece and an imminent threat to the liberty of the Hellenes, Athens' neighbors regarded the two hundred triremes she had recently built as a great boon. Athens' fleet had made the Hellenic victory at Salamis possible. Themistocles' stratagem had worked. It was Athenian cunning that had drawn Xerxes' navy into the narrows where the Greeks were at an advantage. But what was regarded as a godsend while the Persian peril loomed large was perceived as a threat thereafter. Such is the nature of humankind. Athens had provided nearly half of the allied triremes that had fought at Salamis and more than half of those deployed at Artemisium and Mycale, and the marines on Athens' ships had won the last-mentioned of these three battles. Within Hellas, there had been a sudden, dramatic, deeply disturbing shift in the balance of power.

This cannot have pleased the Aeginetans. They had long been hostile to the Athenians. The two cities had fought a series of battles in the 490s and 480s, and they had made peace only because Xerxes was about to invade Hellas.[2] There was every reason to suppose that there would be trouble between the two communities down the line.

The Megarians may have been wary as well. A bit more than a century before, Athens had wrested the island of Salamis from Megara. On the mainland, the two cities bordered on one another; and, as was the norm in Hellas, the boundary between them was in dispute. It was only natural that the Megarians regard their neighbor with distrust.

The Corinthians may also have been nervous and even resentful. Their city was among the most powerful and wealthy in Hellas. It occupied an isthmus of great strategic importance, which separates the Saronic Gulf and the Aegean Sea more generally from the Corinthian Gulf, the Ionian Sea, the Adriatic, and the western Mediterranean as a whole; and this isthmus functioned also as the sole link by land between the Peloponnesus and the rest of the Balkan peninsula. In the Acrocorinth, which towers over the isthmus and the rich farmland within it, the Corinthians possessed an almost impregnable bastion. When occupied by troops, as Philip V of Macedon would later observe, this stronghold could be made to function as "fetters for Greece." The Acrocorinth is, as Plutarch puts it, "a lofty height springing up from the very center of Hellas, which, when garrisoned, blocks and cuts off in its entirety—from intercourse, passage, and martial enterprise both by land and by sea—the territory to the southwest."

As a consequence of her favorable situation and of the dangers associated with attempting to sail around the Peloponnesus, Corinth had long been the crossroads of the northeastern Mediterranean, and she was the chief emporium in the region. The safest way to transport goods from the Black Sea, Asia Minor, and the Aegean to Italy and other points west and vice versa was to take them to Corinth and convey them by one means or another across the isthmus separating the two gulfs. This could be done by carts operating between her port at Cenchreae on the Saronic Gulf and the one at Lechaeum on the Corinthian Gulf, but there was also a slipway [*díolkos*] by which galleys and other small vessels could be shifted from one side to the other. In consequence of their position, the harbor taxes they levied, the goods they produced, and the commerce in which they engaged as middlemen at home and as venturers abroad, the Corinthians grew wealthy.

Theirs was, as one would expect, a mercantile mentality. The city was

known for the work done by her artisans, and Herodotus tells us the Corinthians were less disdainful of those who engaged in the manual arts than any
people in Hellas. Corinth was also famous for the quality and number of her
prostitutes. Her citizens tended to know more about developments abroad
and sooner than any other community on the Greek mainland, and like modern merchant venturers they were exceedingly alert to the drift of events.

In the early archaic period, the Corinthians had been great colonizers,
and for the most part they maintained extraordinarily close ties not only with
the various colonies they had established to the west in Sicily and along the
trade route that ran through the Corinthian Gulf, the Ionian Sea, and the
Adriatic but also with the one colony that they had settled to the northeast on
the Pallene peninsula in western Thrace in the region we now call the Chalcidice. In keeping with their situation and the extensive connections they
maintained abroad, the Corinthians had from very early on established themselves as the leading naval power in the Greek heartland, and they paid close
attention to their security environment and did what they could to shape it.[3]

To this end, when Athens was relatively weak, the Corinthians had con-
sistently championed her cause. In the sixth century—when, at the suggestion
of the Spartan king Cleomenes, the Athenians formed an alliance with the Plataeans on the northern side of Mount Cithaeron, and the Thebans, who were
intent on uniting Boeotia under their leadership, mobilized—the Corinthians
had intervened in defense of Athens and Plataea with an eye to limiting Theban power. Later, in 506, when Cleomenes sought to impose a narrow oligarchy on Athens and make of her a Spartan satellite, they had dug in their heels
and balked. Later still, in 504, when that same Agiad king attempted to rein-
stall Hippias son of Peisistratus as tyrant at Athens, the Corinthians had publicly chided the Lacedaemonians for abandoning the opposition to tyranny that
had long served as a justification for their hegemony. Then, they had ostentatiously withdrawn their contingent from the allied army, and this had precip-
itated a withdrawal by Sparta's other Peloponnesian allies fatal to Cleomenes'
ill-considered scheme. Finally, in the 490s, when the Athenian fleet proved to
be inferior to the Aeginetan navy, the Corinthians had sold them used warships at a nominal price.[4] The fact that Athens' navy now greatly overshadowed
their own fleet may, however, have altered all prior perceptions and given the
Corinthians pause.

In his description of the battles of Artemisium and Salamis in 480, Herodotus has much to say about an antagonism that had purportedly grown up between Athens and Corinth. That decades later such an antagonism existed there can be no doubt. But it is by no means clear that Herodotus' reportage regarding the Corinthians in 480 can fully be trusted—for, in connection with this account, he repeats slander that we know to be untrue. He tells us, for example, that the Corinthians fled the Persian attack at Salamis, and we know that they were singled out and honored for their contribution to the Hellenic victory on this very occasion. He claims that the mound built for their dead at Plataea was empty, and Plutarch tells us that this was not the case.

Of course, Herodotus may well be correct in reporting that the Corinthians favored abandoning Salamis and concentrating the Hellenic fleet in the vicinity of the Corinthiad, where the Peloponnesians were building a wall to keep the Persians out. It is easy to see why they might wrongly suppose such a repositioning in their interest. His claim, however, that their commander Adeimantus expressed seething contempt for the Athenians at the time is apt to be yet another apocryphal tale—for, in the circumstances, such a diatribe would have been impolitic in the extreme. Given the size of Athens' contribution to the allied fleet, it was not in the interest of the Corinthians to infuriate the Athenians at this time. The former could not hope to fend off the Persians without the cooperation of the latter.[5]

Herodotus was a partisan of Athens, and he may have fallen prey to self-justifying tales concocted by the Athenians in later years. Thucydides claims that the deep-seated hatred that the Corinthians later directed at Athens had its beginning almost two decades after 479,[6] and there is evidence suggesting that he was right. We know that Themistocles was chosen to arbitrate a dispute between Corinth and Corcyra. Although we are not told when this took place, it is hard to believe that the Athenian possessed the requisite stature prior to the formation of the Hellenic League. After Salamis, however, Themistocles would have been the natural choice for such a task.[7] But he certainly would not have been selected had his exchanges with Adeimantus on the eve of the battle of Salamis been as bitter as Herodotus claims.

Of course, none of this rules out the possibility that Athens' sudden rise to maritime preeminence worried the Corinthians. When Thucydides tells us that Sparta's allies were "afraid" because of "the number" of ships in Athens' navy and "the daring" that the Athenians had displayed in the war against the Mede and when he adds that they stirred up the Lacedaemonians and per-

Figure 2. Bust of Themistocles (Museo Ostiense in Ostia Antica: Photographer: Sailko, Wikimedia Commons; Published 2019 under the following license: Creative Commons Attribution 3.0 Unported).

suaded them to try to nip Athenian power in the bud by preventing the Athenians from rebuilding the walls of their city, it is no surprise that there is evidence strongly suggesting that Aegina was involved. Her pre–Persian Wars conflict with Athens virtually guaranteed as much. The fact, however, that decades thereafter the Corinthians pointedly criticized the failure of the Lacedaemonians to act decisively on this particular occasion strongly suggests a sense of grievance on their part, which would make especially good sense if they, too, had at the time lodged a complaint. The arrangement proposed— which would have rendered Athens defenseless on land—was, in any case, just the sort of thing that the Lacedaemonians, who were supreme in war on that element, would have preferred; and we can easily imagine their doing precisely what they are said to have done: which was to urge that the Athenians not rebuild their walls but join with them in tearing down the walls of every city on the Greek mainland outside the Peloponnesus.[8]

That this Lacedaemonian appeal was disingenuous was no doubt obvious to all concerned. No one who bothered to think about the matter could seriously suppose that there was any real danger that the Persians would soon launch another invasion of Hellas by land and make use of its fortified cities, as the Spartans claimed. What the request they made to the Athenians did do, however, was offer an opening to Themistocles son of Neocles.

The architect of the Hellenic victory in the battle of Salamis had in the aftermath of that great achievement quickly lost the confidence and support of his compatriots. When, near the gap between Andros and Euboea, Eurybiades, the Spartan commander of the allied fleet, had called off its pursuit of the departing Persian armada, Themistocles had persuaded the Athenians to comply with the man's orders, urging them to put off further campaigning until the spring and to return home and sow their crops. What this man of uncanny foresight failed on this occasion to foresee was that Xerxes would leave Mardonius and an army behind in northern Greece to renew Persia's effort to conquer Hellas. When the Athenians learned that this was the case and, anticipating another invasion of Attica, realized that there was no point in their sowing crops, they were furious—furious at the Spartans and the Peloponnesians for their reluctance to confront the Mede to the north of Attica in Boeotia, and even more furious at the Athenian commander who had so persistently subordinated Athens' efforts in the war to those of these same Spartans and Peloponnesians. It did not help that, at the time, Themistocles himself was lionized at Lacedaemon and elsewhere in the Peloponnesus; and it did not help that, at home, he put on airs and became insufferable. Athens was a democracy. Given his achievements, this great man would, in any case, have been an object of envy. Now, however, he became an object of anger and resentment as well. In consequence, the Athenians deprived Themistocles of his generalship late in 480, and when the time came for the election of those who would hold command in 479, he was passed over.[9]

Now, however, the war was finished and done. The time for fury had passed. His fellow Athenians were once again appreciative of the great statesman who had persuaded them to build their fleet and who had tricked the Persians into fighting in the narrows at Salamis—and, in the circumstances they were even willing once again to heed his advice. When Athens' Odysseus, as he came to be called, took the lead in the assembly, urging that Sparta's ambassadors be dismissed, his compatriots complied. They adopted his suggestion as well when—either in the assembly or, more likely, as one source suggests, in private before the probouleutic Council of 500 that set its agenda and functioned for Athens as an executive—he proposed an elaborate stratagem designed to fool the Lacedaemonians and buy time. On his advice, the Athenians sent him off immediately on an embassy to Lacedaemon. In the meantime, they labored on the walls with their wives, children, and slaves and the city's metics by day and by night, using whatever materials were ready to hand. And they refrained from sending his fellow ambassadors to join him and address the Lacedaemonians until those walls had been raised to a level that made Athens defensible. In places, the surviving remnants of the walls that they constructed at this time reflect the haste with which they had to work and the absence of genuinely suitable materials.[10]

At Sparta, where Themistocles was still revered for his foresight and res-oluteness, for a time he was apparently believed when he begged off speaking to the assembly on the grounds that his colleagues were on their way. When reports came in from Lacedaemon's allies about what was really going on, he lied shamelessly, denying what he knew to be true, and urging the Lacedae-monians to send some Spartans to look things over and report on what was taking place. These men—three former ephors, Cornelius Nepos implies—he then in a message urged the Athenians to detain until he and his fellow am-bassadors should return. And so—when Habronichus son of Lysicles, a close friend of Themistocles who had worked with him at Artemisium, and Aris-teides son of Lysimachus, who had been the Athenian commander at Plataea, arrived with word that the walls were of sufficient height—Themistocles felt free boldly and brazenly to tell the Spartans that Athens was now sufficiently fortified to be defensible and that in the future they should, in sending em-bassies, presume that the Athenians were capable of discerning both their own interests and those that were shared. Along the way, he pointedly reminded the Lacedaemonians that the Athenians had decided to abandon their city and embark on their ships without consulting them, and he argued that the Athe-nians' possession of a fortified city was better not only for them but also for the rest of the Hellenes. "In the absence of a military establishment rivaling those of others," he insisted, "it would not be possible for" his compatriots "to de-liberate regarding the common good [of the Hellenes] in like fashion or with equal weight."[11]

If Thucydides' report regarding what Themistocles had to say is at all cor-rect, the latter's brusque manner and tone must have left the Lacedaemonians nonplussed. They may have refrained from openly displaying anger, as the his-torian reports. But, despite the friendliness they undoubtedly felt with regard to their comrades in arms against the Mede, they surely were "in secret vexed," as he also claims.[12] This would not be the last time that the audacity of Athenian ambassadors reinforced the warnings concerning Athens pressed on the Spartans by their allies.

If the Lacedaemonians nonetheless refused to be provoked and stood idly by while the Athenians reasserted their independence in so blunt and impudent a fashion, they had their reasons. They also looked the other way while— at Themistocles' instigation and with full support from his erstwhile rivals Aristeides and Xanthippus—his fellow citizens went on to complete in a magnificent fashion the walls of the Peiraeus they had begun building in the year of his archonship more than a decade before. If the Spartans watched and waited while the Athenians fortified the three natural harbors on that small peninsula and decided to add annually twenty triremes to their fleet, it was not out of pusillanimity. As the ambassadors sent to Lacedaemon explained, these fortifications were being built in anticipation of a Persian resurgence.[13]

Though spirited and gripped by *phılotımía,* "the love of honor," the Spartans were not hotheads. For the most part, despite their martial character, they were a sensible and sober lot. Thanks to the helot threat, they had a lively sense of their limits. Moreover, they were taught via the *agốgē,* the elaborate system of public education established for their moral formation, an exaggerated respect for the old; and at Lacedaemon the propensities of the young were reined in by the city's *nómoı* and by her constitution. Men under the age of forty-five were barred from public office, denied military commands, and prohibited from traveling abroad. The agenda for what Diodorus Siculus, no doubt following the fourth-century historian Ephorus of Cumae, pointedly calls "the common assembly [*hē koınḗ ekklēsía*]" was set by the *gerousía,* a "council of elders" elected for life from among the well-born over the age of sixty; and this august body was also empowered, if the assembly got out of hand, to veto its decrees.[14]

Age matters. Young men may be "spirited, sharp-tempered, and apt to give way to anger," as Aristotle asserts. They may find it difficult to restrain the spirited part of their souls; and "owing to *phılotımía,*" they may be unable to "endure being slighted and become indignant when they suppose that they have been wronged." The old are differently constituted. "Because they have lived through many years," the peripatetic observes, "they have often been deceived and have made many more blunders than the young." Moreover, most matters involving humankind turn out badly, so that their experience of the world causes the aged to be hesitant.

> They "suppose" only; nothing do they "know." And being of two minds, they always add a "possibly" or a "perhaps." They speak of everything in this fashion and say nothing without reservations. The old are, in addition, ill-disposed—for this trait is grounded in the assumption that all things tend to get worse. They are suspicious because of mistrust and mistrustful because of experience. And because of these things, they neither love nor hate with any vehemence, but . . . they are always loving in the expectation of hating and hating in the expectation of someday loving again. . . . They foresee danger from everything—for they are in temperament opposed to the young. Where the latter are hot-blooded, the former are cold-blooded.

Their excessive caution and their propensity to concern "themselves less with the noble than with the useful" may render the old less than fully useful in the heat of combat. But in deliberations, in the conduct of diplomacy, and in the management of war these qualities can be of benefit to a political community. Nestor was no match for Achilles on the battlefield, but in council he was greatly superior to the young man, as Homer makes abundantly clear. If the Spartans were in fact cautious on the battlefield, if they were more concerned with minimizing losses than with capitalizing on victories, if they were exceedingly cold-blooded in their conduct of foreign affairs, and if they were notorious for supposing the expedient honorable and for being slow to go to war, it was no doubt largely due to their sensitivity to the helot threat. But it also derived from the extreme subordination at Lacedaemon of the young and sanguinary to those old and calculating.[15]

To this, one can add another observation. The Lacedaemonians had never been a people of the sea. Nor were they going to become one anytime soon, and by this point they knew as well as did Themistocles that it would be far, far easier for the Mede to effect a return to Hellas by sea than by land.[16] Put simply, a majority of the leading members of Lacedaemon's ruling order possessed what the Eurypontid king Leotychidas evidently lacked: a good grasp of the geopolitical situation. They desperately needed what the Athenians had to offer, and they knew it. In 479, they were no doubt vexed, as Thucydides claims. They were as apt as any of their allies to resent upstarts; and, more than most human beings, they were prickly and inclined to take offense. But they were by no means fools, and they were anything but suicidal. They knew their strengths. They knew their weaknesses—and they were not apt to be led astray by pique. The Spartans were, as the Athenians later pointedly told the Melians, "conspicuous for thinking the pleasant noble [*kála*] and the advantageous just [*díkaia*]." So in good diplomatic fashion, on this occasion, they consulted their interest, they bit their tongues, and they acquiesced.[17]

Maritime Hegemony

The following spring, the Lacedaemonians dispatched the regent Pausanias son of Cleombrotus, who had led the Hellenic forces to victory at Plataea, to command the Hellenic fleet. Thucydides reports that the Peloponnesians sent twenty ships to accompany him; Diodorus Siculus, who is likely to have been following Ephorus, claims that there were fifty such ships. Both Thucydides and Diodorus report that the Athenians, who were no doubt still pre-occupied with rebuilding their homes and with fortifying the Peiraeus, dispatched thirty. This latter flotilla was led by Aristeides and by Cimon, son of the Miltiades who had defeated the Persians at Marathon. The "multitude" of additional ships said by Thucydides to have been provided by the "other allies" were supplied for the most part, we must suppose, by the islanders just off the Anatolian coast and in the Cyclades and by the Greeks living in what we now call the Chalcidice and on and just off the Thracian coast to that peninsula's east.[18]

Pausanias was fully aware of the geopolitical imperatives, and he did not display any of the reluctance and hesitation that had characterized Leotychidas the year before. Initially, he led the Hellenic fleet to Cyprus—where, in at least some of the Greek cities on the island, there appears to have been an uprising against Persian rule comparable to the one that had taken place twenty years earlier in response to the Ionian revolt. Thucydides tersely reports that he subdued most of the island. Diodorus tellingly adds that his assignment was to liberate the Greek cities "still garrisoned by barbarian troops" and that on Cyprus—where, we have reason to suspect, Soli, Salamis, and Paphos were still held in this fashion—this is precisely what he did.[19]

There was nothing fanciful about this expedition to distant parts. As the Greeks understood only too well, Cyprus was prosperous and strategically located, and the cities on the island were capable of fielding a sizable fleet.[20] Pausanias' aim was presumably to deprive Achaemenid Persia of the considerable contribution which these Cypriot cities could make to its navy, to add their strength to that supplied by the Hellenes, and to bottle up in the Levant

and place permanently at risk the fleets deployed on the Great King's behalf by
Sidon, Tyre, and the other Phoenician ports.

When he was done with Cyprus, Pausanias shifted his attention and that
of the Hellenes some distance away to Byzantium, a city also garrisoned by the
Mede, which was situated on the European shore where the Propontis ends,
the Bosporus begins, and the current from the Black Sea drives ships toward
the great harbor we now call the Golden Horn. Here, too, Pausanias displayed
geopolitical acumen. Like Cyprus, Byzantium—which would later be renamed
Constantinople; then, eventually, Istanbul—was a location of no small strategic importance. Whoever held it was in a position to regulate all trade between
the Mediterranean and the Black Sea and to deprive the cities of the Aegean
of their chief source of imported grain. This city Pausanias seized.[21]

But if no one could fault the strategic judgment of Cleombrotus' son,
much that was critical could be said with regard to his handling of the Hellenic
coalition. His high-handed conduct, especially in the wake of his seizure of
Byzantium, elicited tremendous resentment—particularly on the part of the
Ionians and of the other eastern Greeks newly liberated from the Persian yoke,
whom he roundly abused. To his fellow commanders, he displayed little but
anger. Some of the marines and rowers he had whipped. Others he forced to
stand all day with an iron anchor on their shoulders. Under his command, no
one was allowed to gather bedding or fodder or to draw water from a spring
before his fellow Spartiates had done so; and, if anyone tried, the servants of
the latter, armed with whips, would drive him away. Thucydides tells us that,
in desperation, the Ionians eventually turned to the enterprising Athenian
commanders, begging them for protection and asking that they take over the
leadership of the Hellenic forces. They cannot have found Leotychidas, with
his marked reluctance to take on responsibility for their defense, to their liking; and Pausanias they evidently regarded as worse. Diodorus reports that, in
their frustration, these eastern Greeks were not alone. According to his report,
some of the Peloponnesians actually deserted from the fleet, went home, and
had envoys sent to Lacedaemon to complain about Pausanias' conduct. The
young man was evidently out of control.[22]

There was also another dimension to the complaints lodged at Lacedaemon. Pausanias was suspected of Medism. When he took Byzantium, the son
of Cleombrotus captured a number of Persian notables—some of them close
relatives of the Great King. These men and Byzantium itself he left for a time

in the care of his friend Gongylus of Eretria; and in the Spartan regent's absence, unbeknownst to the other Greek commanders, this Gongylus slipped off with these valuable prisoners in tow and made his way to the Great King. He almost certainly journeyed first to the fortified town of Dascyleium— nearby in Anatolia, inland roughly twenty miles from the Propontis—where Darius' cousin the sometime admiral Megabates held court as the satrap of Hellespontine Phrygia. In the absence of formal sanction from a high official, Gongylus could never have traveled to Xerxes past the elaborate network of guard posts, inns, warehouses filled with provisions, stables, and courier stations spread out at regular intervals along the royal road. Nor could he have made use of the royal pony express to dispatch a message to the Achaemenid monarch.[23]

The story told by Thucydides concerning the Medism of Pausanias has given rise to skepticism and a great deal of speculation.[24] But there can be no doubt that Gongylus did precisely what he is said to have done. More than three-quarters of a century later, his descendants were still living the high life on a fief in the Caicus valley in western Asia Minor that had been awarded the Eretrian by a grateful Great King.[25]

Otherwise, however, it was difficult at the time to separate fiction from fact, and it is virtually impossible to do so now. What can be said with confidence is that many of the Greeks involved in this expedition suspected that it was at the behest of his friend and associate, the son of Cleombrotus, that Gongylus did what he did. Their suspicions were reinforced by a shift that took place in their commander's mode of conduct. When he marched out from Byzantium and through Thrace at this time, Pausanias flamboyantly dressed in Median garb in the manner of a Persian noble and surrounded himself with a bodyguard of Egyptians and Medes drawn from among those captured in the town. Even more to the point, he is said to have dined sumptuously and ostentatiously in the Persian fashion and to have made himself as difficult of access as an Oriental despot. The man—who at Plataea had expressed such astonishment that those who kept table in the manner of Mardonius should come to Hellas to deprive the Greeks of the "dreary mode of living" they possessed— evidently knew which of the two ways of life he preferred.

At this time, Pausanias also apparently conducted negotiations of some sort with Megabates—for Herodotus was told that, as a consequence of "his lust [*érōs*] to become tyrant over Greece," the Spartan regent had actually arranged to marry the man's daughter; and he is said also have had dealings soon thereafter with Megabates' immediate successor as satrap, Artabazus son of Pharnaces, who was also a cousin of Darius. Whatever assessment one reaches concerning the ancient evidence—and Herodotus harbored doubts about the betrothal—there is one conclusion that it is hard to avoid: Pausanias son of Cleombrotus was one strange bird.[26]

At Lacedaemon, the Agiad and Eurypontid kings reigned. They did not rule. They were hereditary magistrates of a sort, endowed with certain political, military, and religious prerogatives and blessed with the prospect of permanence in office; and the powers and prestige they possessed were such that Spartan politics tended to revolve about the two royal houses. The kings were by no means above the law, and they were regularly reminded of the fact. Once a month they exchanged an oath with five annually selected magistrates called ephors or "overseers."

These magistrates—who were chosen from the entire body of the Spartiates who had reached the appropriate age—are said to have exercised an almost tyrannical power. They supervised every aspect of Lacedaemonian life, and, as we shall see, they played a prominent role in the formulation of public policy. Had they been directly elected, as most scholars now assume, and had they been in a position to campaign for office, as we know the *gérontes* did, Sparta would have quickly become a democracy—for the ephors would frequently have come into office endowed with a mandate. They were, however, chosen by a procedure in which chance played so important a role that Plato once remarked that theirs came "near to being an allotted power," and they do not appear to have been eligible to serve a second time. In consequence, the majority of those selected were, as Aristotle repeatedly notes, "nonentities [*hoi túchontes*]"; and, while in office, they tended toward caution and a defense of the existing order. When these magistrates met with the two kings, the latter swore to uphold the laws, and the ephors swore in turn to uphold their prerogatives as kings if they honored their pledge.[27]

This friendly exchange of oaths disguised—or, rather, ostentatiously displayed—a threat. For a king who broke the law, who exhibited softness and cowardice [*malakía*] on the field of battle, or was thought to have betrayed Lacedaemon was subject to trial; and he could be fined, removed from office, exiled, and, in principle, even executed should the ephors bring charges and should a jury made up of the five ephors, the two kings, and the twenty-eight *gérontes* or elders elected for life to the *gerousía* find against him. Nor was this threat merely notional. In the course of the fifth century, there were only three kings who are not known to have been tried on a capital charge.[28] Leonidas, whose reign lasted barely a decade, if that, was one. His son Pleistarchus, who died not long after he came of age and took up his responsibilities as king, was another. And Leotychidas' grandson Archidamus—about whose forty-two-year reign we know only a little, most of it pertaining to the last five years of his life—was the third.[29]

In conducting himself in the outlandish fashion in which he did, Pausanias was trading on his prestige as victor at the battle of Plataea. But that prestige was not enough. As their propensity to put kings on trial suggests, the Spartans were extremely sensitive to the dangers of tyranny; and the arrogance displayed by the son of Cleombrotus had inspired suspicion and dismay. Late in the winter of 477 or early in the spring, the Agiad regent was summarily recalled from his posting. Soon thereafter, he was tried for treason and misconduct, censured and fined for his mistreatment of those under his command, then acquitted on the charge of Medism.[30] The Lacedaemonians were not about to condemn on a capital charge a man of his rank and achievements unless they possessed positive, indisputable proof of his treason—which, at this time, they evidently lacked.

The Lacedaemonians were, however, more than willing to cut this arrogant young man down to size. Pausanias had had inscribed on the tripod dedicated at Delphi as the first fruits of Persia's defeat two lines of verse composed by Simonides, which would most naturally be read as an assertion not only that the dedication was his alone but that the same was also true of the defeat recently inflicted on the Mede. It was at this time or soon thereafter that the authorities at Lacedaemon—spurred on by a complaint lodged by the Plataeans and approved at a meeting of the Amphictyonic League—intervened and substituted for the elegiac couplet their general had chosen a list of the thirty-one Hellenic communities that had helped "save their cities from a hateful subjection" by battling the Mede.[31]

Nor did the authorities at Lacedaemon cease to regard Pausanias as suspect. The fact that the evidence was not, in the judgment of a majority on the jury, sufficient to warrant his conviction for medizing did not mean that it fell short of what was required to justify his trial. Tellingly, they did not restore him to his command but sent another—a Spartan named Dorcis—as navarch in his place.

This newcomer was not, however, destined to take charge. Before Pausanias' recall, the anger directed at him had grown to the point that a leading Chian and a leading Samian were prepared to make a display of their wrath against the Spartan regent by ramming his trireme and forcefully preventing him from taking the lead; and, when Dorcis appeared, the Ionians bluntly refused to accept him as their commander. It is telling that, when their navarch returned home in disgrace, the Spartans sent no one in his stead. "They wished," Thucydides explains, "to be rid of the war with the Mede."[32]

Counsels at Lacedaemon were clearly divided. Some, such as Leotychidas, were reluctant to pay the penalty for sustaining Spartan hegemony on the high seas. Others, such as Pausanias, were eager that Lacedaemon remain at the helm. Many were, we must suspect, of two minds. Pride and a concern with prestige argued powerfully for insisting on Sparta's primacy.[33] Prudence argued for leaving the leadership at sea to the Athenians. More than one powerful argument pointed to the latter conclusion.

To begin with, Pausanias' misconduct was a reminder of something that members of the ruling order at Lacedaemon instinctively understood. The virtue and the discipline on which they so prided themselves were hothouse flowers. They flourished in the favorable climate of what we now call Laconia, where the citizens were subject to oversight—that of the ephors, of course, the "overseers" par excellence, but, more important, that of everyone else as well. For there, as a consequence, shame held sway. But this virtue and discipline were apt to wither in the larger world, where temptation abounded and Spartans not subject to the purview of their peers operated beyond the reach of reproach. Knowing the fragility of the remarkable qualities fostered and sustained by the Spartan *agōgē*, the Lacedaemonians, in most circumstances, prohibited foreigners, apart from a favored few, from visiting their homeland; and they denied their fellow citizens the freedom to travel abroad when and where they wished. The Spartiates "feared," Thucydides tells us, "that those going out would deteriorate," and these fears were redoubled when they "perceived" that this was "the very thing that had happened in the case of Pausanias."[34]

A fear of corruption was not the only motive dictating reluctance on the part of the Lacedaemonians. As we have seen, they were few in number, and their domestic duties were daunting. For obvious reasons, they were inclined to be extremely parsimonious when it came to the expenditure of Spartiate manpower. They had long been prepared, even eager, for others to do their fighting for them. They were, moreover, skilled in getting others to do this, and the Athenians had proved to be exceedingly serviceable in the recent past. In 477, moreover, none but the Athenians had the requisite ships. They had the desire; and, though their pride and assertiveness made them insufferable, they were also indispensable. According to Thucydides, the Spartans not only wished to rid themselves of the war with Persia. "They regarded the Athenians as sufficient for its conduct and they thought them of use to themselves in the present instance."[35]

Some Lacedaemonians were no doubt annoyed, and they may well have been numerous. But to most it seemed obvious how the difficulties they faced should be resolved. In consequence, the members of Sparta's ruling order opted for caution and gave way to the wishes of the Ionians, conceding maritime hegemony to the Athenians—who had arguably earned it at Artemisium, Salamis, and Mycale, and who had long been itching to take it on.[36]

Itching might, in fact, be an understatement. The truth, as we have seen, is that the Athenians connived in Pausanias' fall and arranged for Dorcis' rejection. In and after 478, Aristeides and, at his urging, his much younger colleague Cimon had deliberately handled themselves in their dealings with the Ionians and those newly liberated from Persian rule in a mild and respectful manner designed to inspire confidence and elicit trust. Initially, they had stood idly and to all appearances innocently by while Pausanias blotted his copybook. Then, when the Spartan regent had successfully enraged many of those subject to his command, the two Athenian generals had discreetly encouraged discontent and stoked resentment on the part of those who approached them, while offering Athens' hegemony as an alternative.

The ramming of Pausanias' trireme appears to have taken place at Aristeides' instigation. To those who asked that the Athenians assume the leadership, he reportedly responded that they would have to establish their trustworthiness by a deed which, once done, would by dint of the depth of hostility it evinced rule out their reversing course a second time.[37] It is a reasonable guess that Dorcis' rejection was similarly staged.

A Dual Hegemony

In the aftermath, we are told, almost certainly in the late spring or early summer of 477, the Athenians—with Aristeides in the lead—organized the islanders in the Aegean, the Greeks on the Thracian coast, and those on the Anatolian mainland into a formal alliance, which met in assembly in the temple of Apollo on the island of Delos and there also lodged its treasury. The founding members of what we now call the Delian League began by swearing an oath to have the same friends and enemies as the Athenians, who were accorded the hegemony and given the authority to name both the alliance's commanders and the *Hellenotamíai* entrusted with its funds. As the title of its treasurers suggests, this new league claimed to be acting on behalf of all the Hellenes. Its stated aim was aggression. Its members were to continue the war against the Persians. Their explicit purpose was liberation and revenge. They were pledged to free the Greeks still living under the dominion of the Mede and to ravage and plunder the territory possessed by the Great King in retaliation for the suffering he and his minions had inflicted on the Hellenes.

The larger, if unspoken, purpose of the league was, however, Hellas' defense. Everyone understood that the defeats inflicted on the Great King's forces at Salamis, Plataea, and Mycale might well be, from his perspective, a mere setback. They were not such as to rule out his return. The Persians had staying power. No one at the time contemplated taking from them the vast continental empire they ruled, and the resources they drew from that empire beggared the imagination. Given that money was, even then, the sinews of war—especially, of war at sea—there was every likelihood that Xerxes would rebuild his navy, augment its size, and try once more. There was certainly nothing to prevent him from mounting such an enterprise. As long, however, as the Greeks maintained their dominion over the briny deep, they would be safe—for, in the absence of a fleet dominant on that element, the logistical difficulties that an army would face in invading Hellas were insuperable. In consequence, since there was no reason to expect the Persian peril to disappear in the foreseeable future, the new alliance was intended as a permanent arrangement. When those joining took the requisite oath, they threw iron ingots into the sea and swore to remain faithful until these returned to the surface.

Before leaving Delos for home, the delegates from the new league's constituent cities voted to impose an annual assessment on its members. The cities that wished would provide triremes and crews in numbers soon to be specified. Those communities which preferred to outsource their defense were allowed to supply, in compensation, the equivalent in silver. Part of this *phóros*—the name given their "contribution" to distinguish it from the *dasmós* hitherto exacted as tribute by the Mede—the *Hellenotamíai* were expected to retain and store at Delos as an emergency reserve. Part of it was to be used to defray the cost of constructing triremes additional to those on offer from the alliance's members. Part of it would be used to hire Athenians to officer these additional ships; part, to pay the rowers hired as crew at Athens and elsewhere; and part, to cover the costs of administration. The annual budget constituting the contributions made in specie was to be four hundred sixty talents or a bit more than thirteen tons of silver. This stream of income, in addition to the triremes on offer, is what the members of this new alliance thought that it would take to secure Greece against the Mede. These contributions were also regarded as an investment of sorts—for there was every expectation that ravaging and plundering the Great King's territory would yield booty in ample amounts.

The devil was, as always, in the details—which were left for determination by Aristeides, who had already earned for himself well before this time a reputation for decency and strict honesty. In the aftermath of the foundation of the Delian League, he traveled far and wide, visiting its constituent communities and allocating to each what he estimated to be its just portion of the overall assessment. This task was, to say the least, unenviable. But it may well have been made easier by one peculiar circumstance. After the Ionian revolt, for the purpose of making the assessment of tribute equitable and easier to accept, Darius had commissioned his brother Artaphernes, the satrap at Sardis, to do a land survey in many of the communities concerned. In the cities once under Persian control, Aristeides could without fear of stirring anger frame his allocation of each community's share of the *phóros* largely with an eye to Artaphernes' earlier assessment of that particular city's ability to pay. Elsewhere, however, he had to estimate the carrying capacity of each community's territory himself. That he managed to do all of this without infuriating anyone, that his assessment was in later times universally admired, and that he retained for himself forever after the moniker Aristeides the Just that had been awarded him long before by his compatriots suggests that, as a statesman, Aristeides was a man of exquisite judgment and tact. It is also an indication that everyone involved then regarded the Persian threat as grave and the demand on their resources as reasonable and fair.[38]

Aristeides was also singularly shrewd. He hailed from the Athenian village or deme Alopeke—literally, that of the fox—and a wag named Callaeschrus is said to have remarked at the time that the wily son of Lysimachus was "more of a fox in his *modus operandi* than as a consequence of the deme in which he was born."[39] This canny statesman knew that Athens' turn to the sea and her appropriation of the maritime hegemony would profoundly alter the character of the city. According to Aristotle, he urged the Athenians to leave their fields behind and live in town, where, thanks to Athens' appropriation of the hegemony, there would be "a livelihood for all—for some in the forces sent on expedition, for some in garrison duty, for some in the management of communal affairs." In the end, the peripatetic adds, this enabled "the many"— including a host of officials charged with managing the league—to prosper, just as Aristeides had predicted. From the contributions made by the allies and the taxes they collected, Athens would in time be able to provide remunerative employment for more than twenty thousand men.[40]

While Aristeides was devoting his attention to pressing matters fiscal and administrative, his colleague Cimon collected the Delian League forces that had wintered at Byzantium and led them against the Mede.[41] In Thrace, along the Aegean coast, the Achaemenids had established two great strongholds— the one, a fort at Doriscus near the river Hebrus, sufficient in size for a garrison of ten thousand; the other, a fort to the west at Eion atop a hill on the eastern bank of the river Strymon quite near where it then emptied into the Mediterranean Sea. Both were on the route that Xerxes' army had taken in its invasion of Hellas. Both had served at that time as logistical depots for the storage of food;[42] and at this time, given the circumstances, both were almost certainly well-supplied. With them, if he regained control of the sea, Xerxes could mount another invasion by land. Without them, such an endeavor would have been difficult, if not impossible. It was a strategic imperative for the Hellenes that these Achaemenid outposts be eliminated.

Herodotus tells us that Darius and Xerxes appointed hyparchs—subordinate commanders—to rule the various communities under their control in the Hellespont and Thrace, and he indicates that, in the aftermath of the Persian Wars, the Greeks ousted all of these save one. His name was Maskames son of Megadostes. He had been substituted for Darius' nominee at Doriscus by Xerxes when he passed that way in 480; and, by a grit and determination that earned him the admiration of the Great King and annual rewards, he managed to fend off repeated attacks.[43] Whether one of these was launched by the son of Miltiades at this time we do not know. It would not, however, be surprising—for, late in the campaigning season of 477, he initiated a successful attack on Eion to the west.

From the perspective of the Hellenes, Eion may have been the more important of these two great strongholds. It lay quite near the dense concentration of Greek settlements in what we now call the Chalcidice; and upstream from Eion along the Strymon in the vicinity of Mount Pangaeum, there was not only an abundance of fir trees ideally suited for the building of ships. There were also rich mines, whose yield in silver and gold was also of recognized strategic value.[44]

All of these concerns had no doubt been discussed at the congress on Delos, and Cimon had been sent to deal with them. At Eion this he did—and with admirable dispatch. He landed his marines on the shore; and, with the help of a cavalry force brought from Thessaly by Menon of Pharsalus, he defeated the Persian garrison in battle, initiated a siege of the settlement, and expelled from their homeland the Thracians upriver who were providing the garrison with supplies. Given the costs of conducting such a siege and the fact that the Delian League treasury was not yet a factor, the twelve talents of silver (one-third of a ton) also contributed by this Menon will have been most welcome, and the service rendered by the highly disciplined cavalry he conveyed from his homeland is not apt to have been negligible. The horsemen for which that fertile and well-watered region was renowned were prized at home and celebrated throughout Greece for their exceptional skill and prowess in battle.

Over time, as the winter and spring months passed, the ample stores in the Persian stronghold gradually dwindled. At some point after midsummer 476, it became evident to Boges, the Great King's garrison commander, that Eion could no longer be held. He might have surrendered on terms and returned to Persia, but he chose not to do so. Instead, when the provisions were about to run out, he built a funeral pyre; lit the wood; slit the throats of his children, wife, concubines, and servants; and then hurled their bodies into the fire. The gold and silver he had amassed on his master's behalf he threw into the Strymon, where recovery would be well-nigh impossible. Then, without further ado, he cast himself into the flames.[45]

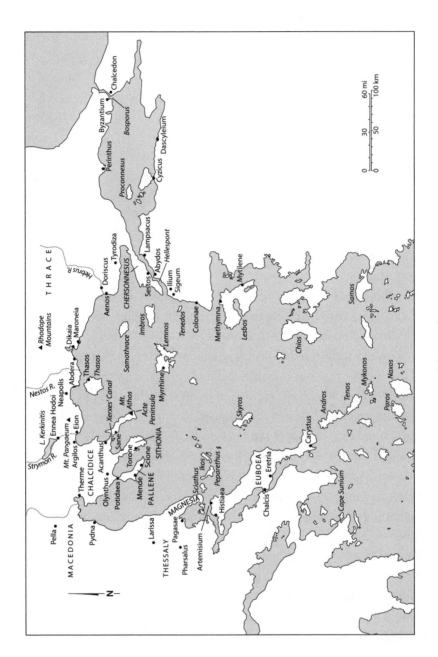

Map 3. The Northern Aegean

After enslaving the survivors, building a fortified emporium and naval base at Eion, and settling a colony of his compatriots on fertile land in the immediate neighborhood,[46] Cimon returned home. The following year he directed his attention to the isle of Skyros—which lay between Euboea and Lemnos, an island which his father had briefly added to the possessions of Athens in the 490s and which, in the aftermath of Mycale, the Athenians had no doubt reacquired. The land occupied by the barbarian population on Lemnos they had confiscated, and on it they had established a cleruchy—a settlement of impecunious Athenians, who, depending on circumstances, either farmed their new allotments themselves with the help of hirelings and functioned as a garrison of sorts or leased them out and returned home to live as rentiers.

Skyros was of interest for three reasons. First, like Lemnos and, for that matter, Imbros and Tenedos, which were even nearer the entrance to the Hellespont, it sat squarely athwart the most direct route leading from Athens to the Black Sea. Second, it was occupied by Dolopians, not Greeks; and this barbarian people was not only given to piracy. They sometimes even plundered merchants who put into their port, and this had made them an object of complaint at a recent meeting of the Amphictyonic League. Third, it was on this island that Theseus, the legendary figure thought to have been the founder of Athens as a unified political community, had purportedly been murdered and buried; and this misdeed was, the Athenians believed, as yet unavenged.

Presumably at the instigation of Cimon, who was a canny political operator, the Athenians had—at some point in the term of the eponymous archon who presided at Athens in 476/5—been instructed by the oracle at Delphi to recover Theseus' bones and bury them honorably in Attica. If they performed this service, they had been told, the island would be theirs. Not long after his compatriots had received this oracle, the son of Miltiades set out to fulfill the terms specified therein; and, in the process, he seized the island, enslaved its population, and established an Athenian cleruchy on the land the Dolopians had long tilled. Skyros and Lemnos—along with Imbros, which appears to have been acquired at about this time—were to become prized possessions of the Athenians.[47]

Our evidence for what followed is sparse. No surviving author, apart from Thucydides, describes the four-decade-long period between 475 and the last few years before the great war between the Peloponnesians and the Athenians in any detail; and he does so sparingly, only by way of brief anecdotes touching on dramatic events in these four decades that illustrate the theme of his narrative: the inexorable growth of Athenian power during the so-called Pentekontaetia after the Persian Wars and the fear to which it eventually gave rise in Lacedaemon.[48] Moreover, Thucydides was far from infallible; many of the events he describes in this section of his history took place before he reached maturity and some, before his birth; and he may on occasion have erred. But his aim was accuracy, as he makes clear; and he was nobody's fool. It is, moreover, a mistake to think him a blind partisan or to suppose his narrative tendentious or dishonest. Athens' power did wax in these years. The Lacedaemonians had good reason to be afraid, as we shall soon see; and Thucydides did what he could to accurately depict this process.

Nevertheless, the story that Thucydides tells concerning these four decades has, from our perspective, more than one grave defect. It is highly selective and has a narrow focus; and, although everything that he has to relate concerning the increase in Athens' power is of the utmost interest, there is much that is not germane to this focus which a student of Sparta's changing security environment and of the grand strategy she adapted to deal with these changes would very much like to know. Concerning, for example, internal developments at Athens in this period that may have had a bearing on the framing of her foreign policy, Thucydides has next to nothing to say. Even more to the point, he mentions Lacedaemon and Persia rarely and, then, only when what they do or suffer has a significant impact on Athens' rise; and he does not supply us with a precise chronology.[49]

To fill out Thucydides' narrative in a such a manner as to take into account Athens' internal politics and to cast light on the changing situation of Sparta and Persia and on their shifting intentions and policy, we will have to attend closely to fragments of information found elsewhere—in Herodotus; in the universal historian Diodorus Siculus, the biographer Plutarch, and the travel writer Pausanias; in a variety of other authors; and in the surviving inscriptions. In some cases, to elicit in full the larger implications of anecdotes that Thucydides actually relates, we will have to consider what can be gleaned from these other sources and from a consideration of the imperatives to which geography gives rise.

At some point, for example, in the years immediately following Cimon's seizure of Skyros, the Athenians turned their attention to Carystus, as Thucydides notes in passing. Although the historian makes no mention of the fact,

The Ongoing War with Persia: A Timetable, 490–465	
490	Helot revolt, battle of Marathon
480	Battles of Artemisium and Salamis
479	Battles of Plataea and Mycale
	Mantineia and Elis late for Plataea
	Islanders admitted to the Hellenic League
479/8	Siege of Sestos
	Walls at Athens rebuilt
478	Pausanias at Cyprus, then Byzantium
ca. 478	Athenians begin in earnest fortifying the Peiraeus
Winter/Early Spring 477	Pausanias recalled, tried, fined for misconduct, acquitted of Medism
Early Spring 477	Dorcis' abortive Navarchy
477	The Delian League founded
477/6	Cimon at Eion
	Pausanias returns to Byzantium
ca. 476/5	Leotychidas in Thessaly
475	Cimon seizes Skyros
ca. 475/4	Hetoemaridas dissuades the Spartans from initiating war with Athens
ca. 475–473	Cimon forces Carystos to join the Delian League
ca. 472/1	News of Achaemenid fleet construction
472, 471, or 470	Ostracism of Themistocles
471/0	Pausanias driven from Byzantium, recalled from Colonae
ca. 470	Rebellion of Naxos
469	Battle of Eurymedon
ca. 468/7	First Peace of Callias
465	Settlement dispatched to Ennea Hodoi
	Rebellion of Thasos
Late Summer 465	Siege initiated at Thasos

the latter *pólis* was, like Skyros, of obvious strategic importance. Carystus was situated near the southern tip of the island of Euboea, and it possessed in Geraistos a port, quite close to Attica, which provided a haven at a crucial point on the maritime byway that ran from the Peiraeus and Phalerum Bay in Attica around Cape Sunium; then, between the islands of Euboea and Andros; and on past Skyros, Lemnos, and Imbros to Tenedos.[50]

It was nearly always from the last of these isles, which lay just twelve miles southwest of the entrance to the Hellespont, that ships set out to work their way up that narrow body of water and on through the Propontis and the Bosporus to the Black Sea. In all seasons, the current running down from the Euxine to the Mediterranean is swift and powerful; and, especially in winter, the prevailing winds blow in the same direction. In antiquity, even on those comparatively rare days when the wind blew from the southwest, sails were insufficient, and it took oarsmen a considerable, sustained effort to overcome the force of the current. Merchant ships wholly reliant on sail—round ships or bathtubs [*gaúloi*], as they were called—tended to drop off their cargoes to be warehoused on Tenedos—whence galleys, rowed by the famed ferrymen of that strategically situated port, would convey them up the Hellespont and through the Propontis to Byzantium on the Bosporus and beyond.[51]

In 490, when Darius sent an expedition by sea to bring the Cyclades under Persian control and to punish the Eretrians and the Athenians for their support of the Ionian revolt, the Carystians resisted and were subdued by force. In 480, mindful of what resistance had cost them in 490, they assisted Xerxes at Salamis; and, in the aftermath, Themistocles had extracted from them as an indemnity of sorts a considerable sum. Apparently, however, the Carystians were not among those who joined Aristeides in founding the Delian League, though, like everyone in the Aegean, they profited from the protection it afforded. No doubt for the purpose of encouraging contributions from other cities which had also held aloof, the Athenians intervened to force the Carystians into line.[52]

Thucydides prided himself on his precision; and, in his account of the early years of the Delian League, he made it a point to discuss events in sequence. The next anecdote he relates concerns the revolt of Naxos, an island *pólis* of some size, blessed with considerable wealth, which was a member of the Delian League. Thucydides does not tell us why Naxos sought to leave the alliance. He singles her out solely because she was the first to try. He does indicate, however, that defections of this sort tended to be the consequence of a desertion from the ranks or of a shortfall in the payment of contributions or provision of ships. In these matters, he tells us, the Athenians were "precise and exacting and made themselves obnoxious by bringing necessity to bear on men unaccustomed to hard labor and unwilling to suffer hardship." He also remarks that the Athenians were no longer as affable and accommodating as they once had been. This change in tone he blames less on the arrogance and ambition of Athens, which he treats as a given, than on the fecklessness of her allies, most of whom preferred to pay their share of the cost of their defense in money—or in empty ships, as Cimon cannily allowed them to do—rather than by supplying naval contingents of their own. "Thus," Thucydides concludes, "while Athens was augmenting her fleet with the money which they contributed, when they did rebel, they lacked the requisite equipment and proved to be inexperienced in war."[53]

Cimon was Athens' principal general throughout this period, and his achievements contributed to his popularity. When, for example, in 476, he made his way back to Athens from the siege at Eion, he was invited to set up in the agora three stone figures of the god Hermes, each adorned with an inscription in verse. In tandem, these celebrated, with a clear reference to Homer and the role thought to have been played by Athens in the Trojan War, the great victory achieved by the Athenians at Eion; and they singled out as worthy of particular honor the benefactors of the city, endowed with great virtue, who had then led their compatriots in war. Though, in deference to Athens' character as a democracy, the latter were deliberately left unnamed, their chief was a man known to one and all.[54]

In similar fashion, after seizing Skyros the following spring, Cimon, in triumph, bore to Athens a large coffin and, within it, a bronze spear, a sword, and the remains of a man of extraordinary size, whom he represented as the hero Theseus. Soon thereafter, with pomp, circumstance, processions, and sacrifices, these remains—the bones of Theseus, as they were called—were solemnly reinterred in the center of the city near the site where a gymnasium would later be built.[55]

While the Athenians and those who had joined the Delian League busied themselves with evicting Persian garrisons and eliminating piracy, with forcing free riders to join the Delian League and share in the costs of collective defense, with suppressing revolts, and with acquiring for Athens territory of strategic value, the Spartans, almost certainly with the help of their Peloponnesian allies, turned their attention to the Medizers on the Greek mainland. Pausanias had dealt with the Thebans in the immediate aftermath of the battle of Plataea. But nothing had been done with regard to Thessaly—where the Aleuads, who had been among the chief instigators of Xerxes' invasion, remained ensconced in their stronghold at Larissa. Leotychidas led the Hellenic forces in this venture; and, on the battlefield, he succeeded gloriously. The Aleuads Agelaos and Aristomenes he deposed. But, although Thessaly was at his mercy, he stopped short of a more general purge when the remaining Aleuads offered him a substantial bribe. Herodotus reports that he was found in his tent sitting on a glove filled with money; that he was carted back to Sparta, tried, and convicted; that his house was torn down and the man himself sentenced to exile; and that he then fled to Tegea seeking refuge.[56]

In the aftermath of this expedition, which almost certainly took place in 476,[57] there appears to have been at Lacedaemon a great gnashing of teeth. At some point, there had to be something of the sort. First, in 479, Pausanias had let the Thebans off the hook. Then, in 478 or quite soon thereafter, he had squandered Sparta's position of leadership on the sea; and, having appropriated her rightful place, Athens was advancing from strength to strength. Now, to make matters worse, Leotychidas had made a hash of the Lacedaemonians' attempt to assert their hegemony on the mainland by dint of a punitive expedition against Thessaly. To describe all of this as a humiliation would be an understatement, and the Spartans are said to have reacted, as spirited men are wont to do, with an irrational burst of anger.

Diodorus Siculus reports that early on, soon after these developments, in 475/4, the Lacedaemonians came quite close to going to war with Athens, the greatest beneficiary of the ineptness, arrogance, and dishonesty that their Heraclid leaders had displayed in their postwar dealings with their fellow Greeks. They thought the loss of "their leadership at sea contrary to reason," and this indignity, he tells us, "they bore ill." They were hostile to "those who had defected from them," and they threatened them "with a punishment befitting what they had done." Moreover,

> when a meeting of the *gerousia* was called together, its members deliberated whether to go to war with the Athenians in a struggle for maritime hegemony. In similar fashion, when the common assembly was convened, the younger men and many of the others displayed an eagerness to recover that hegemony rooted in a love of honor. If they obtained it, they thought, they would become rich, Sparta as a whole would become greater and more powerful, and the households of private individuals would experience an increase in prosperity. They also recalled to mind the ancient oracle in which the god instructed them to take care lest their leadership be "lame." This oracle was uttered, they said, with regard to nothing other than the present circumstances. For their rule would, indeed, be lame if, having hegemony on two elements, they cast it off in one.

According to Diodorus, "virtually all of the citizens" were enthusiasts in favor of this argument. When the *gerousía* then reconvened, presumably to frame a resolution for presentation to the assembly, "no one expected that anyone would dare to advise them to follow any other course." But this is precisely what a member of that august body named Hetoemaridas had the effrontery to do. This Hetoemaridas was no ordinary Spartiate. Like the kings, he was recognized as a descendant of Heracles; and he was, as a consequence of his conduct, a man renowned for virtue. He had a standing among the multitude that enabled him, when he set himself against their opinion, to command their attention and respect—which is what he did when he bluntly told them "to leave the hegemony to the Athenians" and then argued in detail that "it was not in Sparta's interest to wrangle with the Athenians over the sea."[58]

Diodorus Siculus was not a contemporary of the events he describes in this illuminating passage. He lived much later, in the first century. He wrote annals, and he drew on earlier authors—among them, Ephorus of Cumae, the principal (but not the sole) informant on whose work he based his narrative of the period we are now examining, and the likely source of this particular report. Herodotus and Thucydides, who were contemporaries or near contemporaries of the events on which they focus, were in a position to interview eyewitnesses and the children and grandchildren of eyewitnesses. With regard to the period in question, Ephorus, who flourished in the mid-fourth century, was at a disadvantage in this particular. When he took a tack different from the one taken by his two great predecessors, he ordinarily did so on the basis of local lore and of reports found in works, now lost, which were more or less contemporary with the events described. He had, we have reason to believe, a keen interest in the rise and fall of hegemonic powers, as did Diodorus himself; and, as was only natural, the Lacedaemonian regime was one of the chief objects of their research. We should not be quick to dismiss Diodorus' testimony, especially when it pertains to this subject. But we cannot have full confidence in Diodorus' dating of this debate or of any other particular event in this period. Ephorus was not an annalist. He composed his universal history topically, telling one story more or less in full, then another. Diodorus aimed at chronological precision, but it was not always possible for a man in his position to discover exact dates. He was with some frequency confused, and he had a propensity for taking Ephorus' narrative on a discrete topic and reporting it in its entirety as having happened within one of the years it had covered.[59]

All of this notwithstanding, there can hardly be doubt that Diodorus' description of the debate that supposedly took place 475/4 accurately reflects a discussion that actually took place within the first few years following the establishment of the Delian League. That the Spartans were tempted at this time to undertake an imperial venture; that matters came to a head after Leotychidas' disastrous and disgraceful mishandling of affairs in Thessaly; that there really was in the mid-470s a Heraclid in the Spartan *gerousía* named Hetoemaridas; and that, by dint of a sober analysis of Lacedaemon's geopolitical and domestic political situation, he dissuaded his compatriots from flying off the handle and committing themselves to an undertaking apt to end in tears— all of this is highly plausible. If, however, we were to discover somehow that Ephorus invented this particular assembly and this particular debate out of whole cloth and that Hetoemaridas was also a figment of the historian's imagination, unlikely as this would be, it would hardly matter. For we could still be confident that there really was at Lacedaemon someone else of like stature and judgment who made the same arguments at about this time on a similar occasion. As we have seen, powerful arguments were there to be made in defense of Hetoemaridas' position both concerning the geopolitical imperatives Lacedaemon faced and concerning the preconditions for sustaining Sparta's highly disciplined way of life; and both Pausanias and Leotychidas had by their conduct reinforced their compatriots' suspicion that the civic virtue fostered by their regime could not withstand prolonged exposure to the temptations on offer abroad.[60]

Plutarch got it more or less right when he wrote, "Here, indeed, was the mindset of Sparta made manifest in a wondrous way. When the Lacedaemonians perceived that their magistrates were corrupted by the sheer magnitude of the power [entrusted to them], they willingly let go of the hegemony, and they ceased dispatching generals for the war, choosing to have the citizens remain moderate and restrained [*sophronoûntas*] and faithful to custom rather than to rule Hellas in its entirety."[61] This is, indeed, what the Spartans did. But it would be an error to suppose that they were of one mind in settling on this policy.

CHAPTER 2

Persia Redivivus

It is almost impossible that a war can be decided by naval action alone. Un-aided, naval pressure can only work by a process of exhaustion. Its effects must always be slow. . . . The tendency is always to accept terms of peace that are far from conclusive. For a firm decision a quicker and more drastic form of pressure is required. Since men live upon the land and not upon the sea, great issues between nations at war have always been decided—except in the rarest cases—either by what your army can do against your enemy's territory and national life, or else by the fear of what the fleet makes it possible for your army to do.

JULIAN STAFFORD CORBETT

I N 480, after the debacle at Salamis, Xerxes son of Darius, the Achaemenid king of Persia, withdrew to Sardis in western Anatolia. The following year, as events unfolded in mainland Greece and Ionia, he waited patiently in the ancient Lydian capital,[1] providing guidance insofar as communications allowed and anxiously awaiting news—at least until, one must suspect, the arrival from Plataea of Artabazus son of Pharnaces with a report concerning Mardonius' defeat.

In the spring of 478, after weighing the consequences of Plataea and My-cale for his realm, Xerxes made dispositions, we are told, for the defense of Anatolia. Then he departed from Lydia. We do not know where he intended to go—whether toward Susa in Elam, as Herodotus reports, or Ecbatana in Media, as Diodorus claims. But before setting off, he installed as the new ruler of Cilicia a henchman from Halicarnassus who had demonstrated a fierce loyalty to the royal house, and he appears to have taken revenge on the Mile-sians for the support they had lent the Hellenes at Mycale by sacking the tem-ple of Apollo at Didyma and carrying off the bronze statue of the god. Along the way, Xenophon tells us, Persia's king paused for a considerable period of time to fortify the citadel at the strategic city of Celaenae, which lay about a week's march inland from Sardis near the headwaters of the river Maeander in

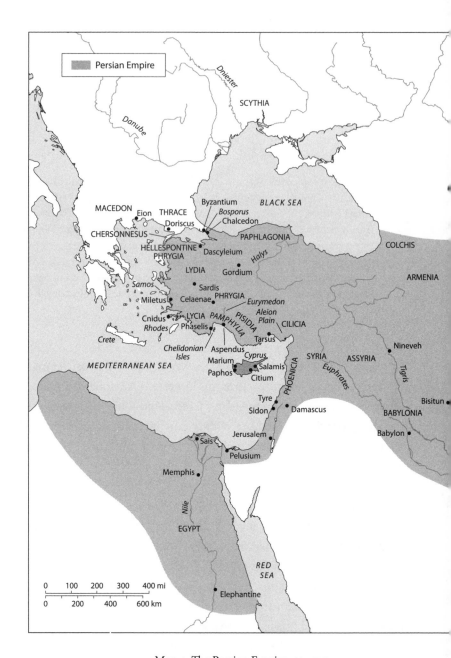

Map 4. The Persian Empire, ca. 475

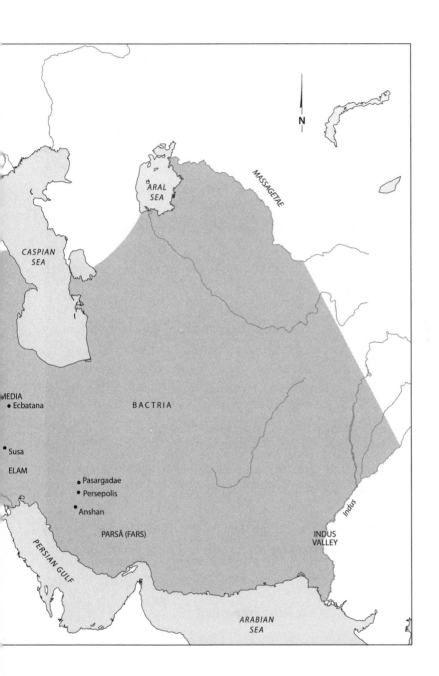

CASPIAN
SEA

ARAL
SEA

MASSAGETAE

MEDIA
• Ecbatana

BACTRIA

• Susa

ELAM

• Pasargadae
• Persepolis
• Anshan

PARSĀ (FARS)

Indus

INDUS
VALLEY

PERSIAN GULF

ARABIAN
SEA

N

southern Phrygia on the border with Lydia. There, at the foot of the acropolis, the Great King is also said to have constructed a royal palace.[2] If Xerxes was dismayed at the outcome of his war with the Hellenes, he certainly did not let on.

There is, in fact, reason to suspect that the Great King and his minions may have represented the Greek campaign to the larger public within the empire as an unmitigated success. Half a millennium after these events—after purportedly hearing a Mede dismiss Marathon as a minor skirmish and sum up the results of Xerxes' invasion with the observation that the Great King had vanquished the Lacedaemonians at Thermopylae and killed Leonidas; then sacked Athens and sold into slavery those of her citizens who had not fled; and, finally, returned to Asia after imposing tribute on the Greeks—the Bithynian orator and philosopher Dio Chrysostom expressed suspicions regarding Xerxes' self-representation of just such a sort.[3]

It would not have been especially hard for Xerxes and his courtiers to spin events in this fashion. After all, he bore with him—on his initial journey to Sardis and on his later travels between Babylon, Pasargadae, Susa, and no doubt Ecbatana and Persepolis as well—proof positive of his glorious victory in the form of statues, images, and votive offerings (including the famous bronze of the tyrant-slayers Harmodius and Aristogeiton) that he had looted from Athens and the other cities he had sacked. Indeed, were we to judge the outcome of the war solely on the basis of the inscriptions that Xerxes himself put up—almost certainly thereafter—at Persepolis, Pasargadae, and presumably elsewhere as well, we would know nothing of his failures at Salamis, Plataea, and Mycale. We would suppose, in fact, that, after the war, he ruled over and collected tribute from not only the "Ionians who dwell by the Sea" but also the Ionians "who dwell beyond the Sea" as well as the peoples of "Thrace," as he claimed.[4]

A King Imperiled

Of course, none of this will have fooled the courtiers who accompanied the Great King on his seasonal peregrinations between Persepolis, Ecbatana, Babylon, and Susa. Nor will it have fooled the great families of Persia. They will have recognized his failure; they will have known that very little tribute was coming in from Ionia, that none was coming in from the islanders and the Greeks who lived in the Balkans, and that Thrace with its gold and silver mines was lost as well. Moreover, in Xerxes' attempts to mislead the public, they will have discerned nothing other than weakness. No one from the high aristocracy who remembered Darius can at this time have harbored much respect for his feckless son. Of course, had Xerxes quickly seized control of the seas once more, had he mounted a second and successful invasion of Hellas, his initial failures would have been forgotten.

But this he did not do; and over time, as Cimon and the forces deployed by the Delian League systematically ousted Persian garrisons and conducted raids into the interior, the Persian defense posture along the coast of Anatolia gradually deteriorated. As Plutarch puts it,

> No one humiliated the Great King and reduced his pride more than did Cimon. For the latter did not allow the former a free and easy departure from Hellas but pursued him, as if at his heels. Moreover, before the barbarians could catch their breath and take a stand, he laid waste, overthrew, and harried them in one quarter, then stirred revolt in another quarter and attached [the rebellious communities] to the Hellenes—so that Asia from Ionia to Pamphylia was entirely emptied of Persian arms.

Cimon's chief aim was the liberation of the Great King's Greek subjects. But he was more than willing to absorb into the Delian League barbarian communities situated in territories of strategic interest. In Caria, we are told, he persuaded the cities long before colonized by the Greeks to revolt against their Persian overlord; and the towns of mixed population, where two languages were spoken and there were Persian garrisons firmly entrenched, he besieged and took by force. In Lycia, to the east along the southern coast of Anatolia, he is said to have done the like. It must have seemed, as Plutarch suggests, as if his object was "the subjection of Asia entire."[5]

In a realm such as that of the Achaemenid kings, in a polity which has expansion as its raison d'être, such a development is apt to have profound consequences—not only abroad, but also at home, where gross personal misconduct on Xerxes' part reportedly compounded his woes by giving rise both to divisions within the royal household and to unflattering talk in other quarters so widespread that it eventually came to the attention of Herodotus.

Contemporary students of Achaemenid history are quick to denounce Plato's contention that the moral formation [*paideía*] afforded Cambyses, Xerxes, and their successors was defective and his suggestion that the spectacular achievements of Cyrus and Darius were made possible by the fact that neither was reared in luxury by women and eunuchs at the court and that both knew little but the hardships of the campaign.[6] There is this to be said for the argument advanced by these scholars. The Persian empire did not collapse after Salamis, Plataea, and Mycale. It survived for another century and a half. It was resilient, and Achaemenid administration appears to have been competent, efficient, and effective throughout.

There is, however, more to be said for Plato's analysis than these scholars are currently willing to admit. The survival of the Achaemenid empire may be a reflection of Darius' genius and of his success in thoroughly cowing its subjects and in setting up institutions more than adequate to insure continued submissiveness on their part. It takes moxie to establish an empire and to defend it in its infancy; it takes very little to sustain it once it is firmly in place. A well-oiled machine can compensate for weakness and self-indulgence on the part of those at the very top. The Roman empire not only survived Tiberius, Caligula, Claudius, Nero, Domitian, Commodus, and the sons of Septimius Severus. For the most part, it flourished under their rule.

To deny that Xerxes was weak, self-indulgent, and more than a bit of a fool, we would have to reject the only real evidence that we have about the man as a man. It would be unwise to do so if we really want to understand his situation. Thanks to the yeoman's work done over the last twenty-five years by the scholars from a great variety of disciplines who regularly attended the annual meetings of the Achaemenid History Workshop, no one now doubts that Herodotus, Xenophon, and even Ctesias, not to mention the others in Hellas who wrote about Achaemenid Persia, knew a great deal. What they have to say about Persian institutions and practices dovetails exceedingly well with the evidence we have from the Jewish Bible; from Achaemenid Egypt and Babylon; from the surviving Old Persian, Akkadian, Elamite, and Aramaic tablets and royal inscriptions; and from the pictorial representations found at Persepolis, Susa, and elsewhere.

The lurid tale that Herodotus tells us concerning Xerxes, his son Darius, his wife Amestris, his brother Masistes, and Masistes' wife and daughter is bizarre, to be sure. But this does not mean that it is wholly or even largely false. Similar tales are known to be true regarding dynasty after dynasty under the Roman principate, and Plato's analysis of the reasons why Cyrus and Darius were so much more impressive than Cambyses, Xerxes, and most of the latter's successors can be applied to the Roman *principes* with no less interpretive force. That a despot's son—reared at court with the expectation that, if he pleases his father, he might well inherit the throne—should come, when king, to entertain a sordid passion for his brother's wife; that he should contrive a marriage between that woman's daughter and his own firstborn son; that he should subsequently seduce the daughter; that his attempts to please the young woman should in time enrage his wife and eventuate in a fatal breach with his brother: this little domestic drama is shocking in the extreme but it is in no way incredible.[7] It does not top what Tacitus and Suetonius have to report regarding the successors of Augustus and their womenfolk at Rome. Where a monarch's word is law, the only discipline to which he will be subject is self-discipline; and those who have not become inured to self-control and self-denial while young are not apt to acquire these qualities later in life.

The fact that there was nothing secret about these events, that they came to Herodotus' attention, and that they must have been discreetly discussed in a disapproving manner behind closed doors in many a noble Persian house-hold can hardly have added to Xerxes' prestige. This he surely knew, and he must also have come to suspect that, if he did not do something to prevent it from happening, his inadequacy as Great King was likely to become a subject of conversation as well. Had the Hellenes, after Mycale, limited their purview to the islands off the Anatolian coast, he might have been able to ignore their dominion over the Aegean. After all, his father had weathered the Scythian disaster, and Darius had not felt the need to return to the northern shores of the Black Sea after suffering defeat on the steppes.[8] But the attacks on Xerxes' Anatolian holdings, especially those situated along the southern coast of Asia Minor, were another matter. He could not afford to ignore the steady assault on his realm mounted by the Delian League and its chief general Cimon son of Miltiades.

As we shall soon have occasion to observe, Xerxes jumped at the opportunity that Pausanias the regent afforded him and did what he could to sow division in Hellas among the victorious Hellenes. But such a venture was, as he no doubt realized, a gamble—which might or might not yield much fruit. And so, after the passage of a handful of years, he once again ordered that a great fleet of triremes be built in Cilicia, Tyre, Sidon, Egypt, and elsewhere. Precisely when he did so we do not with any certitude know. We are not even sure when the great battle that followed was fought—though there is, as we shall in due course see, one datable event, which took place at Athens in the spring of 468, that might reasonably be taken as an indicator that a military encounter of great consequence had been fought in the previous summer.[9]

If so, in 473 or the year following, the Athenians are apt to have begun hearing from merchants who plied the seas in the Levant persistent rumors that the construction of a formidable navy was once again under way. In the 480s, when Xerxes made preparations for his great invasion of Greece, they had had ample warning of this sort. In later times, when the Persians made similar preparations, the Greeks learned what was in store three or four years before the onslaught began. On this occasion, if Plato is to believed (as he should be), they got advance word as well; and they evidently regarded the Mede's return to the Aegean in force as a serious possibility. At this time, while Aristeides was still active in a diplomatic capacity, there was, we are told, a discussion in the synod of the Delian League focused on the question whether the common treasury should be moved from Delos to Athens for safekeeping, and the Samians actually proposed such a move.[10]

If there were Spartans at this time who still harbored resentment at the Athenians' usurpation of the hegemony that they had themselves once exercised at sea, as there surely were, this intelligence may well have been sobering; and it no doubt served to buck up those in Lacedaemon who had favored leaving the war at sea and the considerable risks involved to the city that, in 480 and 479, had provided something like half of the Hellenic fleet and whose leader had maneuvered the Greeks into fighting at Salamis. At Athens itself, this news can only have served to reinforce the conviction, already widespread, that Achaemenid Persia was still by far the greatest threat the city faced. If, from the outset, the Athenians were—as Thucydides tells us they were—"precise and exacting" in collecting the *phóros* on offer from their allies and if they demanded that those who had promised ships actually provide them, it was because they were convinced that the Mede would someday attempt to return. If, moreover, "contrary to" what Thucydides calls "established custom," they ruthlessly attacked Naxos when she sought to withdraw from the Delian League and even subjugated the city for the purpose of making of her a deterrent example, it was arguably because, by the time of that city's rebellion, they knew that the Persians were already in the process of mounting an attempt to restore to Xerxes son of Darius the mastery over the sea that he had inherited from his father.[11]

A Challenge to Cimon's Policy

There was one prominent Athenian who appears to have regarded Lace-daemon as a far greater threat to Athens in the aftermath of the battles of Plataea and Mycale than Persia, and he was a man to be reckoned with. During the war, Themistocles had been the greatest champion of Athenian-Spartan cooperation; and, in his dealings with the Lacedaemonians, he had been a paragon of good judgment, diplomacy, and tact.[12] Afterward, however, when the Mede had retreated from Hellas and the islanders had been liberated from the Persian yoke, he had turned on a dime, as we have seen—shamelessly exploiting the prestige and goodwill he had earned at Salamis in an effort to fool the Spartans while the Athenians rebuilt the walls that had hitherto pro-tected their town, then brazenly asserting Athens' capacity in the postwar world to manage her own affairs and look after the welfare of Hellas as a whole.

The walls about the Peiraeus, which Themistocles had the Athenians fin-ish with great care immediately after their completion of the city walls, were in part designed for the same purpose. Themistocles understood that the Persians could not return until and unless they regained the maritime hegemony, which is why he insisted at this time that his compatriots build twenty additional triremes a year; and he recognized that the Athenians needed a proper forti-fied harbor for quartering and repairing their triremes. This is the argument advanced by the ambassadors he dispatched at this time to Lacedaemon.[13] The Athenian statesman also recognized that, if the Mede ever did regain full con-trol over the sea, the Peiraeus would be useless to the Athenians. What those walls could do, however, was afford the Athenians a place of refuge should the Lacedaemonians and their Peloponnesian allies stage an invasion of Attica by land. As long as Athens controlled the sea, food could be imported, and his fellow citizens could hold out. "The Peiraeus," Thucydides reports, Themisto-cles "thought more useful to the Athenians than the city up-country. Time and again, he urged the Athenians to go down there if they were overpowered on land and withstand all of mankind with their ships."[14]

Themistocles did not stop at this. He attempted to thwart Spartan ambi-tion at every turn. A year or two after persuading his compatriots to fortify the Peiraeus, for example, he was Athens' delegate at a meeting of the council of the Amphictyonic League, which convened twice a year, once in the fall and again in the spring. As we have seen, it was forbidden that a member of this league destroy another member or cut her off from fresh water, even in time of war—which is why Themistocles objected when the Lacedaemonians proposed the expulsion of those cities which had not joined the alliance against the Mede. Plutarch tells us that he feared that—if the Spartans succeeded in excluding the Argives, who had dodged joining the Hellenic League while maintaining friendly relations with the Persians, as well as the Thebans and Thessalians, who had openly medized—they would secure for themselves control of the league and make of it an instrument for their domination of Greece. In consequence, he drew attention to an exceedingly awkward fact—that only three of that ancient league's members were among the thirty-one cities listed on the tripod at Delphi as having resisted Xerxes' invasion. It would be "a terrible thing," he reportedly argued, "if the rest of Hellas was excluded from the treaty and the league council was left to the two or three greatest *póleis*" in Hellas. It was this challenge to their hegemony on the Greek mainland, we are told, that "most gave offense" to the Lacedaemonians and caused them to turn with a vengeance on the Athenian they had once so revered.[15]

After abruptly reversing course and presenting himself as a defender of the Hellenic polities that had medized, Themistocles may have taken an additional step of a similar character. At some point, almost certainly after the Persian withdrawal, Alexander I, king of Macedon, presented himself at the Olympic Games, applied for inclusion, and was acknowledged as a Hellene. It is exceedingly hard to see how the medizing monarch of what was regarded as a barbarian kingdom could have secured recognition in this fashion had he lacked firm support from Athens, which had in the past honored him as a benefactor and named him her *próxenos;* and there is no Athenian who could have been a more effective advocate on his behalf at this time than the architect of the Hellenic victory at Salamis—who was, we know, lionized in 476 at the first Olympic Games subsequent to the great war.[16]

The Spartans may have had additional reasons for fearing Themistocles and even for loathing the man. The son of Neocles appears to have had more in mind than a mere restriction of the Spartan sphere of influence to the Peloponnesus; and, if Plutarch is to be trusted, he was prepared to be ruthless in the extreme. In the year in which Leotychidas led an army into Thessaly in his capacity as the Hellenic League commander, the Athenian statesman tipped his hand. The circumstances deserve attention.

There is reason to suspect that Leotychidas' troops traveled initially by sea.

This was the mode of conveyance employed in 480 when a Spartiate named Euainetos son of Karenos journeyed with just such a force to the Gulf of Magnesia and then marched on through Thessaly to the vale of Tempe in a futile attempt to prevent the Achaemenid army from entering Greece from Macedonia. Moreover, we are told, there was a winter, not long after Xerxes' departure from Hellas, in which the Hellenes lodged a fleet at Pagasae on the northern shore of that same gulf. The only occasion known to us when it would have made sense for such a fleet to sojourn in so remote a place was that of Leotychidas' Thessalian campaign; and, given the burden that the Athenians were shouldering in the ongoing struggle against the Mede in the Aegean, the odds are excellent that most of the triremes involved in this particular venture were supplied by Aegina along with Corinth, Megara, and the other members of the Peloponnesian League. If the Athenians were there at all, it was to keep up appearances. Their aim—that of Cimon, certainly, but surely that of Aristeides as well—was to maintain the alliance with Lacedaemon while continuing the battle with Persia themselves. We do not know who was the Athenian commander on this occasion, but Themistocles was present at Pagasae, as was his former opponent Aristeides. Both may have been generals, and the latter may have been the commander in charge.

In 479 or 478, on an occasion in which Themistocles contemplated a venture that required secrecy and dispatch, he had informed the Athenians that he had a scheme in mind, requiring both, which would be of advantage to them; and they in turn had appointed his erstwhile rivals Aristeides and Xanthippus to vet his proposal. Something of the sort reportedly took place on this occasion at Pagasae as well. Themistocles is said to have concocted another such plan. The Athenians had him divulge it to Aristeides; and, when Themistocles suggested to his counterpart that the allied fleet be burned, Aristeides purportedly responded to his compatriots that "nothing could be more advantageous" to Athens than his comrade's proposal. Then, he added that "nothing could also be more unjust." Thereupon, Themistocles was instructed to desist, and desist he did.[17]

We do not know whether the Spartans ever got wind of Themistocles' scheme, but this does not matter. They were acquainted with the man. They had worked closely with him. They knew him all too well. Most important, they recognized his capacities. They stood in awe of Athens' Odysseus, and they sensed his hostility—even if, at this time, they may not have quite fully plumbed its depths. His response to their proposal that Medizers be expelled from the Amphictyonic League had told the tale. To counter him, those who favored maintaining cordial relations with Athens looked to Cimon son of Miltiades. In those days, there were no permanent ambassadors living abroad to look after the interests of their cities. Instead, the various communities in Greece chose from among the citizens of the communities with which they intended to maintain relations one or more *próxenoi* to function in something like the manner of a modern vice-consul. This was the post of honor that the Lacedaemonians conferred on Cimon at this time, and he signaled his gratitude and delight soon thereafter by naming one of his twin sons Lacedaemonius.[18]

The Spartans chose wisely and well. In the mid- and late 470s, Cimon was ascendant. We do not know the details but there is reason to suppose that, in this and in much of the succeeding decade, he went out as general every year to lead the Delian League fleet against the Mede and that—in his systematic attempt to rid the Thracian coast, the Hellespont, and the Anatolian coast of Persian garrisons—he enjoyed considerable success. If revenge against the Mede was what the Athenians craved, as they surely did, Miltiades' son gave them that revenge and enabled them to taste and savor it.

Themistocles—who had, as we have seen, incurred his compatriots' distrust and resentment in the aftermath of the battle of Salamis—was by way of contrast yesterday's man. He had little in the way of accomplishment that was new to offer and could only hearken back to his achievements in the increasingly distant past. It was, moreover, one thing to try to persuade the Athenians that they needed to fortify their city and the Peiraeus. It was one thing to tell them that they could not entirely trust the Lacedaemonians, the Aeginetans, the Megarians, the Corinthians, and the other Peloponnesians. They were not saps. This much they instinctively understood, and Aristeides, Xanthippus, and no doubt Cimon as well were fully on board. It was another thing, however, for Themistocles to try to persuade his compatriots that their main ally in the recent war against the Mede was really their enemy.

Panhellenic sentiment and a seething hatred of the barbarians who had for a time deprived them of their lands and who had in the process torn down their temples and destroyed their city, their villages, and their homes—these stood in Themistocles' way. Fear played a role as well. The son of Neocles evidently thought the Mede a spent force. On land, the Persians were inferior to

the Greeks. Their archers could not penetrate the armor that the Greek hoplites wore and the capacious shields they bore, and their infantrymen could
not stand up to the Greek phalanx with its wall of interlocking shields and its
ranks eight men deep. This Themistocles had seen with his own eyes at Marathon, and he was probably present as well at either Plataea or Mycale when the
hoplites of the Hellenes shoved their way through a wall of wicker shields set
up by the Persian troops and made mincemeat of the dedicated spearmen
bearing small shields and the shieldless archers doubling as spearmen on the
other side. On the sea, where he had masterminded the Greek victory at Salamis, Themistocles had apparently come to think the Persians inferior as well.
At Mycale, as he knew, they had not even dared to contest the supremacy of
the Hellenes on that element. It was Themistocles' conviction that, if the Athenians and their allies in the Delian League kept the allied fleet in good repair,
they had little to fear.[19] His compatriots, who had suffered grievously at the
hands of the Persians, lacked Themistocles' confidence.

In consequence, when the struggle over policy finally came to a head, the
son of Neocles was at a grave disadvantage. With an eye to reminding the
Athenians of that statesman's achievement at Salamis, Phrynichus could write
and stage *The Phoenician Women* among the tragedies put on at the City Dionysia, and this he did—almost certainly in March 476 when Themistocles, as
his *chorēgós,* is known to have defrayed the cost of producing his plays. Aeschylus could do the same four years thereafter when, at the same festival, he
staged *The Persians* with financial support from the younger of Xanthippus'
two attested sons—a newcomer to public life named Pericles. But neither tragedian could save their friend.[20]

There was considerable irony in the outcome—for Themistocles was hoist
on his own petard. In the 480s, when he had been intent on preparing the
Athenians for a war with the Mede that only he foresaw, he had appropriated
a legal instrument, designed for fending off tyranny, which had been forged
twenty years before but never actually used. The law in question provided for
a procedure by which the Athenians could, if circumstances merited it, vote in
assembly to hold on a specified day two and a half months later what came to
be called an ostracism—which is to say, a referendum in which, if a quorum
of six thousand voters showed up to cast a ballot in the form of a potsherd or
óstrakon with a name scratched on it, the public figure who garnered the most
votes would be banished temporarily from Attica for a ten-year period. In this

fashion, without doing violence or lasting injustice to the man or his family, one could end, at least for a time, the political career of someone of great stature thought to be a danger to the city who had not yet, as far as anyone knew, committed any crime.[21] This instrument Themistocles recast by using it to settle a great policy debate; and, in the wake of the battle of Marathon, he effected one by one the ostracism of those most prominent at Athens who had hitherto favored appeasing the Mede.

First and foremost among those forced to go abroad was Hipparchus son of Charmos, who was a kinsman of Hippias, the erstwhile Peisistratid tyrant who had led the Persian forces to Marathon. After him came Megacles son of Hippocrates, the leader of the Alcmeonid clan, and then an as yet unidentified kinsman of his. In subsequent years, the ostracized included a number of other prominent figures associated in one way or another with that clan—such as Xanthippus son of Ariphron, who had married one of Megacles' sisters; and Aristeides son of Lysimachus, who was a fellow demesman of Megacles and had in days gone by been an ally of his uncle Cleisthenes.[22]

That which began as an expedient seems quickly to have become an ordinary feature of Athenian political life. In the 470s—to judge by the surviving óstraka, which number well over ten thousand—ostracisms took place with some frequency. We know, for example, that the Alcmeonid Megacles son of Hippocrates was sent abroad a second time and that, in the year of his second ostracism, óstraka were cast against Cimon, Themistocles, and a certain Callias son of Cratios who hailed from Alopeke, the deme where Megacles and Aristeides resided. We are told that the treatment meted out to Megacles was visited as well upon Alcibiades son of Cleinias—a prominent figure who bore a Spartan name and inherited a position as one of Sparta's próxenoi at Athens, whose grandfather had been a close ally of the Alcmeonid Cleisthenes, and whose son Cleinias would later marry Megacles' daughter Deinomache. Xanthippus' elder son Ariphron at one point received a handful of votes, and there were a great many others who at one time or another received honorable mention—among them Leagros son of Glaucon; Menon son of Menandrios; the general Myronides son of Callias; Themistocles' friend Habronichus son of Lysikles; Hippocrates son of Anaxileos; Aristeides son of Lysimachus; and Callias son of Hipponicus, a hereditary próxenos of the Lacedaemonians, known for his great wealth, who is said to have been among Aristeides' kinsmen. We are not, however, well enough informed to be able to sort out whether

the contests in which these individuals came under fire arose from policy dis-
agreements or were rooted in nothing more serious than the personal rivalries
that were an enduring feature of Greek life. It may be telling that among the
surviving *óstraka* cast against Megacles in this period are a number which accuse him of luxury, greed, and sexual misconduct but not one that casts asper-
sions suggestive of differences of opinion.[23]

In the 480s, as we have seen, policy differences had trumped personality.
Moreover, in the course of mounting a series of campaigns in the 480s for the
ouster of Hipparchus, Megacles, Xanthippus, Aristeides, and the like, Themistocles and his associates had branded at least some of them "friends of the
tyrant." Some they had also charged with Medism.[24]

At the end of the 470s, as a consequence of his own sudden about-face
regarding the Persian peril, Themistocles himself became vulnerable to a similar smear; and, turnabout being fair play, there is likely to be something to the
report that, at this time, his motives were impugned and someone emerged
to charge in court that the man responsible for Xerxes' defeat at Salamis had
himself in the interim become a Medizer. If so, however, nothing came of the
criminal charges.[25]

Politics is, nonetheless, a rough and ugly business; and lodging charges of
this sort and arguing the case would certainly have served the political purpose of softening up Themistocles as a target. Soon thereafter—in the spring
of 472, 471, or 470, when it had already become abundantly clear that the Mede
really did intend to challenge Athens once again for dominion over the sea—
the debate over policy was thought to be settled; and, naturally enough, it was
Themistocles, not Cimon, who was on this occasion ostracized and sent abroad
for a ten-year term.[26]

A Prince on the Bosporus

There remained one rather large fly in the ointment. In 477, Pausanias the
regent had been tried at Sparta for Medism and for abusing the allies, as we
have seen. At some point—probably some months after he was acquitted on
the first count, found guilty on the second, and had paid his fine—he left Lacedaemon. He purportedly did so on his own and without permission from the
ephors. But we know that there was a faction backing him at Sparta, and he
almost certainly acted with the connivance of the ephors who took office in

the year after his trial. Otherwise, it is hard to explain why the son of Cleombrotus was issued a primitive code machine called a *skutálē*, a transpositional
cryptograph devised by the Lacedaemonians for encoding and decoding con-
fidential dispatches, which they reserved for the use of commanders and diplomats sent abroad on official business.[27] Their aim in conducting what amounted
to a semi-clandestine venture must have been to hedge Sparta's bets while
maintaining what those experienced in covert operations now call "plausible
deniability." In this fashion, the authorities could secure for Lacedaemon a
strategic foothold abroad without provoking an open breach with Athens. They
could also open up communications with the Mede, and on the home front
they could appease those among Pausanias' partisans who favored making
peace with the Persians and turning on Athens.[28]

In keeping with this surmise concerning his mission, Pausanias first journeyed to Hermione on the Saronic Gulf. Then, from there, in a trireme not
owned by Lacedaemon, he made his way back to Byzantium, where—at some
point not long after Cimon had collected the allied fleet, then set off for Eion—
he was received into the city as her liberator, honored as her refounder, and
treated as a hero of sorts. It was from here that he is said to have renewed his
dalliance with the Mede.[29] His immediate aims in doing so overlapped with
the divers aims that can be attributed to the authorities back home and to his
Lacedaemonian partisans, but there is reason to suspect that the son of Cleombrotus had ambitions and a personal agenda all his own.

Late in 478 or early in 477, when Gongylus the Eretrian fled to Xerxes
with the Persian notables captured by Pausanias when he took Byzantium, he
is said to have carried with him a letter from the Spartan regent to the Great
King, indicating that their release was a gift to the Achaemenid monarch from
its author and a token of his eagerness to marry into the royal family of Persia
and to subject Lacedaemon and Hellas to the Great King. Pausanias asked
only that Xerxes dispatch to western Anatolia a man of trust with whom he
could closely work.

It was at this time that Xerxes sent his father's much younger cousin Artabazus son of Pharnaces to Dascyleium to take over from Megabates the satrapy of Hellespontine Phrygia. This Artabazus was, by all accounts, the perfect
man for such a job. He was intimately familiar with Hellas and the Hellenes.
He had accompanied Xerxes on his long march into and out of Greece. After
conducting his master to the Hellespont in 480, he had turned back and be-

sieged Potidaea—a Corinthian colony situated astride the narrow isthmus connecting the Pallene peninsula in what we now call the Chalcidice with western Thrace on the mainland, which had rebelled in the wake of Salamis. Then, in 479, he had commanded a Persian army that had fled intact from the debacle at Plataea. Even more to the point, while in Boeotia, he had tried to persuade Mardonius that the proper way to defeat the Hellenes was not to stage a military confrontation. He had urged him, instead, to employ gold as a means for corrupting their leaders and sowing division within their ranks.

With Artabazus, the Achaemenid monarch is said to have sent to the Spartan regent a letter in reply, thanking him for his benefaction, politely ignoring the proposal for a marital alliance, and indicating that he had instructed Artabazus to do everything in his power to help him achieve his stated aim. This, we are told, is what the new satrap of Hellespontine Phrygia did by providing Pausanias with subventions on a considerable scale.[30]

Among scholars, these reports have for understandable reasons aroused a modicum of skepticism bordering on outright incredulity. Among other things, they say that Thucydides, our most authoritative source, is almost certainly in error in supposing that an exchange took place between Artabazus and Pausanias prior to the latter's initial return to Lacedaemon. For this, there was, they insist, insufficient time. It would have taken Gongylus six to thirteen weeks to make the journey with his charges to Xerxes' court at Ecbatana or Susa. It would have taken Artabazus a similar span of time to make his way back from that court to Dascyleium near the Propontis in Asia Minor—and, in the interim between these two journeys, a week or more would have been needed for deliberation. By that time, Pausanias would have been long gone. Even, they add, if the initial message was conveyed with dispatch via Persia's remarkably efficient pony express, the timetable would have been implausibly tight.[31] If there is anything at all to the stories told concerning the Spartan regent's dealings with the minions of the Mede, some argue, those that involve Artabazus must be located, after Pausanias' trial and partial acquittal, in the six- or seven-year period in which the Spartan regent held court at Byzantium.[32]

These arguments would be dispositive or very nearly so were it established that, in late 478 and early 477, Xerxes was ensconced at Susa, where Persian monarchs tended to spend the winter months, or in a royal palace at Ecbatana, Babylon, or Persepolis. There is evidence, however, strongly suggesting that, at this time, the Great King of Persia was still in Asia Minor, and it is tolerably likely that Artabazus was either with him or still in command of a Persian army stationed elsewhere in Anatolia. In his *Anabasis,* Xenophon mentions in passing that after Plataea, when he headed home from Sardis, Xerxes paused nearby at Celaenae on the Lydian border with southern Phrygia to fortify the citadel and construct a palace. Such a venture was bound to take some months, if not, in fact, a year or more. Major construction projects cannot be accomplished overnight. If, then, Xerxes was tarrying at Celaenae in the fall of 478 and the winter of 477, as seems likely, the letter that Pausanias is said to have dispatched with Gongylus of Eretria at some point after the end of the campaigning season in 478 could easily have been in the Great King's hands within a few days, and Artabazus could have presented himself at Dascyleium with Xerxes' reply in hand in well under a month.[33]

Among the lurid tales told by Thucydides, moreover, there is one set of claims advanced that almost certainly does deserve credence—for these particular charges were based on public conduct visible to all. As we have noted, late in 478 or early in 477, after Gongylus had fled but while the Agiad regent was still in charge of the Hellenic League fleet, Pausanias began to put on Persians airs. This *modus operandi* reappeared with a vengeance after Pausanias' return to Byzantium,[34] when Artabazus was certainly in charge at Dascyleium, and the two men were in a position to have extensive dealings with one another.

The reports concerning Pausanias' mode of conduct—if, as I think, they are accurate—should give us pause. For they suggest that there really was something amiss with the man. The harshness with which he handled Lacedaemon's allies in 478 and 477 may well have been a common enough Spartiate trait—a natural concomitant of the rigors associated with the Lacedaemonian *agōgē* and of the overweening pride instilled in those who survived it. There was, as Aristotle argues, something beast-like about the upbringing or *paideía* that young Spartans were made to endure, and the son of Cleombrotus was by no means the last adult Spartiate to display such qualities.[35] But Pausanias' adoption of Persian dress and of the practices of the Achaemenid court—this was, indeed, peculiar; and it was, to say the least, inconsistent with Lacedaemonian mores and manners. Moreover, the same thing can be said with even greater emphasis regarding the Spartan regent's decision, probably in 478/7, to commit an act of gross impiety—by appropriating, for his own use, a great bronze bowl already dedicated by someone else at the sanctuary of Poseidon located on the cliffs overlooking the entrance from the Bosporus to the Black

Sea; and by having inscribed on it an epigram (which a visitor in the late fourth or early third century could still read), in which the general victorious in the battles that had taken place at Plataea, on Cyprus, and at Byzantium boasted of his own prowess [*areté*] and described himself in ominous terms as "the ruler [*árchōn*] of Hellas extensive in territory."[36]

So inconsistent was Pausanias' public conduct with Spartan customs and ways that it lends credence to what might otherwise be regarded as an outlandish supposition: that, like his father's half-brother Cleomenes, the young man had, in fact, become unhinged and that, as a consequence of his megalomania, he had come to harbor ambitions which could not be realized within the framework of the existing Spartan regime. We should, in sum, be open to the possibility that the bizarre tales told concerning Pausanias and his dalliance with the Mede were by and large true.[37] The Spartans certainly came in time to think them so.

Cimon, who had no desire to cross the Lacedaemonians, appears initially to have kept his distance and to have left Pausanias to his own devices. He no doubt heard complaints concerning the Spartan's brutal mistreatment of the Byzantines, and he cannot have been ignorant of the man's entanglement with the Mede. But he also must have sensed, even if his *xénoi*—his guest-friends— in Lacedaemon gave him no warning, that the Spartan regent was on a semi-official mission and had protectors and partisans at home—as, Thucydides and Aristotle make clear, he did. In about 470, however—as a consequence of the Persian naval buildup unfolding in the Levant—the Athenian commander decided that he could no longer afford to avert his gaze, and he intervened and ousted the Medizing Spartan from the strategic city that he controlled.[38]

Apart from the stories told about his misconduct and his assumption of Persian airs, we hear very little about Pausanias' long sojourn in Byzantium. There is, however, a snippet in a pseudepigraphical letter—composed half a millennium or so thereafter as part of an epistolary novel focused on Themistocles' last years—which may cast some light on the question. We cannot identify the author or authors of these letters. But about them we can say two things: that whoever was responsible for their composition was exceedingly well-informed and aimed at verisimilitude, and that the letters themselves betray a close familiarity with accurate contemporary reportage now lost. The particular letter in question purports to have been written to Pausanias by Themistocles while the latter was in exile at Argos. "I hear," the pertinent snippet reads, "that you rule the Hellespont almost in its entirety up to the Bosporus and that you are making an attempt on Ionia as well."[39]

Were this letter our only source of pertinent information, it would probably be appropriate to give it little, if any, weight. But there is another snippet—this one in Plutarch's *Life of Cimon*—which derives from the memoirs, the *Epidēmíai* or *Sojourns,* penned by Cimon's much younger contemporary and admirer the pro-Athenian Chian tragedian, lyric poet, philosopher, and well-born man-about-town Ion son of Orthomenes.[40] It reveals that, when Miltiades' son recovered Byzantium, he drove the Mede not only from that city but from Sestos in the Thracian Chersonnesus as well. There, in the years in which Pausanias held sway, Xerxes' minions appear to have made dramatic inroads from their stronghold at Doriscus and also from Dascyleium and even Lydia. We are told, in fact, that, on this occasion, the forces of the Delian League captured a host of Persian notables, who fetched a pretty penny when Cimon offered them for ransom by those of their kinsmen and friends who were residing in Phrygia nearby and, at a greater distance, in Lydia as well.[41] The presence of these Persians in both cities suggests not only that Byzantium on the Bosporus and Sestos on the Hellespont were governed in common at this time but also that Pausanias really did rule the little empire described in the Themistoclean epistle—and that he did so in close cooperation with the Mede.

It is no less revealing that, when the son of Cleombrotus was finally expelled from Byzantium, he did not return to Lacedaemon. Instead, he made his way to Colonae in the Troad, a settlement of Aeolic origin which lay slightly inland in a region of Anatolia not at this time likely to have been included in the Delian League. There, moreover, where, we must presume, the satrap of Hellespontine Phrygia held sway, Pausanias lingered for some months, apparently under Artabazus' protection. Then, when a new board of ephors came into office at Sparta, those in charge summoned him home by sending him a brief message on a strip of leather—which he could read if he wrapped it about the *skutálē* issued to him when he left for Hermione six or seven years before. In this message, the son of Cleombrotus was bluntly told that, if he did not return home forthwith, he would be declared a public enemy of Lacedaemon.[42]

There had been, we must suspect, a shift of sentiment at Sparta—occasioned by the naval buildup then known to have been taking place in the Levant, and reflected in the composition of the new board of ephors. It would not do to have a Spartan regent colluding with the Mede at a time when the only thing that stood between Lacedaemon and a second Persian invasion was the fleet fielded by Athens and her allies in the Delian League.

Trireme Warfare

The year of reckoning, if my interpretation of the indicators is correct, was 469; and Miltiades' son was intent on fighting fire with fire. If there was to be all-out war, he did not want it taking place in the Aegean. Audacity could be, he knew, an advantage. The Phoenicians and the others who manned the Achaemenid monarch's fleet had been whipped at Salamis, and they were apt to be afraid of what was in store for them if they battled the Hellenes at sea a second time. It was far better, Cimon supposed, that the Greeks confront the Great King's fleet in waters he regarded as his own. Boldness would buck up their morale. A display of confidence might subvert the morale of their foe.

The fleet of the Delian League was made up of triremes. By this time, ships of this sort had been in operation in the Mediterranean for well over a half century—if not, in fact, for a considerably longer interval. Their deployment in large numbers in the 520s by Cambyses, Great King of Persia, had constituted a military revolution. For, when supported by merchant galleys able to carry provisions and by the even more capacious sailing vessels that the Greeks called "round ships" or "bathtubs [*gaúloi*]," they could sweep the seas of the lesser ships—the thirty-man triaconters and the fifty-man penteconters—that had ruled the deep in days gone by; and they could do something else as well that had never been done before. They could convey overseas an expeditionary force—made up not only of footsoldiers but also of horses and of cavalrymen to ride them—and this they could do on a scale sufficient for this force to constitute an army capable of projecting power from the sea ashore as never before.

In the mid-490s, Darius' triremes had ferried infantrymen, horsemen, and their steeds from the base he maintained on the Aleion plain near Tarsus in Cilicia across to Cyprus to good effect. Even more to the point, however, in 490, his generals Datis and Artaphernes had conveyed from Aleion all the way across the Aegean to Marathon in Attica an army and a unit of cavalry of a size sufficient, at least in principle, for the conquest of Athens. Moreover, in 480, Xerxes had mounted his invasion of Greece as a combined operation. On land, his army marched from Sardis to the Hellespont, which it crossed via two

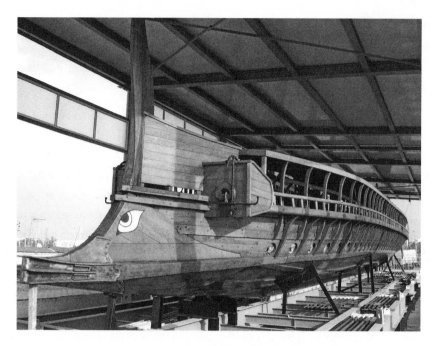

Figure 3. The *Olympias,* Naval Tradition Park, Palaio Paliro, Greece
(Photograph: Χρήστης Templar52, Wikimedia Commons. Published 2019 under the
following license: "The copyright holder of this file allows anyone to use it for any
purpose, provided that the copyright holder is properly attributed. Redistribution,
derivative work, commercial use, and all other use is permitted.").

bridges of boats built from Abydos in Anatolia to a point near Sestos on the
European shore. Thereafter, it marched up the Thracian Chersonnesus, then
west through Thrace to Macedon, and south through Thessaly to Thermopylae
and on to Boeotia and Attica—while his fleet, bearing thousands of marines
and horsemen, made its way along the Thracian and Hellenic shores in tandem with a host of horse transports and of merchant ships carrying supplies.

The Spartans knew that this could happen again—as did the Athenians
and their principal general Cimon. The battle in prospect was to be no minor
affair. Fortunately—thanks to the wisdom that Themistocles had displayed in
and after the 480s and to that evidenced by Aristeides when, in the course of
founding the Delian League, he had made its constituent cities responsible for
providing triremes or for paying for their provision—the Athenians and those
of their allies who had chosen to provide ships had triremes of their own in
considerable numbers, and by this time they had had ample experience in their

handling. Landlubbers in 480 many of them may have been. Landlubbers they were no more.

This was no mean accomplishment. The trireme was a triple-banked shell, shaped like a wine glass. In the manner of the double-banked penteconters that had preceded it, it sported a prow equipped with a bronze-sheathed ram. Its ram, however, had not one, but three horizontal cutting blades capable of slicing through the hull of virtually any vessel equal or smaller in mass that it struck amidships or in the stern. Triremes varied in size—from about one hundred to one hundred thirty feet long and from about fifteen to eighteen feet wide. When fully manned, those known to have been deployed by the Hellenes were powered by one hundred seventy oarsmen facing the stern, each plying a single oar fourteen feet in length, using as a fulcrum a tholepin to which the oar was tied by a well-greased leather oarloop. These rowers, who slid back and forth on cushions of fleece so that they could leverage the muscles in their legs as they pulled the oars, were organized on three levels—with at least two-thirds of them enclosed within the hull and unable to see their own oars.

Some of the triremes in the Persian fleet may have been considerably shorter than those deployed by the Hellenes, and these will have employed fewer oarsmen. In the Phoenician galleys, which sported majestically high bulwarks lined with shields, the third of the rowers on the top level were also situated inside the trireme—some think, at the topwale. In the ships deployed by the Athenians in the late fifth century, however, these oarsmen were perched on outriggers mounted above and outboard from their colleagues on the topwale. Whether those employed by the Athenians and their Hellenic allies at the battles of Artemisium and Salamis in 480, at Mycale in 479, and in the struggle with the Mede in 469 were of a similar character, we do not know.

Within a trireme, there were officers on deck to decide on and direct the ship's course, to dictate and sustain the tempo of the oarsmen's strokes, and to convey to them the orders of the trierarch awarded command. There was also a shipwright on board and a purser, and there were specialists trained in handling the sails as well as archers and marines fully equipped for combat—enough to bring a Greek boat's full complement to two hundred men at a minimum and its weight, when loaded with all of the pertinent equipment and personnel, to something on the order of fifty tons. When fully manned—as it had to be if it was not to be underpowered, slow, hard to maneuver, and

Figure 4. Section of Athenian trireme carved in stone; fragment of
Lenormant relief, ca. 410–400 B.C. (Acropolis Museum, Athens; Photograph:
Marsyas, Wikimedia Commons, Published 2019 under the following license:
Creative Commons: Attribution Share-Alike 2.5 Generic).

unlikely to survive a contest—this newfangled ship was a formidable fighting
machine.

Rowing such a vessel required, as a Phocaean commander told the Ionians on the eve of the battle of Lade in 494, that one embrace "hardship" and
"toil." This was the price, he rightly insisted, that one had to pay for liberty.
It, in fact, took extraordinary grit, determination, discernment, and discipline
on the part of a great many men for a trireme to be operated in battle to advantage. The trierarch in command had to be a man of fine judgment—quick
to sense danger, and no less quick in recognizing opportunity—and he had to
have an intimate knowledge of the capacity of his ship and crew and of their
limits. The helmsman [*kubernétēs*] stationed immediately below the trierarch's perch at the stern was in charge in the trierarch's absence and had to
possess the same capacities. He also had to be skilled and precise in his use of
the vessel's two steering oars. Everything depended on his ability to maneuver
the galley into a position from which it could strike and not be struck in return, and an error or even a measure of imprecision on his part could quite
easily be fatal to all concerned. When the trireme was in motion the archers
and marines on deck had to remain seated lest they destabilize the vessel. In

consequence they had to be able to shoot or hurl projectiles with great accuracy from an uncomfortable, sedentary position. With the help of a flutist [*aulḗtḗs*] located amidships keeping time with his instrument, the exhorter [*keleustḗs*] situated on the gangway near the stern and his colleague, the bow-master [*prōrátēs*] stationed near the prow, had to drill the oarsmen in synchronizing their strokes and in rowing forward now at this pace, now at that. These two also had to teach them how to reverse themselves on the benches and back water without missing a beat, and they had to instruct them in the procedure of partially shipping their oars on command at a time when a few seconds' delay on their part could result in the oars on one side being sheared off, in some of the men wielding them being killed by whiplash, and in the galley itself being left entirely disabled. In time of battle, moreover, these two officers had to convey the helmsman's orders quickly and accurately, and throughout they somehow had to sustain the morale of men whom they were driving quite hard.

The oarsmen themselves had to learn endurance and close coordination. This was no small thing, as scholars first came fully to appreciate in the late 1980s and early 1990s—when, under the guidance of an intrepid group of British classicists and naval experts, a Greek shipyard built a replica of a trireme; and, every other summer, volunteers gathered from far and near to take the *Olympias,* as she was called, to sea and put her through a series of trials. There was, these scholars discovered, a great deal to endure, and everything depended on a precise synchronization of the rowers' strokes.

On journeys, for example—when the sea was becalmed, when the wind blew from the wrong quarter or was insufficient—the oarsmen of ancient times had to row steadily for hours and hours. When the fleet was arranged for battle in line abreast, they had to row gently forward and then back water and do this again and again to maintain their galley's position in the formation. In the battle itself, when maneuvering for advantage, they had to be able to turn the vessel on a dime; and, when closing in for a kill or fleeing attack, they had to drive the vessel forward at maximum speed. If, at the end of such a sprint, their ship succeeded in ramming at high speed an enemy trireme, they had to back water at a moment's notice to prevent the two vessels from being locked together in such a manner that the infantrymen seated on board the damaged ship could attempt to board and seize their own. Alternatively, if the trierarch's aim was to approach an enemy vessel head-on at full tilt, then narrowly dodge a collision and coast along the enemy boat's starboard or port side with an eye to shearing off half of its oars and rendering it defenseless and incapable of maneuver, the oarsmen on the vulnerable side of his own trireme had to be able to partially ship their oars at a moment's notice while their colleagues on the other side of the vessel simultaneously lifted theirs out of the water. For the rowers in a trireme to be able to do all of this with maximum effectiveness, they had to drill and drill and drill once more. Following orders and close co-ordination had to become second nature for each and every one of them.

Prior to the battles of Lade and Artemisium, the rival fleets had practiced a complex maneuver called the *diékplous*. This maneuver consisted, as the etymology of the Greek term suggests, in the galleys belonging to one fleet "rowing through and out" between the ships of the rival fleet. This each galley may have done, as one scholar supposes, with an eye to shearing off the oars on one side of one of the two enemy ships as it passed between. Alternatively, the crews may have "rowed through and out," as most others presume, with the aim of repositioning their ships behind the enemy fleet where each could then swing around [*anastróphē*] and at high speed ram a hostile trireme in the stern, as the Phoenicians had apparently become wont to do. Or they could have carried out this maneuver, as yet another scholar argues, in order to swing around and position themselves at the stern of an enemy trireme, poised for boarding and seizing the vessel. There is also a fourth and, I have argued, more likely possibility: that the *diékplous* was a preliminary maneuver designed to open up all three options, leaving it up to the trierarch to select which of the three modes of attack best suited the occasion and the capacity of his crew.[43]

At Artemisium, the Persian commanders had initially attempted to take advantage of their fleet's superiority in numbers and in skill. To this end, their triremes swarmed around the Greek ships and carried out a maneuver which appears to have been called the *períplous*—in which they surrounded the Greek fleet and rowed one behind another around it in a circle, gradually re-ducing the circumference so that the enemy triremes would be forced back upon one another and eventually run afoul of one another in such a manner that their helmsmen would lose control over their craft. The Greeks responded by forming, when a prearranged signal was given, what was called a *kúklos*—engaging in an exceedingly difficult maneuver that they must have frequently practiced in advance. Each trireme backed water so that their sterns formed a circle. Then, as the Persian fleet tightened the *períplous* and drew nearer, the Greek ships, when a second prearranged signal was given, suddenly shot forward en masse and attempted to hull the ships of their opponents.

On this occasion, after closely observing the conduct of both sides, Themistocles had concluded that the Hellenes were likely to lose if they fought in the open sea—where the ships of the Mede, above all, the triremes deployed by the kings of Tyre and Sidon, were apt to outmaneuver the less experienced crews manning the Greek ships. In consequence, he later sought to lure the Persians into the narrow waters separating Attica from the island of Salamis, where their superiority in numbers would give them no advantage and where crowding would result if they deployed more ships than could operate effectively in the limited space available. This turned out to be a stroke of genius— for the Great King's admirals took the bait; the Greeks, who were familiar with these waters, managed within their confines to ram and disable or board and seize a great host of ships; and the Persian triremes frequently ran afoul of one another. This battle eventuated in a great massacre, which broke the back of the barbarian mariners' morale.[44] Eleven years would pass before the navy of the Great King was ready once again to confront the Hellenes. By then, as we shall soon see, the Persians had already recovered Cyprus.

Eurymedon

The Greeks whom the Great King's fleet did confront on this later occasion were, if anything, more experienced and better prepared in seamanship than the crews deployed by the Mede. For eleven years, they had had the run of the sea, and every summer they were out and about, landing marines, ousting Persian garrisons, and patrolling the Aegean and the waterways leading to the Euxine. The Ionians had never been landlubbers, and it could no longer be said of the Athenians, as the saying went, that they knew neither how to read nor how to swim.[45]

The triremes they rowed were altered as well. Those crafted on Themistocles' behalf prior to Salamis had been only partially decked, and they carried no more than four archers and ten marines [*epıbátaı*] up top. The Athenian statesman's aim had been to make the ships as maneuverable and as light as possible; and he rightly calculated that adding thirty more *epıbátaı* on deck of Iranian stock, as the Persians had done, would make their vessels, which had a draft of no more than three and a half feet, top-heavy and unwieldy, especially if the seas were at all rough.[46]

Cimon opted, nonetheless, to maximize the number of *epibátai* on deck. To this end, he had had full decks added to the Themistoclean triremes still in service. This change he is likely to have effected well before 469. Themistocles' chief concern had been the Persian fleet. In the years following 479, however, the Athenians and their allies had devoted themselves almost entirely to combined operations—aimed at raiding the country districts and at descending on cities and strongholds, assaulting and scaling their walls, and ousting their garrisons—and, for this, they had needed hoplites, light-armed troops, and specialists of various sorts in considerable numbers as well as mariners.[47]

When word came that the Persians had once again launched a great armada, Cimon began by conveying a sizable fleet, amounting to some two or three hundred triremes, to Cnidus on the Triopian peninsula of Asia Minor. From there the Athenians and their allies rowed east between the island of Rhodes and Caria on the mainland of Anatolia, then along the Lycian shore past the Chelidonian isles to Phaselis, a Greek city still loyal to the Great King. By dint of ravaging the city's territory and assaulting her walls, Cimon managed, with the intercession of Athens' Chian allies, to persuade her citizens to make a contribution to the Hellenic cause of ten talents (well over a quarter ton) of silver.[48]

The Persians he found awaiting him in force at the mouth of the Eurymedon River near the Pamphylian city of Aspendus. The surviving reports are not entirely in accord. Ephorus tells us that they had six hundred ships; Phanodemus, that they had three hundred fifty. Ephorus indicates that the commander of the fleet was Tithraustes and that Pherendates commanded the Persian infantry. Aristotle's nephew Callisthenes claims that the overall commander was Ariomandes, the son of Darius' spear-bearer and brother-in-law Gobryas and the brother or half-brother of Mardonius.

Callisthenes reports as well that this Ariomandes was awaiting reinforcements, in the form of eighty additional Phoenician triremes (which were on their way from Cyprus), and that for this reason he was exceedingly eager to delay the encounter. Initially, we are told, he tried to withdraw up the Eurymedon. Cimon, however, whose fleet was outnumbered, saw his opportunity and set off in pursuit. For a time, the Persian navy in the narrows put up a fight. But, as at Salamis, it was bested.

The enemy triremes still intact then fled to the shore; and their crews sought refuge with the Persian infantry, which marched down to the strand. Cimon then had his crews back their triremes onto the shore nearby, and the marines on board poured out of these vessels at the stern, as was their wont. Upon arrival, they formed up in a phalanx, and a great infantry battle took place. As at Marathon, Plataea, and Mycale, it ended with a Greek victory and a great massacre of the Mede.

We are not provided with the details. Given the circumstances and the limited space available for maneuver, however, the naval battle is apt to have been a melée in which some ships were rammed and hulled and others were boarded and seized. The infantry conflict was almost certainly a reprise of what had happened at Plataea and Mycale (and probably Marathon as well)— where, initially, the Persians had set up a wall of wicker shields, from behind which their archers, who doubled as spearmen, had fired arrows at the approaching Hellenes; and the Greek hoplites, in turn, after shoving their way past the wall of shields, had on the other side massacred the handful of dedicated Iranian infantrymen bearing small shields as well as the much larger body of shieldless archers who had dropped their bows and taken up spears. What we do know is that Cimon captured and reportedly demolished two hundred triremes, and we are told that he destroyed thereafter the eighty Phoenician triremes rowing over from Cyprus.[49]

By all accounts, Eurymedon was a great victory for the Greeks. A treasure trove of booty was captured in the Persian camp. Those who died there on Athens' behalf were buried along the road leading from the Academy to the city, where stone slabs bearing inscriptions listing their names were set up. Dedications were made at Delphi and elsewhere, and the proceeds that remained were used by the Athenians to construct the southern wall of their acropolis—while, with his own funds, Cimon, who had garnered great wealth as a consequence of his many victories, laid out in the swamplands stretching in an arc from the bay of Phalerum to the Peiraeus foundations for the Long Walls that would later provide protection for the road linking the city of Athens with the sea.[50]

We can be confident that Cimon's victory at the battle of Eurymedon took place at some point between 470 and 465. We cannot, however, be certain that it happened, as I have suggested, during the campaigning season of 469. Our only reason for preferring that date is the fact that a signal honor was conferred on Cimon and his fellow generals the following spring and that we know of no other event in this period that would have justified so magnificent a gesture. At the City Dionysia that year, when the ten generals entered the theater and poured a libation as was the custom, Athens' eponymous archon intervened and requested that they take the requisite oath and serve themselves as judges of the contest about to take place. This was a memorable event for more reason than one. That year, quite possibly for the very first time, Themistocles' friend and supporter Aeschylus failed to take the prize—which was awarded to a young tragedian on his first outing. The victor, who may well have been a partisan of Cimon, was a young poet named Sophocles.[51]

CHAPTER 3

Shifting Sands

If you can look into the seeds of time,
And say which grain will grow and which will not,
Speak then to me, who neither beg nor fear
Your favors nor your hate.

BANQUO, IN *MACBETH*

EURYMEDON was not as great and glorious a battle as Salamis or Plataea. Nor was it as important. There was, to begin with, a marked difference in scale. There were a great many more Persian and Greek triremes deployed in the engagement off the Attic coast, and there were a great many more soldiers on both sides involved in the conflict in Boeotia. Scale mattered. It always does—but, in this case, it did not matter nearly as much as the fact that the battles at Salamis and Plataea turned the world upside down, defying all expectations, while the sea battle and that on land at Eurymedon served merely to reaffirm and confirm the result achieved a decade before.

This confirmation and reaffirmation was, in and of itself, highly significant, however—for the victory achieved by the Athenians and the other members of the Delian League at Eurymedon was decisive in a fashion in which Salamis and Plataea were not.[1] In the aftermath, it seemed not at all likely that the Persians would try again. In consequence, Eurymedon was a battle more than sufficient to alter the course of subsequent events. If Plataea and Mycale created new standards of values, new moods, and new atmospheres in the eastern Mediterranean, Eurymedon made it abundantly clear that it was to these that everyone would have to conform.

Among the first to recognize and accommodate himself to the new situation was Xerxes himself. Now, for the first time, he saw that the game was up—that, its great wealth and vast resources notwithstanding, there was little, if any, chance that Persia could in the foreseeable future recover its supremacy at sea and once again project power in the Aegean. Salamis may have seemed a fluke, but Eurymedon demonstrated that it was anything but. The Hellenes now possessed a superiority in naval warfare that the Persians were not likely to be able to overcome; and—thanks to Eurymedon—Marathon, Plataea, and Mycale were now seen as similarly decisive. In infantry battles of the sort apt to take place on plains in the rough mountainous or semimountainous country in the Balkans and along the coasts of Thrace and Anatolia, Greek hoplites formed up eight men deep in a phalanx behind a wall of broad shields were a great deal more effective than were the dedicated infantrymen bearing small shields and the archers doubling as spearmen who operated in close cooperation with the cavalry of Persia's Great King.

Achieving a Modus Vivendi with Persia

We do not know when the negotiations began. But it is striking that we hear nothing about an effort on the part of the Athenians and their allies to recover Cyprus at this time. The Greek cities on that island had lent their support to the Ionian revolt in the early 490s. They had rallied to the banner of the Hellenes in the spring of 478 when Pausanias had visited the island; and, after Eurymedon, there was nothing that the Great King or anyone else could have done to prevent Cimon from landing hoplites on the island and once again taking control.

On the two occasions in the past when the Greek cities on the island had rebelled, the Mede had vigorously asserted himself, and in time he had regained dominion. This he had reason to strive for. As everyone understood, Cyprus was strategically vital to the Achaemenid monarchy. If it fell to the Greeks and they fully consolidated control, Cilicia, the Levant, and the Nile basin would be vulnerable to assault, and it would only be a matter of time before the Egyptians—who were, even in the best of circumstances, restive under the Great King's yoke—would revolt and seek the aid of the Hellenes.[2]

Cyprus was far less important to the Greeks. It was not strategically vital, and it lay on the margins of the Hellenic world. There were, moreover, Phoenician as well as Greek settlements on the island. Of course, its acquisition did promise to bring with it one quite considerable advantage. The Mede would never risk his fleet in the Aegean if the Hellenes in his rear could launch a strike from the great island sitting athwart the coasts of the Levant and southern Anatolia. If, then, Cimon failed to seize Cyprus in the wake of Eurymedon, it was perhaps because he suspected that it would be exceedingly difficult, if not impossible, for the Hellenes to sustain control over regions to any considerable degree populated by non-Greeks. It certainly could be argued that, with the acquisition of Phaselis, the Delian League had more or less reached its natural limits. Cyprus was a prize, to be sure. But it may, in Cimon's opinion, have been more valuable as a bargaining chip than as an actual possession; and it is this fact that explains why he exercised restraint and enlisted the services of a man who had done him a good turn two decades before.

Hereby hangs a tale. As a young man, prior to the beginning of his military career, Cimon had found himself in dire financial straits. His father Miltiades, after the victory at Marathon, had persuaded the Athenians to back him in an ill-fated attempt to liberate the Cycladic *póleis* from Persian control and extract from them the silver needed to bolster Athens' defense. In the aftermath, his enemies—led by Xanthippus son of Ariphron—had brought Miltiades to trial on a charge of treason, arguing that he had misled the Athenians and contending that he must have been bribed by agents of the King of Kings to withdraw from Paros, as he had quite precipitously done; and Miltiades, who had been wounded on the island and was too ill at the time to be able even to speak in his own defense, lost the case. He was fined fifty talents of silver, a whopping 1.425 tons—which may have been the estimated cost of the expedition, and which was an enormous sum for an individual to have to cough up. When he was unable to come up with the money on short notice, Miltiades was jailed; and there, after gangrene set in, he died, leaving it to Cimon, who was still in his early twenties, to pay off what remained of the fine. Had it not been, we are told, for his negotiation of the marriage of his younger sister Elpinike to the richest man in Athens, Miltiades' son might never have been able to pay the debt.[3]

The figure said to have rescued Elpinike's older brother from this predicament was Callias son of Hipponicus, the scion of an aristocratic family no less ancient and distinguished than the Philaid clan to which Cimon himself belonged. After Eurymedon, when the son of Miltiades was at the height of his power and influence, there is reason to believe that he generously returned the favor this man had once done for him by singling him out for a signal honor and sending him to Susa to negotiate a cessation of hostilities with Persia's Great King.

We do not know who initiated the bargaining. But the fact that Cimon assiduously kept his hands off Cyprus suggests that he had negotiations in mind from the outset; and from this we can infer that he is likely to have made the first move. The Athenian was, after all, the victor. It was only appropriate that he make the initial friendly gesture. It was the polite—it was the diplomatic— thing to do. It would have cost him nothing. But for a man charged by the great god Ahura Mazda with responsibility for world conquest who styled him- self the King of Kings to abase himself by making such an overture—this would have been exceedingly unpleasant and politically awkward, especially in the wake of a devastating military defeat. Put simply, it would have been a great humiliation, and it would have been perceived as such. The art of diplomacy has as its focus making it as easy and as painless as possible for the other side to give ground. This much Cimon surely understood.

The terms of what modern scholars call the Peace of Callias were dictated by geopolitical circumstance. The Hellenes left Cyprus to the Mede and agreed not to attack his lands; and the Great King agreed in turn to leave to the Greeks Thrace, the Hellespont, the Bosporus, the Aegean, and the Hellenic, Carian, and Lycian cities on the Aegean and Anatolian coasts of Anatolia west of the Eurymedon River and the Chelidonian isles. He promised to launch no attacks on these communities, and he pledged, moreover, to send neither his navy nor his armies anywhere near these cities and to limit the size of any fleets he might have his minions construct.

If there were negotiations in the wake of Eurymedon—as, I believe, there were—it probably took a year or more to work out the details. It was, as we have seen, a six to thirteen-week journey from Ephesus on the Aegean coast to Susa, and it took no less time to return. In the interim, there was no doubt a great deal of pomp and circumstance to be endured, and negotiations re- quire patience. It is a reasonable guess that, sometime late in 468 or early in 467, everything was settled in a manner more or less to the satisfaction of both parties and that Cimon squared it with the Spartans, who had every reason to welcome Persia's withdrawal from the scene. As was the Persian practice, Xerxes presumably provided direction to his satraps as to how they were to conduct themselves—and that may be all that he did. But it is also possible that, from on high, he later issued a formal edict spelling out the terms, which he pretended, justice required that he, as Ahura Mazda's viceroy on earth, dictate to all concerned. Such were the protocols by which the Achaemenid Great

Kings sought to save face and uphold the pretense that everyone was marching to the beat of the great god's drum.[4]

It is highly unlikely that the accord negotiated by Callias was publicly
promulgated as a treaty, formally bringing to a close the Persian Wars.[5] Had
there been solemnities of this sort, a decade or so after Mycale, Herodotus
might well have treated them as the denouement marking the end of his tale;
and, in the fourth century, Theopompus of Chios would not have been so
quick to denounce as a fabrication the story told by Callias' descendants.[6]
Thucydides has rightly been accused of neglecting to tell readers interested in
understanding the geopolitical situation of Athens and Sparta in this period
much of what they need to know concerning Persian affairs.[7] But, this propensity notwithstanding, had there actually been a formal peace, he would surely
have mentioned it in his highly abbreviated account of the inexorable growth
of Athenian power during the Pentekontaetia. Moreover, had there been a
proper peace, at Athens a fifth-century inscription recording the terms would
in all likelihood survive in whole or in part. Callias' handiwork is apt to have
been what we would today call an executive agreement; and it was, I suspect,
analogous to what came, in the age of firearms, to be called a cease-fire. It
signaled the end of open conflict. It embodied a modus vivendi. It was not a
genuine treaty of peace.

It could hardly have been otherwise.[8] The Achaemenid kings were Zoro-
astrians of a sort. In keeping with their political theology, Xerxes' invasion of
Hellas was a holy war—akin to those launched by the early Muslim caliphs. As
the royal inscriptions of the Achaemenid monarchs make clear, the Great
King of Persia was under an obligation to subdue the earth in its entirety, to
put an end to commotion, and to restore to the sway of the Wise Lord Ahura
Mazda the lands which lay within the realm of the evil spirit Ahriman. He
could not make a formal peace with the foe. Behind the scenes he could make
any species of temporary accord he wished, but he could not publicly acknowledge and treat with another power as his equal. He was, after all, the King of
Kings.[9]

The Athenians were in a similar bind. The Delian League had been formed
to liberate the Greeks, to take revenge on the Mede, and continue the war. If
they made a formal peace and renounced this quest, the alliance would lose
its raison d'être, and it would be apt to come apart at the seams—which was not

what the Athenians had in mind. They profited from the alliance. They had come to depend upon it for income and employment, and they knew perfectly well that its collapse would invite a resumption of war on the part of the Great King. It was in everyone's interest that there be a cessation of hostilities and that it not eventuate in a treaty proclaiming peace and amity between the former foes.

There were some at Athens who were less than fully satisfied with the results—some who had their eyes on larger prey, on Cyprus, for example, and on Egypt beyond; and some who were merely hostile to and jealous of Cimon. But, at this time, they were in no position to stand in the way of an implementation of the peace by the general who had gone from strength to strength and who had quite recently won at Eurymedon a magnificent double victory, on two elements in one day. It was elsewhere, we must suspect, that there was genuine bitterness and discontent. The Persians were not used to losing. Theirs was, in principle, a universal empire. Expansion was its sole rationale, and it was only natural that they blame their losses and the contraction of their empire on their leader—Darius' pathetic, feckless son.

Given his penchant for egregious and imprudent personal misconduct, it is hardly a surprise that, in due course, Xerxes fell prey to assassination. Many a self-indulgent Roman *princeps* suffered the like in similar circumstances. But this Great King's domestic travails probably counted for little in this regard when compared with his perceived failures as an empire-builder. The Gallo-Roman historian Pompeius Trogus was surely correct, when, writing in the time of Augustus, he claimed that, after repeated defeats at the hands of the Hellenes, Xerxes came to be held in contempt by his own people. Indeed, it makes perfect sense that, after this Great King had tacitly acknowledged Persia's defeat by ordering a cessation of hostilities and abjectly accepting the humiliating terms proposed by the Athenian Callias, the Chiliarch in charge of court protocol—who controlled access to the monarch, commanded the royal bodyguard, and functioned as the Persian equivalent of the Roman principate's praetorian prefect—should play a prominent role in the conspiracy that brought him down. No one could be better placed to witness and reflect on what Justin, following Pompeius Trogus, rightly calls "the decline day-by-day-by-day in the majesty of the kingship."[10]

Within the Persian empire, the battles of Salamis, Plataea, and Mycale, when viewed in retrospect half a century thereafter, may well have seemed like a mere bump in the road. At the time, however, these defeats are likely to have been seen as a catastrophe by those in the know. For the self-indulgent, out-of-control son and heir of Darius the Great, these battles, his failure to mount a successful expedition soon thereafter, the gradual erosion in subsequent years of Persia's defensive position along the Anatolian coast, the annihilation of his navy and massacre of his army at Eurymedon in 469, and the man's disgraceful acceptance of a humiliating peace thereafter were arguably fatal.

Thasos

In Hellas, the decision at Eurymedon and the negotiation of a settlement with Persia in its aftermath were also sufficient to create new standards of values, new moods, and new atmospheres to which everyone really did have to conform. The Athenians were themselves among the first to adjust to the new situation.

Prior to this time, they had exercised a modicum of self-restraint in their dealings with their allies. They had, indeed, forced Carystus (and, no doubt, induced other free riders) to join the Delian League. They had been rigorous in requiring that the league's members provide each year the ships and the *phóros* that they had pledged, and they were ruthless in crushing Naxos when that island polity failed to deliver on that promise and sought to withdraw from the alliance. They had also looked after their own interests, installing cleruchies—made up of Athenian citizens selected by lot from among those with modest resources—on territory they had seized from barbarians at Eion, on Lemnos and Skyros, and no doubt elsewhere as well. But, hitherto, they had not, as far as we know, trespassed on the possessions of fellow members of the league.

This they now did—and with a vengeance. Thasos, which had been colonized by Paros in the early seventh century, may have been the wealthiest member of the Delian League. There were gold, silver, lead, and copper mines scattered all over this exceedingly mountainous island, and there were rich marble quarries as well. Thasos was, moreover, famous for her wine, which was marketed far and wide. In addition, the *pólis* drew revenues in gold from the Scaptesyle mine on the mainland of Thrace nearby. Early on, almost certainly in cooperation with her mother city, she established trading posts, such as Galepsos, Oisyme, Neapolis (modern Kavala), and Pistyros, in the *peraía*—

the extraterritorial domain—that the two *póleis* had seized along the Thracian coast between the Strymon and the Nestos estuaries; and there is good reason to suspect that, prior to the coming of the Mede, Eion on the Strymon and even Berge, some ten miles upstream, had been theirs as well. By means of these emporia, the citizens of Paros and Thasos and the cities to which they belonged profited handsomely from the gold and silver extraction taking place at a variety of locations in the interior. Herodotus estimated that, at the time of the Ionian revolt, Thasos' annual revenues varied between two and three hundred talents in gold—which is to say, between 5.7 and 8.55 tons.

During the Ionian revolt, the Thasians had leveraged this wealth to build a sizable fleet of triremes for the city's defense. To house them, they had constructed a military harbor equipped with shipsheds, where the galleys could be drawn out of the water for recaulking and repair. This harbor they had then fortified against both tempests and armed assault by building breakwaters and moles and forging a great chain with which to block the narrow entrance left open to the sea. At this time, they had also strengthened the town's walls, which then stretched to a circuit more than two and a half miles in length. The enceinte they built was of such a quality that, on the landward side, much of it is still intact to a considerable height today, more than two and a half millennia after its construction.[11]

This great effort notwithstanding, when Mardonius passed through with a fleet and army in 492, the Thasians calculated the likelihood that they would be able successfully to resist, then despaired, and knuckled under. Moreover, the following year, when their neighbors accused them of plotting a revolt and they were called upon by the Great King himself to tear down a section of their city walls and dispatch their fleet to the base that the Persians were establishing at Abdera, they did so without protest. To Xerxes' subsequent invasion of Hellas proper, they then lent their support.[12]

We know little about the history of Thasos after the battles of Salamis, Plataea, and Mycale. There is every reason, however, to suppose that the city quickly regained from the Mede much of the territory on the continent that she had once controlled as well as the revenues attendant on their possession. Within the Delian League, the Thasians must have been among the major providers of ships. When Cimon besieged and captured Eion on the Thracian coast to their west, the citizens of this island polity must have been overjoyed,

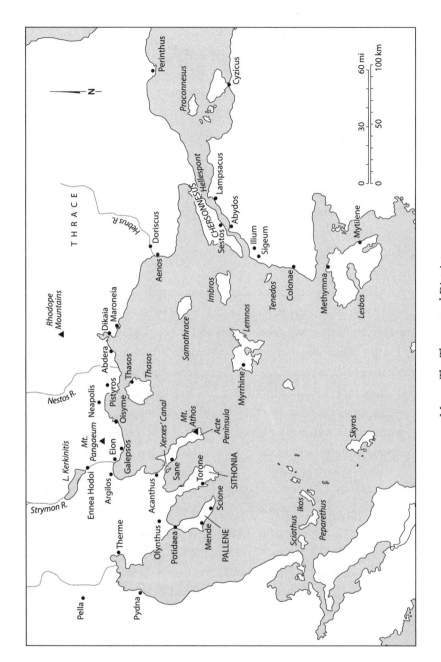

Map 5. The Thraceward District

and they must have welcomed the Athenian generals' gradual elimination of the other Persian garrisons nearby in Thrace and in the Hellespont—though they cannot have been pleased that Athens kept Eion for herself.

If—as a consequence of the peace negotiated after Eurymedon by Callias—Maskames or a successor was forced to relinquish the Persian stronghold at Doriscus to their east, as seems likely, this, too, the Thasians will have cheered. But when, at about the same time, the Athenians and their allies began preparations for the establishment of a colony up the Strymon River, they became disturbed. Mount Pangaeum with its rich mines lay nearby. And when these same Athenians challenged their right to the Scaptesyle mine on the mainland near Neapolis and interfered with the trading posts they maintained on the Thracian coast, the Thasians quite naturally took it ill.

Had this been done in the mid- or late 470s—when a Persian resurgence was in the offing, when the Mede was still perceived as a clear and present danger, and Maskames remained in control of Doriscus—the Thasians might have grumbled bitterly among themselves and acquiesced. After Eurymedon, however, and Callias' negotiation of a cessation of hostilities, their perceptions underwent a change; and, as was predictable, they began to have second thoughts. They, too, recognized that they had to adjust their policy in light of the new circumstances in which they found themselves. The Delian League seemed no longer as much of a necessity as it once had seemed. Athens' hegemony was no longer as welcome as it once had been, and her abuse of the prerogatives attendant on leadership was regarded not as an unfortunate imposition, but as an intolerable affront. In consequence, in 465, the Thasians chose to withdraw from the league and fight for what had long been their property.[13]

We know very little about the Thasians' revolt. They may have taken up the question of Athenian conduct in one of the regular meetings of the league assembly on Delos. If so, they got nowhere. As later rebels would complain, that assembly was rigged. The votes were not weighted. Every member, no matter how tiny, had an equal say. Most of the cities in the Delian League were exceedingly small and desperately in need of protection against their more powerful neighbors. They would support Athens through thick and thin.[14]

Even if they did not take up the matter with the Delian League as such, the Thasians are likely to have approached the Mytilenians, the Chians, the Samians, the Byzantines, the various communities on Rhodes, and the other *póleis* of size and wealth which contributed ships. At one time or another, every one of these cities would stage a revolt. Had they ever coordinated efforts, joined forces, and acted in concert, they might have succeeded. But this they never did. Early on, they were with reason not fully persuaded that the Persian peril had evaporated; and, on this particular occasion as well, no member of Athens' alliance is mentioned as having offered Thasos aid and comfort. In fact, the only *pólis* known to have responded to a plea on her part for help was . . . Lacedaemon.

The magnitude of the Athenian victory must have impressed the Spartans as well. It impressed everyone—as did Xerxes' willingness to ratify the outcome. The strategic situation had altered. It was now possible to imagine that the Persians were more or less off the geopolitical map, at least as far as the Hellenes were concerned; and, as one would expect, the Lacedaemonians were among those who paused to reconsider. The astonishing strength on the high seas displayed by Athens, which had seemed to many Spartans more a consolation and comfort than an offense in 480 and the 470s, they were now more apt to regard as an affront. This was one of the reasons why, as Thucydides informs us, in 465, some time after Athens had defeated Thasos at sea, "the Lacedaemonians"—almost certainly, on this occasion, the "little assembly" consisting of the ephors, the *gérontes,* and the two kings or their regents— secretly promised to come to the support of the islanders and mount an invasion of Attica.[15] There were, as we shall soon see, other reasons as well—powerful reasons—why Sparta came to think Athens a threat. Eurymedon was not the only battle of significance to take place in the early 460s. These years marked the beginning of a period, in which, as Thucydides laconically remarks, the Spartans were "constrained by wars at home."[16]

Although the Athenian historian is exceedingly reticent and casts next to no light on these particular conflicts, piecing together the evidence for what happened in the Peloponnesus in the years to which he refers is, in fact, essential for understanding the divers calculations that governed Sparta's subsequent conduct and that of Athens as well. In both cities, in later years, there were statesmen who were haunted not only by a remembrance of what had actually happened at this time but also, and even more emphatically, by ruminations concerning what had very nearly taken place. Here again Themistocles looms large.

A Lion in Winter

If, when Cimon arranged for the ostracism of Themistocles in the spring of 472, 471, or 470, he calculated that this would settle matters once and for all, he erred grievously. The son of Neocles was a man bigger than life. At Athens, he may have become an object of distrust—a prophet without honor in his own land. Elsewhere, however, the victory over the Mede that he had achieved at Salamis had made him a celebrity. In 480, the Spartans honored him as they never had honored anyone and never would honor anyone again. Four years later, when Themistocles entered the stadium at the Olympic Games, we are told, the audience stood up to applaud. Thereafter, they reportedly neglected the contestants and focused their gaze steadily on him, pointing him out to strangers with expressions of admiration and approval.[17]

It is easy to see why they did so. Pausanias' success at Plataea was a signal achievement, but it did not beggar the imagination. Everyone knew that, if the Mede could be lured onto ground unsuitable for cavalry, he could be defeated. At Marathon, after the Persians had loaded most of their steeds on horse transports, the Athenians had massacred their infantry. The Greek victory at Salamis had, however, seemed impossible. The Phoenicians were the sea dogs of the archaic world, and the Hellenes were greatly outnumbered. Moreover, most of the Greeks rowing and even those officering the triremes at Salamis were rank amateurs. Five years before, apart from the Corinthians, the Aeginetans, and the Athenians, the Hellenic communities that would fight in the straits between Salamis and Attica had possessed hardly any ships of this sort.

Themistocles was not just admired for his tactical brilliance, however. Men also stood in awe of his strategic foresight. He had anticipated Xerxes' invasion, and he had seen to it that the Athenians built the requisite ships. The historian Thucydides was a kinsman of Cimon.[18] By all rights, he should have been the man's partisan. But when he had occasion to record Themistocles' death, the historian intimated that, as a statesman, the son of Neocles was far superior to the son of Miltiades. "Themistocles was a man," he wrote,

> who in a fashion quite reliable displayed strength of nature, and in this regard he was outstanding and worthy of greater admiration than anyone else. By his own native intelligence, without the help of study before or after, he was at once the best judge in matters, admitting of little deliberation, which require settlement on the spot, and the best predictor of things to come across the broadest expanse. What he had in hand he could also

explain; what lay beyond his experience he did not lack the capacity ade-
quately to judge. In a future as yet obscure he could in a preeminent fashion
foresee both better and worse. In short, by the power of his nature, when
there was little time to take thought, this man surpassed all others in the
faculty of improvising what the situation required.[19]

Of no one else did Thucydides (or anyone else of remotely comparable stature
in antiquity) ever speak with commensurate awe and respect. Themistocles
was, in the Athenian historian's estimation, the greatest of statesmen.

When he left Athens after his ostracism, Thucydides tells us, Themistocles
moved to Argos. In two of the pseudepigraphical letters composed half a millennium thereafter, the exiled statesman is depicted as having reported that he
has come under pressure from the Argives to assume public office as a general
or even as the presiding officer of the whole city. On the face of it, this might
seem absurd. Ancient Greek *póleis* were exceedingly jealous of the prerogatives of citizenship. But, in the case of Themistocles, there might be something
to it—for the man was a force of nature. Thucydides, who was in a position to
know, also tells us that, while residing in Argos, Themistocles was in the habit
of traveling throughout the Peloponnesus,[20] and we know that the years that
followed close on his arrival at Argos were a time of trouble and peril in that
great peninsula for the Lacedaemonians. Moreover, it is clear that, in these same
years, the Spartans came to hate and fear the man as never before. Had he
merely operated as a tourist during these years of enforced absence from his
fatherland, it is hard to see why the Lacedaemonians would have even cared.[21]

Sparta's strength derived in part from the discipline her hoplites displayed
on the field of battle. That strength was multiplied many times over by her
ability to leverage the manpower of her neighbors—above all, the Corinthians and the Eleans as well as the Tegeans, Mantineians, and Orchomenians of
Arcadia, and their adherents within that upland region, not to mention the
Phliasians, Sicyonians, Epidaurians, Troezeneans, and Hermioneans. The alliance system that Lacedaemon had constructed within the Peloponnesus
with painstaking care in the sixth century was the bastion of her security. It
was also, however, quite fragile. For the cities that Sparta commanded were
genuine allies, not subjects. Moreover, like all Hellenic *póleis,* they possessed
an agonistic culture likely to give rise to factional strife and bitter disputes
concerning public policy; and within the Peloponnesus lay another powerful
pólis—named Argos—profoundly hostile to Lacedaemon, watching and wait-

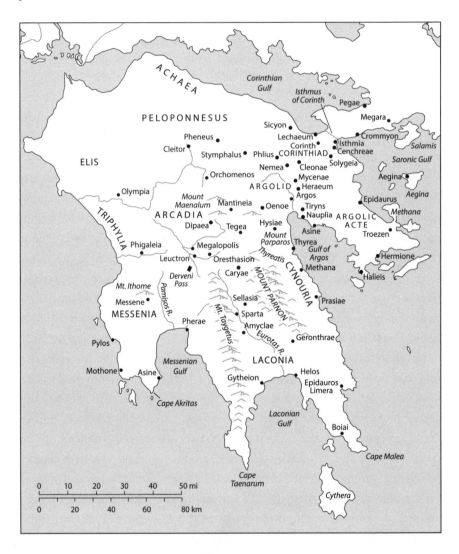

Map 6. The Peloponnesus

ing, hoping to lure away her allies, wrest from her the hegemony, and liberate
the Messenians.

In later years, one Corinthian leader would sum up Sparta's strategic position elegantly by comparing her to a stream. "At their sources," he noted,
"rivers are not great and they are easily forded, but the farther on they go, the
greater they get—for other rivers empty into them and make the current
stronger." So it is with the Spartans, he continued. "There, in the place where

they emerge, they are alone; but as they continue and gather cities under their control, they become more numerous and harder to fight." The prudent general, he concluded, will seek battle with the Spartans in or near Lacedaemon where they are few in number and relatively weak.[22] The structure of Sparta's defenses was fragile in the extreme, and the Lacedaemonians understood from the beginning what history was eventually to reveal: that it took but a single major defeat in warfare on land to endanger the city's very survival.

As Thucydides intimates in his eulogy for the man, Themistocles was also aware of the location of Sparta's Achilles' heel, and this was why, after being ostracized, he accepted an invitation from three of his Argive guest-friends that he situate himself in Argos.[23] Given his predilections, he could hardly have come at a more auspicious time.

The Peloponnesus in Flux

In the decades preceding Themistocles' extended sojourn at Argos, the situation within the Peloponnesus was exceptionally fluid.[24] For example, shortly before the battle of Marathon, when it came to light that the Agiad king Cleomenes had bribed the oracle at Delphi with an eye to ousting his recalcitrant Eurypontid colleague and installing as king someone else who was more pliable, he had fled to Arcadia—where, by sheer force of personality and his charisma as a sacral king, he managed to unite the Arcadians against Lacedaemon on a scale sufficient to persuade his compatriots to recall him from exile forthwith. We are also told that, at some point not all that many years prior to Xerxes' invasion, the Tegeans were not on friendly terms with the Spartans. And yet, in 480, when Leonidas marched to Thermopylae, five hundred Tegeans accompanied him; and in 479, when the battle of Plataea took place, three times as many Tegeans presented themselves. In the latter battle, these men actually distinguished themselves as stalwart, courageous, and enthusiastic allies of the Lacedaemonians.[25]

Mantineia deserves special attention as well. She was said to be the oldest and greatest *pólis* in Arcadia. Her citizens were famous for their prowess in battle—so much so, in fact, that they were sometimes said to have invented the hoplite panoply—and they may well have been the first to treat hoplite warfare as a formal course of study, as was claimed. We are not told that, in the 490s, the Mantineians refused to rally in support of Cleomenes—which suggests that they, too, must have lent him their support. Like the Tegeans, however, they sent five hundred men to Thermopylae. But when the Lacedaemonians later summoned them to Plataea, they balked. They had ample warning, and the battle itself was fought weeks after they were supposed to show up. But they did not arrive until it was over.[26]

A similar tale could be told about the Eleans, who did not present themselves until after the arrival of the Mantineians. That the citizens of these two important cities confessed that they deserved punishment and subsequently banished those responsible for their late arrival strongly suggests that—from the Spartan and, for that matter, the Hellenic perspective—something far more sinister than fecklessness was involved. Between them, these two communities were capable of fielding something on the order of six thousand hoplites.[27]

The situation at Argos was also fluid. There had been an epoch, a century and more before Themistocles arrived in that city, when the Arcadians had been aligned with the Argives against Lacedaemon, and Argos had been the leading power within the Peloponnesus. In those days, the Argives had dominated the Argeia, the Argolic Acte, and much of the world beyond. After seizing Asine in the late eighth century, they had apparently asserted their presidency over the amphictyony of Apollo Pythaeus long based in that city; and, with this as a justification, they had extended their dominion over the Argolic Gulf in its entirety. From this position of preeminence, they had imposed obligations on cities as distant as Sicyon, Epidaurus, Troezen, and Aegina. At this time, the fertile plain of Thyrea and Cynouria to the south along the Aegean coast of the Peloponnesus had been in their grasp along with the island of Cythera opposite Cape Malea—and Sparta's hold on Messenia had been tenuous.[28]

From time to time, in and after the mid-sixth century, the Argives had mounted an attempt to regain their hegemony within the Peloponnesus, but to no avail. In about 494, at Sepeia, they had suffered a particularly severe setback, losing in battle something on the order of six thousand men—a larger number than are known to have been lost by a single city in any other battle in the classical period—and in the aftermath, we have reason to believe, the Spartans had refused to sign with them the customary thirty years' peace.[29]

In the wake of the massacre that took place at Sepeia, a woman named Telesilla is said to have organized the defense of the city walls, rallying the old men, the young, her fellow women, and the underlings attached to their households [οἰκέται] to wield whatever weapons they could find and fend off an assault. Herodotus, our most reliable source, makes no mention of this event. But he appears to be aware of this tradition, for an oracle he cites associates Argos' defeat with a victory and an achievement of glory on the part of that city's women.[30]

It is a reasonable guess that the *oikétai* mentioned by Plutarch in his discussion of Telesilla's achievement were drawn from the city's substantial and downtrodden pre-Dorian population. In the aftermath of the battle, Herodotus tells us, there was a revolution at Argos, and the slaves [*doûloi*] seized power. Aristotle has a different tale to relate. According to his report, the Argives were forced, after their defeat, to accept some of their *períoikoi* into the ruling order. Plutarch confirms what we would in any case surmise: that those whom Herodotus' aristocratic Argive informants disdainfully called *doûloi* outsiders would be inclined to identify as *períoikoi;* and he mentions that, because of a shortage of adult male citizens, the widows and young girls of Argos married these men.

A generation after this development, in the wake of the conflicts to which it gave rise, the citizen body of Argos appears to have been reorganized: a "tribal reform" was carried out on the model of those known (or thought) to have been instituted earlier at Lacedaemon, Corinth, Athens, Samos, Eretria, and Cyrene. In consequence, membership in the political community at Argos came to be redefined, in a manner guaranteeing the inclusion of the pre-Dorian population of the Argeia, either in terms of a citizen's residence in a particular ward or village (as opposed to his membership in one of the three ancient Dorian kinship corporations and the fourth consisting of the pre-Dorian element in the population), or in terms of his assignment to a phratry of the enfranchised included within one of these four tribes.[31]

The catastrophe at Sepeia and Sparta's persistent refusal to agree to a peace of extended duration help explain why Argos dodged joining the Hellenic coalition at the time of Xerxes' invasion; why, without incurring the risks associated with sending soldiers to support Xerxes, it maintained exceedingly cordial relations with the Mede; why Sicyon and Phlius to the north of the Argeia and cities on its periphery near the Saronic Gulf or the Aegean, such as Epidaurus, Troezen, and Hermione, as well as the island of Aegina just off that coast, felt free to ignore the predilections of the Argives and join the Hellenic League; and why small *póleis* deep within the Argeia near Argos itself, such as Mycenae and Tiryns, which had previously been answerable to that great city, were able to participate in the Hellenic League as independent communities.[32] The absorption of the pre-Dorian population into the citizen body at Argos, which may have been a matter of military necessity in 494, also set the stage for a struggle that broke out years later when those whom Herodotus terms "the sons of the slain" reached maturity [*epébēsan*] and carried out a coup d'état that eventuated in an expulsion of at least some of the underlings promoted to citizenship.[33]

By the time that Themistocles reached his intended refuge, Argos must to some extent have recovered from the blow dealt it at Sepeia. Almost a quarter of a century had passed, and a new generation had come of age. At Argos, there had never been a shortage of women able to bear sons. The demographic implosion that had eliminated the better part of a generation of Argive men and that had for a time crippled the city must have been largely past. The only obstacle to an Argive resurgence was the independence of cities within the Argeia which had once been her subjects.

It would be tempting to suppose that, at the time of Themistocles' arrival, "the sons of the slain" had not yet driven out the *períoikoi* and that his activities and those of the Argives within the Peloponnesus had a democratic cast.[34] The Spartans were, as we have seen, *kaloì k'agathoí*. As was only natural, they preferred the company of men like themselves; and, within their alliance, when they had an entirely free hand, they tended to promote oligarchy.[35] Athens was, by way of contrast, a democracy; and, all else being equal, the Athenians tended to promote that form of government.[36] During the great war between Sparta and Athens that sputtered on through most of the last third of the fifth century, the opposed predilections of these two rival hegemonic powers would occasion, within the cities that were up for grabs, bitter quarrels as well as bloody revolutions rooted in class differences and regime preferences.[37]

Themistocles' opponent Cimon was the scion of one of Athens' leading aristocratic clans, as was his sister's husband Callias. When the time came for him to marry, the former chose a wife from the no less distinguished Alcmeonid clan. In the process—by marrying Isodike, daughter of Euryptolemos son of Megacles—he not only put an end to a quarrel between the two families that had given rise in 489 to his father Miltiades' trial and conviction. He also effected a political consolidation of Athens' ancient aristocracy.[38] The Theban poet Pindar—who in this period wrote odes celebrating the accomplishments and family histories of great aristocrats victorious in the athletic contests at

Olympia, Delphi, Isthmia, Nemea, and elsewhere—had occasion to sing the praises of Cimon and his family, of the Alcmeonids, the Spartans, and a distinguished Argive of Tirynthian ancestry named Theaios, who cannot have been one of Herodotus' *doûloi*. But he did not in a similar fashion honor Themistocles, and there is no evidence to suggest that any of the poets who directly or indirectly singled out the son of Neocles for praise—such as Simonides, Phyrnichus, and Aeschylus—had a good word to say about the son of Miltiades.[39]

A decade or so after Themistocles' ostracism, those at Athens who are thought with some reason to have been his allies and who were similarly opposed to Cimon carried out a political reform in the teeth of the latter's opposition that rendered Athens considerably more democratic than it had been in the latter's heyday; and there is evidence, too often dismissed, suggesting that Themistocles and Aristeides had initiated the campaign that those junior to them later carried to a successful conclusion. The Areopagus—a council made up of Athens' former chief magistrates, the archons, who were drawn from among the "fifty-measure men [*pentakosiomédimnoi*]" and the "cavalrymen [*hippeîs*]" who made up the two wealthiest census classes in the city—appears to have been a great source of strength for Cimon and the other great families allied with him. The struggle to clip that body's wings and the attempt to reorient Athens' foreign policy may not in principle have been connected, but in the circumstances they came to be so in practice.[40]

Within the Peloponnesus, only a handful of the cities possessed walls. Argos had them, as did Corinth. But the Spartans had none,[41] and the same held true early on for Elis and for the *póleis* within Arcadia—including Tegea and Mantineia—which consisted of dispersed villages and lacked fully developed urban centers. We know very little about the political and social development of these communities, but there is evidence suggesting that they tended in and after the late archaic period to drift in the direction of urban consolidation, democratic government, and local imperialism.

There are, for example, inscriptions showing that, three decades or more before the time of Themistocles' ostracism, Elis had already become a democracy of sorts and that she was already then a power of some significance—ruling over a regional empire, modeled on that maintained by Lacedaemon in Laconia and Messenia, replete with dependent *póleis* peopled by *períoikoi*. Diodorus tells us that a synoecism—a consolidation of villages and the establishment of an urban center—took place there in 471/0, when Themistocles may already have begun to be active at Argos; and Herodotus reports that in his day the Eleans seized and sacked most of the cities in the region nearby to the south that came to be called Triphylia.[42]

In a passage in which he confirms Diodorus' testimony regarding Elis' synoecism and specifies that it took place in the wake of the Persian Wars, Strabo adds that the Argives effected a synoecism of the five villages of Mantineia, and his phrasing suggests that this, too, may have taken place in the aftermath of the Persian Wars and that the Argives may also have had something to do with the synoecism of the nine villages of Tegea that he mentions next in the same passage. There is, moreover, evidence that Mantineia became a democracy at some point prior to 421; and—at Mantineia and presumably also elsewhere as well—there seems to have been a connection between urban consolidation and democracy and between dispersal into villages and the rule of the few.[43]

This evidence is suggestive, but it is in no way dispositive. We know that Mantineia became a democracy. We do not know when. We have reason to believe that a synoecism took place at Elis in 471/0. We do not know whether Themistocles or the Argives had anything to do with it. We know that the Argives had carried out the synoecism at Mantineia, and there is reason to suspect that they may also have done the like at Tegea. But, apart from the fact that Mantineia was said to have been the oldest *pólis* in Arcadia and to have been governed at some point under a moderate democracy, we have no firm evidence bearing on the question when either synoecism took place. All that we can say is that it is as easy to imagine as it is impossible to prove that Themistocles' travels within the Peloponnesus had something to do with these developments.[44]

It would, in any case, be a grave error to read the ideological polarization of late modernity back into classical antiquity. Democracy cannot have been the principal focus of Themistocles' concerns in these years. This Athenian and those at Athens who supported him were surely favorable to democracy as such. But no one connected with Athens was intent on making of the city's foreign policy an ideological crusade. Nor could the Athenians have afforded one. At this time, most, if not all, of their chief allies within the Delian League—including Chios, Samos, and Mytilene on the island of Lesbos—were oligarchies.[45]

Themistocles and his allies had Sparta as their focus, and they were more than willing to cooperate with any Peloponnesian polity intent on resisting her hegemony. At Argos in particular, it cannot have much mattered to them whether the *períoikoi* still possessed full political rights, and the odds are good that at least some of them were no longer so situated. In the twenty-three or more years that had passed since the disaster at Sepeia, the sons of the men killed there by Cleomenes had without a doubt come of age after having undergone the training and rites of passage associated with late adolescence [*ephēbeía*], and Herodotus' choice of language suggests that by this time they must have seized control and that they must in some measure have purged the citizen body—though the epigraphical record shows that they did not reverse the tribal reform. It is hard to see why this would have mattered to Themistocles. The "sons of the slain" were far more likely to have been itching for revenge than to have sympathized with those responsible for the massacre of their fathers. If, after carrying out a tribal reform and embracing democracy at home, the Argives, with Themistocles' help, staged synoecisms and promoted regime change elsewhere within the Peloponnesus, it was chiefly or even solely because the existing oligarchies were in league with Lacedaemon.[46]

The Argives had two objects in mind—one local and immediate, the other further afield. For obvious reasons, they desperately wanted to reverse the verdict of Sepeia and regain full control of the Argeia and hegemony over the Argolid as a whole,[47] and they were also eager to recover Cynouria and supplant Lacedaemon as the leading *pólis* within the Peloponnesus. For geopolitical reasons, however, the Argives had to attend to Arcadia first. They could not hope to regain Cynouria and replace the Spartans until they had recovered Mycenae and Tiryns in the Argeia and cowed Epidaurus, Troezen, and Hermione further afield in the Argolic Acte. But they could not assert themselves against these *póleis* as long as the Lacedaemonians could march at will through Arcadia into the Argolid to support their clients there. To prevent this from happening, therefore, the Argives forged an alliance with Tegea, which sat athwart the main thoroughfare leading from Lacedaemon to the Argolid.[48]

As Themistocles, the probable architect of this alliance, undoubtedly realized, the emergence of this axis was a development that the Spartans could not afford to ignore. From a military perspective, south-central Arcadia was for Lacedaemon the center of gravity. The Pamisos valley in Messenia, which lay to the west across Mount Taygetus from the Eurotas valley in Laconia, was the principal source of Lacedaemon's wealth. The land there was fertile. It was well

The Peloponnesus in Flux: A Timetable, 494–461

494	Sparta defeats Argos in the battle of Sepeia
Ca. 491	Cleomenes stirs rebellion in Arcadia
490	Helot revolt
479	Mantineia and Elis late for Plataea
Ca. 472–466	Themistocles sojourns at Argos, tours the Peloponnesus
471/0	Synoecism at Elis
	Synoecisms at Mantineia and Tegea? Possible Argive role
469	Battle of Eurymedon
Ca. 469	Argive-Tegean alliance
	Argos and Tegea battle Sparta at Tegea
468/7	First Peace of Callias
467/6	Pausanias executed for Medizing
466	Themistocles accused of Medism, takes flight from Argos
Spring 465	Settlement at Ennea Hodoi
	Rebellion of Thasos
Summer 465	Thasos defeated at Sea, appeal for Lacedaemonian support
	Secret Spartan pledge of aid, siege initiated at Thasos
Early August 465	Assassination of Xerxes
Late Summer 465	Execution of younger Darius, succession of Artaxerxes
Winter 465/4	Great earthquake and helot revolt at Sparta
	Mantineians, Aeginetans, Plataeans, Athenians come to Sparta's aid
Winter–Spring 464	Artabanus' coup d'état thwarted
	Artaxerxes repudiates first Peace of Callias
Spring, 464	Argos, Tegea, and Cleonae attack and defeat Mycenae
	Massacre at Drabeskos
464/3	Argive war against Tiryns begins
463	Battle of Dipaea
	Battle of the Isthmus near Mount Ithome
462	Cimon and the Athenians summoned to Messenia
	Thasos surrenders
	Ephialtes' reform
	Cimon and the Athenians sent home from Messenia
462/1	Athens repudiates alliance with Sparta
	Athens forms alliance with Argos and Thessaly
461	Ostracism of Cimon

watered. But the helots who farmed that land for their Spartiate masters were a nation in bondage, more than capable of revolt, and Messenia was hard to reach. There were paths and even carriage roads across the Taygetus massif that the Spartans sometimes used, and the upkeep of these and other routes of communication was assigned to the two kings in their capacity as generals. But it was much easier for men with equipment and carts loaded with provisions to work their way around the mountain by marching north-northwest along its eastern flank, then west through the highlands of south-central Arcadia, and finally southwest over the Derveni pass into the Pamisos valley via the route followed by the modern road.

In ordinary circumstances, Tegea, which lay directly to the north of Laconia, exercised considerable influence over the districts of Arcadia to her west that bordered on Messenia. In the past, when the Tegeans had been allied to Lacedaemon's Argive enemy, it had for obvious reasons been exceedingly difficult for the Lacedaemonians to sustain their hold on Messenia. It is no wonder, then, that the ephors dispatched the Spartiates and the *períoikoi* of Laconia to Tegea—where, Herodotus tells us, a great battle was fought, pitting the Lacedaemonians against the adherents of this new and threatening alliance.[49]

We do not know whether Tegea's allies elsewhere in Arcadia, who may well have been numerous, rallied at this time to her defense; and we hear nothing of the Eleans or the Mantineians. As we have had occasion to remark, these last two communities had both been at odds with Lacedaemon in 479. If Diodorus' chronology is to be trusted, the Eleans had just undergone a synoecism; and the Argives may recently have effected a synoecism at Mantineia. But Herodotus has nothing to say about the presence of either of these two peoples or that of anyone else, apart from the Argives, at the battle of Tegea—which would be quite telling and perhaps even dispositive were it not for his failure to mention "the Hellenes responsible for keeping Tegea free" and "the Athenians of great prowess who fell at Tegea," whose deeds were celebrated in a poem said to have been composed by Themistocles' friend Simonides. The presence of Athenians at this battle in numbers worth mentioning suggests that there were many at Athens who agreed with Themistocles' analysis of their city's strategic situation and who had volunteered to fight against the Spartans. As everyone no doubt recognized at the time, had the Lacedaemonians, in fact, lost this particular battle, it might well have sealed their doom.[50]

Pausanias and Themistocles

Themistocles reached Argos in the late spring or early summer of 472, 471, or 470. Simonides died in 468/7.[51] The odds are good that the battle of Tegea took place in 469 or in the spring of 468. It was, moreover, later in the latter year or in 467 that the Spartans are likely to have discovered for themselves what might well have been in store for them had they incurred defeat at Tegea.[52]

When Pausanias returned from Colonae, he was reportedly thrown into jail. When he challenged his incarceration by offering to undergo a trial, he was released. But no trial took place—for, although his evident contempt for Spartan custom and his aping of the barbarians gave rise to suspicion, the man responsible for Hellas' victory over Persia at Plataea had admirers. There were, moreover, those who thought that Lacedaemon really should reach an accommodation with the Mede, and the authorities lacked the level of proof required for the conviction of a figure of his stature. Even, we are told, when they were informed by certain helots that the Spartan regent was up to something with their fellows, offering the helots liberty and promising them citizenship if they joined him in an uprising and helped him accomplish his ends, they held back—for they were not about to convict or even try a citizen on the word of an underling.

But then Pausanias asked a slave of his named Argilus to convey a letter to Artabazus; and with an eye to the fact that none of the prior messengers had returned, this Argilus took the precaution of breaking the seal and reading his master's letter. In it, among other things, he found instructions asking that its bearer be killed; and he brought the letter, which made reference to Pausanias' arrangements with the Great King, to the ephors. Even then, Thucydides tells us, they were reluctant to act. So they had Argilus flee to the sanctuary of Poseidon at Taenarum as a suppliant, and there—when Pausanias came to attempt to persuade him to go on the mission and Argilus called him to account for the instructions in the letter—they contrived to listen in on their conversation.

It was only at this point that the ephors, after returning to Sparta and conferring, ordered the renegade regent's arrest—and even then, if Thucydides is to be trusted, one in their number tipped him off, and he sought refuge in the temple of Athena of the Brazen House. There the ephors had him bricked in; and from there, when he was on the verge of starving to death, the authorities committed a sacrilege by having him dragged out to die. We are told that they considered throwing his corpse into the pit reserved for criminals and that they decided, instead, to inter him nearby. We are also told that the oracle at Delphi subsequently instructed the Lacedaemonians to rebury him where he died and to return to the goddess of the Brazen House two bodies to replace the one they took and that there they then dedicated two bronze statues in his stead.[53]

This story—as told by Thucydides and elaborated on by others in his wake—is, to say, the least, bizarre; and, as one would expect, it has been a fruitful source of scholarly speculation.[54] One thing is, however, crystal clear: that, at Lacedaemon, Pausanias was a political lightning rod and that his opponents thought his elimination essential to the city's well-being. This, in turn, suggests that we should not dismiss out of hand the report that he was conspiring with certain helots. Indeed, there is reason to suspect that it was at this time, in connection with Pausanias' flight to the sanctuary of Athena Chalkiokis, that a number of these, known to have been party to his plot, fled as suppliants to the sanctuary of Poseidon at Taenarum—whence, in an act no less sacrilegious than that performed with regard to the renegade regent, they were dragged from the altars and massacred by the Spartans.[55] Moreover, as I have already had occasion to observe, what we know about Pausanias' public conduct while in Byzantium lends powerful support to the suspicion that he really was a Medizer. In short, the tale told (or, as some suppose, taken over from an earlier source) by Thucydides makes a great deal more sense of what was publicly known about Pausanias' conduct and about the response of the authorities at Lacedaemon than any of the alternative modern reconstructions. The Athenian historian was not, in any case, a man easily gulled.

It is also perfectly conceivable that the two letters said to have been found among Pausanias' effects after his death, which Thucydides quotes verbatim, are genuine.[56] Pausanias may well have made a copy of the missive he sent Xerxes, and there is no reason why he should not have kept Xerxes' reply. Their possession was no doubt dangerous—for, read in tandem, they provided proof of his dalliance with the Mede. But, by the same token, when read in tandem, they put him in a position to lure others into the plot they described. Moreover, the marriage proposal contained in Pausanias' message to Xerxes is suitably awkward. It is just the sort of thing that a headstrong young man who has lost all sense of proportion would propose, and Xerxes' response handles this

presumptuous proposition with appropriate tact simply by ignoring it. His letter, moreover, follows with great precision the protocols of the Persian chancel-
lery,[57] and one may wonder whether there was anyone at Lacedaemon capable
of producing so convincing a forgery.

Even the claim that Themistocles was somehow privy to and supportive
of the Spartan regent's plans is apt to be true. The two men could easily have
met in Lacedaemon when the Hellenic League was formed, and they can hardly
have avoided becoming well acquainted when Themistocles visited Sparta in
the wake of the battle of Salamis. At the time, Pausanias' father Cleombrotus,
who had become regent for the Agiad king Pleistarchus son of Leonidas after
the untimely death of the boy's father at Thermopylae, was himself dying or
quite recently dead. Cleombrotus' son and heir, who was about to become
regent or had just assumed the office, would have been expected to play a
prominent role in the entertainment of the city's distinguished guest. Moreover, Themistocles and Leonidas are apt to have become *xénoi* on the eve of
Xerxes' invasion—which would have made of Themistocles and Pausanias
hereditary guest-friends. If the latter pair did not, in fact, inherit such a tie, the
xenía, the guest-friendship, that appears to have linked them must have originated—in accord with ordinary Greek practice—at the time of Themistocles'
visit. The author of the pseudepigraphical letter from Themistocles to Pausanias presumes that they were well acquainted; and the Spartans, in making
their accusation, are said to have laid great emphasis on the fact that the two
were close friends (and presumably guest-friends). It may not be fortuitous
that Simonides wrote in praise of Leonidas and Pausanias as well as his friend
Themistocles.[58]

As we have already had occasion to note, at the end of 470s, when word
reached Athens that the Persians were once again building a great fleet, Themistocles came under attack for his insistence that Sparta, not Persia, was the
true danger to Athens. Cimon and an Athenian bearing the tell-tale name
Alcmaeon—presumably, one of the former's Alcmeonid in-laws—reportedly
seized on the occasion to denounce Themistocles. Then, if the reports are true,
Alcmaeon's son Leobotes initiated the great man's prosecution on a charge of
treason. The fact that Themistocles' prosecutor bore a Lacedaemonian name of
royal provenance, otherwise unattested in Attica, suggests a close connection—
perhaps a long-standing guest-friendship—linking his progenitor's family with
the Agiad house. In all likelihood, Alcmaeon and his son resembled Cimon,

his brother-in-law Callias, and their contemporary the elder Alcibiades in being among the *próxenoi* at Athens charged with looking after Sparta's interests—which is precisely what, we can surmise, the two did on this particular occasion.

The object of their ire was known to have corresponded with Pausanias. So we are told. Alcmaeon charged that the Spartan regent had informed Themistocles of his own collusion with the Mede, that he had more than once invited him to join the conspiracy, and that the Athenian had not only kept the man's confidence but had become a Medizer himself. In reply, Themistocles is said to have acknowledged the truth of the first three of these claims, to have asserted that he had rebuffed Pausanias' offer, and to have explained his failure to sound the alarm on the grounds that he had not taken seriously the Spartan's hare-brained scheme. He had figured that Pausanias would either give up his silly quest or get caught.[59] Themistocles was a man who prided himself on being of service to his friends; and, as everyone understood at the time, the aristocratic ethos militated against guest-friends betraying one another.[60]

It is perfectly possible and even likely that the two old friends remained in touch after the recall of Pausanias while Themistocles was at Argos, as the Lacedaemonians later asserted. Given the Athenian's ostracism, one can easily imagine Pausanias supposing that his counterpart no longer had a stake in the status quo and that he might finally be ready to join in. It would, moreover, be an error to dismiss out of hand the possibility that incriminating letters, exchanged between the two, were found among Pausanias' effects—precisely as the Spartans claimed. Indeed, given Themistocles' conviction that Lacedaemon was at this time a far greater threat to Athens than Persia, there is no reason why he should not have welcomed Pausanias' collusion with the Great King and even encouraged his attempt to stir up a helot revolt. From the perspective of this Athenian Odysseus, what the son of Cleombrotus was trying to do at Lacedaemon was perfectly consonant with what the Argives and Tegeans had attempted at the battle of Tegea. Had either project come off, it would in practice have meant Sparta's elimination as a great power.[61]

There is one other reason for supposing that there might have been something to the charges lodged by the Spartans when, after Pausanias' death, they sent an embassy to Athens to propose that Themistocles be tried before the council at the upcoming meeting of the Hellenic League. The Athenian statesman could have surrendered himself for trial, but this he did not do. Nor did he stay in Argos and await a summons. Instead, fearing conviction and suspecting that the Argives would, if called upon, surrender their guest, he set off for Corcyra, hoping that his service to that city in the past as an arbitrator would persuade the citizens there to harbor him, and perhaps pondering, as Stesimbrotus suggests, the possibility that he might find refuge at the court of the tyrant Hiero in Syracusa further to the west. But the Corcyraeans were no more willing than the Argives to take the risk of protecting their benefactor when faced with demands from both Sparta and Athens; and while on Corcyra, if he ever dreamed of a sojourn in Sicily, Themistocles is apt to have learned of Hiero's quite recent death.

In desperation, therefore, Themistocles fled as a suppliant to Admetus, the king of the Molossians—a man, like Hiero, to whom he had reportedly given offense in days gone by when he was riding high. Although he had reason to spurn the Athenian's plea, Admetus nonetheless received him, refused to turn him over to the Spartans when their embassy arrived, and sent him on from Epirus to Pydna in Macedon, where Alexander I ruled.

From there, no doubt with the connivance of that canny Macedonian monarch, Themistocles took passage, incognito, on a merchant ship headed for Anatolia. We do not know the projected itinerary, and we do not know whether Themistocles traveled in the summer or the winter. At no time was it possible to make such a journey without danger. It is possible that the ship's captain was intent on heading directly south past Pieria and the iron coast of Magnesia and then southeast along the unforgiving eastern shore of Euboea before making his way to Ephesus through the Cyclades past Andros, Tenos, Mykonos, Ikaros, and Samos—always in sight of land. It is also conceivable that he aimed to sail around the Chalcidice. Once past that formidable obstacle, he could take one of two routes—either east along the Thracian coast past Thasos and Samothrace to the Hellespont and then south to Ionia along the Anatolian shore or, more likely, east southeast toward Lemnos and Lesbos and on to Ionia from there.

What we do know is that the man's ship was caught in a storm; that, if the best manuscript of Plutarch is to be trusted as an indication of what that author read in Thucydides, the vessel was driven to Thasos, which Athenians were then besieging; and that, at this point, Themistocles revealed his identity to the captain, promised him a reward if he delivered him to Anatolia, and threatened that, if the man betrayed him, he would tell the Athenians that he had bribed him. In the event, the ship's master opted not to land on Thasos,

Map 7. Themistocles' Flight: From Argos to Corcyra, Epirus, Pydna in Macedonia, Thasos, and Cumae in Anatolia

concealed his passenger, and sailed on by one of the two northern routes to
Cumae in Anatolia, where Themistocles learned that Xerxes had died not long
before—early in August 465.[62]

Themistocles' arrival in Anatolia did not by any means put an end to his
travails. He was as much a marked man in the Achaemenid empire as he was
in Hellas. The Great King had at some point put a price on his head of two
hundred talents (which is to say, 5.7 tons) in silver, and, needless to say, there
were individuals in Anatolia eager to collect that reward. This fact notwithstanding, the Athenian managed to find a hideout not far from Cumae in a little
Aeolic town, where a guest-friend of his, a man of great wealth with close ties
to the district's Achaemenid administration, had his estates. This figure appears
to have put him in touch with the local satrap Artabazus son of Pharnaces—
who had more than a decade before been assigned by Xerxes the management
of the Medizer Pausanias, as the Athenian may well have known. It was, we
have reason to believe, this Artabazus who arranged for the long journey Themistocles then made to Susa, on which he was shepherded, Thucydides reports,
by a Persian—presumably one of the satrap's underlings. It must also have
been through the good offices of Artabazus that the Athenian sent on ahead a
letter offering his services to Artaxerxes, the deceased Persian monarch's successor as the King of Kings. Without authorization from on high, as we have
seen, no one could make such a journey within the Achaemenid realm or
dispatch such a missive. It was in this fashion that Athens' Odysseus made his
way to Susa, trading on the dubious claim that at the time of Salamis he had
shown himself to be a benefactor of the royal house.

In Susa, Themistocles managed by guile or dumb luck to sidestep an exceedingly delicate situation. Xerxes was dead. His firstborn son and prospective heir Darius had been falsely accused of patricide and had himself been
killed in turn. His second son Hystaspes, the satrap of Bactria, was in the
process of asserting his right to the throne; and Artaxerxes, who was a
stripling, was by no means firmly established as king. Thucydides tells us that,
before formally presenting himself at the court, Themistocles tarried for a year
with the permission of the Great King, studying Old Persian. According to another report, penned by a follower of Aristotle named Phanias of Lesbos, the
Athenian was initially received in Susa by Artabanus, the Chiliarch responsible for Xerxes' assassination, the murder of young Darius, and the succession
of Artaxerxes—and it was there that he settled down to learn what he could of

the language spoken by his new master. Scholars have tended to regard the latter report as improbable in the extreme, but we are told by a generally reliable source that Artabanus ruled for seven months after Xerxes' death, and it is plausible to suppose that for a time he managed the realm in the name of the boy king whom he had installed on the throne.

Eventually, we are told, this Artabanus, who bore an Achaemenid name and may have been a descendant of Xerxes' like-named uncle, hatched a plot to eliminate Artaxerxes and take office in his place. In one particular, however, he blundered, and that was by taking into his confidence Megabyzus son of Zopyrus—who had been a figure of great importance at Xerxes' court. This man's like-named grandfather had been one of the seven conspirators who had made Darius son of Hystaspes Great King in 522. His father had for Darius put down a great rebellion in Babylon. As a young man, this Megabyzus had accompanied Xerxes on the march into Greece, and he had served as one of his marshals. At some point, he had even married one of that Great King's daughters; and, in the aftermath of Xerxes' assassination, he stood by his brother-in-law Artaxerxes, divulged the nature of the plot, and saw to it that Artabanus' machinations were thwarted. It is apt also to have been during Themistocles' extended period of study that the authorities in Susa saw off the challenge mounted by Artaxerxes' older brother Hystaspes.

By the time that Themistocles' year of study had come to an end and he had emerged from seclusion, things had to a considerable degree settled down. This much is clear: Artabanus and his sons were dead; Hystaspes was no longer in evidence; Artaxerxes was fully in charge; and a man named Roxanes now served as his Chiliarch. When this Roxanes conducted Themistocles into the royal presence, Plutarch reports, he furiously denounced him as a "wily Greek serpent." And there, this hostile introduction notwithstanding, the man most responsible for Persia's defeat at Salamis secured for himself from Xerxes' son and heir a position of honor and rich reward.[63]

A New Atmosphere and a New Mood

If the chronology of events suggested here is correct or even close to correct, one dramatic development followed another in the early 460s. First, probably in 469, came Athens' stunning victory at Eurymedon and the news that she was in the process of negotiating an accord with the Great King. At about the same time, there came a grave crisis within the Spartan alliance, which eventuated in a great battle at Tegea; and this event was soon followed by a series of unsettling revelations made in quick succession—by reports that the Agiad regent was conspiring to raise a helot revolt, by the presentation of proof that he had offered his services to Xerxes and had long been operating as the Great King's agent, and finally, after the man's death, by the discovery among his effects of correspondence indicating that Themistocles, the wiliest of the Athenians, had for some time been privy to the man's intrigues, confirming that he had failed to divulge what he knew, and suggesting that he may even have encouraged the enterprise.

In circumstances such as these, those who take the lead in determining public policy within a polity are bound to pause and reflect. They see the earth moving rapidly beneath their feet. They have brought home to them in a most unpleasant way the vulnerability of the position their city occupies, and they revisit the calculations on which they had hitherto grounded the foreign policy of the community they govern.

Those at Lacedaemon who were convinced that the pursuit of empire would destroy the Spartan regime and that an alliance with Athens still best served the polity's interests were no doubt exceedingly eager that Themistocles be removed from the scene. On this matter, there was no doubt unanimity among the Spartiates. Those, however, who longed for grandeur and wealth and who resented the rise of Athens can hardly have regarded this as sufficient— and they now had new arguments to make. At the time these must have had considerable purchase.

With Persia more or less off stage, as we have seen, the Delian League now seemed more like a threat than a bulwark of defense. Even more to the point, during his sojourn at Argos, Themistocles had made manifest the fragility of the Spartan alliance. Argos was resurgent. Tegea had been defeated but she was still hostile and defiant. Even if Elis and Mantineia were still loyal, as they may well have been, they could not be fully relied on. Of this their conduct in 479, when they failed to show up in time for the battle of Plataea, was more than sufficient proof.

As long as Athens was a great power, these Spartans could argue, it would be a serious threat. Within every city in the Spartan alliance, there was a faction that resented Lacedaemon. To the extent that Athens represented an alternative, she was a temptation. Cimon might favor peaceful coexistence and cooperation with Sparta. But there were others at Athens who shared the strategic vision of Themistocles. A host of them had come to Tegea as volunteers to fight against Lacedaemon, and the odds were good that at Athens they would someday be ascendant. It made no sense for the Spartans to make their security dependent on the political success of the son of Miltiades and those who shared his views.

When the Athenians encroached on the interests of the Thasians and the latter revolted, were defeated at sea, and appealed to Sparta for aid, we can be confident that in "the little assembly"—consisting of the ephors, the *gérontes,* and the two kings or the regents who stood in for them—these concerns were fully aired.[64] If the authorities secretly opted to promise Lacedaemon's support— as, I suspect, was the case—or if "the common assembly" actually did so, it was because what had happened at Eurymedon and Tegea and in the aftermath of these two great battles had within Hellas created a new atmosphere and had given rise to a new mood—to which the Spartans thought that they, too, would have to conform.

Part II

YOKEFELLOWS NO MORE

It is not by speech-making that the Laconian *pólis* is fortified.
But whenever mutinous Ares falls upon an army,
Counsel rules, and the hand performs the deed.

ION OF CHIOS

I T is an open question whether the authorities at Lacedaemon would have been able to persuade the assembly of the Spartiates to go to war with Athens over the Athenians' mistreatment of the Thasians. There certainly would have been fierce objections raised. Had they persuaded their compatriots, however, and had they been able to rally the support of the communities within the Spartan alliance, there is nothing that would have prevented them from marching into Attica. It is perfectly possible that the Athenians would then have sallied forth from behind the walls of the city and those of the Peiraeus to defend their farmland. That would have been suicidal. But it was the natural thing to do. It is also conceivable that Sparta's intervention would have prompted a rebellion on the part of those of Athens' allies in the Delian League that still had fleets. Athens in 465 was anything but impregnable. The policy persistently pursued by Cimon presupposed Spartan goodwill.

In practice, however, this scenario is pure speculation and the question posed, academic—for the possibility never really presented itself. In 465/4, probably in the winter—after Themistocles had fled, after the Thasians had made their appeal, after the authorities at Sparta had made their pledge, but before the campaigning season when they would have rallied the members of their Peloponnesian alliance and mounted an invasion of Attica—a cataclysm took place which, for a time at least, altered everything.

Greece is subject to seismic upheavals, and the southern reaches of the Peloponnesus are in this particular especially vulnerable. In this case, we do not know the precise date or even the month. All that we know is that, before the Lacedaemonians could come to the support of Thasos, a series of earth-quakes struck Laconia. The epicenter appears to have been near the constitu-tive villages of Lacedaemon. We are told that, at Sparta, these earthquakes left only five houses standing, that twenty thousand Lacedaemonians were killed, and that more than half of the adult male Spartiates (the full citizens of Lace-daemon) lost their lives—and we have excellent reason to believe that many more died in battling the revolt of the helots and the rebellion of the *períoikoi* in Thouria and Aethaea, which followed fast on this event.[1] Some scholars regard the ancient testimony as exaggerated. There is one sign, however, that this is not the case: the Spartans in desperation actually asked for assistance; and, as we shall see in due course, ample assistance they received.[2]

There are two other pieces of evidence that bear on Sparta's straitened circumstances at this time. The first has to do with Argos' close neighbor My-cenae. Thanks to the Spartan victory over the Argives at Sepeia in 494, this small city was independent at the time of the Persian Wars, as we have seen. For some time thereafter, she asserted and managed to retain control over the most prestigious cult site in the Argive plain, the Temple of Hera—which lay considerably closer to Mycenae than it did to Argos. We are told that, at some point subsequent to the withdrawal of the Mede, the Argives—fearing that the entire Argolid would eventually come under Mycenaean sway—attacked and defeated the Mycenaeans in battle; then besieged, conquered, and razed their town before selling most of its inhabitants into slavery. This they did not do entirely on their own. At least initially, when they had to meet the Mycenaeans in the field, they drew support from the Tegeans, whom they had earlier sup-ported at the battle of Tegea. They are also said to have received aid from the citizens of Cleonae in the northern Argeia, which was a rival to Mycenae in asserting a right to control the Nemean Games.

It is the timetable that tells the tale. Diodorus relates the story of Argos' war against Mycenae immediately after describing the earthquake at Sparta and the helot revolt. Then, no doubt following Ephorus, he expressly relates the two sets of events—explaining that the Argives seized on Lacedaemon's tra-vails as an opportunity for the elimination of a local rival that looked to Sparta for support, and asserting that they were correct in their calculations: for the earthquake and the struggles subsequent to it made it impossible for the Lace-daemonians to send a relief expedition.[3]

The second piece of evidence for Sparta's distress at this time is that, quite soon after Mycenae's initial defeat, the Lacedaemonians fought another contest against the Tegeans—this one at a place named Dipaea—and that they fought it in circumstances suggesting on their part a severe shortage of manpower. Herodotus does not mention the Argives as having taken part in this particular battle.[4] This could conceivably be an oversight on his part, but it is also possible—and, indeed, likely—that they were pouring all of their energies into the ongoing siege at Mycenae. It is also conceivable that at this time they were involved in a war with their near neighbor Tiryns. For, when Herodotus reports that—after the sons of the Argives massacred by Cleomenes and the Spartans in 494 came of age—they drove out the *doûloi* who had been admitted to the citizen body in the aftermath of that battle, he adds that those who had been expelled then seized Tiryns and that, after a time, a conflict of some duration and difficulty erupted between "the sons of the slain" who remained in control in Argos and the *doûloi* who had found refuge at Tiryns.

We do not know precisely when this struggle with Tiryns took place, but there is reason to suspect that Lacedaemon may have been the instigator—for it was very much in the interest of the Spartans that the Argives be preoccupied at this time, and Herodotus reports that the war erupted when a seer named Kleandros from Phigaleia in southwestern Arcadia on the border of Messenia induced the Tirynthians to launch an attack. If, at this time, the Argives missed a golden opportunity to strike a blow at Lacedaemon, as Herodotus' failure to mention them in connection with the battle of Dipaea strongly suggests, there must have been some development that precluded their participation. It was not until about 460 that they appear to have been in a position to turn their attention and energy to other matters.[5]

In the Argives' stead, however, others joined the fray. When speaking of the battle of Tegea, Herodotus has nothing to say about any of the Arcadians apart from the Tegeans. When, however, he goes on to allude to the battle of Dipaea, which is the next conflict in a chronologically arranged list of Spartan victories in this period that he quickly reels off, he reports that this time the Tegeans had the support of all of their fellow Arcadians—apart from the Mantineians.[6] When considered in a geopolitical light, the composition of this coalition is revealing, as is the exclusion of the Mantineians: for it suggests that the Spartans intervened in Arcadia for two disparate reasons.

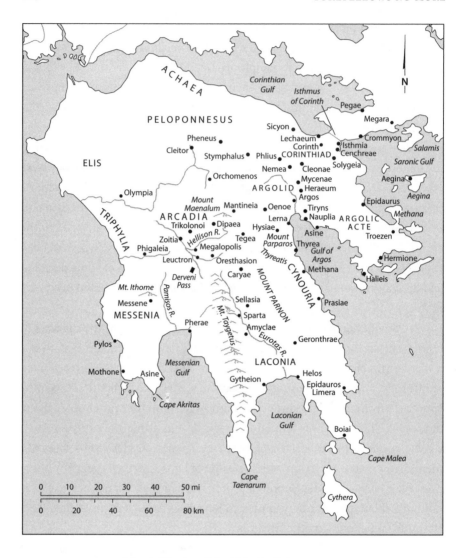

Map 8. The Argolid within the Peloponnesus

Dipaea was located in central Arcadia—well to the south and a bit to the west of Arcadian Orchomenos—in the upper Hellison valley. Its strategic significance stemmed from the fact that it lay directly west across the mountains from the fertile highland plain in eastern Arcadia dominated by Tegea in the south and Mantineia in the north. To reach Dipaea from Laconia, one must first follow the wagon road running up the Eurotas River north-northwest along the eastern flanks of the Taygetus massif toward the sizable highland plateau situated north of Taygetus where—on the banks of the Hellison River, a century after the battle of Dipaea—the Arcadian League and its allies would found the city of Megalopolis as a check on the power of Lacedaemon. From this well-watered region, one must then proceed north-northeast through Zoitia past Trikolonoi and into central Arcadia or make one's way directly up the exceedingly narrow and difficult Hellison gorge.

The Lacedaemonians could not stand idly by while Tegea asserted her control over south-central Arcadia—for through the southernmost reaches of that district, as we have already had occasion to note, ran a strategically vital wagon road which stretched like an umbilical cord between the Spartan heartland on the Eurotas in Laconia and Lacedaemon's rich holdings along the Pamisos in Messenia. Nor can the Spartans have relished the prospect that Mantineia, the one *pólis* of consequence in the strategically vital region of Arcadia still loyal to them, would succumb to pressure from her neighbors—especially, since that one city was the sole obstacle to the unification of Arcadia and its emergence as a regional power with considerable heft. The Lacedaemonians resembled other hegemonic powers in this particular. To rule, they had to divide.

The army that ended up in Dipaea must have initially paused en route to reassert Spartan hegemony over the south-central Arcadian plateau, over Parrhasia to the west, and Phigaleia in the Neda river valley even further to the west—all of which bordered on northern Messenia. Then, it must have retraced its steps back to what would eventually become the Megalopolitan plain; and from there, by one of the two routes mentioned, it must have headed north-northeast to Dipaea with an eye to approaching Mantineia from the west via one of the two passes across Mount Maenalum. By means of this roundabout route, the Spartans could sidestep Tegea, which straddled the direct wagon road leading north from Lacedaemon via Caryae to Mantineia, and avoid thereby a provocation certain to eventuate in a second military confrontation with that formidable Arcadian *pólis*—this time on terms likely to be less favorable to Lacedaemon.[7]

This elaborate evasive maneuver did not, however, fully work as planned. As was only natural, the Tegeans got wind of Sparta's incursion into Arcadia; and, with the help of their fellow Arcadians, they set an ambush and surprised the Lacedaemonians—either when the latter were en route north-northeast from the Megalopolitan valley; or more likely, given the location of Tegea and the time prerequisite for gathering support from the rest of Arcadia, later when the Lacedaemonians were making their way home.

Whether Tegea's success in rallying the other Arcadians should be taken as an indication that there was a formal Arcadian confederacy in the 460s is a matter in dispute. Tegea had no civic coinage until much later in the century, but Arcadian coins were issued on a very substantial scale in the post–Persian War period by three separate mints—with three-obol coins on the Aeginetan standard being predominant. Whether these were produced by a religious amphictyony in connection with a religious festival, as some scholars suspect, or by a political confederacy intent on paying its hoplites the standard three-obol daily allowance, as others with considerable force argue, we cannot be certain. The only thing of which we can be fully confident is that in the classical period, whenever Pan-Arcadian patriotism flared up, it had an anti-Spartan slant.[8]

To this information, the Athenian orator Isocrates adds one other tidbit suggestive of the dire predicament in which the Lacedaemonians found themselves at this time. The Spartans, he reports, were deployed at Dipaea in a single line. If this means what it seems to mean, we must suppose that they fought in that battle on their own—perhaps with the support of those among their *períoikoi* who remained loyal, but certainly without the assistance of any of their Peloponnesian allies—and that, in extending their line to match that of the Tegeans and their fellow Arcadians, the Lacedaemonians were stretched so thin that their phalanx was but one file deep.[9] If so, the number of Spartiates had, indeed, been drastically reduced by the earthquakes and their initial conflict with the helots of Laconia.

Lacedaemon's survival may well have been at stake at Dipaea. Had the Argives been present in force on this occasion, the Spartans would almost certainly have been overwhelmed, and such a defeat would have opened the way for a consolidation of Tegean control over all of Arcadia and for an Arcadian-Argive intervention in Messenia that would have tipped the balance against the Lacedaemonians. But win, on this occasion, the Spartans did, and they did so against all odds, leaving Tegea's alliance in a shambles and Tegea herself chastened. This was by no means the final chapter in this story, however—for, as long as the Argives were on the warpath and Tegea remained in unfriendly hands, south-central and southwestern Arcadia were apt to remain in play.

None of the surviving sources discusses at any length the events that shook the Peloponnesus in this period. None of them has anything to say regarding their impact on the subsequent calculations of the Spartans and the Athenians. But the lack of evidence that these events influenced such calculations cannot in a case like this be taken as evidence that this crisis was inconsequential—for, although we are very poorly informed concerning this period, we do know this: cataclysms are not soon forgotten, and there was much to be gleaned from reflection on these developments. They surely brought home to the Lacedaemonians in a dramatic and painful fashion the vulnerability of their polity. The process of dissolution that Themistocles and the regent Pausanias had initiated did not quickly come to an end—not even when they were both eliminated from the scene. Instead, it came to a crescendo shortly thereafter, and Sparta was repeatedly borne to the very edge of the abyss.

Nor should we assume that the Athenians paid no attention. Themistocles had had supporters at Athens. Some of them had lost their lives at the battle of Tegea. Those who survived that clash of arms must have followed subsequent developments in the Peloponnesus with keen interest. These developments can only have heightened their admiration for the strategic genius who had diagnosed the fragility of the Spartan alliance, recognized just how vulnerable Lacedaemon was, and very nearly brought that polity to its knees; and this realization must also have intensified their regret that his compatriots had not wholeheartedly supported Athens' Odysseus in his Peloponnesian venture. By the time that the critics of Cimon's policy had come to power in that city, however, the opportunity that Themistocles had attempted to seize had vanished. Their aim was to recover the *occasione* that had been squandered, as we shall soon see.

CHAPTER 4

A Parting of the Ways

Great quarrels, it has been said, often arise from small occasions but never from small causes.

WINSTON CHURCHILL

THE first and most severe of the seismic jolts that shook Lacedaemon in 465/4 took place during the day. We are told that it wiped out an entire class of young men on the threshold of adulthood, who were caught at their exercise beneath the colonnade of a gymnasium. Moreover, given the greater likelihood that at that time of day the women and small children were inside their homes, there is reason to suspect that their proportion among the casualties greatly exceeded that of the boys and men, which was itself by all accounts enormous. We must imagine rents opening up in the earth, landslides hurtling down from Mount Taygetus, and nearly all of the houses and public buildings in the villages constituting Sparta collapsing suddenly in a cloud of dust as the ground beneath everyone's feet gave way, turned liquid, and shifted dramatically. The screams of those caught inside and trapped in the debris were no doubt everywhere heard.[1]

In the midst of the chaos, there was one man of consequence who kept his head. His name was Archidamus son of Zeuxidamos. He was the grandson and heir of the disgraced, exiled Eurypontid king Leotychidas, whom his father had predeceased. In 469/8, four years before the earthquake, Leotychidas had reportedly died, and Archidamus, who was barely then old enough to assume office, had been installed as king. When the catastrophe struck, while others were intent on rescuing from the rubble their valuables (and no doubt also their kin), he had the presence of mind to lay hold of his weapons and sound the alarm by having the *sálpinx* blown; and those of his compatriots who were dazed but otherwise unharmed did what they had been, as Spartans, trained to do: they quickly retrieved their arms, rallied, and formed up in a phalanx—

just in time to fend off the attacks which the helots of Laconia soon thereafter mounted. "At the moment of crisis," Plutarch reports, "this saved Sparta—this alone."[2]

Such appears also to have been the judgment of Archidamus' contemporary Ion of Chios, who is in all likelihood the source on whom Ephorus, Cicero, Pliny, Aelian, Polyaenus, and Plutarch later drew for the details they report concerning the earthquake, the damage it did, the loss of life it inflicted, the helot revolt that followed, and Archidamus' alacrity in summoning his compatriots. It was probably soon after these events that Ion penned a drinking song for the Spartans in which, on the most likely interpretation, he had them hail the Eurypontid king as their "savior and father." Looking back some years thereafter, Ion would pointedly celebrate, in his guise as a tragedian, the fact that, in fortifying herself against "mutinous Ares," Lacedaemon relied on deeds guided by sound counsel and not on the mere making of speeches.[3]

The fact that the helots of Laconia were so quick to recognize this seismic catastrophe as an opportunity to wreak havoc is a sign that Aristotle was right when he later described that servile class as a force hostile to their masters, "continuously lying in wait for misfortune" to strike. Of course, their readiness on this particular occasion may as well have had something to do with the unsettling impact on their generation of their discovery, while on campaign with their masters abroad in Boeotia at the time of the battle of Plataea in 479, that elsewhere within Hellas virtually all of the Greeks were free; and it may also be an indication of the effectiveness of Pausanias' efforts shortly before this time to forge them into an instrument for revolution. Had the Agiad regent been alive to witness these events, to rally his supporters among the Spartiates, and provide the helots with leadership, the outcome might well have been fatal to the inherited order at Lacedaemon. As things stood, the Spartans came to think the earthquake and the subsequent revolt a punishment inflicted on them by Poseidon for the sacrilege they had committed when they dragged the helot suppliants from his sanctuary at Taenarum and put them to the sword.[4]

An Appeal for Aid

As one would expect, the revolt quickly spread to Messenia—where the helots were more numerous than in Laconia and far less docile—and there, no doubt to the great consternation of the Spartans, the *períoıkoı* of Thouria and Aethaea joined in.[5] It must have been as this was happening that Archidamus and the ephors dispatched the *próxenoı* of Sparta's allies—those, at least, who had survived the quake and the initial skirmish—to seek support. For, as he was no doubt acutely aware, it was by no means clear that Lacedaemon's remaining manpower was adequate to the challenge the city then faced. The Spartiates had been vastly outnumbered by the helots prior to these events. If, as we are told, half of the former had lost their lives in the earthquake and if two communities of *períoıkoı* reinforced the rebellious helots, the disproportion in numbers and the danger attendant thereon will have increased dramatically.

We do not know which city responded first, but it is a reasonable guess that it was Mantineia. Although—or, rather, because—she shared a fertile plain with Tegea, this city was nearly always at odds with her neighbor to the south.[6] She cannot have been pleased by the alliance of that city with Argos to her east. Nor will she have relished the prospect that Arcadia would find unity under the leadership of her rival. She had a stake in Lacedaemon's survival as a great power. For, in these circumstances, she could hardly remain independent in the absence of Spartan support.

If Mantineia had a motive, she also had the means. In a pinch, perhaps with the help of her dependencies in Maenalia, she could field a hoplite army of three thousand.[7] She was closer to Laconia than any of the other cities known to have sent aid, and the help that she did send apparently made a considerable difference. More than three-quarters of a century later, when Sparta and Mantineia were at odds, Archidamus' younger son Agesilaus asked not to be saddled with the punitive expedition against the latter then in the offing, and he gave as his reason the fact that "the *pólıs* of the Mantineians" had been "serviceable" to his father "in many regards in the wars" he conducted "against Messene."[8]

The Aeginetans were probably the next to arrive—for we know that they, too, earned the gratitude of the Lacedaemonians.[9] They were a wealthy, mercantile people resident on a small island in the Saronic Gulf which could be seen from Athens on a clear day. They had a distinguished maritime tradition and are said to have manned more ships in 480 and 479 than any city in Hellas apart from Athens. In the first of these two years, despite the fact that they had to hold back a squadron of triremes to defend their own island against a surprise attack which might have been mounted at any time by the Persian fleet then harbored at Phalerum, they managed to supply to the Hellenic force that gathered at Salamis thirty triremes—manned by something like six thousand men—and it was to this flotilla that the participants in this fleet action later awarded the prize for valor. The following year, while sending a similar or even larger continent with the Hellenic fleet to the island of Delos and on to Samos and to Mycale on the coast of Asia Minor, the Aeginetans were nonetheless able to dispatch five hundred hoplites to Plataea.[10]

In 465/4, when they had no need to deploy a fleet for battle, the Aeginetans could have come up with a comparable force of infantrymen or even with twice or thrice that number, and they could easily have employed some of their triremes as transports (as they had in the past) to ferry these hoplites down the eastern coast of the Peloponnesus to the plain of Thyrea south of the Argeia, to Prasiae or Epidauros Limera on Laconia's Aegean coast, to Gytheion, Sparta's port on the Laconian gulf, or even to Coryphasium in Navarino bay in Messenia.[11] Something of the sort they probably did with dispatch. For, like the Mantineians, the citizens of Aegina had need of the Lacedaemonians. Prior to Xerxes' invasion of Greece, as we have seen, they had been involved in what must have seemed like an endless, episodic war with Athens—and the emergence of the Athenians at the battles of Artemisium, Salamis, and Mycale as the leading naval power in Greece had not only made them nervous. It had taught them that they needed a counterweight if they were to retain their independence.

The fact that Mantineia and Aegina are the only two *póleis* in or near the Peloponnesus known to have supported the Lacedaemonians in their time of need should not be taken as an indication that Sparta's other allies left her in the lurch. If we know that Mantineia and Aegina were among Lacedaemon's benefactors at this time, it is solely because decades later dramatic occasions meriting mention presented themselves in which reciprocity on some level seemed necessary and appropriate. We are told that the Lacedaemonians sought help from all of their allies,[12] and there was at least one other city belonging to the Spartan alliance that was beleaguered and in need of Sparta's protection. It, too, deserves special notice.

Geographically, the northeastern Peloponnesus formed a unit. There was a thoroughfare, ideal for carts, linking the main districts suited to growing grain; and naturally enough, in the late Bronze Age, the entire region was ruled

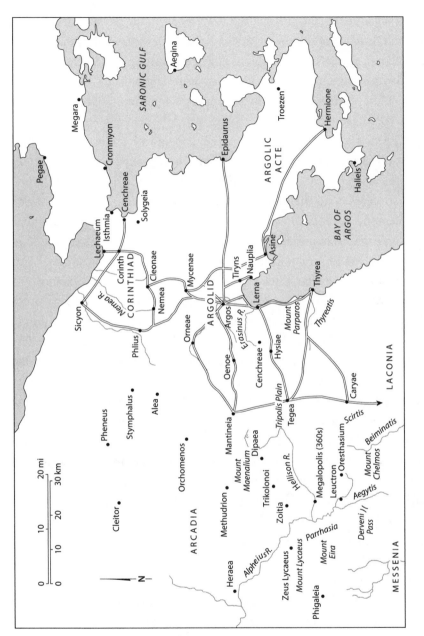

Map 9. The Argolid, the Argolic Acte, the Corinthiad, and the Cities Nearby

from a single center, the great palace at Mycenae. In the archaic period, however, and in much of the succeeding classical period, the region was divided
between two powers of genuine consequence and comparable weight—Argos
and Corinth—and, although both *póleis* were Dorian, they were also in a
variety of ways—religiously, culturally, and economically—distinct and even
opposed.[13]

Prior to 494, the Argives, an agrarian people with a long, distinguished
hoplite tradition, were locally predominant—which helps explain why, in the
early archaic period and in the sixth century, Corinth, a mercantile power
much stronger at sea than on land, sought shelter through an alliance with
Lacedaemon.[14] After Cleomenes' massacre of the Argives at Sepeia that year,
however, Argos went into temporary eclipse, as we have seen; and the Corinthians, who would soon come to be overshadowed at sea by Athens, had a
much freer hand on land in the region than ever before.[15] Sometime not long
thereafter, they appear to have overrun Cleonae, which lay well to the north
of Argos—athwart both the main thoroughfare, which led from Corinth to
Argos and on past Hysiae to Tegea, and the more difficult wagon road leading
from Tenea in the east past Cleonae to Nemea and Phlius further west. For
a time, the Corinthians even usurped from the Cleonaeans the presidency
of the Nemean Games.[16] It was presumably at this time as well that, with full
support from Lacedaemon, they drew, into a regional alliance hostile to Argos,
Cleonae and the other cities in the region once in the Argive orbit—which
helps explain why Sicyon and Phlius a few miles inland from the Corinthian
Gulf; Epidaurus, Troezen, and Hermione on or near the coast of the Argolic
Acte; and Aegina just offshore in the Saronic Gulf joined the Hellenic League
in 481 or 480. It is telling that later, when Tiryns fell to Argos, the surviving
citizens found refuge within the Argolic Acte—initially in Epidaurus and Hermione and ultimately at Halieis on the coast.[17]

Eventually, however, Argos recovered; and, by the time of the helot revolt and the Argive attack on Mycenae, Cleonae was once again an Argive
satellite,[18] as we have seen. By this time, however, the Corinthians had turned
northeast. Centuries before, they had seized Perachora from the Megarians;
and, in the late archaic period, they appear to have made an abortive attempt
to encroach further on the territory of the Megarians—for we have good reason to believe that in the late sixth century, with the help of the Argives, the
Megarians had inflicted on their aggressive neighbor a severe defeat. In the

mid-460s, if not before, the Corinthians renewed the struggle, contesting the southwestern border of the Megarid.[19] In the circumstances, it was only natural that the Megarians look to Lacedaemon, their mutual hegemon, for protection. We are not told that the Megarians responded quickly to the Lacedaemonian appeal for help in 465/4, but, in the circumstances, they certainly had reason to do so.

The odds are also good that cities less obviously in need of Spartan support—such as Corinth herself; her regional allies Sicyon, Phlius, Epidaurus, Troezen, and Hermione; and perhaps even Elis—also responded by sending troops. Mantineia and Aegina may have been enthusiastic and especially quick off the mark. Megara had a powerful motive for being similarly forthcoming. But these three *póleis* can hardly have been alone. In the sphere of foreign affairs, the price for neglecting one's obligations can be quite high. Betting on Lacedaemon's demise was apt to be unwise.

Even outside the Peloponnesus, the *próxenoi* dispatched by Lacedaemon managed to secure support. The Plataeans had not forgotten what the Spartans had done to their advantage in the struggle with Persia a decade and a half before; and, given the proximity of Thebes and the hostility the Thebans continued to display, they had reason to treasure the promises formally made to them after the battle of Plataea in the presence of the Hellenes by Pausanias the Regent. On this occasion, as we have seen, the allied commander had not only conceded to the Plataeans their city and land and formally affirmed their right to live there and conduct their affairs in accord with their ancestral customs and laws. He had also promised that no one would be allowed to attack them unjustly with an eye to their subjection, and he had pledged that, if this occurred, those who had formed the great alliance against the Mede would rally in their defense.[20]

The Plataean contingent at the battles of Marathon and Plataea had been led by a man, sometimes identified in the ancient sources as Arimnestus, whose real name was almost certainly Aeimnestus. Before the latter battle, in the company of the Athenian commander Aristeides, he had scouted out the Pantassa ridge outside Hysiae, identifying it as a place where a hoplite force could deploy for combat and not have to worry about a cavalry assault. When, on the actual day of the conflict, the Spartans retreated from their perch on the ridge running along the south bank of the Asopus River and marched up the slopes of Mount Cithaeron to the outskirts of Boeotian Hysiae, this Plataean was with them, almost certainly functioning as a guide. And at the battle that followed, a combatant bearing his name—who is described by Herodotus as "a man to be reckoned with [*lógimos*] at Lacedaemon"—managed to kill the Persian general Mardonius.[21]

If this Aeimnestus was not already the *próxenos* of the Spartans at Plataea, he was soon thereafter awarded that office, and he clearly delighted in the fact. In celebration of the status conferred on him, he named his son Lakon; and it was almost certainly he who persuaded his compatriots to send one-third of their levy to fight at this time on Sparta's behalf. We are told, moreover, that on the Stenyklaros plain in Messenia the man who had brought down Mardonius in 479 led a band of three hundred against the Messenians and that, on the latter occasion, he and every one of his comrades lost their lives.[22]

The Athenians were not at this time beleaguered; and, thanks to the withdrawal of the remaining Persians from Hellas after the battle of Plataea and to their own valiant efforts at sea thereafter, they no longer had any pressing need for Lacedaemonian support. But they answered Archidamus' summons anyway.[23]

Regarding the details, Plutarch is our chief informant. As we have already had occasion to note, he had access to the memoirs of Cimon's much younger friend Ion of Chios, who resided in Athens in these years. He drew also on the ruminations of Socrates' renegade student Critias and on the testimony of the comic poets, and he was intent on fleshing out in full the remarkable life story of Miltiades' son. In consequence, his account of the interaction of Sparta and Athens in Cimon's heyday is considerably less terse than is the pertinent material found in Thucydides' highly abbreviated and narrowly focused description of the growth of Athenian power during the Pentekontaetia, and there is every reason to suppose Plutarch knew what he was talking about. On this occasion, according to his report, a Spartiate named Pericleidas—whom we have reason to identify as the Athenians' *próxenos* at Lacedaemon and who is known to have named his son Athenaios—suddenly and unexpectedly presented himself at Athens' civic altars, as the comic poet Aristophanes later recalled in his *Lysistrata,* "white-faced, clad in the distinctive purple cloak of the Lacedaemonians, seeking an army."[24]

It goes without saying that there were Athenians vehemently opposed to sending aid. Themistocles had had a following at Athens. Some of his admirers had fought alongside the Argives and the Tegeans at the battle of Tegea just a few years before. Sparta's demise would be, they were convinced, Athens' gain. In the assembly called to consider Pericleidas' request, this was, Plutarch tells us, the position articulated by Ephialtes son of Sophonides—a man of unimpeachable honesty who had been, we have reason to suppose, a close ally of Themistocles in the past. Lacedaemon he identified as Athens' "adversary [*antípalos*]." To aid her, to raise her up made no sense, said he. "Let Sparta in her arrogance lie prostrate and be trampled under foot."[25]

Cimon took the opposite side—as did, we must presume, the other *próxenoi* of the Lacedaemonians at Athens: among them, Alcibiades son of Cleinias, Cimon's brother-in-law Callias son of Hipponicus, and, in all likelihood, Alcmaeon and his son Leobotes. Cimon in particular had his reasons for taking a strong stand. For a decade and a half, he had relied on Sparta's forbearance. In the absence of Lacedaemon's willingness to let Athens take the lead on the sea, it would not have been at all easy for the latter to have founded the Delian League and to have continued the war against Persia in the way she had. Mindful of this, the son of Miltiades had done everything he could to sustain and reinforce the friendship between the two powers, which had made possible the Hellenic victory in the Persian Wars and opened the way for the emergence of Athens' maritime hegemony in the aftermath. Although circumstances had changed dramatically as a consequence of the earthquake and the helot revolt, and, at least for the time being, Athens no longer needed Sparta's forbearance, Cimon was not about to change his stance. He was not as cold-blooded as his erstwhile rival Themistocles. He was restrained by a sense of honor and perhaps by a conviction that Lacedaemon's moment of weakness would soon pass. He could not turn on a dime. And so, according to his friend and admirer Ion of Chios (who in all likelihood witnessed the debate), the Athenian statesman passionately urged his compatriots "not to look on, standing idly by, while Hellas went lame and their own city became ill-matched with her yokefellow." In this fashion, by appealing to Panhellenic sentiment, Cimon secured the support of his fellow Athenians, and to Lacedaemon he soon thereafter led by land a force of four thousand hoplites.[26]

The End of an Alliance

We do not know in detail how events thereafter unfolded. It is conceivable that the Spartans managed to pacify Laconia without outside aid. But the odds

are that the Mantineians, the Aeginetans, and the loyal among the Lacedaemonians' other allies within the Peloponnesus arrived in time to help them
with this formidable task. Messenia was an even harder nut to crack. To begin
with, it was on the other side of the Taygetus massif—an obstacle to the pro-
jection of power almost insuperable—and in Messenia there were no Spartan
settlements. There may have been—there surely were—garrisons, though we
know nothing about them. But the members of these may have been—indeed,
they are likely to have been—massacred at the beginning of the revolt.

We do not know how long the various foreign contingents remained. It is
a reasonable guess that, once Laconia was thoroughly pacified, some of them
returned home. The Mantineians and the Plataeans were present for at least
some of the fighting in Messenia, however. This we know. And the same may
well have been true for the Aeginetans. But we do not hear of the Athenians
doing battle in Messenia at this time. They may have marched back as soon as
Lacedaemon's survival was guaranteed. At this time, they had pressing business
of their own to attend to.

The siege at Thasos was still under way, and the Athenians and their other
allies were also then absorbed in an enormously ambitious and difficult endeavor to establish a colony in a position to exploit the timberlands and the
silver and gold mines of Thrace. Just under three miles up the Strymon River
from Eion—where Xerxes, while en route to Thermopylae and beyond, had
had bridges built to span the stream at its narrowest point—lay a strategic
location called Ennea Hodoi ("Nine Roads"), where travelers tended to con-
verge. At Myrcinus a short distance to the north, Histiaeus of Miletus had once
attempted to build a fort; and it was at another, similar spot, nearer the surviving bridge, that these colonists sought to settle at this time.[27]

Unfortunately for the Athenians and their allies, however, their venture
on the Strymon quickly came a-cropper. Before the colony was firmly established and fully fortified, the Edonians in alliance with the other Thracian
tribesmen of the region ambushed an expedition mounted by the settlers and
massacred "ten thousand" of them—which is to say, an immense number—at
a place further inland called Drabeskos, which lay near the gold mines in the
Daton valley north of Mount Pangaeum. And soon thereafter the survivors
camped at Ennea Hodoi were evacuated.

The colony had been a joint venture, and the Athenians may have been
only a minority among the settlers. But Athens' losses that year in the Cherson-

Map 10. The Strymon Valley and Its Environs

nesus, at Thasos, and, above all, in Thrace must have been deeply felt—for the names of the dead were recorded tribe by tribe in a set of inscriptions carved on stone slabs set up along the road leading from Athens to the Academy, and many scholars suspect that the casualties in this set of campaigns inspired the practice, well attested later, of providing a formal civic burial in the Ceramicus each year for citizens who had died in war. It was presumably with Drabeskos in mind (but clearly not Drabeskos alone) that Aristotle dryly remarks, "The generals given commands in those days were chosen on the basis of the reputation of their ancestors and," apart from Cimon, "tended to be inexperienced in war so that up to two or three thousand of those going out on an expedition always lost their lives, which cost the Athenians the decent sorts—those drawn both from the common people and from the well-to-do."[28]

Cimon's popularity may well have suffered. Up through the Eurymedon campaign, he had gone from strength to strength. But, in some measure, he must have been held responsible for the rebellion of Thasos and the disaster at Drabeskos. His prestige was such, especially after Themistocles' ostracism, that Athens was not apt to have done anything of moment that he did not favor, and we have a confused report attributing to him the foundation of a colony of ten thousand at Ennea Hodoi.[29] But even if we had no information expressly assigning responsibility to him, we would have to suppose something of the sort—for Cimon was certainly active in the region at this time.

After Eurymedon, the Athenian commander is said to have cleared the Persians once again from the Thracian Chersonnesus, to have crushed the Thracians whom they had called in for support, and to have once again opened up that fertile district, which had been a Philaid family fiefdom, for settlement by his compatriots. It may have been at this time and at his instigation that the Persians finally evacuated their stronghold nearby at Doriscus on the Hebron to the west. Cimon also led the Athenian fleet that defeated the Thasians at sea in 465, soon after their rebellion, and he it was who then initiated the siege and seized their settlements along the Thracian coast and their gold mine inland from there.[30] The establishment of a colony at Ennea Hodoi was clearly a central part of his overall scheme.

Envy no doubt also played a role in undercutting Cimon's popularity, as it often had with regard to others similarly situated in the recent past—after Marathon, for example, when Cimon's father Miltiades led the Athenians on an ill-fated campaign against Paros and was fined; and again after Salamis when the Spartans fêted Themistocles, the Athenians learned that he had erred in encouraging them to presume that their victory at sea would induce the Persians to withdraw their army from Hellas, and he was cashiered as general. Envy always plays a role in politics—especially, the politics of democracies, where every form of superiority is an invitation to resentment; and, in Greece, envy's influence was greatly enhanced by the agonistic ethos propagated in Homer's *Iliad* and *Odyssey*—the two books that served as a Bible of sorts for the Hellenes.[31]

In democratic societies, resentment of this sort is apt to find expression in scurrilous taunts with sexual overtones, and we know from the surviving graffiti that Cimon, who was thought to be sexually voracious, and his sister, who sometimes acted as his political agent, were an object of these. Forty years later, the comic poet Eupolis would parody in the following fashion the scuttlebutt retailed at this time regarding the Athenian leader:

> A total disgrace he was not, but he did love his drink and he was careless.
> Moreover, he would often sleep away from home in Lacedaemon,
> Leaving that Elpinike alone with herself.[32]

When a man as successful and as overbearing as Cimon finally stumbled, as stumble he would, he was bound to come under attack.

In the wake of the revolt of Thasos and the massacre at Drabeskos, the son of Miltiades was prosecuted for treason. After defeating the Thasians, investing the city, and seizing their holdings in Thrace, he could easily have invaded Macedonia and hived off much of its territory—or so it was said—but, purportedly in return for a bribe from the Macedonian king Alexander, he had chosen not to proceed. This was the charge he faced. To make sense of this claim, one must attend to the evidence strongly suggesting that Alexander, who had been on good terms with the Athenians before the Persian Wars and who had been singled out at that time as their "benefactor" and made their *próxenos,* had taken Artabazus' headlong retreat from Plataea with the remnants of Xerxes' great army in 479 as an opportunity to assert Macedonian control over the mines in the upper Strymon basin. Thereafter, one must suppose, he had come into conflict with Athens over these mines.[33]

Among those selected at the time of Cimon's annual audit [*euthúna*] as general to argue the case against him was Pericles, son of the Xanthippus who had prosecuted his father Miltiades in 489. As a child, this Pericles had witnessed his own father's ostracism at the hands of Themistocles, the evacuation of Attica in anticipation of Xerxes' invasion, Themistocles' recall of his father from exile, his father's re-emergence as a political force, and his victorious return from the battles at Mycale and Sestos—and all of this no doubt made a strong impression on the young lion. As a young man, Xanthippus' younger son appears to have been a supporter of Themistocles. It is otherwise hard to explain why, in March 472—a couple of weeks, just over a year, or two years before that statesman's ostracism—as *chorēgós* he had defrayed the cost of producing a tragedy by Aeschylus designed to remind their compatriots of Themistocles' achievement at Salamis. In 463, he was aligned with Ephialtes; and, though he reportedly soft-pedaled his rhetoric at the trial and no one can have expected a conviction, the prosecution of Cimon on a charge of treason—like that of Themistocles shortly before his ostracism—was an instrument useful for besmirching the man's reputation and reducing his political support.[34]

According to Plutarch—who is presumably once again drawing on the memoirs of Ion of Chios—Cimon responded by dismissing the indictment as absurd. Money was, he implied, nothing to a man like him. He was not, he proudly noted, the pampered *próxenos* of a rich Ionian *pólis*. Nor did he represent at Athens the fabulously wealthy dynasts of Thessaly. He was neither looked after like others whom he seems to have identified but left unnamed. Nor was he on the take. He was the *próxenos* of the Lacedaemonians. He was a passionate admirer of their frugality and of their moderation, and in his conduct he assiduously imitated both. These qualities he honored far more than wealth, and he prided himself on enriching his own *pólis* at the expense of her enemies.

The prosecution was obviously frivolous, and Cimon's response was an effective riposte. He was not the sort to take a bribe, and everyone knew it.[35] But flaunting his love of all things Spartan, as he did on this and apparently on other occasions as well, was costly to him in the end.

In 462, if Plutarch's report is to be trusted (as it should be), the Spartans once again asked for Athenian help. The year before, if the chronological framework that I have adopted here is correct, the Lacedaemonians had sent a force north—first, to reassert their hegemony over southwestern Arcadia, the Parrhasia, and what would eventually be called the Megalopolitan plain; and, then, as we have seen, to buck up their allies at Mantineia. After weathering the attack the Arcadians mounted against them at Dipaea, the Lacedaemonians had returned; and soon thereafter, with the help of the Mantineians, the Plataeans, and the remainder of their most loyal allies, they had defeated the Messenians in a great battle which took place, we have reason to suspect, near the midpoint of the Pamisos valley—where a ridge, which may then have been called "the isthmus," runs from Mount Ithome eastward toward Mount Taygetus, separating the Stenyklaros plain in the north from the Makaria flats to the south.[36]

This impressive victory did not, however, bring the great revolt to an end. Instead of surrendering, the surviving rebels—helots from Messenia, *períoikoi* from Thouria and Aeathea, and refugees from Laconia—fell back on Mount Ithome and waged a guerrilla war from its heights.[37] It was their continued resistance that induced the Lacedaemonians to turn to Athens once again.

Figure 5. Greek hoplites bearing *aspídes* on the Nereid monument from Xanthos in Lycia, ca. 390–380 B.C. (British Museum, London, Photograph by Jan van der Crabben / Ancient History Encyclopedia [www.ancient.eu], courtesy of the photographer).

The Lacedaemonians excelled at hoplite warfare. In archaic and early classical Greece, there were no heavily armed soldiers worthy of comparison. But—on rough ground where one could not deploy one's heavy infantry in a phalanx, and on hillsides where agility and quickness were required and strength and endurance were not the principal key to success—they were at a distinct disadvantage. The *aspís* borne by the hoplite was designed for use in the phalanx. It had a bronze armband in the center, called a *pórpax*, through which the warrior slipped his left arm, and a leather cord attached to the right rim of the shield, called an *antilabé*, for him to lay hold of with his left hand. Such a shield was not suitable for a solo performer. It left the right side of its bearer's body dangerously exposed. Within the phalanx, however, it provided protection to the right side of the hoplite arrayed to its bearer's left. But on ground unsuited to their joint deployment in a phalanx, where the shields of the infantrymen could not in this fashion interlock, the *aspís* was worse than useless. It was heavy and burdensome—an obstacle to agility—and it rendered its bearer vulnerable to attack on his exposed right side.[38]

Of course, at Plataea and in other battles, the Spartans had sometimes deployed light-armed troops. But these were drawn from among the helot population. To the best of our knowledge, there were no experienced *psíloi* among the Spartiates themselves. The ablest of the residents of Laconia and Messenia possessed of these specialized skills were ranged against them on Ithome. At siege warfare, moreover, the Lacedaemonians were notoriously ineffectual; and, on the slopes of the mountain, the Spartans were seriously outclassed.

Cimon's Athenians were differently situated. They had ample experience in siege warfare. For a decade and a half, they had been busy along the Thracian and Anatolian coasts scaling fortresses, bursting through palisades, and ousting garrisons; and they had among their forces a corps of specialists—light-armed troops picked and trained for this particular task—who had become adept at fighting in the hill country, at skirmishing on rough ground, and at capturing strongholds. It made sense for the Spartans to summon Athenian help a second time and to ask this time that they send these specialists, and they could rely on Cimon, who was a genuine Laconophile, to persuade his compatriots to respond—which is what he did.[39]

This time, however, the Athenians may have been a bit more reluctant. The emergency had passed. Lacedaemon's survival was no longer at stake. Moreover, they had had time to reflect at leisure on their situation and on that of the Spartans. They could now more easily consider what it was that they were being asked to do, and they could question whether Athens had anything to gain from such an effort. Panhellenic sentiment still had a hold on them, of course. But the rebels on Ithome were not barbarians, much less Persians. They were Hellenes, as the Athenians well knew. It was one thing to assist fellow Greeks in subjugating barbarians. This was a matter of ethnic solidarity. The barbarians were, after all, the common foe. Under the leadership of Darius and Xerxes, they had attempted to deprive the Athenians and the other Hellenes of the liberty that had long distinguished the Greeks as Greeks. The veterans of the battles fought at Marathon, Artemisium, Salamis, Plataea, Mycale, Sestos, Cyprus, Byzantium, Eion, Eurymedon, and elsewhere needed no instruction in such matters. But to assist the Spartans in denying other Hellenes the liberty they bravely sought—there was something distasteful about that.

Had abstract justice been their only ground for objection, the Athenians might have been prepared to dismiss the arguments against aiding Sparta that the likes of Ephialtes and Pericles no doubt advanced once again in the assembly. Athens was, after all, deeply indebted to Lacedaemon. Her citizens had not forgotten the battle of Plataea. They were, moreover, deeply indebted as well to the son of Miltiades. He had repeatedly defeated the Persians, and he really had enriched the city at the expense of her foes. Furthermore, he had recently defeated the Thasians at sea and had initiated a siege that was bound to succeed. At Drabeskos, they could remind themselves, he had not been in command; and what had happened there was, in any case, nothing more than a temporary setback. This they understood.

But there was another sphere in which things had also gone wrong. Late in 468 or early in 467, as we have seen, Cimon's brother-in-law Callias had negotiated a peace of sorts with Xerxes, and nearly everyone at Athens had breathed a great sigh of relief. Two or three years later, however—in early August 465, as we have also seen—Xerxes was assassinated. Darius the crown prince was murdered soon thereafter; and Artaxerxes, the youngest of Xerxes' three sons, was installed on the throne. In the fall of 465 or not long thereafter—as soon as the identity of the new Great King was clear—Callias was once again dispatched as an envoy to Susa, presumably for the purpose of renewing the peace with Persia's new monarch. We have reason to suspect that he returned laden with gifts of the sort that Achaemenid monarchs customarily showered on emissaries from abroad—but otherwise empty-handed.[40]

Xerxes had paid dearly for his willingness to treat with the Athenians; Artaxerxes had good reason not to fall into the same trap, and in this and other ways he distanced himself from his father's policies. Within a very short time the Athenians found themselves once again at war with the Mede. It was probably upon the occasion of Callias' return from Susa in or soon after the summer of 464 that the Athenians reacted in anger, as was their wont when they did not get what they desired, and charged that their emissary had been bribed, demanding that he cough up a fifty-talent fine.[41] By 462, Cimon's achievements may have seemed to his compatriots if not tarnished, at least considerably less impressive than hitherto.

Another concern of some moment is apt to have presented itself at this time. Thasos surrendered in 462, and soon thereafter the Athenians are quite likely to have learned that in 465, shortly before the helot revolt, the Spartans had promised the rebels aid. Had the Athenians known of this when Cimon proposed sending a second expedition in support of Lacedaemon, they would surely have refused. We are not told that word came to Athens soon after the expeditionary force left for Messenia. We are not told precisely when the Athenians learned the truth. But that they did so eventually we do know, and the most likely time for the divulging of this information was the immediate aftermath of Thasos' surrender.[42]

It is, I would suggest, in light of this hypothesis that we can most easily make sense of three events—the sudden and total collapse of Cimon's position at Athens, open grumbling on the part of "the picked men" under his command in Messenia, and an overreaction on the part of the Lacedaemonians to this expression of discontent. At Athens, in the absence of Cimon and of the soldiers in this expeditionary force, Ephialtes, with the help of Pericles, managed to push through the assembly a democratic political reform, stripping the Areopagus of the political responsibilities implicit in its charge as "the guardian of the regime [politeía]." Precisely what this involved is by no means certain. After the reform, the Areopagus continued to adjudicate murder trials and at least some cases involving religious infractions. That much is clear. If it had previously conducted the scrutiny [dokimasía], determining whether candidates for office met the necessary legal qualifications, it lost this prerogative. If it handled treason trials or played a preliminary role in their regard (as, for example, it may have done in the cases lodged against Themistocles and Cimon), it no longer did so. If it ordinarily played a role in punishing magistrates for a breach of the law and if (perhaps only as the court of first resort) it audited retiring magistrates, holding a hearing [euthúna] at the end of their term to consider whether the conduct of each in office had been lawful and proper or not, it was deprived of these functions. There can be no doubt that the prerogatives which the Areopagus had previously exercised gave this council of former magistrates considerable political leverage and that its exercise of these prerogatives elicited in some quarters fierce resentment and in others an admiration no less vehement. For when these tasks in their entirety were reassigned to the council, the assembly, and the courts (which acted on behalf of the dêmos as a whole), there was an uproar on both sides of the dispute.[43]

An attack on the Areopagus and its superintending role within the city was an attack on the proud son of Miltiades. This body had been a bastion of his power. This much everyone knew—and it is most unlikely that the Athenians would have turned so savagely on their champion and his associates had there not been a revelation suggesting on his part an improvident stewardship of Athens' affairs.

In the end, however, it was the Spartans who finished Cimon off. A majority of the ephors who had appealed to Athens for help were, we can presume, friendly to the Spartan-Athenian condominium in Greece. Those who succeeded them in September may have been among those hostile to and instinctively distrustful of the Athenians. For understandable reasons, many of their compatriots were unnerved by the pronounced grumbling that erupted at this time within Athenian ranks. These Athenians were not Lacedaemonians, they apparently told themselves. They were not even Dorians. From the Spartan perspective; they were, as Thucydides pointedly puts it, an alien people drawn "from another tribe." In these elite light-armed troops—proud, as they were, of their expertise in unconventional warfare—the Lacedaemonians discerned "a spirit of audacity and a taste for innovation." The word—*neōteropoía*—that I have translated here as "innovation" can also mean "revolution," and that is surely what the Spartans feared. The resentment expressed by these interlopers and their propensity as Athenians to speak their minds were evidently serious enough to cause the ephors to worry that Cimon might soon face a mutiny and to fear that his soldiers might abandon their allegiance and side with the rebels holed up on Mount Ithome. Here again it is unlikely that the authorities at Lacedaemon would have been so nervous had they not become aware that the promises made to the Thasians in 465 had been quite recently divulged.

When the Spartan leaders requested that the man they had made their *próxenos* at Athens lead his soldiers back home, saying that they now had sufficient support from their other allies and no longer needed Athenian help, it was perfectly evident that they were lying—for the Athenians' first attempt to dislodge the rebels from Ithome had failed, and the insurgent helots and their supporters from among the *períoikoi* of Messenia were still firmly ensconced on the mountain. What the Spartans did on this occasion was an expression of distrust, not outright hostility. They were in no position even to think about launching a war, and they did what they could to disguise their distrust. In context, however, their dismissal of the Athenians was tantamount to a confession that the stories these soldiers had recently heard from home were true—that the Lacedaemonians really had promised the Thasian rebels an invasion of Attica. Suddenly, it looked as if Themistocles' assessment of Athens' interests had been right all along, and the indictment that Critias would hand down half a century later now seemed apt. Cimon had "subordinated the augmentation in power of his fatherland to the interests of the Lacedaemonians." This is what an overwhelming majority of his compatriots now believed, and it was on the basis of this conviction that they decided what to do next.[44]

When Cimon reached Athens, he mounted an effort to have Ephialtes' reform reversed—but to no avail. The Areopagus would never again have any considerable political weight. Henceforth everything was to be decided in as democratic a fashion as possible—in the probouleutic Council of 500, in the assembly, and the popular courts.[45]

This was one blow delivered to the son of Miltiades. There would soon be more. First, almost immediately after Cimon's return from Sparta, the assembly voted to effect a diplomatic revolution. It renounced the alliance against the Mede that Athens had forged with Lacedaemon, and it opted to embrace as Athens' new allies the erstwhile Medizers of Thessaly and of Argos. This was a turning point—for, as Thucydides takes care to remind his readers, the Argives were then at war with the Lacedaemonians: the Argives were, he says, the Spartans' *polemíoi*. Then, to confirm the revolution that they had effected, the Athenians voted early in 461 to hold an ostracism, and ten weeks later more than six thousand of the great man's compatriots gathered in the agora, scratched the names of the various rival candidates on potsherds called *óstraka,* tossed them in a pile, and sent Cimon packing.[46]

Whether, in this period, Cimon's associates Alcmaeon and Leobotes and his brother-in-law Callias son of Hipponicus suffered a similar comeuppance we do not know. Callias' close relationship with the illustrious son of Miltiades and his status as hereditary *próxenos* of the Lacedaemonians at Athens must have made him exceedingly vulnerable to attack, and Alcmaeon and Leobotes are apt to have been in a similar plight.

Callias' colleague as hereditary *próxenos,* Alcibiades son of Cleinias, was, in fact, soon made to suffer as Cimon had. The Athenians were clearly furious. This Alcibiades, whom they had reportedly ostracized once already, they easily could have spared. The news that the Spartans had offered aid to the Thasian rebels appears to have been more than he could stomach. For he had taken the dramatic step of breaking all ties with Lacedaemon. No longer, he intimated, could he in good faith continue to do what his ancestors had done for many generations—serve among the Spartans' *próxenoi* at Athens. This gesture did not, however, allay the anger of his compatriots.[47]

If Alcmaeon and Leobotes were spared, it was presumably because the Athenians held only one ostracism per annum. After venting their wrath on Cimon one year and on Alcibiades the next, they seem have turned their minds to matters more pressing. If, moreover, Callias also escaped retribution, it was perhaps because Pericles and the others now dominant in Athens had the good sense to realize that they might in time need the services of an experienced diplomat intimately familiar both with the ways of the Lacedaemonians and with the protocols of the Persian court. As a consequence of the promise that the Lacedaemonians had made to the Thasians and of the breach with Sparta that the Athenians had initiated in the aftermath of Cimon's return from Messenia, a great strategic rivalry had begun, and, as everyone understood, active warfare would soon ensue.[48]

First Blood

Had circumstances been different, the diplomatic revolution staged by Cimon's rivals in 461 and the alliance they had forged with Sparta's foe might well have eventuated in an invasion of Attica by the Lacedaemonians and their allies in the Peloponnesian League. The like had happened in the past, and the Corinthians, who had at the time played a crucial role in thwarting the efforts of Cleomenes to turn Athens into a Spartan satellite, were no longer apt to come to Athens' defense. In 480, there had been an abrupt and dramatic shift in the balance of power at sea; and the Corinthians were now far more wary of the Athenians than of their Lacedaemonian allies.

In 461, however, the Spartiates of Lacedaemon were not in a position to mount such an assault. Thanks to the earthquake of 465/4 and the helot revolt to which it had given rise, their numbers were depleted. Moreover, within their fastness in the southern Peloponnesus, they were still confronted with a rebellion, and they had to be constantly on their guard lest the guerrillas operating from Mount Ithome rouse anew the helots of Laconia and Messenia who had once again submitted to the Lacedaemonian yoke and perhaps draw into revolt those of the *períoikoi* who had thus far remained loyal. To this, one can add that the Argives were still poised, ready to strike, and that the Tegeans, though weakened, remained disaffected. To project power abroad with any real effectiveness, the Lacedaemonians had to be secure at home—and there they were anything but secure. For the time being, at least, the Athenians had a relatively free hand, and they intended to take full advantage of the opportunity they had been afforded.[49]

They were not, however, in a position to directly confront Lacedaemon. Laconia—where, along the Eurotas River, the Spartans resided—was geographically isolated. It was, moreover, "ringed round by mountains, rough, and difficult for foes to enter," as Euripides tells us; and it was aptly described as "an acropolis and guard-post for the entire Peloponnesus."[50] Had the Spartans limited their sphere of control to the Eurotas valley—cut off as it was by Mount Parnon to the east, Mount Taygetus to the west, and rugged hill country to the north—their situation would have been almost impregnable.

But, as we have seen, they did not limit themselves in this fashion. To the west, on the other side of the Taygetus massif, lay the Pamisos river valley in Messenia. "Rich" it was "in lovely fruit," as Euripides would observe,

> Irrigated by a myriad of streams and springs,
> And well furnished with good pasture for cattle and sheep,
> Neither bitter and stormy in the windy blasts of winter
> Nor, on the contrary, rendered excessively hot by the four-horsed chariot
> of the sun . . .
> Possessed of an excellence greater than can be expressed in words.[51]

This region was more vulnerable to invasion than was Laconia—especially from south-central Arcadia via the Derveni Pass—and there were places along its coast where troops could easily be landed. But, at the time of the battle of Dipaea, Lacedaemon had successfully reasserted her dominance in south-central and southwestern Arcadia, and the Athenians and their Argive allies were in no position at this time to make their way through Arcadia to the Derveni Pass. Moreover, while Athens could land hoplites at will on the Messenian shore, her manpower was limited and her capacity to provide logistical support for any length of time to such a force in so isolated a region at so great a distance from Athens was limited. Cape Malea at the tip of the southeasternmost prong of the Peloponnesus, where the prevailing winds and currents clashed and the waves could rise to mountainous heights, and the long lee shore stretching south to it from the plain of Thyrea did not constitute an insuperable obstacle. But in anything other than ideal weather this was a prover-

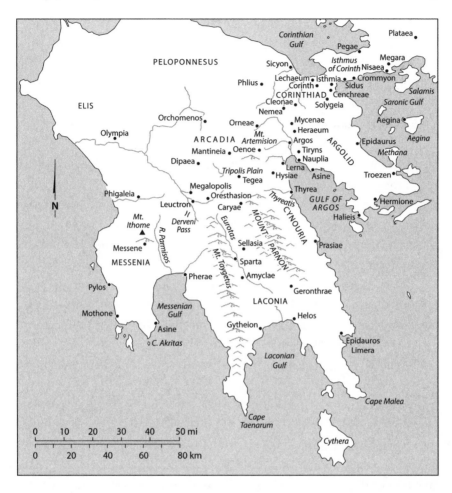

Map 11. Argos, the Argeia, the Argolic Acte, and Their Environs

bially dangerous coast. "Double Malea," they said, "and forget your way home."[52] Like Laconia, Messenia was, for all intents and purposes, a world unto itself.

Furthermore, as a polity, Lacedaemon was virtually an autarchy. Economically, she was inward-looking. There were local sources of iron. Her citizens were gentlemen-farmers. They relied on the land and the helots the city owned for nearly everything that they needed. In the late archaic and classical periods, they had no trading relations worth mentioning, which helps explain why Sparta never had any coinage of her own. Athens could not in any obvious way easily leverage her mastery of the sea in such a manner as to do the Lacedaemonians grave harm.

As Themistocles had recognized, there was just one way in which a sea power, such as Athens, could decisively defeat a land power, such as Lacedaemon. The only available path to victory lay through the Peloponnesus. The analysis provided by a Corinthian leader in the early fourth century applied with equal force in 461, and it bears repeating here. It really was appropriate to think of the power of Sparta as a stream and to remember that, "at their sources, rivers are not great and they are easily forded, but the farther on they go, the greater they get—for other rivers empty into them and make the current stronger. There, in the place where they emerge, they are alone; but as they continue and gather cities under their control, they become more numerous and harder to fight."[53] If one could win over Sparta's allies and turn them against her, one could gather a hoplite army sufficiently numerous to be able to overwhelm the Lacedaemonians quite close to home.

Before, however, the Athenians could fully focus their attention on the Spartan alliance, they had to consider the needs of their own new allies—above all, Argos, their one ally within the Peloponnesus (and, given their aims, an utterly indispensable ally). It is this that explains their descent, early in 459, on the coastal town of Halieis. Originally a Dryopian settlement, Halieis was located within the territory of Hermione near the southeastern tip of the Argolid at the entrance to the Gulf of Argos. Its strategic significance appears to have been recognized quite early on. The archaeological remains suggest that the Spartans had garrisoned the place in the early sixth century and that they had subsequently been driven out. Its fine harbor can hardly have escaped the attention of the Athenians. It was well-suited to serve as base from which a flotilla and the marines it carried could provide assistance to the Argives on short notice, mount operations along the coast of the Argolic Acte, and raid the fertile district of Thyrea as well as Prasiae, Epidauros Limera, and the other towns occupied by Lacedaemonian *períoikoi,* which were nestled in coves to the south in Cynouria at irregular intervals along the rugged Laconian coast.[54]

There is reason to suspect that Argos may have been in need of assistance at this time. By 462/1, when the two cities forged their alliance, the Argives had almost certainly conquered and razed Mycenae. It is not likely that the siege initiated in 465/4 lasted more than a year. Whether, however, the Argives had already also overcome Tiryns, as they eventually would, we do not know. The latter struggle is said to have been quite difficult and to have lasted for some time,[55] and it had probably not yet come to an end. This is likely to have been one difficulty that the Athenians' new ally faced. There was almost certainly another as well.[56]

The cultural geographer Pausanias twice alludes to a battle within the Argeia—commemorated at Athens in the mid-fifth century and by Argos at Delphi at about the same time. In this conflict, the Argives and the Athenians assisting them are said to have defeated the Lacedaemonians. The battle in question was reportedly fought at Oenoe, west of Argos up the valley of the Charadros (now called the Xerias) on a narrow, difficult road—one branch of which runs from Oenoe below Mount Artemision and over the Prinos Pass to the village of Nestane and on to Mantineia, while the other branch makes its way from there across the Artemision massif further south to Nestane by way of the modern village of Tourniki.[57]

Pausanias' report, registered half a millennium after the supposed event, has given rise to considerable scholarly skepticism. As one observer has pointed out, there was no path over Mount Artemision from Mantineia that one would be likely to choose if one were leading a Lacedaemonian army against Argos—for there was a far easier road, a thoroughfare better suited to carts, that ran up to Argos from Lacedaemon via Caryae, Tegea, Hysiae, and Lerna. What this scholar failed to notice, however, is that there was one period in the fifth century in which the Athenians and the Argives were allied and the hostility of the Tegeans precluded Spartan use of the main wagon road—and that this was the very period in question here.[58] The battle described by Pausanias can plausibly be situated in or quite soon after 461—shortly before the fall of Tiryns, which is likely to have taken place in 460, and the Athenian attack on the Tirynthians' ultimate place of refuge at Halieis in the spring of the following year.

Thucydides' failure to mention the battle of Oenoe may but should not seem puzzling. As we have had occasion to observe, his narrative of the period between the Persian Wars and the great Peloponnesian War is highly selective, and he mentions only events that are grist to his mill. If this battle did not in his opinion bear in any significant way on the growth of Athenian power, it is because it was strategically inconsequential. The Messenians were still holed up on Mount Ithome. The Spartans may have felt called upon to relieve the siege of Tiryns, but they could not spare a large host; and, given the roughness of the roads, it would have been hard to provide much in the way of logistical support to an army of any size situated precariously on the Argive side of the Artemision massif. So, with an eye to exploiting the element of surprise and perhaps also inspiring civil strife among the Argives, they launched a commando attack.

That, at the time, the Argives and the Athenians would go to some lengths, as they reportedly did, to commemorate their victory in what was little more than a skirmish is not, however, surprising. They really did have something to celebrate. For it was not every day that either city handed the Spartans a crushing defeat,[59] and the "sons of the slain" at Argos were understandably proud that they had succeeded gloriously where the previous generation had so ignominiously failed. So proud, in fact, were they of this achievement that shortly thereafter in celebration, both at Delphi and at Argos itself, they erected statues of the victorious Epigone of Argive legend, which they juxtaposed with statues of these men's fathers—the Seven, including Oedipus' son Polyneices, said to have fought on his behalf in a vain attempt to conquer Thebes and make him king. It was apparently at this time as well, perhaps to celebrate their success at Oenoe and their achievement in conquering and appropriating Mycenae and Tiryns, that the Argives launched an ambitious campaign of construction, expanding the Heraeum and building a host of temples throughout the Argeia, and that they founded the athletic games in honor of Hera for which Argos would henceforth be known.[60]

In retrospect, however, Oenoe may not have seemed all that memorable—especially, when seen at a distance in time from the perspective of men as hardheaded as were Thucydides, Ephorus, and Plutarch. Their silence is a salutary reminder of the limits to our knowledge of this period. Had it not been for the monuments discussed in passing by Pausanias, we would be completely unaware of what happened at Oenoe.[61]

It is a reasonable guess that the failure of this commando operation occasioned on the part of the Lacedaemonians another surprise attack no less daring. This one is mentioned in passing by Herodotus—who reports that at an unspecified time prior to 430 a Spartiate named Aneristus, whose father Sperthios had gained great fame in the mid-480s, managed to enter the harbor of Halieis on a merchant ship concealing a small contingent of soldiers and seize the town where the refugees driven from Tiryns by the Argives would soon find a home.[62]

If Aneristus' audacious coup preceded the attack that the Athenians launched on Halieis in 459, as seems tolerably likely,[63] that strategic harbor town must have been in hostile hands at the time. This suggests two possibilities: that the Athenians had seized Halieis shortly after forging their alliance with Argos, as they may well have done; or that at this time the Hermioneans—in whose territory, as we have seen, Halieis lay—were already aligned with Athens, as they and the citizens of nearby Troezen certainly would be a few years thereafter. Absent the latter of these two possibilities, it is hard to explain why, when the Athenians launched their attempt to retake Halieis in 459, Hermione was conspicuously absent from among the cities in the Peloponnesus known to have cooperated in fending off Athens' assault; and it is also telling that her near neighbor Troezen passes unmentioned in this regard as well. In this region, the Athenians had apparently seized the initiative almost immediately after forging their alliance with the Argives.[64] From the outset, they sought to attract Lacedaemon's allies into their orbit, offering the carrot but more often wielding the stick.

CHAPTER 5

War in Two Theaters

Never in this city, pray I,
May faction, greedy for evils, rage. . . .
Instead, let the citizens return joy for joy
In a spirit of common love,
And may they hate with a single heart.
For much there is among mortals that such a hate can remedy.

AESCHYLUS

TROEZEN and Hermione were not alone in adjusting with alacrity to the new geopolitical environment. The Megarians did the like at about the same time. It is a reasonable guess that Athens threatened the two cities on or near the coast of the Argolid with the stick. To the Megarians, by way of contrast, they offered the carrot.

Athens and Megara had not been on especially friendly terms in the past. The island of Salamis had been a bone of contention in the early years of the sixth century, and the border between the two cities was contested.[1] In Hellas, next-door neighbors tended to be at odds.

In the aftermath of the Persian Wars, however, the Corinthians, who were also neighbors of the Megarians, had begun bullying their ally to the west, as we have seen. Eventually, we must suppose, the Megarians appealed to Lacedaemon, asking that the hegemon of the Peloponnesian League intervene to rein in her most important ally. This, if the Megarians really did ask, the Spartans were unwilling—and, in the circumstances, quite likely unable—to do, as the Corinthians no doubt knew. The Lacedaemonians were, as we have also seen, preoccupied with wars nearer to home.

The pressure on Megara must have been great and her situation, grim. For, when the Athenians broke off their alliance with Lacedaemon and lined up with Argos and Thessaly, the Megarians, in desperation, did the unthinkable. They withdrew from the Spartan alliance, and they grasped at the opportunity

152

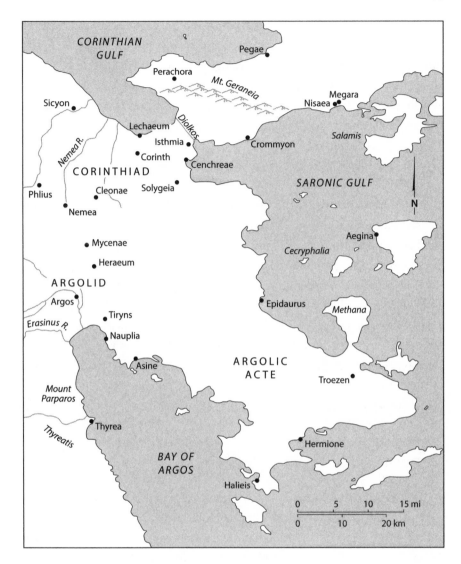

Map 12. The Saronic Gulf

this realignment afforded them. Then, without hesitation, the Athenians did the like, seizing the golden opportunity that the Megarians' appeal afforded them and forging an alliance with that political community.[2]

For Athens, Megara was a strategic prize. Like Corinth, she occupied part of the narrow isthmus that connected the Peloponnesus to the Balkan peninsula and separated the Corinthian from the Saronic Gulf. Between the two

communities situated on this isthmus lay Mount Geraneia, which was tra-
versed by passes that, with light-armed troops, one might be able to close. If
Athens controlled the Megarid and guarded with an adequate force either
these passes themselves or the approaches to them from the northwest, it
would be exceedingly difficult for a Peloponnesian force to invade Attica.[3]
Moreover, if Athens controlled the Megarid, she could also make use of Pegae,
the capacious Megarian port on the Corinthian Gulf.

The Athenians were not behindhand. The news of Lacedaemon's pledge
to the Thasians had shaken them. They knew that the helot rebellion would
someday come to an end, that the Spartans would then find an occasion in
which to march into Attica with their allies, and that they could neither defeat
the Peloponnesians in the field nor withstand a lengthy siege. With this prospect in mind, they garrisoned Megara and Pegae and set about building walls
on either side of a corridor designed to serve as an umbilical cord, linking the
town of Megara, which was just under a mile inland from the Saronic Gulf,
with Nisaea, its port on that body of water.[4] In this fashion, by making it easy
to resupply the Megarians from the sea, they rendered it impossible for Lacedaemon and her Peloponnesian allies to mount a successful siege of their town.
In this fashion, they also arranged that, if the Peloponnesians managed to
force their way through Geraneia and the Megarid and enter Attica, they would
have a sizable Athenian garrison in their rear.

The Year 459

It is to Athens' alignment with Megara chiefly that Thucydides traces "the
violent hatred [*sphodròn mîsos*]" that characterized the disposition of the Corinthians with regard to the Athenians from this time on.[5] Prior to the Persian
Wars, as we have seen, the Corinthians had sided with the Athenians against
the Thebans and the Aeginetans, and they had stood in the way of Spartan
attempts to make Athens a satellite. In 480, the two communities had clashed
over the advisability of staging a battle in the narrows at Salamis; and there is,
as we have also seen, evidence strongly suggesting that the sudden and dramatic shift in the balance of power at sea in Athens' favor effected by Themistocles on the eve of the war elicited from the Corinthians in its aftermath a
measure of wariness and even fear. Like the Spartans, however, the Corinthians may well have been ambivalent—appreciative of the service that Athens

and her Aegean alliance performed in fending off the Persians, and both miffed and nervous at unexpectedly being overshadowed.

Athens' intervention on Megara's behalf in her border dispute with Corinth transformed the Corinthians' wariness, fear, and resentment into fury; and a year later, in 459, when an Athenian fleet descended on Halieis, it was the Corinthians who rallied their Epidaurian and Sicyonian allies and drove off Athens' marines.[6] In, however, the naval battle that followed quite soon thereafter off the little island of Cecryphalia (which lay between Epidaurus and Aegina), the Athenians defeated the Corinthians and their Peloponnesian allies. And not long thereafter, in the same campaigning season, the Athenians and their own allies fought a great fleet action off Aegina against Athens' ancient Aeginetan enemy and her allies in which—under the command of Leocrates son of Stroibos, who had been one of Athens' generals at Plataea—they achieved a decisive victory and captured seventy ships before landing marines on the island and initiating a siege.[7]

These were not the only battles that the Athenians and their allies fought in the campaigning season of 459. They were also engaged in that year with the Mede. In 464, when Artaxerxes repudiated the agreement that his father Xerxes had made with Cimon's brother-in-law Callias in the aftermath of Eurymedon, he was in no position to launch an attack on any of the members of the Delian League. He first needed to consolidate his control of his father's empire, subdue a rebellion that broke out in Egypt that year, and rebuild the Achaemenid navy.[8]

This left the initiative in the hands of the Athenians and their allies. After Eurymedon, Cyprus had been Cimon's bargaining chip. He could have seized it. Instead, as we have seen, he offered to back off—on condition that Xerxes agreed to a cessation of hostilities and to ground rules governing the future disposition of the Greek and the Persian forces. After Callias' return from Susa late in 464 or in 463, the Athenians and their allies began making plans to take the island. At first, they may have been preoccupied—initially, with the siege at Thasos and with evacuating the surviving colonists from Ennea Hodoi; then, with forging alliances with Argos and Thessaly, with asserting control along the Argolid coast, and with building fortifications in the Megarid. But when these operations were all completed—if not, in fact, before—they turned once again to the eastern Mediterranean to demonstrate to Artaxerxes just how much damage they could do. Precisely when they first initiated a campaign we

War in Two Theaters: A Timetable, 464–449

Winter 464	Inaros stages a rebellion in Egypt
Winter–Spring 464	Artaxerxes refuses to renew the Peace of Callias
462/1	Athens repudiates her alliance with Sparta
	Athenian alliance with Argos and Thessaly
461	Athens cows Hermione and Troezen and garrisons Halieis
	Battle of Oenoe
	Athens allies with Megara, garrisons Megara and Pegae
461/0	Athens builds Long Walls from Megara to Nisaea
ca. 461/0	Athens begins constructing Long Walls from Athens to Phalerum and the Peiraeus
460	Fall of Tiryns, refugees flee to Epidaurus and Hermione
	Aneristus' commandos capture Halieis
	Tirynthian refugees resettle at Halieis
459	Athenian fleet dispatched to Cyprus, raids Phoenician coast
	Corinthians, Epidaurians, and Sicyonians defend Halieis against Athens
	Athenians victorious at sea in battles off Cecryphalia and Aegina
	Siege of Aegina initiated
	Persians defeated at Papremis in Egypt
	Athenian fleet shifts from Cyprus to Egypt
	Corinthians cross Geraneia, Athenians defeat them in the Megarid
458	Siege of the White Castle at Memphis in Egypt initiated
	Spartans lead Peloponnesian force to Doris, Delphi, Phocis, and Boeotia
	Athenian Triremes, based at Pegae, institute blockade
	Battle of Tanagra
	Battle of Oenophyta; Athens subdues Boeotia, Phocis, and Locris
	Athens' Long Walls completed, Aegina surrenders on terms
456	Megabyzus mounts Persian invasion of Egypt
455	Tolmides circumnavigates the Peloponnesus, captures Cythera, burns Gytheion
	Withdrawal of Messenian helots from Mt. Ithome negotiated

	Tolmides settles Messenian refugees at Naupactus
	Athenians tighten their blockade in the Corinthian Gulf
	Athenian fleet besieged at Prosopitis in Egypt
454	Athenian force at Pharsalus in Thessaly
	Tolmides quells uprisings in Boeotia and on Euboea, Naxos, and Andros
	Pericles with fleet in the Corinthian Gulf, attacks Sicyon and Oeniadae
	Achaean alliance with Athens
	Athenians captured at Prosopitis, loss of relief squadron
454/3	Cimon recalled from exile
451	Five-year truce
	Battle of Cypriot Salamis
449	Peace of Callias renewed, Congress Decree

do not know. But, in 459, we find them present along the coasts of Cyprus with a fleet of two hundred triremes, which they also used to raid the Phoenician coast.[9]

In the meantime, a Libyan prince named Inaros—who appears to have passed himself off as a descendant of the younger Psammetichus, the last Saite ruler of Egypt—had seized upon the news of Xerxes' death as an opportunity to stage a revolt in lower Egypt. At some point not long after January 464, he managed to lay hold of much of upper Egypt as well, and the man then hailed in Egypt as "the prince of the rebels" is said to have expelled from the valley of the Nile the hated functionaries charged with collecting tribute for the Mede.[10]

In the aftermath, Inaros may have sent an embassy to Athens to forge an alliance. In 459—when he got word that Artaxerxes' uncle Achaemenes, who had been the Persian satrap in Egypt for more than twenty years, was advancing on Egypt with a sizable armada—he appealed for assistance, and the Athenians broke off operations on Cyprus and sailed with their entire force to the Nile. Whether, as Diodorus Siculus reports, they lent a hand when Inaros, his Egyptian subjects, and the mercenaries in his hire defeated the Persians at Papremis and killed Achaemenes is open to question. But with their triremes they did defeat the naval forces of Achaemenes and they seized control of the great river; and with the marines on board, they captured two-thirds of Mem-

Map 13. The Southeastern Mediterranean

phis and initiated a siege of the fortress called the White Castle—where the surviving Persians and Medes and their Egyptian supporters were holed up.[11]

Inaros was a Libyan, not an Egyptian, and his assertion of his right to rule the Nile basin may in some quarters have stirred resentment. It is possible that his hold on upper Egypt, where he was a complete stranger, was tenuous from the outset; and it seems likely that the presence of a large Persian garrison at Memphis and the expectation that an army would be sent for its relief was sufficient to encourage the Iranians still lodged in the region, the mercenaries at Elephantine and elsewhere, and native Egyptians who had benefited from the Achaemenid regime to rebel against his rule. The papyrological evidence indicates that at Elephantine, in and after December 459, Artaxerxes was recognized as king, and the same was evidently true at Aswan in and after 458. North of Memphis, however, in the marshlands of the Delta where little, if any, written evidence from this period has survived, Inaros appears to have retained control. Such is what we would conclude from weighing the testimony of our Greek sources.[12]

At this time, the Athenians were stretched thin; and, with an eye to capitalizing on the fact, the Corinthians and their allies attempted to dislodge them from Megara. First, they dispatched three hundred Peloponnesian hoplites to Aegina to stiffen the resistance to Athens' siege. Then, to the surprise and dismay of their adversaries, they seized the heights of Geraneia and marched into the Megarid, figuring that, with so many heavy infantrymen absent on Aegina and in the southeastern Mediterranean, the Athenians would be incapable of defending the Megarians without lifting the siege on Aegina. The Corinthians were, however, in for a shock—for, at Athens, Myronides son of Callias, who had also shared in the command at Plataea twenty years before, rallied the reserves left behind to defend the town—both those deemed too young to take the field and those regarded as too old—and he led them into the Megarid, where they engaged the Peloponnesians, fought them to a standstill, and sent them packing.

Twelve days later, when the hoplites of Corinth—stung by the taunts they encountered at the hands of their elders—returned to the battlefield to set up a trophy belatedly asserting their claim to victory, Myronides' men sallied out from Megara and inflicted on them a clear-cut defeat. Then, to add injury to insult, when one division of the retreating army lost its way and stumbled into a cul-de-sac, the Athenians blocked the exit and had their light-armed troops stone to death the men they had trapped. The defeat, compounded by this massacre, was for Corinth, Thucydides tells us, "a grave blow," and it greatly buoyed Athenian morale.[13]

All in all, it had been an astonishing year for the Athenians. After the campaigning season had come to an end, they commemorated their achievement by acknowledging the cost. Near the Ceramicus, they erected ten marble slabs—one for each civic tribe—and on these they recorded the names of the men who had given their lives in war for Athens that year. The memorial for the Erechtheid tribe, which survives almost in full, specified that the fallen had died on Cyprus, in Egypt, in Phoenicia, at Halieis, on Aegina, and in the Megarid.

In 480, there had been thirty thousand adult male Athenians. Twenty-one years later, thanks to financial contributions from the members of the Delian League and the employment on offer for those willing to assist with the maintenance and deployment of the fleet, Athens could support a much larger population, and the citizen body appears to have grown dramatically to meet the demand. The losses must nonetheless have been deeply felt. The dead belonging to the Erechtheid tribe exceeded 185 in number. It is conceivable that ten times as many citizens—perhaps 3 percent of a total adult male citizen population numbering sixty thousand—died in service to Athens that one year.[14]

Lacedaemon Awakes

The Athenians must have found the invasion of the Megarid by the Corinthians and their allies unsettling. Hitherto they may have entertained the notion that the guards whom they had installed on or near the passes through the Geraneia would be able to prevent such an invasion, but this pleasing presumption had turned out to be an egregious error. Had the invading force been considerably larger, had the Lacedaemonians joined in, had they brought with them the Arcadians and Eleans as well as the members of Corinth's regional alliance, Attica would have been in grave peril—for the underage and superannuated men under Myronides' command would not have been adequate for homeland defense.

In the past, the Athenians had contemplated joining Athens to the Peiraeus and Phalerum Bay with Long Walls like those which they had constructed at the very end of the 460s between Megara and Nisaea. After Eurymedon, as we have seen, Cimon had even gone to the trouble of laying foundations for the two "legs" (as they would be called) in the marshland lying inland from Phalerum and the Peiraeus.[15] But, if anyone followed up on his preparatory effort, it was in a desultory fashion. The distance and the cost were no doubt daunting. Less than a mile separated Megara from Nisaea. Athens was nearly five miles inland from the Peiraeus. Moreover, the Thebans, who had posed a threat in the past, were no longer dominant in Boeotia to the north. The Boeotian League, if it even existed at the time, was not militarily formidable.[16] And the Athenians had for some time been on friendly terms with the Spartans and their allies. They were not in peril—or so they thought.

When the Athenians learned of the commitments that the Spartans had

Map 14. Attica, Southern Boeotia, and the Eastern Megarid, ca. 457

made to the Thasians in 465, it must have shattered the illusions that they had hitherto entertained. Had the Lacedaemonians with their Peloponnesian allies actually invaded Attica, as they had promised, the Athenians would have been virtually defenseless. They could not hope to defeat an army of that size as well trained as were the Peloponnesians. Nor could they cower for long behind Athens' city walls and outlast a siege. For what was threatened they were woefully unprepared.

It is conceivable, then, and, in fact, quite likely that the Athenians began in earnest building their own Long Walls in the winter of 461/0, shortly after their breach with the Lacedaemonians. Thucydides' choice of language is imprecise. Immediately after describing the events of 461 through 459, he tells us that *katà toutoùs chrónous*—"in these times"—they initiated construction. Given the number of miles involved and the height and breadth of the walls required, it is a reasonable guess that the project, which reached completion in 458, took two or even three years to finish.[17]

All that we can say, however, with any degree of certainty is this: that the Corinthian invasion of the Megarid in 459 must have removed any lingering doubts the Athenians had entertained. The Messenian threat had been contained. Although the rebels holed up on Mount Ithome had not been dislodged, they could not hold out forever. Someday—in all likelihood, someday tolerably soon—the Lacedaemonians would be back in force. It was imperative that the Long Walls connecting the city with the sea be finished before that day came, and everyone at Athens knew it.

Themistocles had foreseen the danger the city now faced, as he had foreseen many another. As we have already had occasion to note, when this great statesman had pressed his compatriots to complete the fortifications around the Peiraeus, he had repeatedly urged that, if they ever found themselves beleaguered on land, they should fall back on the Peiraeus, import food, and rely on their fleet.[18] In the interim, however, the dramatic growth in Athens' population had rendered this expedient untenable. As Cimon may have been the first to recognize, his compatriots were going to need a much larger refuge—one that encompassed the town of Athens as well as the Peiraeus and turned the two into something like an island. To accomplish this and radically alter and improve the strategic situation of the *pólis* thereby, all that they would have to do would be to fortify the thoroughfare linking the town with its port—which is what the Athenians set out to accomplish—in 461, 460, or, at the latest, 459—when they began building formidable fortifications along this route on foundations made up of immense quadrangular blocks of stone roughly twelve feet across.[19]

While the Athenians busied themselves with this ambitious project, the Spartans and their Peloponnesian allies mounted an expedition into central Greece north of the Corinthian Gulf. To the best of our knowledge, the Lacedaemonians had done nothing when Megara withdrew from the Spartan alliance. They had apparently done nothing when Athens attacked Halieis and initiated the siege of Aegina. Moreover, when the Corinthians and their allies had responded to this crisis by sending three hundred Peloponnesian hoplites to Aegina and by invading the Megarid, the Spartans do not appear to have lent a hand.

Now, however, that the Athenians' Phocian allies had attacked Doris—which lay outside the Peloponnesus tucked away in the Cephisus river valley to the south of Thermopylae—the Lacedaemonians and their allies suddenly came to life. Why they did so at this time and not before is a puzzle. The northeastern Peloponnesus was of far greater strategic importance to Sparta than the Dorian tetrapolis could ever be.

It is, of course, true that the Lacedaemonians—and presumably the other Dorians residing within the Peloponnesus—considered Doris their ancestral homeland. It is also true that it was solely by dint of her connection with Doris that Sparta had a vote in the Amphictyonic League, and this surely counted for something. As Herodotus insists, the Lacedaemonians took their religious responsibilities very seriously.[20]

It is nonetheless exceedingly odd that the Phocians' seizure of one of the four *póleis* in the Dorian tetrapolis was accorded greater weight than Athens' acquisition of Megara, her annihilation of the Aeginetan fleet, and her investment of the town of Aegina itself. Lacedaemon's troubles at home may well have eased somewhat by 458, but they were by no means over. The fact that the Eurypontid king Archidamus did not accompany the expedition to Doris strongly suggests that he was still preoccupied with the ongoing efforts aimed at containing the helot revolt and at dislodging the rebels from Mount Ithome—which is what we would expect from reading Thucydides' report that the helot revolt, which began in 465/4, did not end until its tenth year.[21]

By 458, Pleistarchus was dead. Pleistoanax son of Pausanias the regent had inherited the Agiad kingship, but he was still a minor. So, commanding in the latter's stead was his guardian, the regent Nicomedes—who is described in one source as a son of Cleombrotus (and, therefore, a brother of Pausanias) and in another as a son of Cleomenes, and who was no doubt one or the other. The expeditionary force Nicomedes led on this occasion consisted of fifteen hundred Lacedaemonian hoplites and of a great host—"ten thousand" more—drawn from among Sparta's Peloponnesian allies. The number of Lacedaemonians dispatched reveals (and it may to some degree conceal) the severity of the manpower crisis that Sparta faced at this time. At Plataea in 479, Pleistoanax' father had had under his command ten thousand Lacedaemonians—half of

Map 15. Central Greece

them Spartiates. Of the fifteen hundred men that the authorities at Lacedaemon thought that they could spare in 458, the vast majority are apt to have
been *períoikoi*.[22]

There were only two possible routes from the Peloponnesus to Doris. One
could journey initially by sea or one could journey entirely by land. To be precise, one could slip across the Corinthian Gulf by ship and, then, either march
up from Itea on the Gulf of Crisa some twenty-five miles—past the Phocian
city of Amphissa and west of Mount Parnassus—into the upper reaches of the
Cephisus valley, or land at Crisa itself and make one's way on foot up through
Delphi and along the western flanks of Parnassus to Lilaia, which was perched
above the middle of that valley. Alternatively, one could trudge the much longer route through Geraneia and the Megarid, then on through Boeotia, into
eastern Phocis, and up the Cephisus river valley from there. The passes through
Geraneia were, we are told, difficult to traverse and now carefully guarded by
the Athenians—which suggests what we are not expressly told: that Nicomedes
and his men must have journeyed surreptitiously by sea from Sicyon or the
Corinthian port at Lechaeum, perhaps under cover of night.[23] Once in Doris,
they reportedly set things to rights, thrashing the Phocians, restoring to its
rightful owners the town that the Phocians had seized, and settling future relations between the two peoples.[24]

When, however, the authorities at Lacedaemon dispatched this expedition, they may have had more than one aim in mind. In this regard, Thucydides speaks only of Doris—which is no doubt the story he heard more than thirty years after the event from his Spartan informants. Plutarch, however, mentions Delphi where Thucydides had mentioned Doris. On this point, the manuscript tradition of Plutarch is unanimous. There is no reason why one should suppose this a scribal error, and it is unlikely to be an authorial slip. Plutarch was himself one of the two priests at the temple of Apollo at Delphi. He was steeped in local lore, and he was far more attentive to religious motives than was Thucydides.[25] It is, moreover, perfectly possible that the Phocians, who lived nearby, had taken control there (as, we know, they would a few years thereafter) and that they had done so on behalf of the Amphictyonic League, in which they figured prominently. It is even conceivable that, at the instigation of their Athenian allies, they had seen to something apt to anger the Lacedaemonians: that the god should demand of the Spartans that they "release the suppliant of Ithomaean Zeus," as, we know, he did.[26] Delphi was, as we have seen, on one of the two roads leading from the Gulf of Crisa to Doris, and it was only a few miles east of the other path.

Diodorus Siculus and Justin in the material he excerpted from Pompeius Trogus—both in all likelihood echoing Ephorus—also claim that, after settling affairs in Doris, the Peloponnesians attempted to restore the hegemony of Thebes within Boeotia as a counterweight to the Athenians, and Plato reports that they were acting in defense of the liberty of the Boeotians.[27] Not one of the ancient authors asserts that either aim was an object of the expedition from the outset, but their silence in this particular can hardly be judged dispositive. The Spartans were notoriously secretive; and although they customarily said very little, on those rare occasions when they actually did speak up, the authorities at Lacedaemon were famous for saying one thing and doing another.[28] That the liberation of Doris was the stated object of the expedition is virtually certain, but it is not apt to have exhausted the aims contemplated by the closed-mouth older men in charge. Nicomedes is unlikely to have been freelancing, and it is easy to imagine that the Corinthians, who were thoroughly familiar with the geopolitical dynamics of Attica and Boeotia, had recommended something of the sort.

Thucydides also reports that Nicomedes received word after reaching Doris that the Athenians meant to dispute his army's passage home. In the interim, an Athenian fleet made up of fifty triremes had apparently circumnavigated the Peloponnesus and was now stationed in the Corinthian Gulf, almost certainly in the sizable harbor at Pegae;[29] and, thanks to the Athenians' awareness of the presence of the Peloponnesians to the north, this fleet was no doubt on alert. The journey back by sea from the Gulf of Crisa to Sicyon or Lechaeum was now much more perilous than before. There were also Athenians guarding the passes through the Geraneia massif. That road was, in the best of times, difficult, and it would be dangerous for the Peloponnesians to try to force their way back through the Megarid.[30]

There was also dissension at Athens. The political reforms championed by Ephialtes had left some Athenians embittered and apoplectic. The diplomatic revolution that had followed had intensified their dissatisfaction, and they considered the ostracism of Cimon an outrage. Shortly after the passage of his reforms, Ephialtes was discovered one morning dead in his bed. It is conceivable that he died of natural causes, as one scholar has recently suggested. But there is apt to have been clear evidence of foul play—for it was widely assumed at the time that he was assassinated in his sleep, and rumors were rife. Moreover, Aeschylus clearly believed that Ephialtes had been murdered—for he made sleeplessness, the dangers of sleeping, and nocturnal killing thematic in his *Oresteia.*

At some point, a name was assigned the putative assassin. But this only adds to the mystery, for the man mentioned in our sources—Aristodikos—bears a name instanced neither in Tanagra, where he supposedly originated, nor anywhere else in Boeotia. Moreover, no murderers or accomplices were ever apprehended, indicted, or tried; and one fourth-century commentator actually suggested that Ephialtes' friend and political associate Pericles was the culprit.[31] There is one thing, however, that cannot be doubted and that is that there were some at Athens who genuinely hated Ephialtes and his legacy.

Aeschylus was clearly not in their number. He had backed Themistocles; and, as we have just seen, he lent oblique support in his *Oresteia* to the suspicion that Ephialtes had been assassinated. In keeping with this, he warmly welcomed the alliance forged with Argos in 461, and he may also have embraced the reform program carried out by Ephialtes the previous year. In his *Oresteia,* which won the prize at the City Dionysia in March 458, the tragedian staged the epic tale—repeatedly referenced in Homer's *Odyssey*—of Agamemnon, Clytemnestra, Aegisthus, and Orestes, shifting the location for most of the action from Mycenae to Argos, and recasting the story in such a manner as to foreshadow in legend and extol in elegant verse the new ties linking the latter city with Athens. In the *Eumenides,* the final play of that trilogy, he also articulated a new foundation legend for Athens' Areopagus, celebrating that body for the one function left to it by Ephialtes and his allies—its role as a sentinel, watchful over those who sleep, and its responsibilities as a court in which a trial for murder could put a destructive vendetta to rest, as it purportedly had in the case of Orestes.[32]

In the spring of 458, Aeschylus was clearly worried that the discontent to which the diplomatic revolution and the political reform effected by Ephialtes and his allies had given rise would eventuate in civil war. Toward the end of his *Eumenides,* he twice in an unmistakable fashion sounded the alarm. First, he had Athena warn the Furies not to inflict *stásis* on the political community whose patron god she was:

> Do not cast into places that belong to me
> A whetstone to sharpen the taste for blood, damaging to the spleen
> Of young men, driven mad by a spirited anger not due to wine.
> Do not pluck out the hearts of fighting cocks
> And plant with them in my townsmen an Ares
> Operating within the tribe, rendering them brazen in their dealings with
> one another.
> Instead, let there be war abroad, beyond the door, let it come without toil
> or pain.
> In it there will be a wondrous lust for renown;
> But battle with the bird in one's own abode—this I do not sanction.

Then, judging this brief, oblique warning insufficient, the tragedian had the chorus take up the same theme once more:

> Never in this city, pray I,
> May faction, greedy for evils, rage.
> Never may dust drink the black blood of citizens
> And a furious impulse for vengeance,
> Driven by murder to the bane of murder in return,
> Devour the city.
> Instead, let the citizens return joy for joy
> In a spirit of common love,
> And may they hate with a single heart.
> For much there is among mortals that such hatred can cure.

Though heartfelt, Athena's exhortation and this choral prayer appear to have fallen on deaf ears. According to Thucydides, some at Athens from among the disaffected sent an emissary to Nicomedes, inviting him to cooperate with them in effecting a revolution in the city and in putting an end to the Athenians' construction of Long Walls.[33]

This last possibility is apt to have been in contemplation at Lacedaemon well before Nicomedes' departure from the Peloponnesus. The strategic significance of Athens' Long Walls project could not have escaped the notice of the Corinthians, who had responded to Athens' seizure of control in the Saronic Gulf with a project of construction along the same lines—aimed at building Long Walls along the thoroughfare, some two miles in length, linking Corinth with Lechaeum on the Corinthian Gulf. The fact that, a quarter of a century later, we find them bitterly reproaching the Lacedaemonians for having failed to nip the Athenian project in the bud strongly suggests that at the time they had pressed hard for a decisive intervention on Sparta's part.[34] At the time, the Lacedaemonians may have been obsessed with conserving their now meager manpower, with ousting the Messenian rebels from Ithome, and with shoring up their position in Arcadia. But they were neither stupid nor strategically obtuse. If, at acceptable cost, they could prevent the Athenians from making of Athens an island, it would be worth the very considerable risks attendant on sending a hoplite army outside the Peloponnesus.[35]

Nicomedes is said to have tarried for a time near Thebes, expanding the circuit of the town's walls and pressing the other Boeotian cities to unite under her leadership. Then, if I have the order of events right, he shifted his army ten miles to the southeast—away from the Corinthian Gulf, away from the Megarid, away from every conceivable route home—to the environs of Tanagra in southeastern Boeotia, which lay just north of the Asopus River, less than a mile from the border of Attica and quite close to Oropus—Athens' strategically important port of embarkation for Euboea.

There, Nicomedes' immediate aim may have been to overturn or co-opt a regime, hitherto friendly to the Athenians, that had for some time been asserting Tanagra's hegemony over Boeotia. If it had been his intention all along to draw the Athenians into battle, with this act, Nicomedes succeeded gloriously. For they regarded the isolation of his army and its inability to find an unimpeded way home as a welcome opportunity.

The Athenians were still engaged in Egypt, and the siege on Aegina had

Figure 6. Hoplite on Vix Krater, late archaic Laconian ware (Vix Treasure, Musée du Pays Châtillonnais. Châtillon-sur-Seine, France. Photographer: Michael Greenhalgh, Wikimedia Commons. Published 2019 under the following license: Creative Commons Attribution-ShareAlike 2.5 Generic).

not yet been brought to a successful conclusion. But it is virtually certain that by this time the Athenians had completed their circumvallation of the town and had, in keeping with standard operating procedures, reduced considerably their hoplite commitment on the island. In countering the Peloponnesians, they were better situated than they had been vis-à-vis Corinth in 459, and they were even more audacious. The twenty-five miles to Tanagra via Deceleia or Cephisia in northeastern Attica they marched with their entire levy.

This maneuver or something like it they had planned well in advance. For, in addition, the Athenians brought with them one thousand Argive hoplites and an unknown number from Cleonae, a considerable body of infantrymen from their Aegean allies, and a cavalry force from Thessaly. They should have been a match for Nicomedes' Peloponnesians. Their army is said to have amounted to fourteen thousand hoplites, and his, to eleven thousand five hundred. If, as Plato and Pausanias contend, he had some Boeotian support as well, it must have come largely from Thebes; and, given what we are told by Thucydides concerning the makeup of Nicomedes' infantry force, the Theban contribution must have been for the most part composed of cavalry familiar with the Boeotian plain and well-suited to deployment on it—for that is what Nicomedes is almost certain to have lacked, though it could not have been clear that the Boeotians could withstand the celebrated horsemen of Thessaly.

The battle itself was hard fought, and, if Diodorus and Pausanias are not confused, it lasted two days. It was, we must suppose, a classic clash of two long phalanxes made up of heavy infantrymen armed with interlocking shields, thrusting spears, and short swords and variously equipped with metal helmets or caps made of felt and with corslets or cuirasses and greaves made of brass.

We must imagine serried ranks of exhausted hoplites stubbornly pushing, shoving, spearing, and stabbing for hours on end in the hot summer sun while the cavalry forces covered their flanks. In such a battle, everything turned on strength and endurance, and that will have been especially true if the conflict actually continued for two days.

On this particular occasion, we are told, there were a great many lives lost on both sides—including three or perhaps even four hundred of the thousand Argives—and, at a crucial juncture, at least a part of the highly disciplined Thessalian cavalry force shamelessly switched sides. When it was all over, the Lacedaemonians and their Peloponnesian allies, though badly battered, still held the field.

Diodorus reports that, in the aftermath, the two sides negotiated a truce lasting four months and that the Peloponnesians then made their way home via Geraneia and the isthmus. Thucydides confirms the route they took but mentions no truce and asserts that—presumably as a gesture of triumph—the Peloponnesians tarried in the Megarid for some time to cut down the trees bearing fruit.[36] However ambiguous the situation may have seemed in the three years preceding, the Athenians and the Spartans were undoubtedly now at war.

After Tanagra

For the Lacedaemonians, the Athenians, and the Argives, there was a great deal riding on the outcome at Tanagra. Had either side inflicted on the other a genuinely decisive defeat—had the Peloponnesian force overwhelmed and slaughtered its opponents, or had the Athenian-Argive coalition managed to massacre or force a surrender of the Peloponnesians—the battle might well have marked a turning point in Greek history. Churchill was surely right: "Great battles, won or lost, change the entire course of events, create new standards of values, new moods, new atmospheres, in armies and in nations, to which all must conform." But great battles fought to a draw change very little.

To be precise, had the Lacedaemonian allies achieved such a victory, their accomplishment would have prevented Athens' completion of the Long Walls linking the urban center with its port at the Peiraeus. It would have fanned into flames the civil dissension then threatening Athens, and it would almost certainly have forced her to raise the siege at Aegina and agree to a humiliating settlement on Spartan terms. The Athenians had marched out with their full levy. Had they been deprived of a substantial proportion of this force, they would not have been able to defend the territory in which they resided.

By the same token, had the Athenians and Argives triumphed in a similar fashion, their victory would almost certainly have undermined the morale of the Spartan alliance. It would have shaken Corinth and Mantineia. It would have heartened the rebels on Ithome, and it would have encouraged the Argives and Tegeans to attempt a revival in the fortunes of the latter's stillborn pan-Arcadian alliance.

At Tanagra, however, neither side struck anything like a decisive blow. At the end of the struggle, the Peloponnesians held the field. They had won the day, and in triumph they marched home, pausing contemptuously in the Megarid, as we have seen, to ostentatiously display their command of the situation by cutting down the fruit trees of their erstwhile Megarian allies.

Satisfying though their victory must have seemed, it was nonetheless for Sparta a strategic defeat—for her losses and those of her Peloponnesian allies were no less heavy than those of their opponents, and this the Lacedaemonian element at the core of the Peloponnesian army could ill afford. If Sparta was ever in a position to win a war of attrition, it was not at this time. In consequence, once they crossed the Geraneia, the Peloponnesians dispersed to their homes and did not return. In effect, as Plato would later point out, the Lacedaemonians and their allies left central Greece to the mercy of those whom they had just overcome.[37]

The shrewdest of the Athenians were aware of what they had gained. Although they had been defeated in battle and their loss of life had been considerable, they were anything but defeated in spirit. Sixty-two days after Tanagra, Myronides son of Callias led an Athenian army back into Boeotia. So Thucydides tells us, and he adds that the Athenian general defeated the Boeotians at Oenophyta, secured control of Boeotia and Phocis, tore down the walls of Tanagra, and carried off as hostages the one hundred wealthiest Opuntian Locrians.[38]

Diodorus' account deserves attention as well. For, although his treatment of these events is marred by the rhetorical hyperbole and Athenian triumphalism to which Ephorus was prone, and he is clearly confused concerning the order of events preceding the battle of Tanagra and following immediately thereafter,[39] he fleshes out the details regarding Myronides' expedition in a manner suggesting that in the fourth century the historian from Cumae knew more than Thucydides in his highly abbreviated epitome bothers to tell us.

To begin with, Diodorus observes, a good many Athenians were late in arriving at the place where they were instructed to gather before setting off on the expedition, and he tells us that Myronides chose not to tarry and left with a considerably smaller force than expected—confident that enthusiastic hoplites were worth far more than those who were reluctant. If the story that he tells us is true, as I am inclined to suppose, it is indicative of the impact that their grueling defeat at Tanagra had had on Athenian morale. It nonetheless also says even more about Athenian resilience. For Diodorus reports that Myronides and his men, though outnumbered, won a victory at Tanagra, then captured the town, and razed its walls. Myronides' harsh treatment of the citizens of Tanagra suggests the possibility that Athens had earlier sponsored that *pólis'* claim to hegemony within Boeotia and that, when Nicomedes appeared, the ruling order in the city had earned Athenian ire by abandoning their allegiance to Athens and embracing the Lacedaemonian cause.[40]

After dealing with Tanagra, according to this report, Myronides marched throughout Boeotia, ravaging the countryside and collecting booty in such a manner as to force the Boeotians to rally and fight—which is what they eventually did at Oenophyta, where they suffered a decisive defeat. In the aftermath, Diodorus tells us, Myronides firmly took possession of every *pólis* in Boeotia apart from Thebes. Then, the Sicilian historian adds, after marching against the Locrians of Opuntia, defeating them, and taking hostages to guarantee good conduct on the part of those not seized, he did the same in Phocis. Thereafter, Myronides is said to have marched into Thessaly to punish those who had turned coat at Tanagra and to have attempted, in vain by way of a siege, to force the Pharsalians in particular to take back their pro-Athenian exiles.

Diodorus contends that Myronides accomplished all of this in a short span of time. But, given the Sicilian annalist's propensity for summarizing a chronologically extended narrative in a single entry under a particular year, it seems more reasonable to suppose that the pacification process took more than one campaigning season. Moreover, Aristotle's claim that Thebes was governed by a democracy in the immediate aftermath of the battle of Oenophyta suggests that, while she may not have come into the possession of the Athenians, she was among the cities forced to submit. And Thucydides' testimony strongly suggests that Myronides did not reach Thessaly until a few years after Oenophyta.[41]

There is one matter of great importance that Diodorus with his celebratory bombast neglects. We have it on good authority that, in this period, the Boeotians in the various cities were at odds with one another, and it is virtually certain that Myronides and the Athenians more generally exploited their mutual hostility. It was in this period that Pericles son of Xanthippus famously compared the Boeotians with holm oaks, remarking that these trees knocked one another down in the course of falling and that the Boeotians did the like when they warred against one another.[42]

The Spartans appear to have employed an expedition ostensibly sent for the defense of Doris to rearrange affairs in central Greece to the disadvantage of the Athenians. After their withdrawal, Myronides undid nearly everything that they had done. The fact that he found it necessary to intervene in Phocis is especially telling—for it suggests that, after he defeated the Phocians, Nicomedes had left a pro-Spartan faction in command. It was probably also at this time that Athens made an alliance with the Amphictyonic League and that the Phocians recovered control of Delphi.[43]

Late in 458, not long after Myronides' victory at Oenophyta, the Athenians finished their Long Walls; and the Aeginetans surrendered on terms, gave up their surviving triremes, pulled down their walls, and agreed to join the Delian League and pay the *phóros* required of its members. In return, the Athenians may have pledged that they would honor the Aeginetans' right to govern themselves in accord with their ancestral laws. According to Diodorus, the siege had lasted nine months.[44]

The Saronic Gulf was now, for all intents and purposes, an Athenian lake. Thanks to the Long Walls, Athens herself was an island of sorts impervious to assault by land, and the Athenians were now free to turn their attention further afield. It is no wonder that, in his account of the Pentekontaetia, Thucydides reserves the central place for the battle of Tanagra. The tactical victory that was for Sparta a great strategic defeat marked a genuine turning point in the growth of Athenian power.[45]

In 459 or 458, Themistocles died at Magnesia-on-the-Maeander, and there, in the marketplace, a monument was constructed in his honor. After his flight from Argos, there had been a treason trial at Athens, he had been condemned in absentia, his property had been confiscated, and his sons, driven into exile.

In other circumstances, Cimon's ostracism might have paved the way for The-mistocles' recall. But his flight to Persia, which seemed to confirm the charge of Medism, ruled this out. After Themistocles' death, however—perhaps in the wake of Athens' victory at Oenophyta and the surrender of Aegina, when his admirers were riding high—the assembly at Athens voted to recall his sons and restore to them his property. In time, perhaps at the instigation of his off-spring, the great man's remains were reburied in a tomb overlooking that great monument to his foresight: the largest of the three harbors in the Peiraeus.[46]

The Corinthian Gulf

Two years after the fall of Aegina, Tolmides son of Tolmaeus sailed around the Peloponnesus with a force of fifty triremes—half of which must have served as troop transports. For, with him, he brought no fewer than four thousand hoplites—three thousand of whom appear to have been volunteers. Many of these presumably doubled as rowers.

Before departing, Tolmides secured permission to raid Laconia. En route he may have captured Methana in the plain of Thyrea, and he is said to have taken Boiai on the Gulf of Laconia and the island of Cythera a short distance to the south. Thereafter, presumably using Cythera as a base, he descended on the dockyards at the Spartan port of Gytheion, burned them, and ravaged the land nearby. Then, after sailing along the coast of Messenia, he brought over two islands—Zacynthus, which lay off the coast of Elis in the northernmost corner of the western Peloponnesus; and Cephallenia with its four distinct *póleis,* which faced both the Gulf of Patras and, deep within that body of water, the entrance to the Corinthian Gulf. In turn, using the latter of the two islands as a base, he captured both the Corinthian colony of Chalcis—which was situated a short distance north of the Gulf of Patras a few miles west of the mouth of the Corinthian Gulf—and Naupactus, which was located along the latter gulf's northern shore a few miles east of its entrance and narrowest point (where northern Greece and the Peloponnesus are separated by a mile and, in 2004, a suspension bridge bearing a roadway was completed between the two).[47] It was in the strategically vital waters off Chalcis and Naupactus (by then renamed Lepanto) that a naval battle of world-historical importance would take place some two millennia subsequent to Tolmides' arrival.

In the meantime, the Lacedaemonians, who were presumably once again

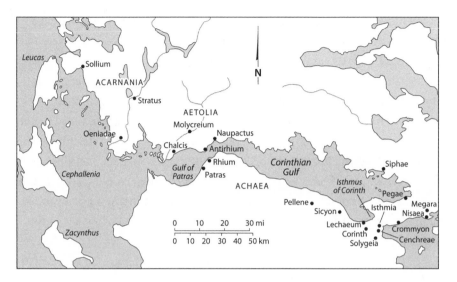

Map 16. The Corinthian Gulf, the Gulf of Patras, Zacynthus, Cephallenia, and Leucas

under pressure from the oracle at Delphi "to release the suppliant of Itho-maean Zeus," came to terms with the rebels on Mount Ithome—who surren-dered their stronghold on condition that the Spartans allow them to depart from Messenia under truce with their children and wives. These refugees the son of Tolmaeus then settled in Naupactus alongside the Ozolian Locrians, who were themselves recent arrivals; and, thereafter, he descended on Sicyon and defeated the citizens of that maritime city in battle.[48]

When Tolmides and his hoplites marched back to Athens, as they pre-sumably did at the end of the campaigning season, he almost certainly left most of his triremes at Pegae in the Megarid. We are not told that, after this, the fifty Athenian triremes present in the Corinthian Gulf since 458 and those left by Tolmides two years thereafter vigorously asserted Athens' control over that body of water. But it stands to reason that they must have done so, and we later learn that the Achaeans, who lived along the northern coast of the Pelo-ponnesus west of Sicyon and opposite Naupactus, had aligned themselves with the Athenians.[49]

Naupactus near the narrows was clearly chosen with an eye to its strategic significance. Twenty-seven years after settling the Messenians on that site, when the Athenians were once again at war against the Spartans and their allies, one of their commanders circumnavigated the Peloponnesus with twenty triremes, based himself at Naupactus, and set out to prevent anyone from sailing in and out of Corinth and the Corinthian Gulf as a whole. It is not at all likely that he blocked only the movement of triremes and troop transports. Merchant galleys and *gaúloi* were easy marks; and, in this later war, we are expressly told, the Athenians were interested in preventing the shipment of grain to the Peloponnesus from Italy and Sicily. Moreover, during this later war, they tried to maintain from Salamis and, in time, the tiny island of Minoa a strict blockade of Nisaea, Megara's port on the Saronic Gulf—which suggests that they must have treated Corinth in much the same fashion, cutting her off, insofar as this was possible, from all commerce with the emporia in the Aegean, on the Ionian Sea, on the Adriatic, in Sicily, Italy, and the western Mediterranean more generally.[50]

If, as seems clear, this is what the Athenians did in the 420s, it seems plausible to suppose that they did the same in their earlier war with the Peloponnesians. It is highly likely that they initiated this project in 458 when fifty Athenian triremes are known to have been present in the Corinthian Gulf; that in 455 they stationed a squadron at Naupactus, and perhaps another at Chalcis, in addition to the one known to have been lodged at Pegae; and that central to the mission they were assigned was to put an end to the lucrative trade with the west that enriched Corinth, supplemented incomes at Sicyon and elsewhere, and supplied foodstuffs to much of the Peloponnesus. To the same end, the Athenians may also have lodged a squadron of galleys in the harbor of Patras on the Achaean shore. It is striking that in 419—when an Athenian general once again intervened in Achaea, built long walls from the city of Patras to the gulf bearing her name, and attempted to construct a fort at Achaean Rhium where, at the narrowest point between the northern and southern shores, the Gulf of Patras gives way to the Gulf of Corinth—the Corinthians and Sicyonians became agitated and intervened to put a stop to construction. If, as I suppose, the Athenians in the 450s actually mounted a blockade, using these ports, the suffering they inflicted in this manner on the Corinthians in the latter part of that decade would go a long way toward explaining the depth and persistence of "the violent hatred" that the latter contracted for the Athenians in these years.[51]

Even more to the point, had the Athenians not imposed a blockade on Corinthian trade in the late 450s, it would be hard to explain what the Corinthians had in mind when, two decades thereafter, in speaking to the members of the Spartan alliance, they adopted a didactic tone, alluded cryptically to their own bitter experience with the Athenians, and then went on to issue a warning to the cities that lay in the interior of the Peloponnesus—in which they stressed the great damage that the Athenians could do them in battle far less than the economic hardship they could inflict if ceded command of the sea. "It is necessary," the Corinthian delegates insisted on this occasion, "that those who occupy the interior [*mesógeia*] and reside off the beaten path recognize that, if they do not rally to the defense of those down-country on the shore, they will have greater difficulty both in exporting by sea the produce which in season they gather [*hè komidè tôn hōraíōn*], and in receiving again as a return [*antílēpsis*] those things that the sea has to offer to the lubbers on land." Theirs was, as these Corinthians clearly imply, the voice of experience—and that experience appears to have been exceedingly unpleasant.

One could exercise considerable leverage if one controlled the sea. As an acute Athenian observer would note at some point in the decades that followed, among the Hellenes and the barbarians none but his compatriots were really "capable of amassing the wealth" attendant on overseas commerce. "If a city is rich in timber for ships," he asked,

> where will she dispose of it, if she does not persuade the rulers of the sea? If a city is rich in iron, copper, or flax, where will she find a market, if she does not persuade the rulers of the sea? . . . Moreover, we will not allow men, on pain of losing the use of the sea, to conduct trade elsewhere with those at odds with us. . . . And near every mainland district there is a headland sticking out, an island lying offshore, or a choke point so that it is possible for those ruling the sea to lie in wait and wreak harm on those who make their homes on land.

In short, in the 450s, when the Athenians were riding high, a blockade that would have been a hardship for those who resided in the *mesógeia* would have been a disaster for a city famous for the wealth she elicited from trade.[52]

The Athenians were also active on land. In the spring of 454, the Athenians —probably under the command of Myronides—made an attempt with the help of their Boeotian and Phocian allies to install Orestes son of Echecratides as the ruler of Pharsalus, but to no avail. The Thessalians—who were superior in cavalry, as the Athenians should have foreseen—confined them to their camp, and they were unable to storm the town. A short time thereafter, we are given to understand, there was trouble in Boeotia, which Tolmides was sent to quell.

While the son of Tolmaeus was thus preoccupied, Pericles son of Xanthippus took to the sea. First, he marched to Pegae with a thousand Athenian hoplites. Then, he embarked on the triremes lodged there, sailed along the coast to Sicyon, marched inland either to Nemea or along the Nemean River, and inflicted a defeat on the Sicyonians. And finally, he reembarked, took with him a host of Achaeans, induced most of the Acarnanians to align with Athens, and unsuccessfully laid siege to the stronghold of Oeniadae, a short distance upstream from the coast.[53]

In these years, the Athenians may not have been in a position to put real pressure on Lacedaemon's allies in the interior of the Peloponnesus. But they did everything they could to force the cities on the coast to abandon the Spartan alliance, and it is a reasonable guess that they made life miserable for the Epidaurians, the Sicyonians, and the Corinthians in a multitude of minor ways that Thucydides, Diodorus, and Plutarch have no occasion to mention.

A Reversal of Fortune

A quarter of a century after these events, the Corinthians, looking back, tried for the benefit of the Lacedaemonians to describe what they were like themselves and what with Athens they were up against. "The Athenians," they reportedly remarked, "are innovators." They are

> keen in forming plans, and quick to accomplish in deed what they have contrived in thought. You Spartans are intent on saving what you now possess; you are always indecisive, and you leave even what is needed undone. They are daring beyond their strength, they are risk-takers against all judgment, and in the midst of terrors they remain of good hope—while you accomplish less than is in your power, mistrust your judgment in matters most firm, and think not how to release yourselves from the terrors you face. In addition, they are unhesitant where you are inclined to delay, and they are always out and about in the larger world while you stay at home. For they think to acquire something by being away while you think that by proceeding abroad you will harm what lies ready to hand. In victory over the enemy, they sally farthest forth; in defeat, they give the least ground. For their city's sake, they use their bodies as if they were not their own; their intelligence they dedicate to political action on her behalf. And if they fail to accomplish what they have resolved to do, they suppose themselves deprived of that which is their own—while what they have accomplished and have now acquired they judge to be little in comparison with what they will do in the time to come. If they trip up in an endeavor, they are soon full of hope with regard to yet another goal. For they alone pos-

sess something at the moment at which they come to hope for it: so swiftly do they contrive to attempt what has been resolved. And on all these things they exert themselves in toil and danger through all the days of their lives, enjoying least of all what they already possess because they are ever intent on further acquisition. They look on a holiday as nothing but an opportunity to do what needs doing, and they regard peace and quiet free from political business as a greater misfortune than a laborious want of leisure. So that, if someone were to sum them up by saying that they are by nature capable neither of being at rest nor of allowing other human beings to be so, he would speak the truth.[54]

This is an apt description of the Athens that the Corinthians encountered in the 450s, and it captures as well the character of their Lacedaemonian opponents. If Sparta was a tortoise—slow, steady, methodical, and cautious in the extreme—Athens was a hare. Her citizens were quick, nervous, brilliant, and bold almost to the point of madness.

At the same assembly, the members of the Athenian delegation present did everything they could to reinforce the impression left by the Corinthians and to overawe the Lacedaemonians. Their hegemony—which by this time they were prepared to concede was, in fact, an empire—they boldly defended, asserting that at Marathon and Salamis and in the struggles that followed Lacedaemon's withdrawal from the fray they had earned the right to rule. Their audacity in this regard they openly celebrated. In one passage, they asserted that they had been "compelled to advance their dominion" to its present extent "above all by fear, then also by honor, and subsequently by advantage." In another passage, they tellingly put fear in second place. "We have done nothing wondrous," they insisted, "nothing contrary to human ways, in accepting an empire given to us and in not yielding it up, having been conquered by the three greatest things—honor, fear, and advantage. Nor were we the first such, for it has always been the case that the weaker are subject to those more powerful. In any case, we think that we are worthy. Indeed, we seemed so to you—at least until now when, after calculating [*logizómenoi*] your advantage, you resort to the argument from justice [*díkaios lógos*]." When one has weighed the realities, the Athenians asserted, one must conclude that "those are worthy of praise who, while following human nature in ruling over others, nonetheless are more just [*dikaióteroi*] than is required by a concern for retaining power. We certainly think that others, taking our place, would show very clearly whether we are measured [*metriázomen*] in our conduct of affairs."

The delegates conceded that Athens' allies were restless under her yoke, but this they attributed to their failure to recognize and properly assess the only viable alternative to Athenian rule. "If you were to overcome us and to take up an empire," they remarked, "you would swiftly lose all the goodwill which you have secured because of the fear we inspire—that is, if you hold to the pattern of conduct that you evidenced in the brief span when you were the leaders against the Mede. You have institutions, customs, and laws [nómima] that do not mix well with those of others; and, in addition, when one of you goes abroad he follows neither his own customs and laws nor those employed in the rest of Hellas." There is a boldness, a baldness, and an insolence evident in the Athenian speech for which there is no Spartan counterpart. It is hard to imagine a Lacedaemonian statesman openly acknowledging that it is a law of nature that the strong rule the weak. If anything, in its intellectual audacity, this speech was a demonstration of the disturbing qualities that the Corinthians had singled out.[55]

The weakness of Athens derived from her strengths. Her successes—from Marathon, Salamis, and Mycale to Eurymedon and the war she conducted in these years against the Peloponnesians in Hellas and the Persians in Egypt—stemmed from her energy, her audacity, her resolve. And her magnificent success in all of these ventures served only to make the Athenians more energetic, audacious, and resolute. But energy, audacity, and resolve untempered by prudence can also lead to disaster, and this is what happened in 454.

It was one thing to harry the Persians when one had the Lacedaemonians guarding one's back. It was another to do so when one was at daggers drawn with Sparta and her Peloponnesian allies. The Athenians were far more numerous than the Lacedaemonians, but, as we have seen, the city's manpower was nonetheless quite limited. It did not compare with what the Peloponnesians were capable of putting in the field. Achaemenid Persia had what must have seemed like an infinite supply of men, and it possessed financial resources and a capacity to build and field fleets that beggared the imagination.

Egypt was important to the Great King. It was one of the wealthiest satrapies in his vast empire. He was not going to give it up without a tremendous fight, and that is precisely what was required—for the reconquest of Egypt was a monumental task, as Artaxerxes' uncle Achaemenes by his failure had shown. First, one had to brave the heat, the sandstorms, the quicksand, the lack of water and make one's way through Sinai. Then, one had to force one's way past the massive fortifications built near Pelusium by Necho at the very end of the seventh and the very beginning of the sixth centuries. Finally, one had to march a considerable distance up the Nile, seize Memphis, and extend one's control hundreds of miles south throughout upper Egypt.[56] For this, the Great King had the requisite resources. On land, in a place like Egypt, with sufficient preparation, he was apt to be able to overwhelm whatever forces Inaros could deploy. The Libyan rebel had defeated Achaemenes at Papremis, and he had killed the man. But, despite repeated efforts and the passage of something on the order of two or three years, he and his Athenian allies had not been able to take or force the surrender of the White Castle at Memphis; and, after Papremis, Inaros appears to have lost control of upper Egypt. "The prince of the rebels" was in Egypt an interloper of sorts himself—and this made him vulnerable.

At this stage, there was perhaps no great danger involved in the Athenians' providing Inaros with aid. The Great King could send a minion such as Megabazos with gold to the Peloponnesus for the purpose of bringing the Lacedaemonians onto the field, as he did. But although by the end of 455 the Messenian rebels had withdrawn, within that great peninsula the Argives remained hostile, as did the Tegeans; and, outside it, Athens still controlled and patrolled the Geraneia in the Megarid as well as the Corinthian Gulf. Tanagra had been costly enough, and by this time the Athenians had finished their Long Walls. For an invasion of Attica, in 456 and 455, the circumstances were anything but propitious; and, gold or no gold, the Spartans were not about to do anything without carefully calculating the likelihood of success, which was not high, and the attendant risks, which were considerable.[57]

The danger for Athens lay less in her meddling in Egypt than in the level of her commitment there. According to Thucydides—with whom, for what it is worth, Diodorus in one passage concurs—the fleet near Cyprus that was summoned by Inaros in 459 consisted of two hundred ships.[58] The manpower required for such an enterprise amounted to more than two-thirds of the entire adult male population of Athens. As we have seen, it took one hundred seventy oarsmen to power a Greek trireme, and there were at least thirty more men on board each ship, serving as officers, specialists, archers, or marines. If, initially, it was intended that this fleet be able to deploy hoplites in any numbers on the island of Cyprus, as seems likely, there may have been as many as thirty extra marines on board each galley. If Thucydides' report is accurate—

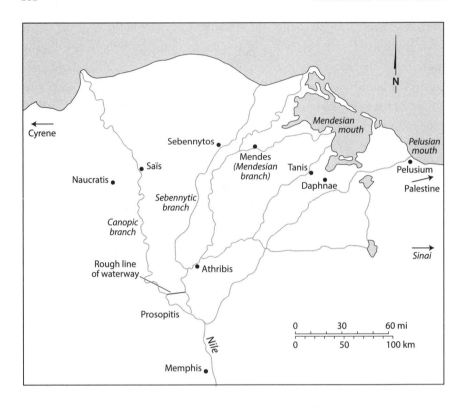

Map 17. Lower Egypt

as it is apt to be—the Delian League's commitment to Inaros at this time consisted of forty to forty-six thousand men.

Of course, some of the triremes and crews were supplied by Samos. This we know.[59] Some no doubt were provided by Mytilene, Methymna, and the smaller *póleis* on the island of Lesbos. Chios was almost certainly represented as well; and, although the officers, specialists, and marines on Athens' triremes were all Athenians, some of the rowers in those galleys were, we can be confident, volunteers from abroad—men with little or no property, drawn from every corner of the Aegean, who earned their livelihood plying an oar. A great many, however, were without a doubt Athenians in straitened circumstances. It is, in fact, hard to believe that the citizens of Athens serving with the fleet numbered fewer than twenty thousand, and they may have been considerably more numerous.[60] In Egypt, the Athenians were playing for high stakes—which is what they nearly always did.

It took Artaxerxes and his underlings some years to gather the forces requisite for succeeding where Achaemenes had failed, but this they did. In time, almost certainly in 456, yet another Achaemenid army marched on Egypt. This time, the leader was Megabyzus son of Zopyrus, the man who had thwarted Artabanus' plot. In the interim, he had reportedly been named satrap of Syria.[61]

Thucydides tells us that the army brought to Egypt by Megabyzus was large, but he does not say how large it was. We know only that it was sufficient. The Athenians can hardly have been unaware of the preparations required for the dispatch of an expeditionary force on this scale. Their chief task will have been to overawe the Phoenician fleet and to deny Megabyzus access to Egypt by sea, and for this they will have needed a fleet of considerable size.

The Achaemenid army arrived, Thucydides pointedly reports, by land— presumably because at the time the two hundred triremes deployed in this theater by the Athenians still commanded the approaches to Egypt from the sea. Megabyzus' army then defeated in battle the partisans of Inaros and their allies—presumably at Pelusium, the gateway of Egypt, near where the easternmost branch of the Nile flows alongside the Sinai desert and into the Mediterranean. Thereafter, having entered Egypt, it marched upriver to Memphis in time-honored fashion, put an end to the siege of the White Castle, and drove Inaros' forces and those of his Greek allies from the city.

In the interim, in the midst of the chaos associated with Megabyzus' victory at Pelusium and the fighting at Memphis, the Great King's fleet must have defeated the Greek squadron assigned to deny it access to the Nile. For, after the fall of Memphis, Megabyzus' forces managed to trap the surviving Greeks in the delta on the island of Prosopitis. Fifty to sixty miles in circumference, this island was located some sixty miles downstream from Memphis, and it was set off from the mainland by a canal constructed on its northern side for the purpose of linking the Canopic and Sebennytic branches of the great river.

In the 1940s of the modern era, Prosopitis was capable of supporting more than a million souls. In Megabyzus' day, however, before the drainage projects carried out in later times, it cannot have been even remotely as populous. But, in an era in which lower Egypt seems to have been for the most part sparsely populated, this particular island must have been well-tilled—for Herodotus, who visited this part of Egypt, tells us that Prosopitis was replete with villages. In the early and mid-450s, the Athenians and their allies will have needed a base within the delta from which to operate and a reliable source of provisions; and this island, which was strategically located athwart the two main branches of the river, may have served their turn.

At Prosopitis, deep in the delta—far, far from the sea—Megabyzus subjected the surviving Hellenes to a siege lasting eighteen long months. So Thucydides tells us. We have reason to suppose that the Athenians lodged most, if not all, of their fleet along the shores of the canal linking the Canopic and Sebennytic branches of the great river. After their victory downstream, the Phoenicians must have sailed up both branches from the Mediterranean. Their way further south along the eastern and western shores of the island must have been blocked at the two points where the canal met the branches of the river; and where these two streams ran alongside the island, the land must have been too marshy for the Persians to cross on a great host of rafts. The Athenians presumably had ample stores, but to hold out for eighteen months they must have been able to requisition produce from the villagers who resided on the island, as the pharaohs of Egypt had always done.

Finally—either in the winter of 454 or, more likely, in the following fall, when the inundation produced by the annual flood was no longer in evidence—Megabyzus and his men drained the canal by diverting the water within it into another channel and left the Greek triremes lodged along its shores stranded in the mud high and dry. It was at this point, Thucydides reports, that the soldiers of the Great King made their way across the muddy channel on foot and captured the Greek crews.[62]

This was not, Thucydides tells us, the final blow delivered to the Greeks. Not long thereafter, when a relief squadron of fifty triremes supplied by Athens and the other members of her confederacy put into shore at the Mendesian mouth of the great river—where the Athenians and their allies, with an eye to denying the Persian fleet access to Egypt, are apt to have maintained another base—it was caught unawares. By land Megabyzus' infantrymen attacked the Greek camp and from the sea a naval squadron descended on the fleet. Most of the Greek galleys were destroyed. Only a handful managed to escape.[63]

Thucydides leaves us with the impression that the fleet originally diverted to Egypt remained there for five full years and that, at Memphis and Prosopitis, the Athenians and their allies lost something on the order of two hundred triremes—which is the number mentioned by his younger Athenian contemporary Isocrates and by Aelian half a millennium later.[64] All in all, then, the

Athenians and their allies appear to have lost something not far short of two hundred fifty triremes in this venture—which means that the number of Greeks captured and killed must have approached, if it did not in fact exceed, fifty thousand and that Athens herself must have sacrificed something on the order of one-third of her adult male citizens, if not a greater proportion.

As one would expect, there are numerous scholars who find these numbers incredible. They cannot believe that, in 459, Athens managed to deploy two great fleets—one in and near the Saronic Gulf to attack Halieis, defeat the Corinthians and their allies, annihilate the Aeginetans and their supporters; and the other in the eastern Mediterranean—and they cannot imagine that the Athenian alliance could have survived a blow as severe as the one that, Thucydides deliberately leads us to presume and Isocrates and Aelian openly assert, they suffered in 454.[65]

For support some of these skeptics look to Ctesias of Cnidus, who served as a physician at the court of Artaxerxes II in the last years of the fifth and the first years of the fourth century, and to the account that Diodorus Siculus cribbed from Ephorus. From Ctesias, we have only fragments—often, salacious tidbits which caught the fancy of later authors, many of them preserved in an epitome by the Byzantine scholar Photius—and these may not fully do the man justice. There is no reason to doubt his familiarity with the Achaemenid court in the time in which he served there, and what he has to report concerning the marriage of Megabyzus with Xerxes' daughter and the role he played in the affairs of the first Artaxerxes may well be reliable. But what he adds concerning the identity of the Persian commander who led the first expedition against Inaros and the size of the armies at Megabyzus' disposal is demonstrably false; and, given what Thucydides and Diodorus report concerning the number of triremes diverted to Egypt in 459, it is hard to credit Ctesias' claim that only forty triremes were dispatched on this occasion.[66] His account and that of Diodorus concerning the ultimate fate reserved for the Greeks fighting in Egypt are no less suspect. Thucydides was a child, perhaps even an infant or a toddler, in 454. As he was growing up, he was surely made aware of what had happened to his compatriots on this particular occasion, and he had ample opportunity to speak with the survivors in the first three decades following that disaster. It is hard to believe the assertion of Ctesias and Diodorus that Megabyzus negotiated an armistice with the Greeks at Prosopitis, allowing them to withdraw, when we have in hand Thucydides' blunt testimony that only "a few from the many" on "the great expedition [*megálē strateía*]" dispatched by the Hellenes managed to escape to Cyrene, well to the west in Libya, and make their way home. There is, moreover, a later passage in Diodorus in which he has a Syracusan speaker attribute to the Athenians on this occasion the loss of three hundred triremes and their crews.[67]

The real question, which was already raised in the extracts Justin made from Pompeius Trogus, is whether Athens and her allies had the resources with which to fight a major fleet action in the Saronic Gulf and to deploy two hundred triremes far afield at the same time—for, if they did (which Pompeius Trogus very much doubted), they clearly had the resources to weather the loss of two hundred thirty or thirty-five triremes in 454. We know that they had enough triremes in reserve to do the like forty years later, and I see no reason to suppose this impossible in and after 461 when they deliberately launched war on a grand scale in two far-distant theaters. It is, as Athens' opponents learned repeatedly in the course of the fifth century, a grave error to underestimate the capabilities of the Athenians and to overestimate those of their adversaries. The fact that, in speaking of its conclusion, Thucydides emphasizes the magnitude of the Egyptian expedition and quite deliberately uses language in his narrative that anticipates his description of the catastrophe suffered by Athens and her allies forty years later in Sicily suggests that we would be ill-advised to downplay the severity of the losses inflicted on the Athenians and their allies in Egypt in 454.[68]

All of this is a reminder that—in political affairs, in diplomacy, and war—the unforeseen is always lurking just around the corner. By overreaching in a fashion that had always in the past served them well, the Athenians inflicted on themselves damage comparable to what the great earthquake of 465 and the subsequent helot revolt had done to Lacedaemon.

CHAPTER 6

Back to Square One

A republic that is wise should hazard nothing which exposes it to good or to bad fortune: the only good to which it ought to aspire is the perpetuation of its condition.

CHARLES LOUIS DE SECONDAT, BARON DE LA BRÈDE ET DE MONTESQUIEU

EGABYZUS' victory in Egypt in 454 was as decisive as it was dramatic. It threatened to change the entire course of events, and for a time within the eastern Mediterranean it fostered new expectations and a new mood and atmosphere to which, all suspected, they might eventually have to conform. Most prominent among those who had to adjust their presumptions, reconsider their options, and rethink the geopolitical imperatives that they faced were the Persians, the Athenians, and the Lacedaemonians.

In the immediate aftermath, Megabyzus was no doubt too busy eliminating pockets of resistance and consolidating Persia's control over Egypt to contemplate any other task. Inaros he captured, but we know that a rebel prince named Amyrtaeus managed to maintain his independence for years in the marshlands of the western Delta. Moreover, Herodotus reports that the Persians allowed Thannyras son of Inaros and Pausiris son of Amyrtaeus to succeed their fathers as dynasts in that region, and there is no reason to suppose these men the sole holdouts. Egypt was immense. It was complex; and given its importance and its propensity for rebellion, for a time at least, it must have required close attention.

For the task facing Megabyzus, however, the Achaemenid fleet was of limited use. What he needed to do was to establish firm control over the main channels of the Nile. There was no shortage of river boats in Egypt and no shortage of men skilled in their management, and by this time both were for the most part under Persian control. The marshlands as such were of little interest.[1]

At sea, however, in the eastern Mediterranean, the fleet of triremes supplied chiefly by the Phoenicians was now for the first time in a quarter-century unopposed. It cannot have taken Artaxerxes and his minions long to realize that Persia was now well-situated for going on the offensive.

We have reason to believe that in and after the late 460s the Athenians had begun encroaching on cities, at least partially Greek in population, hitherto relegated to Persia's domain—such as Aspendus, which lay in Pamphylia along the southern shore of Asia Minor to the east of Phaselis; Celenderis further east in Cilicia; and perhaps even Dorus, a harbor town situated on the Palestinian coast in the shadow of Mount Carmel—and they may have made similar progress in Cyprus prior to being lured by Inaros to the banks of the Nile.[2] These gains Artaxerxes will surely have set out to reverse. Whether he was also intent on recovering the Aegean we do not know, but it is hard to believe that he had abandoned the quest for world domination dictated by the species of Zoroastrianism that had animated his father and grandfather. This ambition was a central feature of the political theology that served as the raison d'être of the Achaemenid monarchy; and we know that, like his forebears, Artaxerxes drew a sharp distinction between the realm he governed on behalf of the great god Ahura Mazda and the realm still under the control of the evil spirit Ahriman.[3] Nonetheless, all that we can say with any degree of confidence is that the Athenians and their allies thought such an incursion perfectly possible. In the circumstances, it made sense for them to anticipate the worst.

The Five-Year Truce

And this they appear to have done. As we have seen, when the Delian League was first established, its council met on the island of Delos; and there, on that same island, the *Hellenotamíai* appointed by the Athenians looked after the *phóros* contributed by those within the confederacy who chose not to supply ships and their crews. As we have also had occasion to note, in the late 470s, when the Persians began once again to build a great fleet for the purpose of challenging the forces of the Delian League in the Aegean, the members of that body considered shifting its treasury to Athens; and we are told in a late, chronologically unreliable literary source that this was eventually done in 461. It is highly unlikely, however, that the move took place at either time. Diodorus, who is no doubt following Ephorus, reports that such a shift was carried out when Pericles was in charge. Plutarch implies that it preceded the early 440s by no more than a handful of years; he reports that the Athenians justified the shift with an eye to the seriousness of the barbarian threat; and it is not until 454/3 that, for the first time, we have clear-cut epigraphical evidence that the contributions as yet unspent had actually been moved to Athens for safekeeping. All that can be said is that, when the Aegean became exceedingly vulnerable to a Persian attack, such a transfer was imperative; that the Athenians defended the move on these very grounds at the time that the move was proposed; and that it was immediately after the Egyptian catastrophe that we have the first undeniable proof that such a shift had taken place.[4]

The money held in reserve in this treasury was of vital importance for the defense of Hellas. After the debacle in Egypt, the Athenians and their allies had many fewer ships than before, and they no doubt set out immediately to build a host of new triremes—which was an expensive proposition.[5] But a shortage of galleys may not have been the greatest difficulty they faced. They had captured a great many at Eurymedon; and, although they are said to have destroyed them all, they may well have salvaged some of those that could serve their turn. In 459, when the confederacy deployed two hundred triremes in the eastern Mediterranean, the Athenians and their allies were still able to field a fleet in the Saronic Gulf capable of defeating the Corinthians and their allies at Cecryphalia and then, in short order, the Aeginetans and their allies at Aegina. Moreover, in the latter battle, they captured seventy triremes; and, when the Aeginetans surrendered on terms after Oenophyta in 458, they handed over to the Athenians what remained of their fleet. Prior to the debacle in Egypt, the Athenians and their allies had something on the order of one hundred triremes in the Corinthian Gulf and perhaps as many as one hundred more stored as a reserve at the Peiraeus with an eye to emergencies such as the one they now faced.

The real problem the Athenians confronted was a lack of manpower. In Egypt, they had lost not only the rowers—quite a few of them citizens. They had also lost trierarchs, helmsmen, flutists, exhorters, bow-masters, and the other specialists needed for maritime operations—as well as the archers and marines carried on deck (the latter apt to have been quite numerous given the aims of the expedition). To put themselves in a position once again to take on the Achaemenid fleet would take an immense effort. The Athenians would have to add to their fleet; they would have to hire able-bodied men to row from here, there, and everywhere; and they would have to train another generation of their compatriots to serve as officers.

All of this the Athenians could do—but it would be a great deal easier if somehow the war in Greece could be put on hold. To this end, Pericles acted with regard to the most important of his erstwhile political opponents just as Themistocles had done on the eve of Xerxes' invasion of Greece with regard to Pericles' father and the others whose ostracisms he had engineered in the years preceding. In the assembly, after working out in private a modus vivendi with Cimon's sister Elpinike, the son of Xanthippus proposed that the son of Miltiades be recalled to Athens.[6]

We do not know with any precision when he did this. Shortly before the battle of Tanagra, Cimon had, Plutarch tells us, made a demonstration of his patriotism by showing up in Boeotia fully armed and prepared to fight alongside his tribesmen on Athens' behalf against the Lacedaemonians and the other Peloponnesians. When sent away at the behest of the Council of Five Hundred at Athens, he is said to have urged those among his friends and supporters who were most sympathetic to Lacedaemon to remain loyal to Athens, and many of these are said to have sacrificed their lives on the city's behalf in the extremely bloody battle that followed. According to Plutarch, it was in the aftermath of this struggle and in the expectation that the Spartans would return the following spring that Pericles secured Cimon's recall. Cornelius Nepos dates the return of Miltiades' son to the fifth year of his ostracism, and Theopompus of Chios asserts that it took place before five years of the war with Lacedaemon had passed. Whether Theopompus dated the beginning of this war to Athens' alliance with Argos in 461, to her attack on Halieis in 459, or to the battle of Tanagra the following year we do not know. What we do know is that all three of these writers claim that Miltiades' son was recalled for the purpose of reaching a rapprochement with Lacedaemon. All three report that he journeyed to Sparta and negotiated a truce, and they imply that he did so tolerably soon after his return.

There is no good reason to doubt the colorful tale told concerning Cimon's conduct at Tanagra. It is the sort of story that would have delighted Ion of Chios, and we know that Plutarch drew extensively on his *Epidēmíai*. Nor is there any reason to suppose Cimon's recall and his negotiation of a truce with Lacedaemon a figment of the fourth-century literary imagination. In an oration, Thucydides' younger contemporary the orator Andocides tells a version of the story—which, though confused, is clear enough on the crucial point. Plutarch and Nepos err, however, in one particular. If Cimon was recalled with an eye to reaching an accord with Sparta, as all insist, the occasion cannot have been the immediate aftermath of the battle of Tanagra. For, as we have seen, the Athenians pursued an exceedingly aggressive policy against Lacedaemon and her allies in the period stretching from 458 to 454. Cimon's conduct at Tanagra may well have figured in the rhetoric later deployed in favor of his recall, but, if Pericles' aim was the negotiation of an extended truce with Lacedaemon, he can hardly have had any reason to make such a proposal before the news reached Athens of the catastrophe in Egypt.[7]

Thucydides says not one word about Athens' activities in the aftermath of the Egyptian debacle—presumably because there was nothing that took place in this period that was germane to his theme. We have reason, however, to think that the Athenians faced ongoing troubles in Boeotia. There is evidence suggesting that the cities in this region may have been inducted into the Delian League and made to pay *phóros*—which, if true, is apt to have stirred resentment. We have scattered reports that democracies may have been set up in the cities of the region but that they did not last long and that Athens' relations with the oligarchies that then took over were fraught. From Tolmides' presence there in 454, we can infer that Boeotia required attention. There is also evidence for this period suggesting revolts on Euboea, Naxos, and perhaps even Andros; troubles elsewhere in the Delian confederacy; and Persian meddling in the affairs of the cities on Anatolia's west coast.[8] Like the battle at Oenoe, however, these developments were of passing importance and did not illustrate in any significant way the growth in Athenian power. The first event subsequent to the disaster in Egypt that Thucydides even deigns to mention is the five-year truce that was negotiated with Sparta in the summer of 451, three years after Myronides' abortive campaign in Thessaly, Pericles' visit to Acarnania, and the debacle in Egypt.[9]

If Theopompus supposed that Athens' war with Sparta began with the shedding of blood at Tanagra—the central event in Thucydides' account of the growth of Athenian power—his dating of Cimon's recall makes excellent sense. For the odds are good that the son of Miltiades returned to Athens late in 454 or early in 453—not in the fifth year subsequent to his ostracism, but in the fifth year after his appearance on the battlefield in Boeotia.

If this was, in fact, the moment when this great statesman reappeared, it will have taken him some time to get the Lacedaemonians to agree to a truce. That they should be reluctant is what we ought to expect. Their allies—especially, the Aeginetans and the Corinthians—had suffered grievously at the hands of the Athenians, and they themselves had been subject to attack. At Oenoe, the Athenians had helped the Argives fend off the raid the Spartans had mounted. At Tanagra, the Lacedaemonian losses must have been considerable; and two years later Tolmides, while circumnavigating the Peloponnesus, had not only overrun Boiai and Cythera; he had also destroyed the Spartan fleet, burned the dockyards at Gytheion, and ravaged the countryside in its vicinity. On the day that the news arrived concerning Athens' great defeat in Egypt, there must have been rejoicing in Lacedaemon.

Soon, however, the Spartans or, at least, the more astute members of Lacedaemon's ruling order must have begun entertaining second thoughts. It was one thing to see Athens brought low. It was another to witness a Persian resurgence. The resentment that the Lacedaemonians harbored for the Athenians must have been tempered by a renewed realization that the fleet deployed by Athens and her allies was the only obstacle standing in the way of a second Persian invasion of Greece. It was on this point that the son of Miltiades must have harped; and if word reached Lacedaemon at this time, suggesting that a major ship-building campaign was under way in the Levant, as it may well have done, it will have considerably eased his task. Cimon was in his person the embodiment of a policy, favorable to the interests of Sparta, that the Athenians were about to revive; and, in time, he was able to overcome the misgivings of the Lacedaemonians and to persuade a majority of the Spartiates that the threat posed by Athens was nothing in comparison with that posed by the Great King.[10]

For the truce, the Lacedaemonians exacted a price. If Athens was to be allowed a free hand in the eastern Mediterranean, the Athenians were going to have to abandon, at least for the nonce, their Argive allies. It was, we must suspect, the prospect that in the interim—while Athens was preoccupied with Persia—Sparta and her Peloponnesian allies would march against them that persuaded the Argives to agree at this time, in 451, to a truce of thirty years' duration with the Lacedaemonians.[11]

It was quite likely in the wake of their forging of this agreement that the Spartans managed to bring Tegea back into their alliance. Our sole source for their achievement of this goal is a passage in the *Stratagems* composed by a figure named Polyaenus, who grew up in Macedonia six centuries after the reported event. Under the command, he tells us, of a Spartiate of some prominence named Cleandridas—who was, we know, a senior figure of great weight and quite likely an ephor at Lacedaemon in 446—the Spartans managed by a ruse to sow dissension within Tegea between the rich and the poor and to secure the city's betrayal.

This event—for there clearly was some such event—marked a real turning point in the relations between Sparta and this Arcadian community. For a number of decades thereafter, when trouble for Sparta once again erupted within the Peloponnesus, the Tegeans remained firmly loyal to Lacedaemon. It is a reasonable guess that, at this time, Cleandridas installed an oligarchy in Tegea fully to the liking of his compatriots and that he did so ruthlessly and without compunction in a manner not easy to reverse.[12]

The Spartans knew what they were doing. The alliance that the Athenians had formed with Megara was an encroachment, to be sure. Their support for Argos at Oenoe, modest though it may have been, was most unwelcome. The attacks that they had launched on the Corinthians, the Epidaurians, and the Sicyonians were an outrage. It was an affront that they had disarmed Aegina and regrettable that they had conquered Boeotia and Locris and restored control of Delphi to the Phocians; and the arrangements that Athens had made with Troezen, Hermione, and the cities of Achaea were also an offense. But none of this—not even the blood shed at Tanagra, the seizure of Cythera, and the attack on Gytheion—mattered nearly as much as the hostility of the Tegeans, the influence they threatened to exercise throughout Arcadia as a whole, and the support lent them locally by the Lacedaemonians' age-old foe the Argives. As the Spartans had forcefully been reminded in 465, the helots (especially those in Messenia) were the city's Achilles' heel, and her alliance with the Arcadians—the Tegeans, first and foremost—was their aegis.

The events of the 460s had very nearly done the Spartans in. Patiently, step by careful step, in the years following, however, they had regained their footing. Initially, they had defeated the Argives, the Tegeans, and the Athenian volunteers at Tegea. Not long thereafter, they had managed to contain the helot revolt. They had also given the Mantineians the support requisite to keep them loyal; they had defeated Tegea and her Arcadian allies at Dipaea; and they had settled things to their liking in south-central and southwestern Arcadia. Thereafter, they had defeated the rebellious helots and *períoikoi* at Ithome in

Messenia. In later years, they had seen to the withdrawal of the remnants of this rebel force; and, finally, they had induced the Argives to sign on to a peace of long duration, and they had reconfigured the polity at Tegea in such a fashion as to render it a Spartan satellite. In the face of a great host of vicissitudes, the Lacedaemonians had not only endured. They had won a reprieve.

A Reckoning with Artaxerxes

After negotiating an accord with Lacedaemon, Cimon turned his attention to the Achaemenid empire. As in the past, Miltiades' son adopted an aggressive posture. He might have done otherwise. He might have bided his time. He might have chosen to wait for the Mede in the Aegean. But, as we have seen, this was not his modus operandi. Nor did it accord with the temperament of his compatriots. The Athenians were not known for their patience. Audacity was for them the norm, and for the most part it had served them well.

Athens and those of her allies who supplied ships had had an interval of three years in which to build triremes, recruit rowers, and train helmsmen, flutists, exhorters, bow-masters, marines, and the like while drilling a new crop of oarsmen in the art of rowing in unison, of reversing positions and backing water, and of performing the *períplous,* the *kúklos,* the *diékplous,* the *anastróphē,* and the other intricate maneuvers developed for combat at sea. By the spring of 451, in the opinion of the son of Miltiades and of his fellow citizens, the Athenians and their allies were ready.

We have three sources of information for the campaign that followed—Thucydides, Diodorus Siculus, and Plutarch. None of them is entirely satisfactory. Thucydides' account is extremely terse, and those of Diodorus and Plutarch are, at least in some particulars, confused. Where they are at odds, there can be no doubt that Thucydides' narrative should be preferred. He was, at the time, a child, but he may have been old enough to be aware of what was at stake and to be attentive to developments. Even more to the point, in the aftermath for decades, he was in a position to consult those who had served in the expedition; and we must never forget that its leader was his kinsman. He is not apt to have been uninterested in Cimon's fate or unaware of the course of events.

What Thucydides tells us is simple. Shortly after negotiating the truce with Sparta (presumably that very spring), in his capacity as the principal com-

Map 18. Cyprus and Its Environs

mander, Cimon led an armada of two hundred triremes, supplied by Athens and her allies, to Cyprus—which once again was to be the fulcrum of war. There he divided his fleet, dispatching sixty triremes to Egypt in response to a request from Amyrtaeus, who ruled, in defiance of Persia, the marshlands in the western Delta. With the remainder, the son of Miltiades besieged Citium, a Phoenician settlement on the southeastern coast of the island, where the city of Larnaca is now located—and there he died.

In the aftermath, the unnamed individual or individuals who succeeded Cimon in the command opted to lift the siege. The surviving manuscripts of Thucydides specify that the allied force was short of food. Some scholars believe that, where the scribes attributed the withdrawal to *limós* or famine, Thucydides had actually written *loimós*—plague. This is perfectly possible. Errors of this sort can easily creep in over the generations as manuscripts are copied, recopied, and recopied again and again; and expeditionary forces are notoriously vulnerable both to shortages of food and to the ravages of disease.

What matters, however, is that, shortly after withdrawing, the Athenians and their allies encountered an Achaemenid fleet—supplied by the Phoenicians and Cilicians and perhaps, as some of the manuscripts say, by the Cypriots as well. The encounter took place just off Cypriot Salamis, which was situated on a bay on the eastern coast of the island where Famagusta lies today. There the Hellenes reportedly fought the barbarians on both land and sea, and there they were victorious on both elements, as they had been at Eurymedon. When it was over, Thucydides tells us, the victors headed home, taking with them the ships that had returned from Egypt.

Diodorus tells a more elaborate tale. He confirms the size of the allied fleet and makes a point of the fact that the crews were well-trained and that the supplies provided were ample. He makes no mention of the squadron sent to Egypt. He reports, instead, that Cimon besieged and seized Marium, a Greek city on Cyprus' northwestern coast. He claims also that the son of Miltiades then conquered Citium. Soon thereafter, according to his account, the Athenian commander led the fleet to victory against a force of three hundred Phoenician and Cilician triremes mustered by the satraps Artabazus and Megabyzus; captured one hundred of these; and pursued the remainder all the way to Phoenicia and also, apparently, to Cilicia—where the Greeks landed their marines and defeated an army of three hundred thousand marshaled in the latter district by Megabyzus. There, he tells us, the deputy commander Anaxicrates lost his life. Diodorus also asserts that, in the following year, Cimon initiated a siege of Cypriot Salamis, where the Persians maintained a large garrison, and died there shortly after the end of the war.

Plutarch's account is even more elaborate—for he reports a great variety of omens and portents. He also claims that the allied fleet numbered three hundred triremes. He mentions the dispatch of sixty ships to Egypt. He refers to a great battle at sea in which Cimon defeated the Phoenicians and Cilicians. He mentions his death at Citium, indicating that he is not certain whether he died from disease, as most of the reports claim, or from a wound, as some say. And he adds, citing the fourth-century Atthidographer Phanodemos, that on his deathbed the son of Miltiades urged his compatriots to keep his passing a secret and to effect an immediate withdrawal, which they did.

It is possible that the allied fleet consisted of three hundred ships and that

Cimon's death at Citium was kept a secret, as Plutarch claims. It is no less possible that the Athenian commander seized Marium shortly after reaching Cyprus in the manner suggested by Diodorus. This prosperous town, which was Greek in population, was the first landfall that a fleet sailing in from the Aegean would encounter, and its possession would have been a real asset. It is also conceivable that there was at some point a battle on land near the Persian base in Cilicia outside Tarsus in which a general named Anaxicrates lost his life. The Achaemenid fleet may, moreover, have been as large as Diodorus claims, and Cypriot Salamis may have been subject to siege in the year following the Hellenic victory on land and sea. But the battle in the bay of Famagusta and onshore nearby was not fought prior to the siege of Citium, as Plutarch asserts. Nor was that city taken in the course of this expedition, as Diodorus contends. Moreover, neither of the victories won on land and sea was the handiwork of Cimon himself, and Megabyzus did not have an army of three hundred thousand. Apart from the insuperable obstacle posed for the Persians by the logistical imperatives, there is no way that six to nine thousand hoplites—the maximum number of marines apt to have been on board the two to three hundred triremes of the Delian League fleet—could have defeated so immense a force. In short, nothing that Plutarch has to add to Thucydides' story can be regarded as certain, and everything that Diodorus and Plutarch say contrary to his testimony is false. Were it not for the survival of a commemorative epigram confirming Diodorus' claim that the allies captured one hundred triremes, it would be tempting to dismiss his entire account as a fanciful tale concocted by a eulogist intent on praising Miltiades' son.[13]

Cimon's larger purpose remains a mystery. On this subject, where Thucydides and Diodorus are silent, Plutarch is voluble. In his estimation, Cimon was intent on redirecting the irrepressible aggressive energy of his compatriots away from their fellow Hellenes against the barbarian, on providing the Athenians and their allies with an opportunity to enrich themselves at the expense of their natural enemy, and on effecting the wholesale destruction of the Great King's empire. One scholar suggests a more modest aim—the acquisition of Cyprus both as a source of triremes and as a forward base for ongoing Athenian operations in the eastern Mediterranean and its denial to the Persians. Another is inclined to emphasize the Athenians' growing need for imported grain and the fact that Cyprus and Egypt were capable of exporting a surplus of that commodity. There may be something to this speculation. Cyprus and Egypt certainly served as temptations. Missing, however, is a proper appreciation of the severity of the damage done Athens by the debacle in Egypt three years before, of the danger that she and her allies faced as a consequence, and of her exhaustion and need for peace.[14]

Cimon had defeated the Persians once before in a decisive fashion in the eastern Mediterranean. In the aftermath on that occasion, as we have seen, he had ostentatiously exercised restraint—holding back when he could have wrested Cyprus from Achaemenid control; and, if Plutarch is to be trusted, supporting negotiations that eventuated in a cessation of hostilities and in an agreement aimed at preventing their renewal. The odds are good that Cimon's purpose in initiating the siege of Citium and in sending a substantial fleet to Amyrtaeus in Egypt had little, if anything, to do with a desire on his part to reorient his compatriots' imperial impulse, gather booty, acquire Cyprus as a base and source of triremes, extend Athenian power to the Levant and the valley of the Nile, and secure grain for the city. He knew better than to suppose that Athens, with her meager population (much reduced as a consequence of the Egyptian catastrophe), could establish her dominion over the barbarian peoples residing in western Asia and along the Nile. What he wanted was to repeat what he had achieved at Eurymedon. He wanted to reassert Athens' supremacy at sea, to provide thereby for her security and that of her allies, to humiliate the Persians, and to draw the Great King into negotiations. If he carried the war into the eastern Mediterranean, attacked a Phoenician city on Cyprus, intervened again in Egypt, and threatened to wrest both Cyprus and Egypt one more time from the grasp of the King of Kings, it was for the purpose of forcing the Achaemenid monarch and his minions to launch the Persian fleet and mount a counterattack. Only by inflicting on Artaxerxes a defeat like the one he had inflicted on Xerxes at Eurymedon could Cimon induce the son to do what his father had done and reach a modus vivendi with the Athenians and their allies.

The Cimon who journeyed to Cyprus in the spring of 451, after negotiating a truce with Lacedaemon, was no longer a young man. He was approaching, if he had not recently passed, his sixtieth birthday; and, Diodorus to the contrary notwithstanding, he did not live to see this scenario take place. Others did, however. For, soon after the Athenian statesman's death, the Persians did launch their fleet, and they did suffer a decisive defeat, as we have seen. And, like the double victory at Eurymedon, that at Cypriot Salamis dispelled illusions entertained by the Achaemenid court and once again within the eastern Mediterranean radically altered expectations.

In the immediate aftermath, if Diodorus—who is once again summarizing Ephorus—is to be trusted, Artaxerxes pondered the matter, consulted his councillors, and then without further ado seized the initiative by authorizing terms. At his urging, Artabazus and Megabyzus sent ambassadors to Athens to open negotiations, presumably in the spring of 450. The Athenians responded with alacrity by once again dispatching, probably to Susa, an embassy led by Callias son of Hipponicus; and the arrangement originally negotiated with Xerxes was perhaps tweaked, and it was certainly renewed.

By the end of 450, hostilities had come to an end. The Athenians withdrew from the eastern Mediterranean and agreed that henceforth they would not attack any of the territories ruled by the Great King. Artaxerxes, for his part, pledged that he would leave Caria, Lycia, and the Greek cities in Anatolia to their own devices; bar his satraps and their armies from approaching within a day's ride of the territory of these communities; limit the size of his fleet; and refrain from dispatching warships south from the Black Sea into the Bosporus and west from the Levant past Phaselis and the Chelidonian isles, which were situated just off the south coast of Asia Minor. This time, the two former antagonists may even have promised mutual friendship. But it is hard to believe that the Persian chosen by Ahura Mazda to bring order to a disordered world, the man who styled himself the King of Kings, deigned to take any sort of oath, and it is quite unlikely that the arrangement was formally promulgated as a treaty between equal powers on the same footing. As in the past, the pretensions of the Achaemenid regime and the rules of decorum are apt to have ruled this out.[15]

Genuinely cordial relations were, in any case, impossible. The regime differences and the manner in which the ruling order in the monarchy and that in the democracy each justified its right to rule precluded the requisite mutual respect and posed insuperable obstacles. Naked self-interest was the only available glue. In the event, however, it proved sufficient. Now and again, as one would expect, one side or the other breached the agreement's terms, and covert or semicovert warfare on a modest scale erupted with some frequency in Anatolia. In no case, however, during the thirty-seven or thirty-eight years that followed did a general war ensue. If, for more than three and a half decades, there was a cold peace between Athens and Persia, it was because the agreement originally forged by Callias with Xerxes in the early 460s and, after a lengthy hiatus, revised and renewed in 449 accurately reflected the balance of power in the region. Painful experience had taught both sides that neither was capable of establishing and sustaining its dominion over the territory claimed and effectively controlled by the other. Persia lacked the wherewithal to recover its hegemony on the high seas and never again made the attempt. Although, with the help of their allies, the Athenians could project power almost anywhere along the coasts of Asia Minor, they lacked the manpower needed for seizing and retaining Cyprus, let alone Egypt, Syria, and the interior of Anatolia.[16]

Most scholars acknowledge that there was such a peace. Some are, nonetheless, skeptical. No surviving fifth-century author mentions the agreement. Herodotus' failure to do so means little, however. He ends his narrative shortly after the battle of Mycale with the siege of Sestos, and given that narrative's focus he could not have touched on the peace in a digression without altering the architecture of his *Historíai* and providing a lengthy explanation of how it came about. Thucydides' silence is, in contrast, passing strange. He describes Cimon's expedition, his death, and the battle by land and sea at Cypriot Salamis, then shifts abruptly back to events in Hellas. He could easily have cited Persia's abandonment of the war as a sign of Athens' growing power and even as a development that greatly enhanced her power.

The first known to have mentioned the peace was Isocrates in 380, who speaks of it in such a manner as to suggest that he is alluding to an event known to his readers from an inscription in the Agora at Athens, which they could peruse for themselves. He and the other Athenian orators who followed his lead tended to cite the agreement polemically as an example worthy of imitation, contrasting the commitments that the Athenian Callias had extracted from the Persians in Athens' heyday with what the Spartiate Antalcidas in the time of Lacedaemon's hegemony had recently conceded to them.

Although the polemical character of these references has given rise to suspicion, it would be a mistake to suppose the peace a fraud. Apart from Thucydides, there is no surviving fifth-century writer whose failure to mention the agreement is in any way odd, and orators who deploy examples from the past for the purpose of belittling the accomplishments of those in the present are far more likely to exaggerate the achievements of men in the days of yore than to invent them out of whole cloth. If, moreover, we are to judge the charge of fraud advanced by the fourth-century writer Theopompus of Chios in light of the argument he made by way of justifying his claim, we would have to reject that charge on its merits. For the fact that the stele in Athens recording the agreement was inscribed in Ionic lettering can hardly be taken as proof that the document was a forgery. In that city, the occasional use of Ionic lettering in inscriptions pertinent to the Ionians predates by decades the decision made in 403/2 to employ henceforth only that script. Moreover, inscriptions of historical importance were often recopied in the fourth century, and there is reason to suspect that the particular inscription read by Isocrates and Theopompus recorded a renewal of the peace in 423—on the occasion of Artaxerxes' death and Darius II's succession to the Achaemenid throne.[17]

In any case, as we have seen, Thucydides' history as it pertains to the Persians is notoriously deficient, and the peace negotiated by Callias in 449 is but one of many important developments in the period between Xerxes' invasion of Greece and the coming of the great Peloponnesian War that the Athenian historian fails to mention. Even more to the point, Thucydides' narrative presupposes that there was a cessation of hostilities after the double victory achieved by Athens and her allies at Cypriot Salamis. Thereafter, he makes no further reference to any campaign directed at Persia until after the Sicilian Expedition thirty-seven or thirty-eight years later; and, under the year 428, he reports a speech delivered by the Mytilenians in which they allude to Athens' suspension of the war with Persia.

Moreover, when Thucydides reports on the negotiations that took place in the winter of 411 between the Athenian leaders then operating in Ionia and the Persian satrap Tissaphernes, we learn that, under previously existing agreements, the Persians were excluded from Ionia and their fleet was restricted in size and barred from entering the Aegean; and a later agreement between the Spartans and Tissaphernes presupposes that there had hitherto been restrictions on what the Great King could and could not do in Anatolia within his own domain. Had there been no such restrictions and had they not been for the most part honored, it is hard to believe that, even if they did fear rebellion, the Athenians would have dared to have the cities in Ionia along the Anatolian coast tear down a stretch of their walls—as they evidently did.[18] In short, even if the orators Isocrates, Demosthenes, and Lycurgus; the historian Ephorus, and the fourth-century Atthidographer Aristodemos had made no reference to an agreement reached between Athens and Persia in the wake of the double

victory at Cypriot Salamis, we would be unable to make sense of what Thucydides does tell us about subsequent events without assuming that, soon after
451, the two powers had negotiated a cessation of hostilities and agreed on a
set of ground rules defining distinct spheres of influence and specifying a pro-
hibition on trespass, which would, in fact, be honored in the breach.

Postwar Challenges

The victory that the Athenians and their allies won at Cypriot Salamis
and their subsequent success in forcing a settlement on Artaxerxes confirmed
within Hellas the impression suggested by their earlier victory over the Persians at Eurymedon and their fleeting achievement of a modus vivendi with
Xerxes; and they had an even greater impact than those earlier developments.
This time—precisely because, after a second round of conflict, the intercommunal system in the eastern Mediterranean had returned to the same equilib-
rium—it looked as if the arrangement with Persia might be tolerably stable;
and for this reason Athens' achievement once again altered expectations and
encouraged on the part of every community concerned a resort to rumination
and a reconsideration of the dictates of self-interest. In this sense, it really did
foster within Hellas a new standard of value, a new mood, and a new atmosphere to which, everyone now knew, they would have to conform.

The Athenians were, for understandable reasons, ecstatic. The fear gener-
ated by the debacle in Egypt dissipated; and, in celebration, they dedicated at
Delphi a bronze column in the shape of a palm tree or *phoînix* (which punned
on the name in Greek given the Aramaic-speaking peoples of the Levant).
Adorning its top was a statue of Athena in gold, and inscribed on the dedication was the following epigram:

> Since first the sea did Europe from Asia in twain divide
> And furious Ares laid hold of cities belonging to those destined to die,
> No deed such as this was accomplished among the men dwelling on
>   the earth
> None such at the same time upon the land and at sea.
> For in Cyprus these men destroyed many a Mede
> And at sea they captured one hundred Phoenician ships
> Stuffed with men, whom Asia greatly mourned,
> Struck down with both hands in the violence of war.[19]

The Athenians had reason to be proud of their accomplishment.

For Athens, however, this victory, though welcome, merely meant the re-placement of one set of difficulties with another. On the one hand, when Athens ushered Persia offstage, it relieved anxiety on the part of nearly everyone in Greece. On the other, it heightened the fear and the resentment inspired by the Athenians themselves, and it posed a question of vital importance to the members of the Delian League.

In principle, this alliance was meant to be permanent. Its members had hurled iron ingots into the sea, and they had sworn that they would act as one until those ingots returned to the surface. In practice, however, the alliance must have seemed to many of its members obsolete. Its stated purpose was unending war against the Achaemenid monarchy, aimed at vengeance and at liberating the Greeks under the Persian yoke. Its chief, if unstated, function was to prevent a return of the Mede, and everyone knew it. The war of liberation and revenge they had pledged was now no more, and Hellas no longer seemed in any obvious way to need a defense. The day after victory is achieved by a coalition in a great war, that coalition almost always begins to unravel.

In this case, however, the victory was far from complete; and, in fact, there was no prospect that it would ever be complete. Achaemenid Persia had not been conquered. It had not been deprived of its manpower. Nor was it ever going to be short of the silver and gold that served as the sinews of maritime war. It had not even been reduced to a state of relative impotence. It had merely been fended off—once, twice, and finally thrice. The Achaemenid realm was still the greatest empire in the world, and it still commanded a greater proportion of the world's wealth and population than any empire before or since. If the Delian League collapsed or if its members dramatically reduced the number of ships and fully trained crews they deployed, the Persians would certainly make mischief; and if and when an ambitious and spirited monarch came to the throne, they might well return in full force. The Athenians could not afford to allow their league to dissolve. Somehow or other, they had to hold it together.

There was no one at Athens who had the *auctoritas* that Themistocles and Cimon had once exercised. Ephialtes had been preeminent in 462/1, but he had been dead now for twelve years; and, though Pericles had been closely as-sociated with Ephialtes in the latter's heyday, he had been a junior partner in the enterprise, for he had been just over thirty at the time. In the 450s, he was but one among a handful of figures who were influential. Men like Tolmides,

Leocrates, and Myronides were not to be trifled with, and there were others also—Cimon, after his return, and Cimon's much younger kinsman by marriage Thucydides son of Melesias, who was a rough contemporary of Pericles.[20]

The odds are good that there was now near unanimity in Athens in favor of detente with Persia. The losses in Egypt were sobering and no doubt concentrated the mind wonderfully. What to do next, however, is apt to have been a matter of dispute.

A City of Salarymen

In the event, it was Pericles who took the lead. He was in his forties now. In the early years of the previous decade, when others were more visible at the head of the army and the fleet than he was, he seems to have concentrated his attention on completing the program of democratic reform initiated by his former colleague Ephialtes. To this end, in 458/7, he sponsored legislation opening to the *zeugítai*—the prosperous smallholders of Athens who formed the backbone of her hoplite armies—the archonship, a magistracy hitherto filled solely from the handful of wealthy Athenians classed via the census as *pentakosiomédimnoi* or *hippeîs*. To this end—either before Cimon's ostracism or shortly after his return—he secured the passage of laws providing pay for those who served on Athens' juries, and it may have been at this time and at his urging that Athens began providing a salary for the multitude of men needed, in the midst of a war with Athens' Peloponnesian neighbors, to guard the dockyards and the walls against surprise attack and to do active service abroad as cavalrymen, archers, and hoplites. Given the size of Athenian juries, which provided six thousand Athenians with occasional employment and given the number of citizens who already drew pay for service in the fleet and in the administration of the Delian League; the number who served in wartime as infantrymen, archers, cavalrymen, and guards; and the number who labored in the city's dockyards, it is fair to say that Athens was well on her way to becoming, as Pericles reportedly put it, a "salaried city."[21]

It was surely with this last fact in mind and with an eye to the opportunities afforded Athenians by the installation of cleruchies that, in 451, Pericles ushered through the assembly a law tightening the requirements for citizenship, which stipulated that henceforth one could not be registered as an Athenian citizen unless both of one's parents were Athenian. In the years following

Figure 7. Bust of Pericles (Museo Pio-Clementino, Muses Hall, Vatican City. Photographer: Jastrow. Published 2019 under the following licensed issued by Jastrow [Marie-Lan Nguyen]: "I, the copyright holder of this work, release this work into the public domain. This applies worldwide. In some countries this may not be legally possible; if so I grant anyone the right to use this work for any purpose, without conditions, unless such conditions are required by law").

Xerxes' invasion and the establishment of the Delian League, the material benefits attendant on Athenian citizenship had become more and more attractive, and there is reason to suspect that, in the last few years prior to the passage of the new citizenship law, there had been an upsurge in the number of Athenian women forming liaisons with men from abroad. After the Egyptian debacle, the former no doubt outnumbered their male compatriots by a considerable margin; and, given Athens' desperate need for manpower at this juncture, there must have been a dramatic increase in the number of foreigners who took up residence in Attica for the purpose of securing employment as rowers in Athens' fleet.[22]

The reforms carried out by Pericles at this time brought to completion a complex transformation initiated almost three decades before. Prior to Xerxes' invasion of Greece, Themistocles and Aristeides had been rivals at odds with regard to public policy. In the aftermath of the battles of Plataea and Mycale, however, the two discovered that they were for the most part of one mind in their assessment of Athens' new strategic environment and of the unprecedented challenges she faced. To cope with this new environment and meet these challenges, they not only cooperated in rebuilding the city's walls and fortifying the Peiraeus. They also worked in tandem to reorient Athens to the sea, seize from Sparta the maritime hegemony, and turn a population of landlubbers into one of mariners. Thereby, with full awareness, the two initiated a revolution in the skein of relations linking Athenian citizens with one another. Subsequently, when he led out each year the fleet Athens contributed to the forces of the Delian League, Cimon unwittingly accelerated the gradual sociopolitical metamorphosis initiated by these two erstwhile rivals. Then, in finishing off the reform program begun by Ephialtes, Pericles deliberately fashioned political institutions to fit the character of this altered civic association, which would make it easier for the poor to participate fully in its governance. Under his guidance, the *pólis* underwent an almost noiseless change of regime, and a new ruling order emerged and took charge.

In the late sixth century, thanks to the efforts of Cleisthenes, Athens' ancient aristocracy had given way to the smallholders who dominated the city's hoplite phalanx. Now the hoplites had to make way for the landless men called *thetes*—who had migrated in large numbers from the countryside into the Peiraeus and Athens to row in and officer the city's fleet; to serve as marines, archers, light-armed troops, and specialists of various kinds in the expeditionary forces of the Delian League; to labor in the city's dockyards and serve on her juries; and to engage in manufacturing and trade. As one nameless Athenian, who heartily disliked the new order, was forced to acknowledge in the aftermath of Pericles' completion of Ephialtes' reform program,

> There [in Athens], it is just that the poor and the *dêmos* have the advantage over the well-born and the rich, and the reason is this: the members of the *dêmos* man and row the ships and confer strength on the *pólis*. The helmsmen and the exhorters and the commanders of fifty and the bow-masters and the shipwrights—these are the ones who confer strength on the city, and they do so far more effectively than do the hoplites, the well-born, and the worthy. Since this is so, it seems just that any one of the citizens wishing to speak up be allowed to do so and that everyone share in the magistracies—in those filled by lot and also in those filled by election.

Although the thetes did not and could not supply Athens with her generals, cavalry commanders, and statesmen, they would henceforth sit in judgment on these men, and it was to their tune, with their material interests in mind, that the city's leaders would have to dance.

It is this fact, which everyone understood at the time, that explains both why Athens was so bitterly divided in the late 460s and the early 450s and why the construction of the Long Walls proved so controversial. Henceforth, the well-to-do *pentakosiomédimnoi*, the *hippeîs,* and the *zeugítai* who served as cavalrymen and hoplites in Athens' armies were not only to be overshadowed by the penurious thetes who labored for the city, built her ships, worked on her construction projects, and engaged in manufacturing and commerce within the great emporium that grew up within the Peiraeus and in Athens as a consequence of the city's imperial venture. The interests of these prosperous farmers were also to be given short shrift, and those who recognized the consequences of their marginalization did not relish the fact. The Long Walls were, as they knew, the visible, material embodiment of a new policy. Thanks to the revolution initiated by Themistocles and Aristeides and completed by Ephialtes and Pericles, if the Lacedaemonians and their Peloponnesian allies were ever to invade Attica, the well-stocked farms of those who tilled the soil would go undefended. There was no longer to be any pretense. Athens had ceased to be a resolutely agrarian republic, and there was a symbiotic relationship between the new order that emerged in Attica in these years and the city's dominion abroad. For the well-being of her new ruling order, Athens looked chiefly to imperial expansion and her rule over the sea.[23] As Pericles understood, she could not let the new arrangement with Persia become an occasion for the dissolution of her empire.

Reaping the Advantages of Empire

By 454, if not well before, Pericles had turned his attention from domestic reform to the management of foreign affairs. In that year, as we have seen, he conducted a military campaign in the Corinthian Gulf; and, that year or the next, he sponsored the recall of Cimon. By 449, however, Cimon was dead, as was Leocrates. After 454, we hear nothing of Myronides, who may have died that year during the expedition against Pharsalus. The only figures of import, known to us, who were at this time in a position to rival Pericles were Tolmides and Melesias' ambitious son Thucydides.[24]

From the time of the foundation of the Delian League, Athens had presented herself—with some justice—as the defender of Hellas as a whole. As we have seen, this is why the treasurers of the Delian League were called the

Hellenotamíai; and it also explains why, in the wake of the settlement with Artaxerxes, Pericles persuaded his compatriots to convoke a Panhellenic congress at Athens so that representatives from all of the Greek cities, both great and small, could discuss what in the new circumstances should be the policy of the Hellenes.

This was done with great fanfare and formality. According to Plutarch, who is clearly restating the formulae of a decree, the Athenians sent out twenty men, each over fifty years in age. Five journeyed to the Ionians and Dorians in Asia and to those on the islands lying between Lesbos and Rhodes; five, to Thrace and the Hellespont all the way up to Byzantium; five, to Boeotia, Phocis, the Peloponnesus, Ozolian Locris, Acarnania, and Ambracia; and five, to Euboea, Oetaea, the Gulf of Malia, Phthiotic Achaea, and Thessaly. The Hellenes living in these parts they invited to deliberate in common concerning three matters: "the Greek sanctuaries burned down by the barbarians, the sacrifices owed the gods in fulfillment of the vows made on Hellas' behalf when they were battling the barbarians, and the manner in which all might without fear sail the seas and maintain the peace."

The first of these three concerns is clear. The oaths that the Hellenes had taken shortly before the battle of Plataea called upon them to leave in ruins the temples destroyed by the Mede as a reminder of Persian impiety—which is what the Athenians and quite possibly the Phocians, Thespians, and Plataeans had done. Now that the war was finally over and a satisfactory settlement had been reached with the Great King, Pericles and his compatriots wanted sanction for a celebratory reconstruction of these sanctuaries.

The same can be said for the third concern. The Delian League had eliminated piracy from the waters in which its members were to be found, and this had proved to be a great boon. Thanks to the Athenian peace, intercommunal trade flourished in and beyond the Aegean as never before. This was true to such an extent that it produced a noiseless revolution in the circulation of currency. Gradually, without any fanfare, the smaller cities ceased to mint coins in the larger denominations. Given the scale of intercommunal commerce and the transaction costs this entailed, it was more convenient for them to make use of the owls produced in Athens and of the silver and electrum specie minted by the wealthiest of their local trading partners.[25]

Mindful of the damage that a renewal of piracy would pose and sensitive to the need to enforce the terms of the peace made with Artaxerxes, Pericles wanted sanction and no doubt funding for the maintenance of a Hellenic fleet capable of policing the seas and deterring Persian encroachment. He was also no doubt interested in the welfare of his fellow citizens. In keeping with Aristeides' prediction, the war with Persia had become a jobs program for Athens' poor. At its high point, twenty thousand Athenians are said to have earned their livelihood from service in the fleet, in the administrative apparatus required for running the Delian League, and in managing the city of Athens.

The second concern set for discussion at the proposed congress may have had to do with the responsibilities taken on by the Plataeans when, after the battle of Plataea, they agreed to tend the graves of those who died there. They may also have agreed—though there are grounds for wondering whether this was really so—to hold a recurring festival called the *Eleuthería* (Liberty or, perhaps, Liberation) in commemoration of the Hellenic victory, at which, on Hellas' behalf, there would be solemn sacrifice to Zeus Eleutherios—Zeus the Liberator. There may have been much more involved—for a great many vows were no doubt made in the course of the various campaigns constituting Hellas' thirty years' war against the Mede, and the time had come for their fulfillment.

Pericles cannot have been oblivious to the fact that it was highly unlikely that the Spartans and their allies would be willing to attend such a gathering. To do so would be to accept Athens' claim to hegemony and to confer legitimacy on her continued collection of *phóros* from those who had joined or been forced into the Delian League, and this would be tantamount to surrender. The prospect was rendered doubly odious by the fact that the Persian threat had receded and that Athens was once again perceived—by the Lacedaemonians, by their allies, and by many of the communities within the Delian League—more as a menace than as a defender (and with some reason). After all, the Athenians still controlled not only their league, but also Megara, Boeotia, Locris, and Naupactus as well as Molycreium further west on or inland a bit from the north shore of the Corinthian Gulf, and Chalcis in the Gulf of Patras; and they had drawn into alliance by force and by other means of persuasion Aegina, Hermione, Troezen, Achaea, Phocis, and Acarnania.

The maneuver devised by Pericles was an ingenious ploy. The issuance of the invitation—coming as it did in the immediate aftermath of the Great King's defeat and his acceptance of a humiliating settlement—enabled the Athenians to stage an elaborate celebration of their achievement and to make a display of their magnanimity, reasonableness, and willingness to consult everyone with a stake in the outcome of the proposed deliberations. This they were able to do while at the same time putting the Lacedaemonians (and those in Athens who desperately longed for a rapprochement with Sparta) in an impossible position. The Athenian gesture forced the former to choose between an acknowledgment of their status as a secondary power and a rejection of what looked—at least to the unsuspecting glance—like a generous offer, and it isolated Lacedaemon's admirers at Athens. The Spartans' selection of the second option made them seem petulant and ungrateful. It put on them the onus for the collapse of the Panhellenic project, and it provided excuse for what Athens did in the aftermath—which was to take unilateral action with regard to the array of issues they had shown to be in need of resolution.[26]

How this resolution was effected lies for the most part beyond our ken. But we do know this. From 454/3 on, each and every year the Athenians set aside for the goddess Athena one sixtieth of the *phóros* collected from the members of their alliance; and, in the agora on stone, they meticulously recorded under the name of each *pólis* the sum subtracted for this purpose from her contribution. There was, however, one year for which no record was kept—either the year 449/8, 448/7, or 447/6 (most likely the first of these years).[27] Some scholars suppose that, shortly after peace was made with Persia, the collection of *phóros* was suspended pending the results of the congress that the Athenians then called. Others cannot believe that the Athenians would take such a risk—given their financial needs and the awkwardness that resuming collection would involve. Some suggest, instead, that all of the *phóros* for that year must have been set aside for the construction of the temple of Athena Nike—Athena the Victor. But this hypothesis is also open to objection—for the Athenians did not begin to build the temple until 435. The truth is that we do not know what occurred. All that we can safely infer is that the gap in the record was somehow connected with the end of the war and the adjustments attendant on that.

After the gap, the records resume. But it is noteworthy that throughout this period—after the Egyptian debacle and again after the making of peace—there are numerous irregularities. Cities appear on the list of contributors, then disappear. Cities contribute different amounts in different years. In any given year, a city may contribute twice or may contribute well after what appears to

have been the deadline. It is a reasonable inference that in many quarters there
was a certain, resentful dragging of the feet.

We also know that the Athenians began rebuilding their temples in 447/6.
We have reason to believe that to cover the cost they drew freely on the reserves that had built up over the years in the treasury of the Delian League,
and it is clear that, when it came to expenditures on the project, the Athenians
did not stint. It was in the decades following that the Parthenon, the Propylaea, the Hephaesteum, the Odeum, the Eleusinion, the temple of Athena Nike,
and other monuments of note were constructed on the Acropolis and elsewhere in Attica.[28]

This use of the money contributed by Athens' allies must have been a
source of bitterness throughout the alliance. Even among the Athenians, it was
controversial. According to Plutarch—whose arresting account is likely to de-
rive from one of the lively anecdotes told in Ion of Chios' *Epidēmíai*—Pericles'
opponents made a concerted attempt in assembly after assembly to use the
embarrassment the expenditure of this money occasioned to undercut his influence. But this they did to no avail. First, they drew attention to the decision
to shift the Delian League treasury from Delos to Athens and to the reason
given at the time—the barbarian threat. Then, they charged that the people of
Athens had incurred a bad reputation because Pericles had laid hold of "the
money belonging in common to the Hellenes." Greece, they said, will suppose
herself "subject to terrible insolence [*húbris*] and to brazen tyranny" as she
"looks on while we expropriate resources, which she has been forced by necessity to contribute for the war effort, and then use these resources to coat our
pólis with gold and doll her up like a vain, pretentious bitch who pretties herself up with precious stones, expensive statues, and temples costing a thousand
talents."

To this, Pericles is said to have responded contemptuously, in the manner
of a schoolteacher addressing students very much in need of instruction, that
the Athenians did not owe an accounting to allies who had chosen to supply
money to the Delian League rather than ships and crews—not at least as long
as they carried on the war for them and warded off the barbarian. "Not a horse,"
he reportedly said,

> not a ship, not a hoplite do they provide, but solely money—which belongs
> not to those giving it but to those receiving it if the latter deliver that in
> exchange for which they took the cash. It is fitting, once the *pólis* has secured

Figure 8. (*Top to bottom*) *Óstrakon* naming Themistocles son of
Neocles, 480s B.C. (Ancient Agora Museum at the Stoa of Attalus, Athens:
Photographer: Marsyas, Wikimedia Commons; Published 2019 under the following
license: Creative Commons Attribution-ShareAlike 3.0 Unported); *óstrakon* naming
Cimon son of Miltiades (Kerameikos Archaeological Museum, Athens. Photographer:
Giovanni Dall'Orto, Published September 2019 under the following license issued
by Giovanni Dall'Orto: "I, the copyright holder of this work, hereby publish it under
the following license: The copyright holder of this file allows anyone to use it for any
purpose, provided that the copyright holder is properly attributed. Redistribution,
derivative work, commercial use, and all other use is permitted."); *óstrakon* naming
Pericles son of Xanthippus (Ancient Agora Museum at Athens. Photographer:
Wally Gobetz, Wikimedia Commons. Published September 2019 under the
following license: Creative Commons Attribution 2.0 Generic).

a sufficient supply of the equipment necessary for war, that she employ the superfluity belonging to her for projects from which, when they are completed, she will gain eternal fame and from which, while they are being completed, an assured prosperity will arise—with all sorts of commerce and productive labor making an appearance as well as a diversity of needs which will excite and awaken every craft and every art and set in motion every hand, making Athens, almost in her entirety, a salaried city so that from this superfluity the *pólis* will at the same time secure nourishment and attain the splendor that arises when things are put in proper order.

This struggle apparently went on for a number of years. Again and again, Pericles' opponents charged him with profligacy in the expenditure of the public funds, and in the end he responded by offering (presumably in a particular case) to shoulder the burden himself and to make the dedication in his own name if that is what the people of Athens preferred. The struggle did not fully come to an end, we are told, until 444 or 443 when Thucydides son of Melesias was ostracized.

If Plutarch's account is an accurate report, as I think it is, Pericles was a visionary with an understanding of the dynamics of trade and industry unsurpassed not only in his time but for a very long time thereafter. The biographer certainly supposed as much—for he went on to argue that what Pericles forecast at the time of these debates is what actually happened and then to describe in accurate detail the energies unleashed, the materials gathered, the enormous diversity of craftsmen and artisans put to work, and the general prosperity throughout Attica to which all of this feverish activity gave rise.[29]

There was, of course, more to Pericles' initiative than a jobs program. As Plutarch maintains, he wanted to make of the city an object of unforgettable beauty; and, as the funeral oration he delivered at the end of the first year of Sparta's second Attic war makes clear, he also wanted to make it a focus of the longing for grandeur and the aspiration to immortality that, he hoped, would animate his compatriots. When he encouraged them to look upon the *pólis* and give way to *erós,* he meant precisely what he said.

Fix your gaze daily on the power that actually belongs to the city, and become her lovers—her *erastaí!* And, when you have realized her greatness, keep in mind that those who acquired this were men of daring, men who knew what was demanded, men who were ashamed to be found wanting in action. . . . They gave their lives in common; and each on his own received in return both a praise that never grows old and the most remarkable of tombs—not that in which they lie buried, but rather that in which their reputation [*dóxa*] is laid up forever, always to be remembered on every occasion which calls for speech or for deed. For men graced with fame have the entire earth for a tomb: not only does the inscription on the columns in their own land mark them out, but, in foreign climes, an un-written remembrance lives on in men's hearts though not graven on stone. Let these men be your model; and, supposing happiness to be freedom and freedom to be stoutness of heart, take no notice of the dangers of war.[30]

The Parthenon, the most conspicuous temple built on the acropolis as part of Pericles' program, may also have been designed, at least in part, with an eye to instilling in that statesman's compatriots the public-spiritedness subsequently celebrated in this funeral oration. Inside the temple's colonnade, a continuous Ionic frieze ran around the entire building. If the latest interpretive study of this frieze is correct, as I suspect it may well be, its subject was self-sacrifice in the city's interest.

The story now, in some quarters, thought to be illustrated on this partic-ular frieze deserves attention. Fortunately for us, Euripides related it at length and in detail in his tragedy *Erechtheus,* good parts of which we now possess. According to what we can piece together from this and other sources concern-ing the tale, some years after the Athenians chose Athena as the city's divine patron in preference to Poseidon, the latter's son Eumolpus was thought to have set out with a band of Thracians and with support from the people of Eleusis in Attica to reclaim Athens for his father. When he learned what was to come, Erechtheus, who was Athens' king, reportedly consulted the oracle at Delphi and was told that he could save the city if and only if he sacrificed one of his daughters. Upon his return, he informed his wife Praxithea, who gave a patriotic speech, urging that this be done. The youngest daughter, the one chosen, then enthusiastically embraced the mission she had been assigned, and her two older sisters chose to die alongside her.

Whether, according to the story, Erechtheus killed with his own hand his youngest daughter or she and her sisters committed suicide by casting them-selves off the acropolis we cannot now ascertain. But this much is clear: the king's daughters were said to have died of their own volition; the king himself, to have fallen in the battle; and Athens, to have been saved by the sacrifice of the daughter whom he had singled out. The Athenians also believed that the Erechtheum on the acropolis was built over the grave of Erechtheus and the Parthenon over that of his daughters, and they supposed that the first priestess of Athena Polias, who managed both cults, was Erechtheus' wife Praxithea. It makes sense, then, that the Ionic frieze within the latter of the two temples should relate in detail the story of the young girl's sacrifice, of Erechtheus' death in battle, of Athens' victory on the same occasion, and of the triumphal procession that followed. And everything that we know about the actual frieze is consistent with the supposition that these were, in fact, its themes—which is what we would expect given what we know about Pericles' eagerness to impress upon his compatriots the necessity that they be ready to risk and even give up their lives on the community's behalf.[31]

Although promoting public-spiritedness appears to have been one dimension of the Parthenon's purpose, it did not by any means exhaust its didactic aim. With the help of his friend Pheidias, Pericles also sought to teach the Athenians that theirs was a *mission civilisatrice.* On the east pediment of the Parthenon, one could observe the birth of Athena. On the west pediment, the first element that would catch one's eye as one passed through the acropolis gateway, one could trace the contest between Athena with her olive tree and Poseidon, the god of horses and the sea, for the divine patronage of the political community. Below the pediments, there was a Doric frieze made up of ninety-two metopes, alternating with triglyphs, replete with sculptures. The metopes on the south side of the Parthenon depicted the Theseus, king of Athens, aiding the Lapiths in a fight against the Centaurs; those on the east side, the Olympian gods battling the Giants; and those on the west side, Theseus and his fellow Athenians confronting the Amazons. Each set of metopes celebrated the victory of civilization over barbarism, and those on the north side told the story of the Trojan War—a confrontation between Europe and Asia thought to have prefigured Athens' defeat of the Persians.[32]

Thucydides son of Olorus witnessed the building of the Parthenon and the Propylaea, the acropolis' monumental entrance. He was an adolescent when the work commenced; and, when the two were completed, he was old enough (or almost old enough) to hold the *strategía* and command a fleet or an army—which, in time, he would do. Years later, when he composed his account of the great Peloponnesian War, he penned a poignant passage in which he asked his readers to pause for a moment and imagine a future age in which Athens was abandoned and nothing remained to interest a visitor other than the temples and the foundations of her public buildings. These visitors would, he warned, be inclined to conclude from what met the eye that in Thucydides' day the city's power had been twice as great as it really was.[33]

It was this conviction that Pericles, with his building program, wanted to impress on his fellow citizens, on their allies and their prospective enemies throughout Hellas, and on anyone who passed through Athens. In the last oration that he delivered—when disease afflicted the city, when his compatriots were most apt to despair, and he wanted to restore their spirits, he is said to have returned to the theme that he had announced earlier in his funeral oration:

> Remember that this city has the greatest name among all mankind because she has never yielded to adversity, but has spent more lives in war and has endured severer hardships than any other city. She has held the greatest power known to men up to our time, and the memory of her power will be laid up forever for those who come after. Even if we now have to yield (since all things that grow also decay), the memory shall remain that, of all the Greeks, we held sway over the greatest number of Hellenes; that we stood against our foes, both when they were united and when each was alone, in the greatest wars; and that we inhabited a city wealthier and greater than all. . . . The splendor [*lamprótēs*] of the present is the glory of the future laid up as a memory for all time. Take possession of both, zealously choosing honor for the future and avoiding disgrace in the present.

The vision of the good life articulated in this speech and that conveyed by the stories retold via the sculpture on the Parthenon were one and the same, and they help explain the inflated sense of their own importance within the larger scheme of things that generally had the Athenians in its grip.[34]

Things Come Apart

In the haunting passage in which he discussed the likelihood that, in later times, Athens' power would be overestimated, Thucydides issued a second warning. Travelers who visited Lacedaemon at a time when that city was desolate would be apt to infer from the absence of a city center, from the fact that her population had been dispersed in villages, and from the lack of magnificent temples and grand public edifices that the Spartans had been considerably less powerful than was suggested by ancient report. This mistake was apt to be made, he added, in spite of the fact that the Lacedaemonians had occupied two-fifths of the Peloponnesus, had exercised hegemony over that great penin-

sula in its entirety, and had secured numerous allies in the larger world beyond.[35] To this, we—who live in the age imagined by the Athenian historian—
can add that the disproportion between the literary monuments produced in
Athens and those produced in Lacedaemon, the relative dearth of reportage
in the ancient sources concerning the latter, and the decided bias against her
that colors some (but, thankfully, by no means all) of the ancient sources and
that mars much of the modern commentary reinforces our propensity to underestimate the Spartans.

Pericles may have done the same. He may have fallen prey to his own
rhetoric, to his own longing for glory, and to the aspirations he wanted to instill in his fellow citizens. And, in the process, he may have forgotten just how
fragile Athens' position was. The city's accomplishments were breathtaking.
Marathon, Salamis, Mycale, Eurymedon, and Cypriot Salamis—the list of her
victories over the greatest empire known to man is long. But triumphalism
can all too easily become an obstacle to a sober appreciation of the realities
of power. In and immediately after 449, when Athens was at the height of
her power, she was unchallenged in the Aegean, along the coast of Caria and
Lycia, and in the Hellespont, the Propontis, and the Bosporus. At this time,
she controlled much of central Greece—and Troezen, Hermione, and Achaea
within the Peloponnesus, as well as Naupactus and Molycreium north of the
Corinthian Gulf, Chalcis on the Gulf of Patras, and most of Acarnania, which
stretched from south to north along the Ionian Sea, were among her allies. All
of this was true. But a net assessment of her situation would have to consider
the sharp decline in manpower that she had suffered just five years before, the
restiveness of her allies, the jealousy inspired by her ascent and the outburst
of vainglory that accompanied it, the resentment to which her continued collection of the *phóros* gave rise, and the residual strength of her adversaries.
When Cimon negotiated a truce with the Spartans, they had given that instrument a term of five years. When these five years were over, there was every
reason to suppose that there would be a renewal of war.

Athens was still overextended. Myronides' foray into Thessaly in 454,
which was his last known campaign, had come to naught. The Boeotians—who
appear to have been required to contribute *phóros*—were resentful and restive,
and the Athenians had had to intervene repeatedly. Euboea, the largest and
most fertile island within Athens' dominion, lay for the most part along the
Boeotian coast; and the scant evidence that we possess suggests that, in the

five years leading up to 449, the cities there and on Naxos, a sizable island nearby, were also inclined to rebellion. Tolmides, who was active in Boeotia in 454, is said to have dealt with the problem. In retaliation, he reportedly confiscated land on Euboea and Naxos, and he may have done the like for the same reason on Andros at about the same time. On this land—although it had belonged to Greeks, not barbarians—he then installed cleruchies, as the Athenians were now wont to do in such circumstances.[36]

The Spartans, who were exceptionally god-fearing, were not disposed to break the truce negotiated with Cimon. As we have seen, however, they had in the early years of that truce put their house in order within the Peloponnesus by reaching an accord with Argos and by luring Tegea back into their alliance. This left them free for the first time in nearly two decades to devote more attention to the world outside that peninsula. In 448, we are told, they sent an expedition to Delphi once again—to oust the Phocians, whom the Athenians had apparently put back in charge of the sanctuary not long after Oenophyta, and to place the sanctuary, as they had shortly before the battle of Tanagra, in control of the population of that city. That this intervention in central Greece was an oblique attack on the interests of Athens is clear, and it was perceived as such. Almost immediately after the Lacedaemonian withdrawal, the Athenians, under Pericles' command, restored Delphi to the control of their Phocian allies and secured for themselves the right of first response from the oracle.[37]

Lacedaemon's brief foray into central Greece on this occasion may have been intended in part to serve as an encouragement of those in that region hostile to the Athenians, who were, in fact, numerous. If so, the expedition was a tremendous success. Quite late in 447 or very early in 446, trouble erupted for Athens in northwestern Boeotia, not far from Delphi, at Chaeronea, Orchomenos, and elsewhere in their vicinity—when Boeotian exiles, who had presumably been driven out earlier by the Athenians, seized control. According to Plutarch, Pericles urged caution, suggesting that Tolmides, who appears to have been Athens' point man in Boeotia, listen to "the wisest of counsellors—time." Whether he had doubts about the wisdom of Athens' attempting to sustain a land empire in central Greece, as some suspect, we do not know. It is perfectly possible that he merely preferred that his colleague take the time to gather a larger force.[38]

Tolmides, however, lived up to his father's name and his own. Like Myronides, the son of Tolmaeus was a man of great daring [tólma], and his record in the field was such that the Athenians were inclined to give him free rein. The troops assigned him he gathered. He is said to have recruited one thousand more, as was his wont, from among those most eager for honor; and he drew some support from Athens' allies—in all likelihood, from the Plataeans and the Thespians and perhaps from other communities in Boeotia controlled by Athens' partisans.

Chaeronea Tolmides and the Athenians under his command seized, and we are told that they enslaved those whom they captured and installed a garrison in the town. Orchomenos was apparently too well defended for them to attempt, for they then turned back in the direction of Athens. Thereafter, as they worked their way along the southern shore of Lake Kopais, the Athenians and their allies were ambushed at a site near Coronea, which lay in between Lebadeia to the west and Haliartos to the east. Thucydides reports that the force that conducted this operation was largely made up of the Boeotian exiles who had taken control of Orchomenos, of Locrians who had joined them, and of exiles from the cities of Euboea. Within their ranks, he tells us, there were others "of the same mind"—who apparently came to be called "Orchomenizers."

In this enterprise, exiles from Thebes appear to have played an especially large role. Plutarch—a native of Chaeronea who was especially well-informed concerning Boeotian affairs—tells us that the general who staged the ambush bore the name Sparton, which was a Theban name. Twenty years later, the compatriots of this Sparton would claim the victory as their own; and this assertion Xenophon treats as uncontroversial. Moreover, in the aftermath, if we are to judge by the coins they and they alone issued on behalf of the Boeotian League, the Thebans quickly and successfully reasserted their hegemony within the region as a whole.

At Coronea, the Athenian losses were considerable. Among the dead were a number of prominent citizens, including Tolmides himself and Pericles' close friend Cleinias, who was a son of the Alcibiades who had earlier renounced the *proxenía* that his family had maintained at Athens for many generations on Lacedaemon's behalf. There were survivors, too, and they were all or nearly all captured. To secure their recovery, we are told, the Athenians agreed to evacuate all of the cities of Boeotia.[39]

Their defeat the Athenians did not take to heart. They considered it what the Hellenes termed "a theft of war." It was not due to the superiority of their foe. It was, they told themselves, the work of a god or hero of the land. Tolmides and his seer Theainetos they did not blame. Subsequently, in fact, they erected at Athens statues of the pair.[40]

Athens' decision to withdraw from Boeotia is puzzling. To the best of our knowledge, she still controlled most of the cities. Of course, the Athenians may have been especially sensitive at this time to the loss of life. Many had been killed at Tanagra a bit more than a decade before. A great many more had died in the interim in Egypt. Others had lost their lives in the battle near Coronea, and the number of Athenians captured may have been considerable. It is also possible that the death of Tolmides had removed from Athens the last great champion of the land empire in central Greece that Myronides had secured at and after the battle of Oenophyta. Pericles, who was now without a question the leading figure at Athens, may have long regarded that venture as a dangerous distraction from more pressing exigencies—from the need, for example, to shore up Athens' maritime alliance and to isolate and destroy Lacedaemon.

The Athenians may, however, have had another, genuinely compelling reason for staging a retreat. In 446, not long after their delivery of that year's *phóros*, Histiaea, Chalcis, Eretria, and Carystus on the island of Euboea nearby revolted in tandem. This may have taken place after the evacuation of Boeotia, as Thucydides' narrative might seem to suggest. It is also possible, however, that the Athenian's order of presentation reflects an eagerness on his part to wrap up one story before launching into another. After all, his focus is the growth of Athenian power—not the Boeotian and Euboean rebellions and their interconnection; and, although he proceeds to present the most illustrative events of the period in chronological order, he nowhere indicates that each and every sequence of events related was complete before the next sequence began.

The revolt on Euboea was surely inspired by Athens' loss at Coronea and fomented by the Euboean exiles who fought in that conflict. If it took place in the immediate aftermath of that battle while the Athenians were negotiating with the Boeotian rebels, as I suspect it did, Pericles and his compatriots may have been confronted with an exceedingly unpleasant choice—between devoting their limited remaining manpower to shoring up their position in Boeotia and deploying that manpower for the recovery of Euboea.

If this is the dilemma that they then faced, the choice will have been easy. Athens was first and foremost a maritime power. Her strength derived from

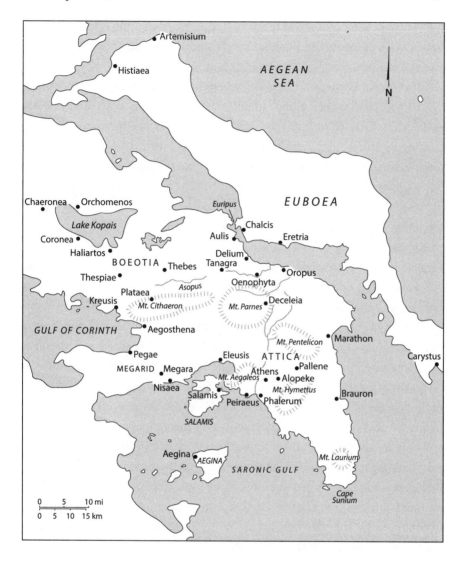

Map 19. The Megarid, Boeotia, Euboea, and Attica

her hegemony over the northeastern Mediterranean and the waterway linking it with the Black Sea and from the leverage she exercised over the islands in the Aegean; over the coastline of Thrace, stretching from what we now call the Chalcidice past Byzantium to the Euxine; and over that of Anatolia, stretching from Phaselis in Pamphylia past Chalcedon on the Bosporus again to the Black Sea. Euboea was Athens' most prized possession. It was the largest island in the Delian League, and it was the closest to Attica. Retaining it was a strategic necessity. In comparison, Boeotia, Locris, and Phocis must have seemed like an extravagance.

If this reconstruction is correct, when the island revolted, the Boeotians agreed to abandon their Euboean allies;[41] the Athenians evacuated Boeotia, and Pericles crossed over to the island with an army of Athenians. Then, according to Thucydides, news reached him that—with the help of a force of Corinthians, Sicyonians, and Epidaurians whom they had admitted into their city—the Megarians hostile to Athens had also staged a revolt; that, in the process, they and the Peloponnesians introduced into the town had slaughtered the Athenian garrison in their city (apart from a handful who escaped to Nisaea); and that the Spartans and their Peloponnesian allies were on the verge of invading Attica. In response, we are told, Pericles returned in haste.

Thucydides does not tell us that the ambush at Coronea, the rebellion in Euboea, and the Peloponnesian seizure of Megara were coordinated. He says nothing to suggest a connection between this set of events and the Spartan intervention at Delphi. But his silence can hardly be regarded as dispositive. He is interested in the results, which were pertinent to the larger question of the growth in Athenian power, and not, at least at this stage, in an assessment of the sources of Lacedaemon's strength. It is, of course, conceivable that what happened was only loosely connected—that the victory of Athens' enemies at Coronea inspired the rebellion on Euboea, which in turn encouraged the revolt at Megara. It is more likely, however, that these events were concerted, that plans and preparations were made well in advance, and that one rebellion followed quickly upon another because Athens' enemies recognized the value of simultaneity. They can hardly have failed to recognize that their chance of success would be reduced considerably if Athens was in a position to deal with the rebellions in Boeotia, on Euboea, and at Megara seriatim. The fact that Pleistoanax, the Agiad king of Lacedaemon, marched into Attica with an army of Peloponnesians not long after the Megarian revolt suggests that the Spartans were party to the plot and had in all likelihood engineered the predicament in which the Athenians unexpectedly found themselves.[42]

Thucydides' account is incomplete. Diodorus claims that, in the immediate aftermath of the Megarian revolt, the Athenians sent an infantry force into Megara, which plundered her territory and carted off a great deal of booty, and that—when the Megarians (and presumably the Corinthians, Sicyonians, and Epidaurians supporting them) sallied forth to defend their property—the Athenians defeated them and chased them back to the city. And the tale he tells is evidently true. For there is epigraphical evidence that—when Pleistoanax and the Peloponnesians actually did invade Attica—an Athenian force of two thousand men, consisting of three tribal regiments commanded by the scion of a great aristocratic family named Andocides son of Leogoras, was operating within the Megarid in the vicinity of Pegae. According to the pertinent inscription, these Athenians then found themselves cut off from Attica, and they were led to safety by a Megarian named Pythion, who conducted them via Aegosthena into Boeotia—either to Kreusis in the territory of Thespiae or to Plataea in the southeast.[43]

The outcome of all of this maneuvering is also a puzzle. Thucydides tells us that Pleistoanax and the Peloponnesians marched into Attica as far as Eleusis and the plain of Thria and that they ravaged the countryside and then returned home without going deeper into Attica. He adds that Pericles then led the Athenians back to Euboea, where they expelled the Histiaeans from their city, seized the territory for their own citizens, and subdued the rest of the island, which surrendered on terms. Then, he reports that, shortly after the Athenians had returned from Euboea, they agreed to a peace with the Spartans and their allies and, in accord with its terms, withdrew their garrisons from Nisaea and Pegae, the two ports of Megara, and from Troezen in the Argolic Acte and Achaea on the Corinthian Gulf.[44]

Diodorus (whose chronology of events is, as usual, confused) adds a few details—that the Megarians, upon revolting, made an alliance with Lacedaemon, that the loss of prestige suffered by the Athenians at Coronea inspired the revolts in Euboea, that the Athenians eventually stormed Histiaea, and that the Spartan *próxenos* Callias son of Hipponicus and an unknown figure named Chares negotiated with Sparta what came to be called the Thirty Years' Peace. To this, the orator Andocides adds that there were ten Athenians on the negotiating team and that one of these was his like-named grandfather Andocides son of Leogoras, the general who had been cut off at Pegae with a force of two thousand men.[45]

Plutarch tells us that, when he brought back his soldiers from Euboea, Pericles did not dare to enter into battle, hand-to-hand, with the multitude of brave hoplites who had been summoned by the Megarians; that he bribed both Pleistoanax, who was, we know, in his twenties, and Cleandridas, who had been sent by the ephors to serve as his advisor and was probably that year an ephor himself; and that the Agiad king then led the Peloponnesian army out of Attica. He indicates as well that, when Pleistoanax and Cleandridas returned home, the Lacedaemonians—in fury at their failure to drive deeper into Attica, to force the Athenians to fight, and to inflict on them a humiliating defeat—imposed so heavy a fine on the Agiad king that, unable to pay, he withdrew from Laconia; and he reports that Cleandridas fled into exile and was condemned to death. Moreover, according to Plutarch's testimony, when Pericles presented his accounts at the end of his year of office, he listed ten talents (more than a quarter of a ton) of silver spent "out of necessity"; and when he subdued Euboea, he banished from Chalcis the *Hippóbotai*, seized their land, and settled Athenian cleruchs on it as well as on the land of the Histiaeans, who had gratuitously massacred the crew of an Athenian trireme.[46]

Two questions remain unanswered. The first has to do with the Athenians, who had long before completed the Long Walls linking Athens with the Peiraeus. These had been built for just such an emergency. It should have been possible for the Athenians to withdraw behind the walls, import food by sea, and defy an invading army. But, on this occasion, Pericles apparently did not call upon his compatriots to rely on this formidable system of defense. Why he made this choice we do not know.[47]

It is, of course, possible that Pericles was in a perilous situation; that he had invaded the Megarid, as Diodorus seems to suggest; and that the units under his direct command, like the regiments led by Andocides, had been outmaneuvered, were cut off from the city, and, if challenged, would have had to fight. Even, however, if his men were safely ensconced behind the Long Walls, it is likely that Pericles was aware of Andocides' plight and that he feared for the safety of his men. He may have thought that Athens could not, in the wake of the disaster in Egypt and the losses sustained at Tanagra and Coronea, afford to abandon two thousand hoplites, and it is likely that he did not relish the prospect that the Peloponnesians would strip Attica bare. The Athenians may have had time to flee their farms, but it is unlikely that they had had an opportunity to collect their valuables and safeguard their oxen, cattle, sheep, and goats. Finally, as one scholar has suggested, Pericles may have worried that Pleistoanax would dispatch a substantial Peloponnesian force to Euboea and station it there at least temporarily as a garrison to give the anti-Athenian leaders in the various cities on the island time in which to consolidate control and prepare for the island's defense. The only thing of which we can be certain, however, is that the Athenians were caught in a terrible bind and forced to make concessions they would never have otherwise made.[48]

The second unanswered question has to do with Pleistoanax. In one fashion or another, as we have seen, he and the Peloponnesians accompanying him must have had the Athenians at their mercy. If the entire levy of the Spartan alliance was present, as is likely, the Peloponnesians will have greatly outnumbered the Athenians; and, as hoplites, they were almost certainly better trained. Had there been a battle, they might well have annihilated the army under Pericles' command; and, had they done this, the cities on Euboea would have remained free and, in virtually every other *pólis* of any consequence within the Delian League, men hostile to Athens would have seized power and effected a withdrawal from Athens' alliance. Had the Athenians chosen to remain behind the Long Walls, Andocides and his soldiers would have been easy pickings, and Euboea would have beckoned, as we have seen.

Pleistoanax had the means with which to do Athens great harm, and the Spartans and their Peloponnesian allies had the motive. They had suffered grievously in the years subsequent to the diplomatic revolution initiated by Ephialtes in 462/1, and they surely knew that the only way to guarantee that there would not be a reprise was to eliminate Athens as a great power by destroying her hegemony. Why Pleistoanax let this opportunity slip, however, we are not told. If it had something to do with the solar eclipse that took place on 2 September 446—as may well have been the case—it is odd that no ancient source even mentions the event.[49]

There is a consideration, however, as yet unmentioned, and it may have been decisive—for we know that, in the past, the Spartans had accorded it great weight. If the Athenian hegemony at sea were eliminated, if each *pólis* in the Delian League were allowed to go her own way, the door would be open for a return of the Mede. Of course, Lacedaemon could have resorted to the sea and mounted an attempt to take up the hegemony herself, but Pleistoanax and Cleandridas may not have been prepared to contemplate that possibility. Like Hetoemaridas two decades before, they may have been of the view that Sparta was constitutionally ill-suited to such an enterprise and that its attempt would be apt to subvert the regime and ultimately destroy the Lacedaemonian way of life.

Of course, the two men may well have been offered a sweetener, and it is perfectly possible that they accepted what was on offer. The Lacedaemonians were notoriously vulnerable to pecuniary temptation. It is, nonetheless, hard to believe that personal profit was the sole or even the chief motive of Pleistoanax and his advisor; and, although their compatriots were for understandable reasons enraged at their failure to seize for their fatherland the opportunity afforded them by the situation, they nonetheless agreed in the aftermath, after they had had sufficient time for rumination, to accept the terms on offer from Callias, Chares, Andocides, and their fellow diplomats—terms which, in rough outline, Pericles must have offered Pleistoanax and Cleandridas.[50]

The citizens of Lacedaemon were not stupid. They were, in fact, exceptionally canny; and, though they may have been more apt to give way to anger than men less spirited, they nonetheless tended toward political sobriety. Long before, in the middle of the sixth century, Chilon the ephor had crafted for them a grand strategy grounded in an appreciation for what they possessed and a prudent acknowledgment of the grave dangers inherent in seeking more. *Mēdèn ágan*—"nothing too much"—was the principle he had taught them, and they had taken it to heart. Henceforth, moderation [*sophrosúnē*] was the virtue that they trumpeted as peculiarly their own; and, although they may rarely have achieved genuine *sophrosúnē* as individuals, collectively, as Thucydides points out, they managed the feat, almost unheard of in Greece, of combining that quality with general prosperity.[51]

In their time of troubles—the two decades following the earthquake of 465/4 and the helot revolt that it inspired, and the fifteen years that had passed since Ephialtes effected the diplomatic revolution that had prepared the way for their war with Athens—the citizens of Lacedaemon had exercised remarkable patience. As we have already had occasion to observe, they had defended their stronghold deep in the Peloponnesus, they had reasserted their hegemony in south-central and southwest Arcadia, they had repeatedly defeated the Tegeans, they had defended the Mantineians, and step by careful step they had recovered control in Messenia while containing and ultimately taming the Argives and then drawing Tegea back into their alliance. Finally, at a moment when the Athenians, supposing themselves triumphant, jubilantly lorded it over most of Hellas, the Spartans seized an opportunity that with their encouragement presented itself; and they pounced, turning everything suddenly upside-down and confronting their opponents unexpectedly with the likelihood that they would be dealt a crippling strategic defeat. In the process—with the help of their allies in the Peloponnesus, in Boeotia, and beyond—the Lacedaemonians forced the Athenians to abandon Megara and her ports, Achaea and Troezen in the Peloponnesus, and Boeotia, Locris, and Phocis in central Greece. Despite everything that they had suffered as a consequence of the great earthquake and the helot revolt and despite the prospect that they might be stripped of their allies, deprived of Messenia, and forced to knuckle under, the Spartans had emerged victorious. They had met the Athenian challenge—as, a few decades previously, they had also met the Persian challenge—and once again, with bravery, cunning, and grace, they had driven off the challenger.

Epilogue
A Fragile Truce

Athens was necessary to Sparta, in the exercise of her virtue, as steel is to flint
in the production of fire; and if the cities of Greece had been united under one
head, we should never have heard of Epaminondas or Thrasybulus, of Lycurgus
or Solon.

ADAM FERGUSON

C ALLIAS son of Hipponicus was not just the wealthiest man in Athens.
He was also among the most canny. As a diplomat, he demonstrated
consummate skill. The arrangement that he negotiated initially with
the Persian monarch Xerxes and then with his son Artaxerxes was well crafted.
As we have had occasion to note, in leaving the Aegean and much of the coastline of Anatolia to the Athenians and their allies, and in relegating the interior
of Anatolia and the eastern Mediterranean to the Persians and their subjects,
the arrangement reflected a balance of power between the two rivals that had
proved enduring. On three separate occasions when the Great King had issued
a challenge—at Salamis, at Eurymedon, and Cypriot Salamis—the Hellenes
had demonstrated their decisive superiority at sea; and, along the way, they
had discovered in a highly painful manner that they did not have the resources
with which to wrest Egypt, much less Asia Minor and the Levant, from Achaemenid control.

The agreement also met the genuine security needs of the two parties.
Under its terms, neither had reason greatly to fear the other. In addition, it
fulfilled part of the purpose for which the Delian League had been founded.
It guaranteed the Greeks of Anatolia and their neighbors on the islands of the
Aegean freedom from the barbarian yoke. Of course, in the aftermath, there
were episodes of skirmishing in Anatolia; and, on occasion, the Athenians
provided aid and comfort to rebellious satraps and the like while the satraps

loyal to the Great King were similarly helpful to dissident Greeks resentful of Athens' hegemony. In modest ways, the longtime antagonists probed for weakness and maneuvered for advantage. But, in the end, whenever out-and-out war presented itself as a genuine option, caution prevailed; and, for more than thirty-five years, the terms of the pact were honored in the breach. As diplomatic endeavors go, the peace negotiated by Callias was a signal accomplishment.

The arrangement that Callias and his colleagues worked out with the Spartans late in the fall of 446 or the winter of 446/5 was no less well crafted. It, too, reflected an enduring balance of power. It acknowledged the facts and left the Spartans and their allies supreme on land and the Athenians supreme at sea. In the aftermath, neither was in a position to strike terror into the other. The Peloponnesus was once again a bastion of defense for Lacedaemon, and Athens retained her Long Walls, her maritime allies, and her great fleet. Furthermore, neither Sparta nor Athens nursed a grievance. Apart from Aegina and Naupactus and perhaps Molycreium to the north of the Corinthian Gulf and Chalcis to the west on the north shore of the Gulf of Patras, Athens relinquished everything that she had seized. None of her remaining acquisitions lay within Lacedaemon's natural sphere of influence; and, to head off possible objections on the part of the Spartans, she may even have reiterated that she would honor the autonomy of their sometime allies the Aeginetans.

The terms of the agreement were in other ways sensible as well. There was not to be another Megara, for the treaty listed the allies of each of the two parties and specified that neither city could accept into her confederacy a community allied with the other. It also allowed a measure of flexibility. Both parties were free to admit into their alliances communities hitherto neutral; and, although Athens was barred from making a formal alliance with Argos, she was free to have close and friendly relations with that city. There was even provision for quarrels unforeseen in a clause stipulating that disputes be settled by arbitration.

The handiwork of the diplomats of Lacedaemon and Athens differed, however, from the accord worked out by Athens with Persia in two important particulars. It was not, as the latter appears to have been, an informal arrangement. It was a formal treaty, which both parties solemnly swore to honor; and its duration was not indefinite. Like the agreements forged in the past between those perennial rivals Sparta and Argos, it had a specified term. At the end of thirty years, it would fall into abeyance. In short, it was not a putatively perpetual pact like the agreement founding Athens' Delian League. There was no pledge of friendship, and the accord was not, strictly speaking, a treaty of peace. It was a truce between once and future foes, albeit an extended truce; and it expressly advertised itself as that and as nothing more.[1]

The instrument recording the agreement reached by the Lacedaemonians and the Athenians reflected a brute fact. Both parties were exhausted. Although nearly twenty years had passed, the Lacedaemonians had not fully recovered from the demographic damage inflicted on them at the time of the earthquake and in its aftermath; and the Athenians still felt the cumulative impact of the dramatic losses they had suffered in Egypt as well as at Drabeskos in Thrace, at Tanagra, and Coronea. Those who forged the deal were persuaded that each of the two parties needed a generation in which to recover. No one even imagined that the two would henceforth be on amicable terms and that the deadly rivalry between them had come to an end.

This may seem strange to us. When we forge a peace agreement, it is nearly always meant to last. Or, at least, that is the pretense. We piously presume that peace is the norm and war, an almost unthinkable, highly regrettable exception. Under the influence of Immanuel Kant, many in our number even dream that peace can be made perpetual.[2] We fight wars to end all wars and to make the world safe for democracy. These are the lies we tell ourselves.

The ancient Greeks did not anticipate our optimism in this particular. They told themselves and others no such tales. For moral guidance, they looked not to a god who had suffered crucifixion and died on their behalf; who had urged them to love their neighbors, turn the other cheek, and themselves take up the cross; and who came to be called the Prince of Peace. They looked, instead, to Homer, and from this poet—whom Plato rightly termed "the education of Hellas"—they learned to take war for granted, to thrill to prowess in battle, and to admire canniness in council. In consequence, ordinary Hellenes would have nodded their heads in approval of the opinion attributed by Plato to the lawgiver of Crete: "What most men call peace, he held to be only a name. In truth, for everyone, there exists by nature at all times an undeclared war among cities." And they were less inclined to mourn this fact than to embrace it with excitement and without regret.[3]

In the event, as we shall see in this volume's successor, the cessation of hostilities negotiated by Callias and his colleagues was short-lived. It did not last even half of the thirty years stipulated. This should come as no surprise.

For, however well-crafted the treaty may have been, one insuperable obstacle stood in the way of its success, distinguishing it sharply from the agreements Callias had reached with the Mede. Xerxes and Artaxerxes undoubtedly regretted Persia's inability to project power overseas, but repeated, decisive defeats had persuaded each in turn to eschew ambition, at least for the time being, and to put on hold the dictates of Ahura Mazda; and the Athenians, by this time a people of the sea, had grown wary of troop commitments ashore in Africa and Asia. By way of contrast, however, within Hellas, Athens remained an unsatisfied—some would say, an insatiable—power.

Athens might sidestep Peloponnesian entanglements for a time, but she was still governed by the spirit of ambition, innovation, and audacity that had made so great an impression on the Corinthians. If the Egyptian debacle had left the Athenians chastened, their victory on both land and sea at Cypriot Salamis had in considerable measure restored their confidence; and, thanks to the restraint foolishly exercised by young Pleistoanax, it was easy for them to suppose their defeat at the hands of the Peloponnesians a mere "theft of war." In the late summer of 446, they had been outwitted and outmaneuvered. This was undeniable. The Spartans had snatched from them an impressive victory, but they had not overpowered, defeated, and humiliated them on the field of battle. They had not demonstrated their superiority and forced the Athenians to grovel, beg, and acknowledge the fact.[4]

After ratifying the Thirty Years' Peace, the Athenians may not have been spoiling for a fight. But their morale was intact. No less than in the past, they were "keen in forming plans and quick to accomplish in deed what they" had "contrived in thought." As events would confirm, they were still "daring beyond their strength" and "risk-takers against all judgment." For, "in the midst of terrors," as always, they remained "of good hope"; and it was still appropriate to say of them what the Corinthians reportedly would soon say to the Lacedaemonians regarding the threat they posed: "They are by nature capable neither of being at rest nor of allowing other human beings to be so."[5]

Thucydides' narrative is structurally defective in one particular. If he is correct in asserting that it was the growth in power achieved by Athens in the course of the Pentekontaetia that forced Lacedaemon to initiate the war which terminated the Thirty Years' Peace—above all, if he is right in contending that it was inevitable from the outset that the war fought in the 450s and 440s be renewed—he erred when he treated the bloody struggles between the Athenians and the Peloponnesians prior to and subsequent to the ratification of that treaty of peace as distinct episodes. As Dionysius of Halicarnassus intimates, the logic of the Athenian historian's argument requires that we regard the interlude between the Peloponnesians' first two Attic wars as a respite and as nothing more.[6]

Abbreviations and Short Titles

In the notes, I have adopted the standard abbreviations for classical texts and inscriptions, for books of the Bible, and for modern journals and books provided in *The Oxford Classical Dictionary*, 4th edition revised, ed. Simon Hornblower, Antony Spawforth, and Esther Eidinow (Oxford, UK: Oxford University Press, 2012); *The Chicago Manual of Style*, 15th edition (Chicago: University of Chicago Press, 2003), 15.50–53; and the bibliographical annual *L'Année Philologique*. Where possible, the ancient texts are cited by the divisions and subdivisions employed by the author or introduced by subsequent editors (that is, by book, part, chapter, section number, paragraph, act, scene, line, Stephanus page, or by page and line number). Cross-references to other parts of this volume refer to book, and chapter and specify whether the material referenced can be found above or below.

Unless otherwise indicated, all of the translations are my own. I transliterate the Greek, using undotted i's where no accent is required, adding macrons, accents, circumflexes, and so on. When others—in titles or statements quoted—transliterate in a different manner, I leave their transliterations as they had them.

For other works frequently cited, the following abbreviations and short titles have been employed:

ASI	*Ancient Society and Institutions: Studies Presented to Victor Ehrenberg on his 75th Birthday*, ed. Ernst Badian (Oxford: Basil Blackwell, 1966).
Badian, *FPP*	Ernst Badian, *From Plataea to Potidaea: Studies in the History and Historiography of the Pentecontaetia* (Baltimore: Johns Hopkins University Press, 1993).
Badian, *Outbreak*	Ernst Badian, "Thucydides and the Outbreak of the Peloponnesian War: A Historian's Brief," in *Conflict, Antithesis and the*

	Ancient Historian, ed. June W. Allison (Columbus: Ohio State University Press, 1990), 46–91.
Briant, *CA*	Pierre Briant, *From Cyrus to Alexander: A History of the Persian Empire,* tr. Peter T. Daniels (Winona Lake, IN: Eisenbrauns, 2002).
Cawkwell, *CC*	George Cawkwell, *Cyrene to Chaeronea: Selected Essays on Ancient Greek History* (Oxford: Oxford University Press, 2011).
DAA	*Defining Ancient Arkadia,* ed. Thomas Heine Nielsen and James Roy (Copenhagen: Det Kongelige Danske Videnskabernes Selskab, 1999).
DS	*Diodorus Siculus, Books 11–12.37.1: Greek History, 480–431 B.C.—The Alternate Version,* trans. Peter Green (Austin: University of Texas Press, 2006).
Fornara/Samons, *ACP*	Charles W. Fornara and Loren J. Samons II, *Athens from Cleisthenes to Pericles* (Berkeley: University of California Press, 1991).
Frost, *PT*	Frank J. Frost, *Plutarch's Themistocles: A Historical Commentary* (Princeton, NJ: Princeton University Press, 1980).
Holladay, *AFC*	A. James Holladay, *Athens in the Fifth Century and Other Studies in Greek History: The Collected Papers of A. James Holladay,* ed. Anthony J. Podlecki (Chicago: Ares, 2002).
Kagan, *Outbreak*	Donald Kagan, *The Outbreak of the Peloponnesian War* (Ithaca, NY: Cornell University Press, 1969).
Lendon, *SoW*	Jon E. Lendon, *Song of Wrath: The Peloponnesian War Begins* (New York: Basic Books, 2010).
Lewis, *OFPW*	David M. Lewis, "The Origins of the First Peloponnesian War," in *Classical Contributions: Studies in Honour of Malcolm Francis McGregor,* ed. Gordon Spencer Shrimpton and David Joseph McCargar (Locust Valley, NY: J. J. Augustin, 1981), 71–78.
Lewis, *SP*	David M. Lewis, *Sparta and Persia* (Leiden: Brill, 1977).
Lewis, *SPGNEH*	David M. Lewis, *Selected Papers in Greek and Near Eastern History,* ed. Peter J. Rhodes (Cambridge: Cambridge University Press, 1997).
Marr, *Commentary*	John L. Marr, "Commentary," in Plutarch, *Life of Themistocles,* ed. and trans. John L. Marr (Warminster, UK: Aris & Phillips, 1998).
Morton, *RPEAGS*	Jamie Morton, *The Role of the Physical Environment in Ancient Greek Seafaring* (Leiden: Brill, 2001).

O&R	*Greek Historical Inscriptions, 478–404 BC,* ed. Robin Osborne and Peter J. Rhodes (Oxford: Oxford University Press, 2017).
Podlecki, *PHC*	Anthony Podlecki, *Perikles and His Circle* (London: Routledge, 1998).
Rahe, *PC*	Paul A. Rahe, *The Grand Strategy of Classical Sparta: The Persian Challenge* (New Haven, CT: Yale University Press, 2015).
Rahe, *SR*	Paul A. Rahe, *The Spartan Regime: Its Character, Its Origins* (New Haven, CT: Yale University Press, 2016).
Rahe, *SSAW*	Paul A. Rahe, *Sparta's Second Attic War: The Grand Strategy of Classical Sparta, 446–418 BC* (New Haven, CT: Yale University Press, forthcoming).
Raubitschek, *SH*	Antony E. Raubitschek, *The School of Hellas: Essays on Greek History, Archaeology, and Literature,* ed. Dirk Obbink and Paul A. Vander Waerdt (New York: Oxford University Press, 1991).
SAGT	W. Kendrick Pritchett, *Studies in Ancient Greek Topography* (Berkeley: University of California Press, 1965–89; Amsterdam: J. C. Gieben, 1991–92).
Ste. Croix, *OPW*	Geoffrey Ernest Maurice de Ste. Croix, *The Origins of the Peloponnesian War* (Ithaca: Cornell University Press, 1972).
Salmon, *WC*	John B. Salmon, *Wealthy Corinth: A History of the City to 338 B.C.* (Oxford: Clarendon Press, 1984).
Samons, *EO*	Loren J. Samons II, *Empire of the Owl: Athenian Imperial Finance* (Stuttgart: Franz Steiner Verlag, 2000).
Samons, *PCH*	Loren J. Samons II, *Pericles and the Conquest of History: A Political Biography* (New York: Cambridge University Press, 2016).
Stadter, *CPP*	Philip A. Stadter, *A Commentary on Plutarch's Pericles* (Chapel Hill: University of North Carolina Press, 1989).
Wade-Gery, *EGH*	Henry Theodore Wade-Gery, *Essays in Greek History* (Oxford: Basil Blackwell, 1958).

Notes

Introduction. From One War to the Next

1. Winston S. Churchill, *Marlborough: His Life and Times* (London: Harrap, 1947), II 381.

2. A part of the Green Pamphlet was eventually published as an appendix to the 1988 reprint of Julian Stafford Corbett, *Some Principles of Maritime Strategy* (London: Longmans Green, 1911), where he had elaborated on the idea of grand strategy without using the term: see Julian Stafford Corbett, *Some Principles of Grand Strategy*, ed. Eric J. Grove (Annapolis, MD: Naval Institute Press, 1988), 305–25. For the history of the term, see Lukas Milevski, *The Evolution of Modern Grand Strategic Thought* (Oxford: Oxford University Press, 2016).

3. See J. F. C. Fuller, *The Reformation of War* (London: Hutchinson, 1923), 211–28 (esp. 218–21). For a recent discussion of the pertinent concept's application to ancient history, see Kimberly Kagan, "Redefining Roman Grand Strategy," *Journal of Military History* 70:2 (April 2006): 333–62 (esp. 348–50).

4. See Edward N. Luttwak, *The Grand Strategy of the Roman Empire: From the First Century A.D. to the Third* (Baltimore: Johns Hopkins University Press, 1976), and *The Grand Strategy of the Byzantine Empire* (Cambridge, MA: Harvard University Press, 2009), as well as A. Wess Mitchell, *The Grand Strategy of the Hapsburg Empire* (Princeton, NJ: Princeton University Press, 2018).

Part I. Yokefellows

Epigraph: Pl. *Leg.* 3.692e–693a.

1. For the details, see Rahe, *PC*, Epilogue. On the spoils, see Margaret C. Miller, *Athens and Persia in the Fifth Century BC: A Study in Cultural Receptivity* (Cambridge: Cambridge University Press, 1997), 29–38.

2. Pausanias' pledge to the Plataeans: Thuc. 2.71.2–4.

3. Oath of Hellenic League vs. Medizers: Hdt. 7.132.2, Diod. 11.3.1–5, as interpreted in *A Commentary on Herodotus*, ed. Walter Wyberg How and Joseph Wells (Oxford: Clarendon Press, 1912), II 177–78. On the so-called Oath of Plataea, the authenticity of which is disputed, see Rahe, *PC*, Chapter 8.

4. Earth and water: Hdt. 7.132.1. Presence of Thebans at Thermopylae: 7.202, 205.2–3, 233. Theban participants drawn from minority hostile to the Mede: Diod. 11.4.7. Oath of the Amphictyonic League: Aeschin. 2.115 with François Lefèvre, *L'Amphictionie pyléo-delphique: Histoire et institutions* (Athens: École française d'Athènes, 1998), passim (esp. 147–51). Note also Aeschin. 3.108–12.

5. Actual handling of Thebes in 479: Hdt. 9.86–88.

6. Juxtaposition of Spartan and Persian meal: Hdt. 9.82.

7. Marriage of Leonidas and Gorgo: Hdt. 7.239.4. Pleistarchus son of Leonidas too young to command at Plataea: 9.10.2.

8. Charismatic Heraclid kingship: Rahe, *SR*, Chapters 2–3. Leotychidas at Mycale: Rahe, *PC*, Chapter 8.

9. For further details and a full citation of the primary sources and the secondary literature, see Rahe, *SR*, Chapter 1 and Appendix 1.

10. Aristotle on Laconian helots: *Pol.* 1269a36–39. Note Critias ap Lib. *Or.* 25.63.

11. Helot revolt at time of Marathon: Rahe, *PC*, Chapter 4. Two thousand helots liberated and made to disappear: Thuc. 4.80.3–4 with Andrewes, *HCT*, V 366. Various dates suggested: Charles D. Hamilton, "Social Tensions in Classical Sparta," *Ktema* 12 (1987): 31–41 (esp. 34–36); Borimir Jordan, "The Ceremony of the Helots in Thucydides IV, 80," *AC* 59 (1990): 37–69 (esp. 55–58); and Hornblower, *CT*, II 265–67. The actual creation of the *neodamôdeis* along the very lines pretended on the occasion described in Thuc. 4.80.3–4, an event which appears to have followed the Athenian construction of the fort at Coryphasium in Messenia, and the institution of the *Brasídeioi* on similar lines in 424 seem to me to rule out situating at that time the massacre described in this passage: consider the timing of Thuc. 4.80.1–2, 5, and that indicated at 5.34.1, in light of the events described in Rahe, *SSAW*, Chapter 5; Part II, preface; and Chapters 6 and 7.

12. For further details and a full citation of the primary sources and the secondary literature, see Rahe, *SR*, Chapter 1.

13. For the details and a full citation of the primary sources and the pertinent secondary literature, see Rahe, *SR*, Chapters 3 and 4.

14. See Rahe, *SR,* passim.

15. See Rahe, *PC*, Chapters 3 through 6.

16. Cleomenes' policy and his relations with Leotychidas: Rahe, *PC*, Part I.

17. Cleomenes and Athens: see Rahe, *PC*, Chapter 2.

18. Evidence Athens the mother city of Ionia: Carl Roebuck, "Tribal Organization in Ionia," *TAPhA* 92 (1961): 495–507. Weight given ethnicity: John Alty, "Dorians and Ionians," *JHS* 102 (1982): 1–14, and Naoíse Mac Sweeney, *Foundation Myths and Politics in Ancient Ionia* (Cambridge: Cambridge University Press, 2013). That the foundation myths simplified what was a messy process is no surprise: Irene S. Lemos, "The Migrations to the West Coast of Asia Minor: Tradition and Archaeology," in *Frühes Ionien: Eine Bestandsaufnahme,* ed. Justus Cobet, Volkmar von Graeve, Wolf-Dietrich Niemeier, and Konrad Zimmerman (Mainz am Rhein: Von Zabern, 2007), 713–27, and Naoíse Mac Sweeney, "Separating Fact from Fiction in the Ionian Migration," *Hesperia* 86:3 (July–September 2017): 379–421.

19. Imported grain: for a citation of the evidence and the pertinent secondary literature, see Rahe, *PC*, Chapter 3, note 3.

20. Leotychidas and the other Peloponnesian leaders notwithstanding, islanders admitted to Hellenic League: Hdt. 9.106.2–4, Diod. 11.37.1–3. Bridges gone, Peloponnesians sail home: Hdt. 9.114.1–2; Diod. 11.37.4. Xanthippus and Athenians besiege and seize Sestos: Hdt. 9.114.2–121.1, Thuc. 1.89.1–2, Diod. 11.37.5. Dinner table of the Peiraeus: Arist. *Rh.* 1411a14. See also Schol. Ar. *Eq.* 262. On the Hellenic League itself, I do not think the positions argued by Dietmar Kienast, "Der Hellenenbund von 481 v. Chr.," *Chiron* 33 (2003): 43–77, and David Yates, "The Tradition of the Hellenic League against Xerxes," *Historia* 64:1 (2015): 1–25, are mutually exclusive. The considerable authority accorded the hegemon is compatible with a recognition that the members of the league collectively wield the ultimate authority.

Chapter 1. The Postwar Settlement

Epigraph: Thuc. 1.77.6.

1. Note Rahe, *PC,* Chapters 7 and 8, and see, now, Robert Garland, *Athens Burning: The Persian Invasion of Greece and the Evacuation of Attica* (Baltimore: Johns Hopkins University Press, 2017).

2. Aeginetan-Athenian hostilities: Rahe, *PC*, Chapters 4 and 5. Residue of resentment, Rahe, *PC*, Chapter 7.

3. Fetters for Greece: Polyb. 18.11.4–5. Plutarch on the Acrocorinth: *Arat.* 16.5. Corinth as naval and commercial center collecting tolls: Thuc. 1.13.2–5, Strabo 8.6.20–25. Note Catherine Morgan, "Corinth, the Corinthian Gulf, and Western Greece during the Eighth Century BC," *ABSA* 83 (1988): 313–38. Colonizer, military power: Salmon, *WC*, 81–185, and *IACP* no. 227. There is also material of value in Donald W. Engels, *Roman Corinth: An Alternative Model for the Ancient City* (Chicago: University of Chicago Press, 1990). Respect for artisans: Hdt. 2.167. *Díolkos:* Georges Raepsaet, "Le Diolkos de l'Isthme à Corinthe: Son Tracé, son fonctionnement, avec une annexe, Considérations techniques et mécaniques," *BCH* 117:1 (1993): 233–61, and Walter Werner, "The Largest Ship Trackway in Ancient Times: The Diolkos of the Isthmus of Corinth, Greece, and Early Attempts to Build a Canal," trans. Timm Weski *IJNA* 26:2 (1997): 98–119. Attempt to shape security environment: Rahe, *PC*, Chapter 1. That Pallene was thought to lie in Thrace (and not in territory belonging to Macedonia) and that when the ancients spoke of the Chalcidice they had in mind only Sithonia and the area directly north of it is clear: Pernille Flensted-Jensen, "The Chalkidic Peninsula and Its Regions," in *Further Studies in the Ancient Greek Polis,* ed. Pernille Flensted-Jensen (Stuttgart: Franz Steiner Verlag, 2000), 121–31.

4. Corinth long favorable to Athens: after reading Hdt. 6.108.2–5, see 5.74.1–75.1, 90–93, 6.89; Thuc. 1.41.1–2. Spartans hostile to tyranny: Thuc. 1.18.1, Arist. *Pol.* 1312b7–8. Overthrow tyrants, sponsor oligarchies: Thuc. 1.19, 76.1; Arist. *Pol.* 1307b23–24.

5. For the stories told by Herodotus, some of them undeniably false, see Rahe, *PC*, Chapters 7 and 8.

6. Late origins of Corinthian-Athenian antagonism: Thuc. 1.103.4.

7. Themistocles as arbitrator: Theophrastus ap. *POxy.* 1012, F9.23–24, with Luigi Piccirilli, "Temistocle evergetes dei Corciresi," *ASNP* 3 (1973): 317–55, and *Gli Arbitrati interstatali greci* (Pisa: Marlin, 1973), 61–66, and Plut. *Them.* 24.1. Cf. Marr, *Commentary,* 138–39, who joins Piccirilli in crediting Herodotus' claims concerning Adeimantus and therefore thinks Theophrastus' report fictitious, with Thuc. 1.136.1, which confirms that he really was considered a "benefactor" of the Corcyraeans, and see Frost, *PT,* 200–203. For the timing, however, see Salmon, *WC,* 258 (with n. 5).

8. Opposition to Athens' rebuilding her city walls: Thuc. 1.90.1–2, Diod. 11.39.1–3, Nep. *Them.* 6.2–4, Plut. *Them.* 19.1–2. As these passages suggest, prior to the Persian Wars, it was the norm for a *pólis* to enjoy the protection of walls: Rune Frederiksen, *Greek City Walls of the Archaic Period, 900–480 BC* (Oxford: Oxford University Press, 2011). Evidence strongly suggesting (but not proving) Corinthian pressure at this time: Thuc. 1.69.1. Aeginetan role: Plut. *Them.* 19.2. As Marr, *Commentary,* 120, points out, the emendation suggested long ago by Schaefer is attractive: the otherwise unknown Polyarchus mentioned in Plutarch's text could well be the Aeginetan Polycritus mentioned at Hdt. 8.92. Note also 6.49–50, 65.1, 73, 85–86.

9. See Rahe, *PC*, Chapter 8.

10. Themistocles the Athenian Odysseus: Plut. *Mor.* 869f. His diplomatic stratagem at Lacedaemon: Thuc. 1.90.2–4, 93.2; Diod. 11.39.4–40.1; Nep. *Them.* 6.2–5; Plut. *Them.* 19.1–2 with Richard E. Wycherley, *The Stones of Athens* (Princeton, NJ: Princeton University Press, 1978), 7–25.

11. Themistocles at Sparta: Thuc. 1.90.5–91.7, Diod. 11.40.2–4, Nep. *Them.* 7. Plutarch's contention (*Them.* 19.1–3) that he bribed the ephors in charge may well be right. Themistocles was undoubtedly capable of such a thing, and the Spartans were notoriously susceptible. Cf. Marr, *Commentary,* 118–19, who thinks this implausible, with Frost, *PT,* 173–74, who points to the story's early provenance: see Andoc. 3.38 with Theopompus of Chios *FGrH* 115 F85. Role of Aristeides: Arist *Ath. Pol.* 23.3–4 with Rhodes, *CAAP,* 292–95. Abronichus and Themistocles: Hdt. 8.21. For the friendship between the latter two, see [Them.] *Ep. Gr.* 4.743–44, 10.751 (Hercher) = [Them.] *Ep.* 4.10, 21–26, 10.1–3 (Doenges), which should be read with an eye to Chapter 2, note 39 and its context, below.

12. Spartans in secret vexed: Thuc. 1.92, Plut. *Them.* 19.3. Cf. Fornara/Samons, *ACP,* 118–21, who dismiss the entire episode.

13. Themistocles' archonship and date: Thuc. 1.93.3 and Dion. Hal. *Ant. Rom.* 6.34.1 with T. J. Cadoux, "The Athenian Archons from Kreon to Hypsichides," *JHS* 68 (1948): 70–123 (at 116, with note 252), and David M. Lewis, "Themistocles' Archonship," *Historia* 22:4 (4th Quarter 1973): 757–58. The Peiraeus and fleet: Thuc. 1.93, 2.13.6–7 with Ar. *Eq.* 813–16, Diod. 11.41–43, Nep. *Them.* 6.1, Plut. *Them.* 19.3–5. See Johannes S. Boersma, *Athenian Building Policy from 561/0 to 405/4 B.C.* (Groningen: Wolters-Noordhof, 1970), 46–50; Robert Garland, *The Piraeus: From the Fifth to the First Century B.C.* (Ithaca, NY: Cornell University Press, 1987), 14–22, 163–65; and the judicious remarks of Frost, *PT,* 175–77, and Marr, *Commentary,* 120–22.

14. Spartan *philotimía:* Arist. *Pol.* 1271a14, Plut. *Ages.* 5.5. *Agōgē:* Rahe, *SR,* Chapter 1. Exaggerated respect for the old: Hdt. 2.80.1; Xen. *Mem.* 3.5.15; Plut. *Lyc.* 15.2–3, 20.15, *Mor.* 227f, 232f, 235c–f, 237d; Just. *Epit.* 3.3.9 with Ephraim David, *Old Age in Sparta* (Amsterdam: Adolf M. Hakkert, 1991). Young barred from public office: Xen. *Lac. Pol.* 4.7 with 2.2. Denied commands: Thuc. 4.132.3. Prohibited from traveling abroad: Isoc. 11.18, Pl. *Prt.* 342b–d. The "common" assembly: Diod. 11.50. Role of *gerousía* within the Spartan *politeía:* Rahe, *SR,* Chapter 2, to which I would now add the telling discussion in Borimir Jordan, "The Ceremony of the Helots in Thucydides IV, 80," *AC* 59 (1990): 37–69 (at 57–69).

15. Aristotle on the propensities of the young and the old: *Rh.* 1389a2–1390a22. Spartans cautious in battle: Hdt. 9.46–48 and Thuc. 5.63–65. Spartans more concerned with minimizing their own losses than with making their victory complete: cf. Thuc. 1.70.2–5 with 5.73.4, and see Paus. 4.8.11; Plut. *Lyc.* 22.9–10, *Mor.* 228f. For similar reasons, the Lacedaemonians were prohibited from dispersing to strip the bodies of the enemy dead: Plut. *Mor.* 228f–229a and Ael. *VH* 6.6. Propensity to confuse the expedient with the honorable: cf. the charge made at Thuc. 5.105.3–4 with the pattern of behavior evidenced at 3.52–68. Slow to go to war: 1.23.6, 68–71, 88, 118.2, 5.107, 109.

16. Themistocles on likely mode of Mede return: Thuc. 1.93.7.

17. Athenian characterization of the Spartans: Thuc. 5.105.4. For a fully articulated argument diametrically opposed to the one unfolded in this volume and its successor, cf. the work of Jon E. Lendon—"Spartan Honor," in *Polis and Polemos: Essays on Politics, War, and History in Ancient Greece,* ed. Charles D. Hamilton and Peter Krentz (Claremont, CA: Regina Books, 1997), 105–26; "Athens and Sparta and the Coming of the Peloponnesian War," in *The Cambridge Companion to the Age of Pericles,* ed. Loren J. Samons (New York: Cambridge University Press, 2007), 258–81; and *SoW,* passim—who contends that, collectively, the Spartans were far more like Achilles than Nestor. For an appreciative and, I think, judicious critique of Lendon's argument, see Karl Walling, "Thucydides on Policy, Strategy, and War Termination," *Naval War College Review* 66:4 (Autumn 2013): 47–85 (at 83–84, n. 25).

18. Pausanias' fleet: Thuc. 1.94.1; Diod. 11.44.1–2; Plut. *Arist.* 23.1, *Cim.* 6.1.

19. Cypriot campaign and aims: Thuc. 1.94.1–2; Diod. 11.44.1–2; Nep. *Paus.* 2.1, *Arist.* 2.2. Soli, Salamis, and Paphos: Aesch. *Pers.* 891–92. See Meiggs, *AE,* 38–39, 482. There is reason to suppose that on the island Panhellenic sentiment was stronger than Franz Georg Maier, "Factoids in Ancient History: The Case of Fifth-Century Cyprus," *JHS* 105 (1985): 32–39, is inclined to acknowledge.

20. Strategic significance of Cyprus: Diod. 14.98.3.

21. Strategic importance of Byzantium and role played by current: Polyb. 4.38.2–44.11 (esp. 4.38.2–11, 44.1–11). Its capture: Thuc. 1.94.1–2, Nep. *Paus.* 2.2, Diod. 11.44.3 with Meiggs, *AE,* 39.

22. Pausanias' misconduct and the complaints it elicited: Hdt. 8.3.2; Thuc. 1.95.1–5 (with 75.2, 96.1); Diod. 11.44.3–6; Nep. *Paus.* 2.2–6; Plut. *Arist.* 23.1–5, *Cim.* 6.1–3; Aristodemus *FGrH* 104 F6.2–3, 8.1.

23. Gongylus medizes: Thuc. 1.128.4–7, Diod. 11.44.3, Nep. *Paus.* 2.2–4. Dascyleium: Takuji Abe, "Dascylium: An Overview of the Achaemenid Satrapal City," *Acta Academiae Antiquitatis Kiotoensis* 12 (2012): 1–17. Road system, pony express, and the need for formal sanction: Hdt. 5.52–54, 8.98; Xen. *Cyr.* 8.6.17–18 with David Graf, "The Persian Royal Road System," *Achaemenid History* 8 (1994): 167–89; Briant, *CA,* 364–87; and Pierre Briant, "From the Indus to the Mediterranean: The Administrative Organization and Logistics of the Great Roads of the Achaemenid Em-

pire," in *Highways, Byways, and Road Systems in the Pre-Modern World,* ed. Susan E. Alcock, John Bodel, and Richard J. A. Talbert (New York: John Wiley & Sons, 2012), 185–201. The precise route followed by the Sardis-Susa road through and beyond Anatolia is disputed: David H. French, "Pre- and Early-Roman Roads of Asia Minor: The Persian Royal Road," *Iran* 36: (1998): 15–43.

24. See, for example, Adolf Lippold, "Pausanias von Sparta und die Perser," *RhM* n.f. 108:4 (1965): 320–41.

25. Descendants of Gongylus in western Asia: Xen. *An.* 7.8.8, *Hell.* 3.1.6 with Giovanni Fogazza, "Sui Gongilidi di Eretria," *PP* 27:142–44 (January–June 1972): 129–30, and Lewis, *SP,* 54 (with n. 29).

26. Pausanias' conduct inspires charge of Medism: Thuc. 1.95.1–5, 128.3–131.1; Diod. 11.44.3–6; Nep. *Paus.* 2.2–6; Plut. *Cim.* 6.1–3; Aristodemus *FGrH* 104 F6.2–3. Adoption of Persian mores and manners: Thuc. 1.130.1–131.1; Diod. 11.44.5, 46.1–3 read in light of Hdt. 1.96–101. Supposed betrothal to daughter of Darius' cousin and admiral, the satrap Megabates: 5.32 with Rahe, *PC,* Chapter 6, n. 27, where I discuss the Greek and Persian evidence concerning Megabates' career.

27. Balance of powers at Lacedaemon: Rahe, *SR,* Chapter 2. Chance, for the most part, governs the selection of ephors, who tend to be "nobodies": Pl. *Leg.* 3.692a and Arist. *Pol.* 1270b29, 1272a27–34, 1272b33–37 with Peter A. Brunt, "Spartan Policy and Strategy in the Archidamian War," *Phoenix* 19:4 (Winter 1965): 255–80 (at 278–80), reprinted in Brunt, *Studies in Greek History and Thought* (Oxford: Clarendon Press, 1993), 84–111 (at 110–11), and Paul A. Rahe, "The Selection of Ephors at Sparta," *Historia* 29:4 (4th Quarter 1980): 385–401. For further discussion of this controversial question and for additional secondary literature, see Rahe, *SR,* Chapter 2, note 51 (in context). Monthly exchange of oaths: Xen. *Lac. Pol.* 15.7 with Rahe, *SR,* Chapter 2, note 46.

28. Ephors can arrest and indict kings on capital charges: Hdt. 6.82, Plut. *Agis* 18–19. Note Thuc. 1.131. Fate of fifth-century kings: Ste. Croix, *OPW,* 350–53, and Anton Powell, "Divination, Royalty and Insecurity in Classical Sparta," in *Sparta: The Body Politic,* ed. Anton Powell and Stephen Hodkinson (Swansea: Classical Press of Wales, 2010), 85–135.

29. Fifth-century Spartan kings not known to have been indicted on a capital charge: see Rahe, *SR,* Chapter 2, note 48.

30. Pausanias' recall, partial acquittal, and fine: Thuc. 1.95.3–5, Nep. *Paus.* 2.6, Aristodemus *FGrH* 104 F6.2–3. It is possible that the Persian hyparch in command at Byzantium surrendered quickly. If, however, there was a siege, it is likely to have lasted well into the winter or even into early spring when provisions will have begun to run out: William T. Loomis, "Pausanias, Byzantion and the Formation of the Delian League: A Chronological Note," *Historia* 39:4 (1990): 487–92.

31. Simonides authors the couplet: Paus. 3.8.2. Inscription altered: *ML* no. 27 with Thuc. 1.132.2–3, Nep. *Paus.* 1.3. Plataean complaint embraced at meeting of the Amphictyonic League: Dem. 59.96–98 with Plut. *Mor.* 873c–d. Regarding the date, cf. Charles W. Fornara, "Two Notes on Thucydides," *Philologus* 111:3 (January 1967): 291–95 (at 291–94), with Jeremy Trevett, "History in [Demosthenes] 59," *CQ* n.s. 40:2 (1990): 407–20 (at 409–11).

32. Pausanias' trireme rammed: Plut. *Arist.* 23.4–6. Dorcis' leadership rejected, no successor sent: Thuc. 1.95.6–7. Note Xen. *Hell.* 6.5.34.

33. Concern with prestige: Detlef Lotze, "Selbstbewusstsein und Machtpolitik: Bemerkungen zur machtpolitischen Interpretation spartanischen Verhaltens in den Jahren 479–477 v. Chr.," *Klio* 52 (1970): 255–75, and Antony Andrewes, "Spartan Imperialism?" in *Imperialism in the Ancient World,* ed. Peter D. A. Garnsey and C. R. Whittaker (Cambridge: Cambridge University Press, 1978), 91–102 (at 91–95).

34. Spartans fear corruption: Thuc. 1.95.7, Plut. *Arist.* 23.7.

35. Maritime hegemony willingly relinquished to Athens by Sparta: Thuc. 1.95.7 and Xen. *Hell.* 6.5.34. The Spartans are apt to have been of two minds, however: Arist. *Ath. Pol.* 23.4–5 with Rhodes, *CAAP,* 294–96. Note also Isoc. 4.72, 7.79–80, 12.67. Cf. Fornara/Samons, *ACP,* 121–22.

36. Athenian eagerness for maritime hegemony: Hdt. 7.161, 8.2–3; Plut. *Them.* 7.3–4.

37. Machinations of the Athenian commanders: Hdt. 8.3; Thuc. 1.95.1–2, 96.1; Arist. *Ath. Pol.* 23.4–5; Diod. 11.46.4–5; Nep. *Arist.* 2.2–3; Plut. *Arist.* 23.1–6, *Cim.* 6.1–3 with Rhodes, *CAAP,* 294–95. Note also Aristodemus *FGrH* 104 F7.

38. Foundation and putative aims of Delian League, pretext for levying of assessments, Aristeides' accomplishment: Thuc. 1.96, 3.10.3–4, 5.18.5, 6.76.3–4; Arist. *Ath. Pol.* 23.4–5; Diod. 11.44.6, 47; Nep. *Arist.* 2.3; Plut. *Arist.* 25.1–3; Aristodemus *FGrH* 104 F7 with Jakob A. O. Larsen, "The Constitution and Original Purpose of the Delian League," *HSCP* 51 (1940): 175–213; Nicholas G. L. Hammond, "The Origins and the Nature of the Athenian Alliance of 478/7 B.C.," *JHS* 87 (1967): 41–61; Meiggs, *AE*, 42–67, 459–64; Kurt Raaflaub, "Beute, Vergeltung, Freiheit? Zur Zielsetzung des Delisch-Attischen Seebunden," *Chiron* 9 (1979): 1–22; and Rhodes, *CAAP,* 294–96. Cf. Raphael Sealey, "The Origins of the Delian League," in *ASI,* 233–55, who overstates the significance of the quest for booty; and Noel D. Robertson, "The True Nature of the 'Delian League,' 478–461 BC," *AJAH* 5:1–2 (1980): 64–96, 110–33 (esp. 64–78), who unwittingly demonstrates that one must engage in special pleading on a very great scale if one is to make a case against the view advanced by Thucydides and Aristotle and supported by Herodotus that the islanders and the Ionians were, with rare exceptions, enthusiastic supporters of the new league and the continued war against the Mede. Aristeides' reputation already existent in the 480s: Plut. *Arist.* 7.5–8. Note Hdt. 8.79.1, 95. Artaphernes' earlier assessment: 6.42.2. In this connection, see Lucia Nixon and Simon Price, "The Size and Resources of Greek Cities," in *The Greek City from Homer to Alexander,* ed. Oswyn Murray and Simon Price (Oxford: Oxford University Press, 1990), 137–70; Lisa Kallet-Marx, *Money, Expense, and Naval Power in Thucydides' History 1–5.24* (Berkeley: University of California Press, 1993), 21–56; David Whitehead, "*HO NEOS DASMOS:* 'Tribute' in Classical Athens," *Hermes* 126:2 (1998): 173–88; and Samons, *EO,* 84–91.

39. Callaeschrus ap. [Them.] *Ep. Gr.* 4.743 (Hercher) = Them. *Ep.* 4.12 (Doenges), which should be read in light of Chapter 2, note 39 and its context, below.

40. Aristeides on Athens' likely transformation: Arist. *Ath. Pol.* 24 with Rhodes, *CAAP,* 296–309, who is less willing than I am to join Aristotle in crediting Aristeides with prescience. Transformation effected: Meiggs, *AE,* 255–72; Jack M. Balcer, "Imperial Magistrates in the Athenian Empire," *Historia* 25:3 (3rd Quarter 1976): 257–87; Moses I. Finley, "The Athenian Empire: A Balance Sheet," in *Imperialism in the Ancient World,* 103–26, reprinted in Finley, *Economy and Society in Ancient Greece,* ed. Brent D. Shaw and Richard P. Saller (London: Chatto & Windus, 1981), 41–61; and the evidence collected in Chapter 6, note 23, below.

41. Fleet collected from Byzantium: Ephorus *FGrH* 70 F191.6, Diod. 11.60.1–2.

42. Fort at Doriscus and garrison: Hdt. 7.59.1, 105–6; Livy 31.16.4. Capacity: Pliny *NH* 4.43. Fort at Eion: Hdt. 7.107. Both serve as depots: Hdt. 7.25.

43. Maskames at Doriscus: Hdt. 7.105–6.

44. Strategic significance of mines and timber near Mount Pangaeum well known: Hdt. 1.64.1, 5.23–24, 7.112; Thuc. 4.108.1; Xen. *Hell.* 5.2.17; Arist. *Ath. Pol.* 15.2. See Paul Perdrizet, "Skaptésylé," *Klio* 10 (1910): 1–27 (esp. 9–11); Russell Meiggs, *Trees and Timber in the Ancient Mediterranean World* (Oxford: Clarendon Press, 1982), 118–20, 126–28, 356–57; and Errietta M. A. Bissa, *Governmental Intervention in Foreign Trade in Archaic and Classical Greece* (Leiden: Brill, 2009), esp. 33–42 107–25.

45. Siege of Eion: Thuc. 1.98.1, Ephorus *FGrH* 70 F191.6, Aeschin. 3.183–85, Diod. 11.60.1–2, Plut. *Cim.* 7.1–8.2. Note Nepos' confused reference to Cimon's defeat of the Thracians: *Cim.* 2.2. Menon of Pharsalus' contribution: Dem. 13.23, 23.199. Exceptional quality and military prowess of Thessalian cavalry: Emma Aston and Joshua Kerr, "Battlefield and Racetrack: The Role of Horses in Thessalian Society," *Historia* 67:1 (2018): 2–35. Boges' dramatic end: Hdt. 7.107, Polyaen. *Strat.* 7.24. Cimon is also said to have diverted the river Strymon and to have used it to undermine the burnt brick walls at Eion: Paus. 8.8.7–9. Date of siege and capture: Schol. Aeschin. 2.31 with *ATL,* III 158–60. Cf. J. D. Smart, "Kimon's Capture of Eion," *JHS* 87 (1967): 136–38, who prefers the date under which Diodorus (11.60) lists the siege of Eion and all of Cimon's other ventures down to and including Eurymedon.

46. Eion captured, and agricultural settlement established nearby: Thuc. 1.98.1, Plut. *Cim.* 7.3. Character of Eion itself: Thuc. 4.102.3, 106.3–107.2; Diod. 12.73.3 with *IACP* no. 630

47. Seizure of Skyros (*IACP* no. 521), occasion and reasons for doing so: Thuc. 1.98.2; Ephorus *FGrH* 70 F191.6; Nep. *Cim.* 2.5; Paus. 1.17.6, 3.3.7; Plut. *Thes.* 35.1–36.1, *Cim.* 8.3–6; Schol.

Ael. Aristid. *Or.* 3.561 (Dindorf). Date of oracle: Plut. *Thes.* 36.1–2 with *ATL,* III 160. A dedicatory inscription found at Delphi may be related to the putative recovery of Theseus' remains: W. G. Forrest, *RBPh* 34 (1956): 541–42. Miltiades' seizure of Lemnos (*IACP,* 756–57): Hdt. 6.137–40. Skyros, Lemnos, and Imbros (*IACP* no. 483) as prized Athenian possessions: Andoc. 3.12; Xen. *Hell.* 4.8.15, 5.1.31. For the geopolitical logic dictating their acquisition that emerged when the trireme supplanted the pentekonter as the ship of the line, see John K. Davies, "Corridors, Cleruchies, Commodities, and Coins: The Pre-History of the Athenian Empire," in *Handels-und Finanzgebaren in der Ägäis im 5. Jh. v. Chr./Trade and Finance in the 5th Century BC Aegean World,* ed. Anja Slawisch (Istanbul: Deutsches Archäologisches Institut, 2013), 43–66. Note also Gerassimos G. Aperghis, "Athenian Mines, Coins, and Triremes," *Historia* 62:1 (2013): 1–24.

48. Focus on growth in Athenian power: Thuc. 1.23.5–6, 33.2–33.3, 88, 118.2–3 with P. K. Walker, "The Purpose and Method of 'The Pentekontaetia' in Thucydides, Book I," *CQ* n.s. 7:1/2 (January-April 1957): 27–38, and Philip A. Stadter, "The Form and Content of Thucydides' Pentecontaetia," *GRBS* 34:1 (Spring 1993): 35–72.

49. Precision Thucydides' stated aim: Thuc. 1.22. Brevity, omissions, chronological imprecision: Gomme, *HCT,* I 361–413. It is, I think, telling that those who accuse Thucydides of tendentiousness and special pleading tend to fall prey to both themselves: cf., for example, Robertson, "The True Nature of the 'Delian League,' 478–461 BC," 64–96, 110–33; Badian, *Outbreak,* reprinted in Badian, *FPP,* 125–62; Johan Henrik Schreiner, "Anti-Thukydidean Studies in the Pentekontaetia," *SO* 51 (1976): 19–63, "More Anti-Thukydidean Studies in the Pentekontaetia," *SO* 52 (1977): 19–38, and *Hellanikos, Thukydides and the Era of Kimon* (Aarhus: University of Aarhus Press, 1997); and Robert D. Luginbill, *Author of Illusions: Thucydides' Rewriting of the History of the Peloponnesian War* (Newcastle: Cambridge Scholars, 2011), 39–59, with W. Kendrick Pritchett, "Thucydides' Pentekontaetia," "Thucydides 1.61.3–5," and "Diodoros' Pentekontaetia," in Pritchett, *Thucydides' Pentekontaetia and Other Essays* (Leiden: Brill, 1995), 1–171, and "Historians of the Pentekontaetia," in Pritchett, *Greek Archives, Cults, and Topography* (Amsterdam: J. C. Gieben, 1996), 40–91, and see Chapter 3, note 15, below. For an extended discussion of what Thucydides had in mind when he spoke of the growth in Athenian power, see Kallet-Marx, *Money, Expense, and Naval Power in Thucydides' History 1–5.24,* 21–69; and for the logic underpinning his selection of the events to relate, see Tim Rood, *Thucydides: Narrative and Explanation* (Oxford: Oxford University Press, 1998), 225–48.

50. The proximity of Carystus (*IACP* no. 373) to the Doros channel between Euboea and Andros with its difficult currents no doubt enhanced its importance: Morton, *RPEAGS,* 90–91 (with n. 36).

51. Tenedos: *IACP* no. 793. Strategic importance: Christopher L. H. Barnes, "The Ferries of Tenedos," *Historia* 55:2 (2006): 167–77. Strength of current and winds in the Bosporus and Hellespont: Morton, *RPEAGS,* 42–45, 87–90. Having gone swimming in the Bosporus myself and having witnessed from the safety of a motorboat a friend's failed attempt to swim the Hellespont, I can testify to the strength of this current.

52. Athens at Carystus: Thuc. 1.98.3 with Hdt. 9.105 and Roger Brock, "The Tribute of Carystos," *EMC* 40 n.s. 15:3 (1996): 357–70. For the city's experience with the Persians and with Themistocles, see Hdt. 6.99, 8.66.2, 112.2, 121.1. For its strategic importance, note Hom. *Od.* 3.173–79, and see Xen. *Hell.* 3.4.4, 5.4.61; Plut. *Ages.* 6.1–6; Dem. 19.326; Arr. *Anab.* 2.1.2. See Malcolm B. Wallace, "Herodotos and Euboia," *Phoenix* 28:1 (Spring 1974): 22–44 (esp. 38–41).

53. The revolt of Naxos (*IACP* no. 507) and of other cities: Thuc. 1.98.4–99.3. Silver or empty ships: Plut. *Cim.* 11.

54. Herms: Aeschin. 3.183–85, Dem. 20.112, Plut. *Cim.* 7.4–8.2 with Robin Osborne, "The Erection and Mutilation of the Herms," *PCPhS* 211, n.s. 31 (January 1985): 47–73 (esp. 58–64), reprinted in Osborne, *Athens and Athenian Democracy* (Cambridge: Cambridge University Press, 2010), 341–67 (esp. 355–62).

55. Bones of Theseus: Paus. 1.17.6; Plut. *Thes.* 36.2–5, *Cim.* 8.5–7 with Anthony J. Podlecki, "Cimon, Skyros and 'Theseus' Bones,'" *JHS* 91 (1971): 141–43.

56. Aleuad Medizers: Hdt. 7.6, 130, 9.58. Leotychidas in Thessaly and his fate thereafter: 6.72,

Paus. 3.7.8–10, Plut. *Mor.* 859d with W. Robert Connor, "The Razing of the House in Greek Society," *TAPhA* 115 (1985): 79–102.

57. The date of 476/5 that Diodorus (11.48.2) provides for Leotychidas' death is, in all likelihood, that of his banishment. The historian's claim (11.48.2) that Leotychidas reigned for twenty-two years and his later report (12.35.4) that his grandson Archidamus did so for forty-two years are consistent with the evidence from other sources indicating that Leotychidas reigned from ca. 491 (Hdt. 6.65–72 with N. G. L. Hammond, "The Expedition of Datis and Artaphernes," in *CAH* IV² 491–517 [at 498–99, 502]) to 469 and that the latter succeeded him that year and died in 427/6. It, moreover, makes good sense to suppose that a punitive expedition of the sort that Leotychidas led against the Thessalians would have been mounted by the Hellenes relatively soon after the Persian Wars: see Joseph Johnston, "Chronological Note on the Expedition of Leotychidas," *Hermathena* 21:46 (1931): 106–11, who lays out the evidence in detail. Note also Connor, "The Razing of the House in Greek Society," 99–102: and David M. Lewis, "Chronological Notes," in *CAH* V² 499. Cf., however, Andre S. Schieber, "Leotychidas in Thessaly," *AC* 51 (1982): 5–14, who argues for a slightly earlier date (478/7), and Marta Sordi, "Atene e Sparta dalle guerre persiane al 462–1 a.C.," *Aevum* 50:1/2 (January–April 1976): 25–41, who argues for a considerably later date (469).

58. Spartan deliberations: Diod. 11.50 with Kagan, *Outbreak*, 51–52, 378–79.

59. Diodorus as an epitomator and his use of Ephorus for this period: Peter Green, "Introduction," in *DS*, 1–47, who cites the pertinent secondary literature and is more appreciative of Diodorus' virtues than are most scholars—apart from Kenneth S. Sacks, *Diodorus Siculus and the First Century* (Princeton, NJ: Princeton University Press, 1990). For a useful, if somewhat exaggerated, reminder of Diodorus' defects, see Pritchett, "Diodoros' Pentekontaetia," 163–71, and "Historians of the Pentekontaetia," 48–77. See also Walther Kolbe, "Diodors Wert für die Geschichte der Pentekontaetie," *Hermes* 72:3 (1937): 241–69, and Meiggs, *AE*, 447–58. Ephorus as an historian of hegemonic regimes and their decay: Rahe, *SR*, Introduction, n. 8. As Sacks, *Diodorus Siculus and the First Century*, 42–49, demonstrates, however, although Diodorus shared Ephorus' interest, he did not slavishly follow his judgments in every particular.

60. Cf., however, Fornara/Samons, *ACP*, 122–24.

61. Plut. *Arist.* 23.7.

Chapter 2. Persia Redivivus

Epigraph: Julian Stafford Corbett, *Some Principles of Maritime Strategy* (London: Longmans Green, 1911), 15–16.

1. Xerxes at Sardis: Hdt. 8.117, 9.3.1, 107.3–108.1.

2. Xerxes awaits news at Sardis: Hdt. 9.107.3. Artabazus brings news to Anatolia: 9.89.1–90.1. Xerxes makes dispositions for defense of Anatolia: Diod. 11.36.7. Dispute whether heads for Susa or Ecbatana: Hdt. 9.108.2, Diod. 11.36.7. Installs new ruler of Cilicia: Hdt. 9.107. Sacks Didyma: Paus. 8.46.3 (with Ctesias *FGrH* 688 F13.31, where, as the context suggests, Didyma, not Delphi, is intended). Tarries to fortify citadel and construct palace at Celaenae: Xen. *An.* 1.2.7–9, read in light of Hdt. 7.26–29, with Briant, *CA*, 559; Lâtife Summerer, "Die Persische Armee in Kelainai," and Christopher Tuplin, "Xenophon at Celaenae: Palaces, Rivers, and Myth," in *Kelainai-Apameia Kibotos I: Développement urbain dans le contexte anatolien*, ed. Lâtife Summerer, Askold Ivantchik, and Alexander von Kienlin (Bordeaux: Ausonius Éditions, 2011), 33–49, 71–92; Elspeth R. M. Dusinberre, *Empire, Authority, and Autonomy in Achaemenid Anatolia* (Cambridge: Cambridge University Press, 2013), 54; and Christopher Tuplin, "The Persian Military Establishment in Western Anatolia: A Context for Celaenae," in *Kelainai-Apameia Kibotos II: Une Métropole achéménide, hellénistique et romaine*, ed. Askold Ivantchik, Lâtife Summerer, and Alexander von Kienlin (Bordeaux: Ausonius Éditions, 2016), 15–27.

3. Mede's statement to Dio Chrysostom: 11.149 with Briant, *CA*, 541–42. Students of Achaemenid history are similarly inclined to underestimate the significance for Persia of Xerxes' defeat: see, for example, Matt Waters, *Ancient Persia: A Concise History of the Achaemenid Empire, 550–330 BCE* (New York: Cambridge University Press, 2014), 132.

4. Xerxes' loot: Hdt. 8.53.2; Plut. *Them.* 31.1; Arr. *An.* 3.16.7–8, 7.19.2; Paus. 1.8.5. Xerxes' inscription: *The Persian Empire: A Corpus of Sources from the Achaemenid Period,* ed. Amelie Kuhrt (London: Routledge, 2007) 7:88. In this connection, see Gojko Barjamovic, "Propaganda and Practice in Assyrian and Persian Imperial Culture," in *Universal Empire: A Comparative Approach to Imperial Culture and Representation in Eurasian History,* ed. Peter Fibiger Bang and Dariusz Kolodziejczyk (Cambridge: Cambridge University Press, 2012), 43–59.

5. Cimon's progress: Plut. *Cim.* 12.1. Efforts in Caria and Lycia: Diod. 11.60.4–5, Frontin. *Strat.* 3.2.5. Asia entire: Plut. *Comp. Cim. et Lucull.* 2.5. Cf. Anthony G. Keen, "Eurymedon, Naxos, and the Purpose of the Delian League," *JAC* 12 (1997): 57–79 (esp. 71–78), who interprets the absence of detail in our sources as an indication that the Athenians failed, after the seizure of Eion, to follow through on their pledge to harry the Mede. The fact that we know so little is a function of Thucydides' decision to restrict his purview to events that dramatically illustrate the growth in Athenian power and of the fact that Plutarch preferred a brief, dramatic summary.

6. Achaemenid raison d'être: Rahe, *PC,* Chapter 1 and Part II, preface. Plato on defective moral formation of Cambyses, Xerxes, and those of their successors reared by the women at court: *Leg.* 3.694c–696a. Scholars dismiss: for example, Briant, *CA,* 515–68. The pertinent passage from Plato's *Laws* is notably absent from *The Persian Empire: A Corpus of Sources from the Achaemenid Period,* and the same can be said for the passage from Herodotus that I am about to discuss.

7. Herodotus on Xerxes and his brother's wife and daughter: 9.108–12. As Lewis, *SP,* 21–22, observed some years ago, "I am myself disposed to take seriously stories of the irrational caprice and wanton cruelty of monarchs. Nothing is reported of Periander, tyrant of Corinth, which does not find ready parallels in well-attested information about Ali Pasha of Iannina at the beginning of the nineteenth century, and allowing for some differences of institutions, the Persian court will be subject to the same kind of pressures and insecurities which have afflicted the courts of absolute monarchs down to the time of Stalin and perhaps beyond."

8. See Rahe, *PC,* Chapter 2.

9. Xerxes once again prepares for war: Just. *Epit.* 2.15.17–20. Event taken as indicator that a great battle had been fought the summer previous to the spring of 468: Plut. *Cim.* 8.7–9, as interpreted in *ATL,* III 160, and W. Kendrick Pritchett, "Thucydides' Pentekontaetia: 5. Naxos, Thasos, and Themistokles' Flight," in Pritchett, *Thucydides' Pentekontaetia and Other Essays* (Leiden: Brill, 1995), 81–94 (at 93–94).

10. Persian preparations and Greek intelligence well in advance of 480: Hdt. 7.20.1, 138.1, 239; Thuc. 1.14.3. Similar conclusions drawn from the preparations under way in 397/6: Xen. *Hell.* 3.4.1. Note also Diod. 16.22.2: Rumor traveled fast. In his fourteenth oration, which was delivered in 354/3, Demosthenes evidenced knowledge concerning the Great King's preparations for the invasion of Egypt that took place in 351/0: George L. Cawkwell, "The Fall of Themistocles," in *Auckland Classical Essays Presented to E. M. Blaiklock,* ed. B. F. Harris (Oxford: Oxford University Press, 1970), 39–58 (at 47–48), reprinted in Cawkwell, *CC,* 95–113 (at 106–7). Advance word before Eurymedon: Pl. *Menex.* 241d–e. Shift of Delian League treasury discussed in synod before 467 (while Aristeides alive), Samians at time propose move: Plut. *Arist.* 25.2–3 read in light of Nepos' dating of Aristeides' death to the fourth year subsequent to the ostracism of Themistocles (*Arist.* 3.3). Cf. W. Kendrick Pritchett, "The Transfer of the Delian Treasury," *Historia* 18:1 (January 1969): 17–21, who argues that the shift took place at this time, with Plut *Per.* 12.1–2 and Diod. 12.38.2, 12.40.1, 54.3, 13.21.3; Isoc. 8.126, 15.234; Nep. *Arist.* 3.1–2, which presuppose that the move took place much later at a time when Pericles was in charge, and see Meiggs, *AE,* 48.

11. See *ATL,* III 160, and Pritchett, "Thucydides' Pentekontaetia: 5. Naxos, Thasos, and Themistokles' Flight," 93–94, where it is plausibly argued that the revolt by Naxos was crushed in 470. Breach of established custom: Thuc. 1.98.4.

12. Themistocles and Athenian-Spartan cooperation: Rahe, *PC,* Chapters 5, 6, and 7.

13. Ambassadors' argument: Diod. 11.43.

14. The Peiraeus: Thuc. 1.93.3–7.

15. Themistocles and the Amphictyonic League: Plut. *Them.* 20.3–4 with Hermann Bengtson, "Themistokles und die delphische Amphiktyonie," *Eranos* 49 (1951): 85–92, reprinted in

Bengtson, *Kleine Schriften zur alte Geschichte* (Munich: Beck, 1974), 151–57; Frost, *PT,* 179–80; and Marr, *Commentary,* 124–25. List of its members: François Lefèvre, *L'Amphictionie pyléo-delphique: Histoire et institutions* (Athens: École française d'Athènes, 1998), 11–139. Note also Georges Daux, "Remarques sur la composition du conseil amphictionique," *BCH* 81 (1957): 95–120, and Simon Hornblower, "Thucydides and the Delphic Amphiktiony," *MHR* 22 (2007): 49–51, reprinted with added material in Hornblower, *Thucydidean Themes* (Oxford: Oxford University Press, 2011), 54–58.

16. Alexander justified his participation in the games by claiming Argive descent: Hdt. 5.22 with 8.137–39. Note also 9.45.2. Benefactor of Athens and her *próxenos:* 7.173, 8.143, 9.44–45. Themistocles at Olympia: Plut. *Them.* 17.4, Paus. 8.50.3. See Ernst Badian, "Greeks and Macedonians," in *Macedonia and Greece in Late Classical and Early Hellenistic Times,* ed. Beryl Barr-Sharrar and Eugene N. Borza (Washington, DC: National Gallery of Art, 1982), 33–51 (at 34, 45, n. 9).

17. Euainetos' expedition: Hdt. 7.173.1–2. Themistocles and Aristeides at Pagasae: Plut. *Them.* 20.1–2, *Arist.* 22.2–4. Cf. Cic. *Off.* 3.49 and Val. Max. 6.5 ext.2, who place the fleet in question at Gytheion in Laconia, and Marr, *Commentary,* 123–24, who (wrongly, in my opinion) thinks this and many another story in Plutarch apocryphal. Vetting by Aristeides and Xanthippus in the past: Diod. 11.42.

18. Spartans out of anger at Themistocles embrace Cimon: Plut. *Them.* 20.3–4, *Cim.* 16.1–3, with Marr, *Commentary,* 124–25. Cimon names son Lacedaemonius: Thuc. 1.45.2 with Schol. Ael. Aristid. *Or.* 3.515 (Dindorf); Stesimbrotus of Thasos *FGrH* 107 F6; Plut. *Cim.* 16.1, *Per.* 29.1.

19. Cf. Frost, *PT,* 186–87, who thinks that Themistocles harped on the Spartan threat solely because Aristeides, Xanthippus, and Cimon were now the leaders of the struggle against the Mede.

20. Timing and sponsorship of Phrynichus' *Phoenician Women* and of Aeschylus' *Persians* and their political import: Plut. *Them.* 5.5 with Anthony J. Podlecki, *The Political Background of Aeschylean Tragedy* (Ann Arbor: University of Michigan Press, 1966), 1–26, and Marr, *Commentary,* 81. For further evidence pertinent to Aeschylus' friendship with Themistocles, see [Them.] *Ep. Gr.* 1.741, 11.751 (Hercher) = [Them.] *Ep.* 1, 11.5 (Doenges), which should be read with an eye to note 39 and its context, below. Three *óstraka* from the 470s testify to the fact that Pericles' older brother Ariphron (Pl. *Prt.* 320a, Plut. *Alc.* 1.2) was active in public life at that time: David M. Lewis, "Megakles and Eretria," *ZPE* 96 (1993): 51–52. See Davies, *APF* no. 11811, I–II.

21. Decision to hold ostracism: Arist. *Ath. Pol.* 43.5, read in light of 22.3, with Rhodes, *CAAP,* 267–71, 526. Quorum for ostracism itself: Plut. *Arist.* 7.5–6, Poll. *Onom.* 8.20, Schol. Ar. *Eq.* 855, Philochorus *FGrH* 328 F30.

22. Ostracism of Hipparchus and Megacles as friends of the tyrant and of Xanthippus and Aristeides: Arist. *Ath. Pol.* 22.4–7, Plut. *Arist.* 1.1–2.1, 5.1–7.7 with Rhodes, *CAAP,* 271–81 and, on Xanthippus in particular, James P. Sickinger, "New *Ostraka* from the Athenian Agora," *Hesperia* 86:3 (July–September 2017): 443–508. Marriage of Xanthippus into the Alcmeonid clan: Hdt. 6.131.2 with Davies, *APF,* nos. 9688, X and 11811, I. Aristeides and Cleisthenes: Plut. *Arist.* 1.1–2.1, *Mor.* 790f–791a, 805f with Davies, *APF* no. 1695, I–II.

23. Candidates for ostracism in the 470s: Stefan Brenne, *Ostrakismos und Prominenz in Athen: Attische Bürger des 5. Jhs. v. Chr. auf den Ostraka* (Vienna: A. Holzhausens, 2001), 46, 81–84, 95–97, 114–17, 153–54, 177–81, 209–11, 225–28, 235–38, 239–40, 245–47, 377–81. Ariphron among them: note 20, above. Megacles' second and this Alcibiades' first ostracism: Lys. 14.39, Andoc. 4.34 with Peter J. Bicknell, "Was Megakles Hippokratous Alopekthen Ostracised Twice?" *AC* 44:1 (1975): 172–75. Grandfather of this Alcibiades an ally of Cleisthenes: Isoc. 16.26 with *SEG* XXVII 135. Marriage alliance between the two families: Plut. *Alc.* 1.1, Pl. *Alc.* I 105d, Lys. 14.39. Alcibiades a Spartan name: Thuc. 8.6.3. Hereditary *próxenos* of the Lacedaemonians: 5.43.2, 6.89.2. Callias son of Hipponicus wealthy, said to be a kinsman of Aristeides: Plut. *Arist.* 25.4–9. *Proxenía* of Lacedaemon hereditary within his family: Xen. *Hell.* 6.3.4. See also Davies, *APF* no. 7826, V–X. There is reason to suspect that Callias son of Cratios was both an Alcmeonid and a kinsman of the son of Hipponicus: see Peter J. Bicknell, "Kallias Kratiou," in Bicknell, *Studies in Athenian Politics and Genealogy* (Wiesbaden: Franz Steiner Verlag, 1972), 64–71; H. A. Shapiro, "Kallias Kratiou

Alopekethen," *Hesperia* 51:1 (January–March 1982): 69–73, the latter with Davies, *APF* no. 7826, III–IV; and Brenne, *Ostrakismos und Prominenz in Athen,* 179–81.

24. Friends of the tyrant: Arist. *Ath. Pol.* 22.4–6 with Rhodes, *CAAP,* 271–77. Medizers: *ML* no. 21; Hdt. 6.115, 121–24.

25. Charges lodged in court: Arist. *Ath. Pol.* 25.3, Diod. 11.54.3–6, Hyp. Isoc. 7. Cf. Plut. *Them.* 23, who dates the charges he mentions solely to the period of Themistocles' sojourn in Argos, with John F. Barrett, "The Downfall of Themistocles," *GRBS* 18:4 (Winter 1977): 291–305, who defends Diodorus' claim that these charges were first lodged prior to Themistocles' ostracism. Cf. Marr, *Commentary,* 133–35, and Arthur Keaveney, *The Life and Journey of Athenian Statesman Themistocles (624–460 B.C.?) as a Refugee in Persia* (Lewiston, ME: Edwin Mellen Press, 2003), 105–8, with Peter Green, "Commentary," in *DS,* 114–16, nn. 203–5. Note also Rhodes, *CAAP,* 319–20.

26. Ostracism of Themistocles: Thuc. 1.135.3; Aristodemus *FGrH* 104 F6.1; Pl. *Grg.* 516d; Nep. *Them.* 8.1, *Arist.* 3.3; Diod. 11.54.1–55.3; Plut. *Them.* 22.3; Cic. *Amic.* 12.42; Euseb. *Chron.* 2.102–3 (Schoene-Petermann) with Anthony J. Podlecki, *The Life of Themistocles: A Critical Survey of the Literary and Archaeological Evidence* (Montreal: McGill-Queens University Press, 1975), 30–37, 185–94; Marr, *Commentary,* 130–33; Keaveney, *The Life and Journey of Athenian Statesman Themistocles,* 104–12; and Green, "Commentary," 116–20, nn. 206–13. The timeline that Robert J. Lenardon, "The Chronology of Themistokles' Ostracism and Exile," *Historia* 8:1 (January 1959): 23–48, proposed and that Cawkwell, "The Fall of Themistocles," 39–58, reprinted in Cawkwell, *CC,* 95–113, later embraced cannot be sustained given what Mary E. White, "Some Agiad Dates: Pausanias and His Sons," *JHS* 84 (1964): 140–52, in the interim demonstrated regarding the longevity of Pausanias. I do not find the attack on White by Frost, *PT,* 188–91, cogent. The argument that Cawkwell, "The Fall of Themistocles," 48, 52–53, reprinted in Cawkwell, *CC,* 107, 113, made regarding the relationship between the Persian naval buildup and Themistocles' final fall from grace (which he dated wrongly to 470) applies with no less and, I think, even greater force to his ostracism (which is properly dated to 472, 471, or 470). See Ste. Croix, *OPW,* 175, and Frost, *PT,* 188.

27. Faction at Lacedaemon backing Pausanias: Arist. *Pol.* 1306b22–1307a4. Note also Thuc. 1.134.1. Private expedition, but equipped with *skutálē:* Thuc. 1.131.1, interpreted in light of Plut. *Lys.* 19.7–12, Aul. Gell. 17.9.6–15, Schol. Thuc. 1.131.1, *Suidas* s.v. *skutálē.* For doubts as to the character of the *skutálē,* as well as an impressive display of learning, cf. Thomas Kelly, "The Spartan Scytale," in *The Craft of the Ancient Historian: Essays in Honor of Chester G. Starr,* ed. John W. Eadie and Josiah W. Ober (Lanham, MD: University Press of America, 1985), 141–69. It is clear that the word had divers meanings. It is not clear, however, that Plutarch, Aullus Gellius, Thucydides' scholiast, and the *Suidas* are in error with regard to Spartan usage.

28. Hedging of bets: Józef Wolski, "Pausanias et le problème de la politique Spartiate (années 480–470)," *Eos* 47 (1954–1955): 75–94 (at 88–89); Alec Blamire, "Pausanias and Persia," *GRBS* 11:4 (Winter 1970): 295–305 (at 299); and James Allan Stewart Evans, "The Medism of Pausanias: Two Versions," *Antichthon* 22 (1988): 1–11 (at 7), reprinted with added material in Evans, *The Beginnings of History: Herodotus and the Persian Wars* (Toronto: University of Toronto Press, 2006), 305–20 (at 313). Cf. Ulrich Kahrstedt, "Sparta und Persien in der Pentekontaetie," *Hermes* 56:3 (July 1921): 320–25, who goes too far in suggesting that the authorities at Sparta were fishing at this time for a secret, separate peace with Persia, with Werner Judeich, "Griechische Politik und persische Politik im V. Jahrhundert," *Hermes* 58:1 (January 1923): 1–19. It is, of course, perfectly possible and even likely that Pausanias and his supporters had something of the sort in mind.

29. Pausanias' return to Byzantium: Thuc. 1.128.3, 131.1; Pompeius Trogus ap. Just. *Epit.* 9.1.3, with Adolf Lippold, "Pausanias von Sparta und die Perser," *RhM* 108:4 (1965): 320–41 (at 339–41), whose reliance on Justin's claim that Pausanias' sojourn in Byzantium lasted seven years squares nicely with what White, "Some Agiad Dates," 140–52, has shown regarding the regent's longevity. Pausanias presumably arrived at Byzantium not long after Cimon had collected the allied fleet and set off for Eion: Ephorus *FGrH* 70 F191.6, Diod. 11.60.1–2. Cf. *ATL,* III 158–59; Wolski, "Pausanias et le problème de la politique Spartiate," 75–94; Raphael Sealey, "The Origins of the

Delian League," in *ASI*, 233–55 (at 249); Blamire, "Pausanias and Persia," 299–300, esp. n.17; and John F. Lazenby, "Pausanias, Son of Kleombrotos," *Hermes* 103:2 (1975): 235–51 (at 239–40), where this possibility is not even canvassed. On the character of Pausanias' initial reception at Byzantium, see Christopher F. Lehmann-Haupt, "Pausanias: Heros Ktistes von Byzanz," *Klio* 17 (1921): 59–73 (at 59–66), who may well be right.

30. Story told concerning Pausanias' Medism and the dispatch of Artabazus: Thuc. 1.95.5, 128.3–131.1; Diod. 11.44.3–6; Nep. *Paus*. 2.2–5. In this connection, see Gabriel Herman, *Ritualised Friendship and the Greek City* (Cambridge: Cambridge University Press, 1987), passim (esp. 41–42, 47, 89, 91). Artabazus in Greece: Rahe, *PC*, Chapter 8 and Epilogue.

31. Six to thirteen weeks: Hdt. 5.52–54, 8.98; Xen. *Cyr.* 8.6.17–18. Skepticism: Charles W. Fornara, "Some Aspects of the Career of Pausanias of Sparta," *Historia* 15:3 (August 1966): 257–71, whose critique of Thucydides' testimony in this particular is endorsed by Mabel Lang, "Scapegoat Pausanias," *CJ* 63:2 (November 1967): 79–85 (at 79), reprinted in Lang, *Thucydidean Narrative and Discourse*, ed. Jeffrey S. Rusten and Richard Hamilton (Ann Arbor: University of Michigan Press, 2011), 37–47 (at 37–38); Peter J. Rhodes, "Thucydides on Pausanias and Themistocles," *Historia* 19:4 (November 1970): 387–400 (at 389, n. 12); Blamire, "Pausanias and Persia," 297–98, esp. n. 7; Antony Andrewes, "Spartan Imperialism?" in *Imperialism in the Ancient World*, ed. Peter D. A. Garnsey and C. R. Whittaker (Cambridge: Cambridge University Press, 1978), 91–102 (at 302–3, n. 5); Andre S. Schieber, "Thucydides and Pausanias," *Athenaeum* 58 (1980): 396–405 (at 397, with n. 5); Evans, "The Medism of Pausanias," 3 (esp. n. 15), 5–6, reprinted with added material in Evans, *The Beginnings of History*, 308 (esp. n. 15), 311–13; and Badian, *Outbreak*, 52–54 with 167–68, n. 17, reprinted in Badian, *FPP*, 130–32 with 225, n. 17. Note also Cawkwell, "The Fall of Themistocles," 49–51, reprinted in Cawkwell, *CC*, 108–10; and Lazenby, "Pausanias, Son of Kleombrotos," 238–39.

32. Six- or seven-year period at Byzantium (depending on whether we suppose that inclusive or exclusive reckoning was used): Pompeius Trogus ap. Just. *Epit.* 9.1.3 with Fornara, "Some Aspects of the Career of Pausanias at Sparta," 267–71; Lang, "Scapegoat Pausanias," 79, reprinted in Lang, *Thucydidean Narrative and Discourse*, 38; Meiggs, *AE*, 71–74, 465–68; W. G. G. Forrest, "Pausanias and Themistokles Again," *Lakōnikaí Spoudaí* 2 (1975): 115–20 (at 117); Evans, "The Medism of Pausanias," 3, reprinted with added material in Evans, *The Beginnings of History*, 309; and Ernst Badian, "Toward a Chronology of the Pentecontaetia down to the Renewal of the Peace of Callias," *EMC* 32 n.s. 7:3 (1988): 289–320 (at 300–302), reprinted in Badian, *FPP*, 73–107 (at 86–88). Note also David M. Lewis, "Chronological Notes," in *CAH* V² 499. The argument advanced by White, "Some Agiad Dates," 140–52, concerning Pausanias' longevity lends considerable support to the supposition that Pompeius Trogus' claim could well be chronologically correct.

33. Xerxes pauses to fortify citadel of Celaenae: Xen. *An.* 1.2.7–9. Efficiency of Achaemenid communication network: Henry P. Colburn, "Connectivity and Communication in the Achaemenid Empire," *JESHO* 56 (2013): 29–52.

34. Pausanias and Persian airs: Thuc. 1.130.1–131.1, Nep. *Paus.* 3.1–3.

35. Aristotle on the Spartan *agógē*: *Pol.* 1338b9–38. The harshness displayed by Pausanias reminds one of Xenophon's depiction of the Spartan Clearchus: *Hell.* 1.3.14–19, *An.* 2.6 with Diod. 13.66.5–6. Note also Thuc. 2.67.4, 3.32.1–2, 93.2, 5.51.1–52.1. See Simon Hornblower, "Sticks, Stones, and Spartans: The Sociology of Spartan Violence," in *War and Violence in Ancient Greece*, ed. Hans van Wees (London: Duckworth, 2000), 57–82, reprinted with added material in Hornblower, *Thucydidean Themes* (Oxford: Oxford University Press, 2011), 250–74.

36. Pausanias has epigram inscribed on bronze bowl: Hdt. 4.81.3. Nymphis of Heracleia *FGrH* 432 F9 reports that it was still there in his own day.

37. It is worth noting that Briant, *CA*, 560–63, thinks Thucydides' report consistent with Xerxes' *modus operandi*.

38. Pausanias' misconduct: Thuc. 1.128.3–131.1; Nep. *Paus.* 3.1–3; Paus. 3.17.7–9; Aristodemus *FGrH* 104 F6.2–3, 8.1; Plut. *Cim.* 6.2–6, *Mor.* 555c. Partisans in Lacedaemon: Thuc. 1.134.1, Arist. *Pol.* 1306b22–1307a4. Expulsion from Byzantium: Thuc.1.131.1, Just. *Epit.* 9.1.3, Plut. *Cim.* 6.5–6 with Meiggs, *AE*, 71–73, 465–68.

39. Pseudepigraphical letter to Pausanias: [Them.] *Ep. Gr.* 2.741–42 (Hercher) = [Them.] *Ep.* 2.5 (Doenges). For a critical edition of the letters, an English translation, a discussion of their character and provenance, a detailed commentary, and a suggestive essay on the principal fifth-century source used by the author, see *The Letters of Themistocles*, ed. Norman A. Doenges (New York: Arno Press, 1981). For another, in large part complementary overview, see Robert J. Lenardon, "Charon, Thucydides, and 'Themistokles,'" *Phoenix* 15:1 (Spring 1961): 28–40, who provides his own translation in Lenardon, *The Saga of Themistocles* (London: Thames and Hudson, 1978), 154–93. As both of these scholars demonstrate, the letters in question contain accurate information not found in the histories of Herodotus or Thucydides or in any other surviving work. Note also [Them.] *Ep. Gr.* 14.754 (Hercher) = [Them.] *Ep.* 14 (Doenges).

40. Cimon's admirer: Ion of Chios F105–6, 109 (Leurini) = *FGrH* 392 F12–13, 15 ap. Plut. *Cim.* 5.3, 9.1–6 and *Per.* 5.3 with Felix Jacoby, "Some Remarks on Ion of Chios," *CQ* 41:1/2 (January–April 1947): 1–17, reprinted in Jacoby, *Abhandlungen zur grieschischen Geschischtscriebung*, ed. Herbert Bloch (Leiden: E. J. Brill, 1956), 144–68, George L. Huxley, "Ion of Chios," *GRBS* 6:1 (1965): 29–46; Martin L. West, "Ion of Chios," *BICS* 32:1 (December 1985): 71–78, reprinted in West, *Hellenica: Selected Papers on Greek Literature and Thought* (Oxford: Oxford University Press, 2011–13), III 424–36; and Christopher B. R. Pelling, "Ion's *Epidemiai* and Plutarch's Ion," and Anne Geddes, "Ion of Chios and Politics," in *The World of Ion of Chios*, ed. Victoria Jennings and Andrea Katsaros (Leiden: Brill, 2007), 75–138. For a thoughtful exploration of Ion's ambiguous status as a Chian and a supporter of Athens, see Alastair Blanshard, "Trapped between Athens and Chios: A Relationship in Fragments," in *The World of Ion of Chios*, 155–75.

41. Byzantium, Sestos, and Persian captives: Ion of Chios F106 (Leurini) = *FGrH* 392 F13 ap. Plut. *Cim.* 9.1–6, Polyaen. *Strat.* 1.34.2. Cf. A. G. Woodhead, "The Second Capture of Sestos," *PCPhS* 181, n.s. 1 (1950–51): 9–12, and Sealey, "The Origins of the Delian League," 248–52, who hold the view that there was no second capture of Sestos and that these passages refer to the capture of Sestos engineered by Xanthippus in 479, with Miroslav Ivanov Vasilev, *The Policy of Darius and Xerxes towards Thrace and Macedonia* (Leiden: Brill, 2015), 218–25, who shows that this assertion is unfounded.

42. Pausanias' eventual recall from Colonae and mode by which message sent: Thuc.1.131.1, Nep. *Paus.* 3.3–4 with Meiggs, *AE*, 71–73, 465–68. Location of Colonae: Xen. *Hell.* 3.1.13, 16; Strabo 13.1.19, 47, 62 with John M. Cook *The Troad: An Archaeological and Topographical Study* (Oxford: Clarendon Press, 1973), 219–21, 360–62, and *IACP* no. 782. Status vis-à-vis the Delian League: *ATL*, I 316–19, III 203–7. Significance of its likely inclusion within the satrapy governed by Artabazus: Briant, *CA*, 560–63.

43. The account I give here regarding the trireme, its crew, and the tactics developed is an abbreviated restatement of the analysis I presented in Rahe, *PC*, Chapter 1 (with notes 31–36, where I cite the evidence and the pertinent secondary literature). Triremes in Persian fleet vary in size: Fabrice Bouzid-Adler, "Les Marines des peuples d'origine louvite à l'époque achéménide," *Res Antiquae* 11 (2014): 1–18, and "Les Navires des Grecs d'Asie au service des Grands Rois perses," *Res Antiquae* 12 (2015): 1–16. Some as short as one hundred feet: Judith McKenzie. "Kition," in *Shipsheds of the Ancient Mediterranean*, ed. David Blackman and Boris Rankov (Cambridge: Cambridge University Press, 2013), 349–62. Phocaean advice before Lade: Hdt. 6.11.

44. Artemisium and Salamis: Rahe, *PC*, Chapters 6 and 7.

45. Proverb: Pl. *Leg.* 3.689d.

46. Themistocles' triremes only partially decked: Thuc. 1.14.3, Plut. *Cim.* 12.2 with John S. Morrison, John F. Coates, and N. Boris Rankov, *The Athenian Trireme: The History and Reconstruction of an Ancient Greek Warship*, 2nd edition (New York: Cambridge University Press, 2000), 153–61. Persian triremes top-heavy: Hdt. 8.118.1–4, Plut. *Them.* 14.1–3 with Lucien Basch, "Phoenician Oared Ships," *MM* 55:1 (January 1969): 139–62 and 55: 3 (August 1969): 227–45.

47. Cimon's triremes fully decked, number of marines maximized: Plut. *Cim.* 12.2. I see no reason for supposing that Cimon's motives were political. Given the character of the operations he conducted in this period, hoplites in considerable numbers were needed; and, as we shall see, at Eurymedon, as at Mycale, their presence was a boon. Cf., however, Barry S. Strauss, "Democracy,

Kimon, and the Evolution of Athenian Naval Tactics in the Fifth Century BC," in *Polis and Politics: Studies in Ancient Greek History Presented to Mogens Herman Hansen on His Sixtieth Birthday,* ed. Pernille Flensted-Jensen, Thomas Heine Nielsen, and Lene Rubinstein (Copenhagen: Museum Tusculanu Press, 2000), 315–26. The fact that light-armed troops are rarely mentioned tells us a great deal about the ideological hegemony of the hoplite ethos. It should not be taken as an indication that they were not employed. See Matthew Trundle, "Light Troops in Classical Athens," in *War, Democracy and Culture in Classical Athens,* ed. David M. Pritchard (Cambridge: Cambridge University Press, 2010), 139–60, on whose passing remarks in this regard one could expand. *Epibátai:* Tristan Herzogenrath-Amelung, "Naval Hoplites: Social Status and Combat Reality of Classical Greek *Epibatai,*" *Historia* 66:1 (2017): 45–64.

48. From Cnidus to Phaselis: Plut. *Cim.* 12.2–4. Note also Aristodemus *FGrH* 104 F11.1.

49. Battle of Eurymedon: Thuc. 1.100.1, Plut. *Cim.* 12.5–13.3, Nep. *Cim.* 2.2–3 (where Eurymedon is confused with Mycale). Ephorus or an epitomator (*FGrH* 70 F191.9–10) and, thereafter, Diodorus (11.60.4–62.3) appear to have conflated this battle with a later struggle of a similar character that took place in the vicinity of Cypriot Salamis in 451: Eduard Meyer, "Die Schlacht am Eurymedon und Kimons cyprischer Feldzug," in Meyer, *Forschungen zur alten Geschichte* (Halle: Max Niemeyer, 1892–99), II 1–25. See also Aristodemus *FGrH* 104 F11.2; Frontin. *Strat.* 2.9.10; Aristid. *Or.* 13.152, 46.156 (Dindorf). Cf. Keen, "Eurymedon, Naxos, and the Purpose of the Delian League," 57–67, who denies that Xerxes had ordered a buildup of forces in preparation for an attempt to retake the Aegean and suggests that Cimon's initial purpose was a raid for plunder and that he opted for a preemptive attack when the Persians rallied to drive his armada back to the Aegean. The fact that Cimon had so large a fleet shows that, from the outset, he had far more in mind than a mere raid for plunder.

50. Booty, burial, dedications, acropolis wall, and foundations for Long Walls: Plut. *Cim.* 13.2, 5–7; Paus. 1.28.3, 29.14 with Margaret C. Miller, *Athens and Persia in the Fifth Century BC: A Study in Cultural Receptivity* (Cambridge: Cambridge University Press, 1997), 38–40. Cimon becomes wealthy: Matthew A. Sears, *Athens, Thrace, and the Shaping of Athenian Leadership* (New York: Cambridge University Press, 2013), 69–74. With regard to the decision to bury the dead from Eurymedon in the public cemetery, see Pritchett, *GSAW,* IV 123–24, 177–78. For another species of commemoration, see Margaret C. Miller, "I Am Eurymedon: Tensions and Ambiguities in Athenian War Imagery," in *War, Democracy and Culture in Classical Athens,* 304–38. For exceedingly muddled accounts of Cimon's role vis-à-vis the Long Walls, see Andoc. 3.5, Aeschin. 2.172–73. There is no reason to doubt Plutarch's testimony in this regard: David H. Conwell, *Connecting a City to the Sea: The History of the Athenian Long Walls* (Leiden: Brill, 2008), 1–64 (esp. 4–7, 19–54). For further muddle, see Nep. *Cim.* 2.5.

51. Cimon and the generals as judges, Sophocles' victory, and the date: Plut. *Cim.* 8.8–9 with Podlecki, *The Political Background of Aeschylean Tragedy,* 42. Likelihood that Eurymedon was fought the previous campaigning season: *ATL,* III 160, and Pritchett, "Thucydides' Pentekontaetia: 5. Naxos, Thasos, and Themistokles' Flight," 93–94. Procedures for judging: Maurice Pope, "Athenian Festival Judges: Five, Seven, or However Many," *CQ* n.s. 36:2 (1986): 322–26. To suppose that Eurymedon was fought later than 466, one must suppose Thucydides an ignoramus or a liar and Ephorus and Plutarch in error: see, for example, Johan Henrik Schreiner, *Hellanikos, Thukydides and the Era of Kimon* (Aarhus: University of Aarhus Press, 1997), 38–49. This I find implausible.

Chapter 3. Shifting Sands

Epigraph: William Shakespeare, *Macbeth* 1.3.56–59, in Shakespeare, *The Complete Works,* ed. Stanley Wells and Gary Taylor (Oxford: Clarendon Press, 1988), 978.

1. Import of Eurymedon: Moses I. Finley, "The Fifth-Century Athenian Empire: A Balance Sheet," in *Imperialism in the Ancient World,* ed. Peter D. A. Garnsey and C. R. Whittaker (Cambridge: Cambridge University Press, 1978), 103–26 (at 105–6), reprinted in Finley, *Economy and Society in Ancient Greece,* ed. Brent D. Shaw and Richard P. Saller (London: Chatto & Windus, 1981), 41–61 (at 42–44).

2. Egypt prone to revolt: Stephen Ruzicka, *Trouble in the West: Egypt and the Persian Empire, 525–332 BCE* (Oxford: Oxford University Press, 2012).

3. Miltiades wounded, tried, fined, jailed, dead: Rahe, *PC,* Chapter 5, note 32. Cimon, Elpinike, Callias, and the payment of the fine: Nep. *Cim.* 1, Plut. *Cim.* 4.4–8, Dio. Chrys. 73.6 with Davies, *APF* nos. 7825, 8429. Ephorus *FGrH* 70 F64 emphasizes in this regard Cimon's own marriage to a wealthy wife—presumably, Isodike daughter of the Alcmeonid Euryptolemos.

4. Terms of peace and timing: Pl. *Menex.* 241d–242a, Isoc. 4.120, Lycurg. *Leocr.* 72–73, Plut. *Cim.* 13.4–5, Just. *Epit.* 2.15.17–20, Ammian. Marc. 17.11.3, Aristodemus *FGrH* 104 F13, *Suda* s.v. *Kallías* and *Kímōn* with Ernst Badian, "The Peace of Callias," *JHS* 107 (1987): 1–39, reprinted with added material in Badian, *FPP,* 1–72 (at 1–60). Cf. Pétros J. Stylianou, "The Untenability of Peace with Persia in the 460s B.C.," *Meletai kai Upomnemata* 2 (1988): 339–71, and Fornara/ Samons, *ACP,* 171–75, with Badian, "The Peace of Callias: Appendix," *FPP,* 61–69, and see Stadter, *CPP,* 150–51, and Jonathan M. Hall, "Eleusis, the Oath of Plataia, and the Peace of Kallias," in Hall, *Artifact and Artifice: Classical Archaeology and the Ancient Historian* (Chicago: University of Chicago Press, 2014), 55–76. Note John Walsh. "The Authenticity and the Dates of the Peace of Callias and the Congress Decree," *Chiron* 11 (1981): 31–63 (esp. 31–41), who—wrongly in my view—supposes that the treaty was negotiated with Artaxerxes shortly after Xerxes' death. Persian protocol: Xen. *Hell.* 5.1.31 with Victor Martin, "Quelques remarques à l'occasion d'une nouvelle édition des *Staatsverträge des Altertums,*" *MH* 20 (1963): 230–33. Note John O. Hyland, *Persian Interventions: The Achaemenid Empire, Athens and Sparta, 450–386 BCE* (Baltimore: Johns Hopkins University Press, 2018), 164–68 (with 7–10). When the terms were renewed with Artaxerxes in 449 after the battles at Cypriot Salamis, Callias was once again the Athenian interlocutor in the negotiations: Chapter 6, note 15, below. They were also renewed and perhaps revised at the behest of an Athenian diplomat named Epilycus, not long after the winter of 424/3 when, Artaxerxes having died, Darius II fought his way to the throne: Rahe, *SSAW,* Chapter 6. If the timing of the original peace and even its existence is in dispute, it is because, in his great history, Thucydides fails to give due weight to Persia and, in consequence, omits matters of real importance: note 7, below. Most scholars think there was no such peace until 449: Henry Theodore Wade-Gery, "The Peace of Callias," in *Athenian Studies Presented to W. S. Ferguson, HSPh* Supplement I (1940), 121–56, reprinted in Wade-Gery, *EGH,* 201–32; Kagan, *Outbreak,* 107–9; Ste. Croix, *OPW,* 310–14; Meiggs, *AE,* 128–51; Stylianou, "The Untenability of Peace with Persia in the 460s B.C.," 339–71; David M. Lewis, "The Thirty Years' Peace," in *CAH* V2 121–46 (at 121–27); George L. Cawkwell, "The Peace between Athens and Persia," *Phoenix* 51:2 (Summer 1997): 115–30, reprinted in Cawkwell, *CC,* 151–69; and Loren J. Samons II, "Kimon, Kallias and Peace with Persia," *Historia* 47:2 (2nd Quarter 1998): 129–40. Some think there was none until 423 or thereafter: Raphael Sealey, "The Peace of Callias Once More," *Historia* 3:3 (1955): 325–33, and Harold B. Mattingly, "The Peace of Kallias," *Historia* 14: 3 (July 1965): 273–81, reprinted in Mattingly, *The Athenian Empire Restored: Epigraphical and Historical Studies* (Ann Arbor: University of Michigan Press, 1996), 107–16. Others doubt whether there was ever an agreement at all: see note 6, below. Although Callisthenes made no mention of the accord negotiated in the wake of Eurymedon, it is a mistake to read Plut. *Cim.*13.4 as asserting that he expressly denied its existence: see A. Brian Bosworth, "Plutarch, Callisthenes, and the Peace of Callias," *JHS* 110 (1990): 1–13. As Badian, "The Peace of Callias: Appendix," 71–72, observes, Plutarch's point is merely that Callisthenes is silent about the peace and attributes the Great King's subsequent self-restraint to fear (which was no doubt the reason why he agreed to a cessation of hostilities). Cimon's failure to follow up on his victory at Eurymedon weighs strongly against our supposing that he thought it possible and desirable to launch a general assault on the Persian empire as such. Cf., however, George Cawkwell, *Thucydides and the Peloponnesian War* (London: Routledge, 1997), 38, and Michael Flower, "From Simonides to Isocrates: The Fifth-Century Origins of Fourth-Century Panhellenism," *CA* 19:1 (April 2000): 65–101 (at 77–89), who think otherwise.

5. On this point, I agree with Fornara/Samons, *ACP,* 171–74. I would go beyond them only in asserting that there must have been negotiations and an informal agreement.

6. No treaty: Theopompus of Chios *FGrH* 115 F153–54. Some scholars side with Theopompus: David Stockton, "The Peace of Callias," *Historia* 8:1 (January 1959): 61–79; Christian Habicht,

"Falsche Urkunden zur Geschichte Athens im Zeitalter der Perserkriege," *Hermes* 89:1 (1961): 1–35; and Klaus Meister, *Die Ungeschichtlichkeit des Kalliasfriedens und deren historische Folgen* (Wiesbaden: Franz Steiner Verlag, 1982).

7. Thucydides' neglect of Persian affairs: Antony Andrewes, "Thucydides and the Persians," *Historia* 10:1 (January 1961): 1–18.

8. The argument so ably advanced by A. James Holladay, "The Détent of Kallias," *Historia* 35:4 (4th Quarter 1986): 503–7, reprinted in Holladay, *AFC*, 55–60, with regard to the agreement made in 449 applies with even greater force to the accord reached, I believe, ca. 468 or 467.

9. Achaemenid Zoroastrianism and the obligations of Ahura Mazda's viceroy on earth: Rahe, *PC*, Chapter 1, the preface to Part II, and Chapter 5. For further discussion and a citation of the secondary literature that has appeared since my volume, see Robert Rollinger, "Royal Strategies of Representation and the Language(s) of Power: Some Considerations on the Audience and Dissemination of the Achaemenid Royal Inscriptions," in *Official Epistolography and the Language(s) of Power*, ed. Stephen Procházka, Lucian Reinfandt, and Sven Tost (Vienna: Österreichschen Akademie der Wissenschaften, 2015), 117–30; Matt Waters, "Xerxes and the Oathbreakers: Empire and Rebellion on the Northwest Front," in *Revolt and Resistance in the Ancient Classical World and the Near East: In the Crucible of Empire*, ed. John J. Collins and J. G. Manning (Leiden: Brill, 2016), 93–102; and Hyland, *Persian Interventions*, 1–14 (esp. 7–10).

10. Xerxes assassinated: *The Persian Empire: A Corpus of Sources from the Achaemenid Period*, ed. Amelie Kuhrt (London: Routledge, 2007) 7:90–91; Ctesias *FGrH* 688 F13.33–F14.34; Diod. 11.69; Ael. *VH* 13.3. Pompeius Trogus attributes assassination to decline in majesty of his kingship (Just. *Epit.* 3.1.1–2), as does Aelian (*VH* 13.3). The commander of the bodyguard may have had other motives as well: Arist. *Pol.* 1311b36–39. For another view, cf. Josef Wiesehöfer, "Die Ermordung des Xerxes: Abrechnung mit einem Despoten oder eigentlicher Beginn einer Herrschaft?" in *Herodot und die Epoche der Perserkriege: Realitäten und Fiktionen*, ed. Bruno Bleckmann (Cologne: Bohlau, 2007), 3–19. Xerxes' death appears to have taken place quite early in August 465: Matthew W. Stolper, "Some Ghost Facts from Achaemenid Babylonian Texts," *JHS* 108 (1988): 196–98; Christopher Walker, "Achaemenid Chronology and the Babylonian Sources," in *Mesopotamia and Iran in the Persian Period: Conquest and Imperialism, 539–331 B.C.*, ed. John Curtis (London: British Museum Press, 1997), 17–25; and Leo Depuydt, *From Xerxes' Murder (465) to Arridaios' Execution (317): Updates to Achaemenid Chronology* (Oxford: BAR, 2008), 9–12. For further discussion, see Briant, *CA*, 563–67. On "the Chiliarch [commander of the thousand]," see Arthur Keaveney, *The Life and Journey of Athenian Statesman Themistocles (624-460 B.C.?) as a Refugee in Persia* (Lewiston, ME: Edwin Mellen Press, 2003), 119–29. Cf., however, Michael B. Charles, "The Chiliarchs of Achaemenid Persia: Towards a Revised Understanding of the Office," *Phoenix* 69:3/4 (Fall–Winter 2015): 279–303.

11. Wealth of Thasos, strengthening of walls, building of triremes, construction of military harbor: note Hdt. 6.28.1, 46.2–47.2 with *IACP* no. 526. Empória: Hdt. 7.109.2, 118; Thuc. 1.100.2, Ps.-Skylax 67 with Alain Bresson, "Les Cités grecques et leurs *emporia*," in *L'Emporion*, ed. Alain Bresson and Pierre Rouillard (Paris: Diffusion de Boccard, 1993), 163–226 (esp. 201–4); Mogens Herman Hansen, "*Emporion*: A Study of the Use and Meaning of the Term in the Archaic and Classical Periods," in *Yet More Studies in the Ancient Greek Polis*, ed. Thomas Heine Nielsen (Stuttgart: Franz Steiner Verlag, 1997), 83–105; and *IACP* nos. 628, 630–631, 634–35, 638. Their significance for Athens: Christophe Pébarthe, "Thasos, l'empire d'Athènes et les *emporia* de Thrace," *ZPE* 126 (1999): 131–54 (esp. 132–35); Lisa Kallet, "The Origins of the Athenian Economic *Arche*," *JHS* 133 (2013): 43–60 (esp. 46–48); and Zosia Halina Archibald, *Ancient Economies of the Northern Aegean: Fifth to First Centuries BC* (Oxford: Oxford University Press, 2013), passim (esp. 258–68). Note also the *empórion* at Pistyros in the interior: Matthew A. Sears, *Athens, Thrace, and the Shaping of Athenian Leadership* (New York: Cambridge University Press, 2013), 25–31. Role of Paros in colonizing the region: Michalis Tiverios, "Greek Colonisation of the Northern Aegean," in *Greek Colonisation: An Account of Greek Colonies and Other Settlements Overseas*, ed. Gocha R. Tsetskhladze (Leiden: Brill, 2006-8), II 1–154 (at 68–91). Mines and marble quarries on island, wine trade, commercial orientation, length of walls, and military and commercial harbors at Thasos: Robin

Osborne, *Classical Landscape with Figures: The Ancient City and Its Countryside* (London: G. Phillip, 1987), 75–81 (esp. 79–81); Yves Granjean and François Salviat, *Guide de Thasos* (Paris: Diffusion de Boccard, 2000), 43–192; and Robin Osborne, "The Politics of an Epigraphic Habit: The Case of Thasos," in *Greek History and Epigraphy: Essays in Honour of P. J. Rhodes*, ed. Lynette Mitchell and Lene Rubinstein (Swansea: Classical Press of Wales, 2009), 103–14. Mines on the mainland: note Strabo 7 F34, and cf. Paul Perdrizet, "Skaptésylé," *Klio* 10 (1910): 1–27, with Meiggs, *AE*, 570–72. Note also Lucia Nixon and Simon Price, "The Size and Resources of Greek Cities," in *The Greek City from Homer to Alexander*, ed. Oswyn Murray and Simon Price (Oxford: Oxford University Press, 1990), 137–70 (esp. 152–53). As I learned when I sojourned on Thasos from 29 June–3 July 2017, the remains there are sufficient to enable one to trace the entire circuit of her walls, the moles and breakwaters of her military harbor, and at least some of the shipsheds contained therein.

12. Thasos submits to Mardonius, cooperates with Darius and Xerxes: note Hdt. 6.43.4–44.2, 46.1, 48.1, 7.118.

13. Revolt of Thasos and its occasion: Thuc. 1.100.2–3, Nep. *Cim.* 2.5, Diod. 11.70.1, Plut. *Cim.* 14.2 with Pébarthe, "Thasos, l'empire d'Athènes et les *emporia* de Thrace," 135–39, and Kallet, "The Origins of the Athenian Economic *Arche*," 43–60. Note Thuc. 4.102, Schol. Aesch. 2.31.

14. One city, one vote in Delian League and the consequences: Thuc. 3.10.5–11.4 with Gomme, *HCT*, II 262–65, and Hornblower, *CT*, I 394–95.

15. Lacedaemon secretly promises Thasos aid: Thuc. 1.101.1–2 with Kagan, *Outbreak*, 61–62, and Ste. Croix, *OPW*, 178–79. That this was done in strict secrecy strongly suggests that the promise was proffered on this occasion, as a similar promise would be thirty-three years later, by "the authorities [*tà télē*]": consider Thuc. 1.58.1, which, I believe, should be read in light of 4.15.1; and see note 64, below. Although I think Andrewes, *HCT* IV 23, 134–35, and Hornblower, *CT*, I 102, right in the abstract, I do not believe that their treatment of the meaning of *tà télē* in Thuc. 1.58.1 correct: see Ste. Croix, *OPW*, 203–4. Nor do I see reason to suppose Thucydides in error with regard to the Spartans' response to this situation, as do Fornara/Samons *ACP*, 127, and Lendon, *SoW*, 55. As Ste. Croix, *OPW*, 179, points out, Thucydides owned a mining concession in the Thraceward region and was intimately familiar with developments there: Thuc. 4.105.1. Cf. Badian, *Outbreak*, esp. 52–60 with the attendant notes, reprinted in Badian, *FPP*, 125–62 (esp. 130–37 with the attendant notes), who denies the credibility of Thucydides' report on the implausible conviction that his history is little more than pro-Athenian propaganda, and Robert D. Luginbill, *Author of Illusions: Thucydides' Rewriting of the History of the Peloponnesian War* (Newcastle: Cambridge Scholars, 2011), 39–59, who holds a similar opinion, with Tim Rood, *Thucydides: Narrative and Explanation* (Oxford: Oxford University Press, 1998), 205–48, and Christopher B. R. Pelling, "Explaining the War," in Pelling, *Literary Texts and the Greek Historian* (London: Routledge, 2000), 82–111 (esp. 94–103), who demonstrate that the Athenian historian was a discerning critic of, not a shameless apologist for Athens; and with C. A. Powell, "Athens' Difficulty, Sparta's Opportunity: Causation and the Peloponnesian War," *AC* 49 (1980): 87–114, and Salmon, *WC*, 297–300 (with 420–21), who argue with considerable intelligence that the Spartans were apt to concert an attack on Athens whenever it seemed likely to succeed. My contention here is that the motives of the Lacedaemonians were more complex than Powell and Salmon realize: that the Spartans were nearly always of two minds—appreciative of the role played by the Athenians in shielding them from Persia, and nervous and resentful regarding the growth in Athens' power—and that this perfectly rational ambivalence played as large a role in their calculations as ambition and opportunism. On this point, see George Cawkwell, "Thucydides' Judgment of Periclean Strategy," *YClS* 24 (1975): 53–70, reprinted in Cawkwell, *CC*, 134–50. On the "little assembly," consider Xen. *Hell.* 3.3.8 in light of Rahe, *SR*, Chapter 2, note 39.

16. Sparta's wars at home: Thuc. 1.118.2.

17. Spartans honor Themistocles in 480: Hdt. 8.124.2–3, Thuc. 1.74.1, Plut. *Them.* 17.3, Aristid. *Or.* 46.289 (Dindorf) with Borimir Jordan, "The Honors for Themistocles after Salamis," *AJPh* 109:4 (Winter 1988): 547–71. Applauded at Olympic games: Plut. *Them.* 17.4, Paus. 8.50.3, Ael. *VH* 13.43.

18. Thucydides kinsman of Cimon: Eugene Cavaignac, "Miltiade et Thucydide," *RPh* 3 (1929): 281–85, and Davies, *APF* no. 7268, IV-VII.

19. Thucydides on Themistocles: 1.138.3. For at least some of the events that Thucydides has in mind, see Hdt. 7.143–44, 8.22, 56–64, 74–83, 108–10, 123–25; Thuc. 1.137.3–138.2. For a perceptive article, appreciative of Themistocles' display of genius in and before 481, that I neglected to cite in Rahe, *PC*, Chapter 5, note 67, see A. James Holladay, "The Forethought of Themistocles," *JHS* 197 (1987): 182–87, reprinted in Holladay, *AFC*, 33–42. See also Richard Cox, "Thucydides on Themistocles," *Politikos* 2 (1992): 89–107.

20. Themistocles at Argos, travels within the Peloponnesus: Thuc. 1.135.3. Pressure to assume high office: [Them.] *Ep. Gr.* 1–2.741–42 (Hercher) = [Them.] *Ep.* 1.7–8, 2.2–3 (Doenges).

21. See W. G. G. Forrest, "Themistokles and Argos," *CQ* n.s. 10:2 (November 1960): 221–41, and "Pausanias and Themistokles Again," *Lakōnikaí Spoudaí* 2 (1975): 115–20. Note also Ste. Croix, *OPW*, 173–77, and Katherine M. Adshead, *Politics of the Archaic Peloponnese: The Transition from Archaic to Classical Politics* (Aldershot: Avebury, 1986), 86–103.

22. Corinthian leader on Spartan weakness nearer home: Xen. *Hell.* 4.2.11–12.

23. According to the pseudepigraphical letter from Themistocles to Aeschylus, three of his guest-friends—Nicias, Meleagros, and Eucrates—proffered the invitation: [Them.] *Ep. Gr.* 1.741 (Hercher) = [Them.] *Ep.* 1.2–7 (Doenges).

24. This was especially true, as we shall see, in Arcadia: see Antony Andrewes, "Sparta and Arcadia in the Early Fifth Century," *Phoenix* 6:1 (Spring 1952): 1–5.

25. Cleomenes and the Arcadians: Hdt. 6.74.1–75.1. Tegea (*IACP* no. 297) hostile to Lacedaemon: Hdt. 9.37.4. Tegeans at Thermopylae: 7.202. Tegeans at Plataea: 9.26.1–28.3, 31, 53–71. Culture of Tegea: Maria Prezler, "Myth and History at Tegea—Local Tradition and Community Identity," in *DAA*, 89–129.

26. Mantineia (*IACP* no. 281) the oldest Arcadian *pólis*: Phylarchus *FGrH* 81 F53. Mantineians and hoplite warfare: Ath. 4.154d. Cf. Xen. *Hell.* 4.4.13–18 (esp. 17) with 4.5.18, and see Thomas Heine Nielsen, "The Concept of Arkadia—The People, Their Land, and Their Organisation," in *DAA*, 16–79 (esp. 52–53). Service at Thermopylae: Hdt. 7.202. Late for Plataea: 9.77.1–2.

27. Eleans also late: Hdt. 9.77.3. Both cities banish generals: 9.77.1–3. Military capacity of Elis and Mantineia: Thuc. 5.58.1, 65–74, 75.5; Diod. 12.78.4; Lys. 34.7. See, however, Chapter 4, note 7, below.

28. Ancient Argive hegemony within the Peloponnesus: Thuc. 5.69.1. Seizure of Asine: Rahe, *SR*, Chapter 4, note 33. Indications that early on Sicyon (*IACP* no. 228 with Yannis A. Lolos, *Land of Sikyon: Archaeology and History of a Greek City-State* [Princeton, NJ: American School of Classical Studies, 2011], esp. 59–65, 124–25) and Aegina (*IACP* no. 358) recognized Argos' preeminence: Hdt. 6.92. Epidaurus (*IACP* no. 348) and Troezen (*IACP* no. 357) as well: Thuc. 5.53 and Diod. 12.78. Religious dimension in latter case: William S. Barrett, "Bacchylides, Asine, and Apollo Pythaieus," *Hermes* 82:4 (1954): 421–44 (esp. 426–29, 438–42), reprinted in Barrett, *Greek Lyric, Tragedy, and Textual Criticism: Collected Papers*, ed. Martin L. West (Oxford: Oxford University Press, 2007), 289–313 (esp. 295–97, 306–11); Marie-Françoise Billot, "Apollon Pythéen et l'Argolide archaique: Histoire et mythes," *Archaiognōsía* 6 (1989–90): 35–100; Barbara Kowalzig, *Singing for the Gods: Performances of Myth and Ritual in Archaic and Classical Greece* (Oxford: Oxford University Press, 2007), 132–60 (esp. 142–60); and Clémence Weber-Pallez, "L'Identité ethnique au service de la définition d'un ensemble territorial: Doriens et Dryopes en Argolide," *Revue Circe* 6 (March 2015): http://www.revue-circe.uvsq.fr/numeros-publies/numero-6/. Argive control of Cythera and coastline from Cynouria to Malea: Hdt. 1.82.2. Note Paus. 3.2.7. In this connection, see Matt Kõiv, "Cults, Myths and State Formation in Archaic Argos," in *When Gods Spoke: Researches and Reflections on Religious Phenomena and Artefacts,* ed. Peeter Espak, Märt Läänemets, and Vladimir Sazonov (Tartu: University of Tartu Press, 2015), 125–64 (esp. 126–40). Thyrea: *IACP* no. 346.

29. Battle of Sepeia and loss of six thousand men: Hdt. 6.76–80, 7.148.2 with Richard A. Tomlinson, *Argos and the Argolid: From the End of the Bronze Age to the Roman Occupation* (Ithaca, NY: Cornell University Press, 1972), 93–97. No thirty years' peace: Hdt. 7.148.4–149.1. Note Paus. 3.4.1, who intimates that the Argives lost over 5,000 men; Polyaen. *Strat.* 8.33, who asserts that they lost more than 7,000 men; and Plut. *Mor.* 245d, who claims that they lost 7,777 men.

30. Contingent said to approach city walls: Socrates *FGrH* 310 F6. Telesilla rallies old men,

the young, women, and servants: Plut. *Mor.* 245c–f. See also 223b–c, Paus. 2.20.8–10, Polyaen. *Strat.* 8.33, Clem. Al. *Strom.* 4.19.120.3–4. Oracle and achievement of Argive women: Hdt. 6.77.2.

31. Argive *doûloi* take over: Hdt. 6.83.1. *Períoikoi* admitted to ruling order: Arist. *Pol.* 1303a6–8 with Detlef Lotze, *Metaxu Eleutherôn kai Doulôn: Studien zur Rechtsstellung unfreier Landbevölkerung in Griechenland bis zum 4. Jahrhundert v. Chr.* (Berlin: Akadmie Verlag, 1959), 8–9, 53–54, 79. Plutarch, following Socrates of Argos *FGrH* 310 F6, resolves difference—widows and girls marry *períoikoi: Mor.* 245f. See Detlef Lotze, "Zur Verfassung von Argos nach der Schlacht bei Sepeia," *Chiron* 1 (1971): 95–109. For other views on the character of the outsiders admitted to the ruling order: see Ronald F. Willetts, "The Servile Interregnum at Argos," *Hermes* 87:4 (December 1959): 495–506; Forrest, "Themistokles and Argos," 222–26; Tomlinson, *Argos and the Argolid,* 97–100; Antony Andrewes, "Argive *Perioikoi,*" in *"Owls to Athens": Essays on Classical Subjects Presented to Sir Kenneth Dover,* ed. E. M. Craik (Oxford: Clarendon Press, 1990), 171–78; Charalambos Kritzas, "Aspects de la vie politique et économique d'Argos au Ve siècle avant J.-C.," in *Polydipsion Argos: Argos de la fin des palais mycéniens à la constitution de l'État classique,* ed. Marcel Piérart (Athens: École française d'Athènes, 1992), 231–40 (esp. 232–34); Marcel Piérart, "L'Attitude d'Argos à l'égard des autres cités d'Argolide," in *The Polis as an Urban Centre and as a Political Community,* ed. Mogens Herman Hansen (Copenhagen: Munksgaard, 1997), 321–51 (esp. 327–31); Eric W. Robinson, *The First Democracies: Early Popular Government outside Athens* (Stuttgart: Steiner Verlag, 1997), 82–88; and Cinzia S. Bearzot, "Argo nel V secolo: Ambizioni egemoniche, crisi interne, condizionamenti esterni," and Paolo A. Tuci, "Il Regime politico di Argo e le sue istituzioni tra fine VI e fine V secolo a.C.: Verso un'instabile democrazia," in *Argo: Una Demcrazia diversa,* ed. Cinzia S. Bearzot and Franca Landucci Gattinoni (Milan: Vita e pensiero, 2006), 105–46 (esp. 106–22), 209–71 (at 216–38). Evidence for mid-fifth-century tribal reform: *SEG* XXIX 361, XXXIII 295, XXXIV 295, XXXV 273, XLI 282, 284, 288, 291; and Thuc. 5.59.5, 72.4 with Michael Wörrle, *Untersuchungen zur Verfassungsgeschichte von Argos im 5. Jahrhundert vor Christus* (dissertation; Nuremberg: University of Erlangen-Nuremberg, 1964), passim (esp. 101–32); Andrewes, *HCT,* IV 121–23; Kritzas, "Aspects de la vie politique et économique d'Argos au Ve siècle avant J.-C.," 231–40; Piérart, "L'Attitude d'Argos à l'égard des autres cités d'Argolide," 332–36; Hartmut Leppin, "Argos: Eine griechische Demokratie des fünften Jahrhunderts v. Chr.," *Ktema* 24 (1999): 297–312 (esp. 297–303); and Marcel Piérart, "Argos: Une Autre Démocratie," in *Polis and Politics: Studies in Ancient Greek History Presented to Mogens Herman Hansen on His Sixtieth Birthday* (Copenhagen: Museum Tusculanum Press, 2000), 297–314 (esp. 307–10). Note also Eric W. Robinson, *Democracy beyond Athens: Popular Government in the Greek Classical Age* (Cambridge: Cambridge University Press, 2011), 6–21 (esp. 6–9). For the tribal reforms that took place elsewhere, see Rahe, *SR,* Chapter 4, n. 16.

32. Argive neutrality: Hdt. 7.145.2, 148–51, 9.12. Sicyon, Phlius, Epidaurus, Troezen, Hermione, and Aegina in Hellenic League: 7.202, 8.1, 42.1, 43, 72, 9.28–30, 85.2–3. Mycenae at Thermopylae, and Mycenae (*IACP* no. 353) and Tiryns (*IACP* no. 356) at Plataea: 7.202, 9.28.4, 31.3. Prior close connection between Mycenae, Tiryns, and Argos and dependence early on of the second and perhaps also the first on the last: Piérart, "L'Attitude d'Argos à l'égard des autres cités d'Argolide," 334–36.

33. Sons of the slain: Hdt. 6.83.

34. The case is made by Forrest, "Themistokles and Argos," 221–41. Note also Forrest, "Pausanias and Themistokles Again," 115–20 (esp. 119, n. 2).

35. Lacedaemon promotes oligarchy: consider Hdt. 5.92α.1, Polyaen. *Strat.* 2.10.3, Thuc. 5.81, Xen. *Hell.* 5.2.7 in light of Thuc. 1.18.1 and Arist. *Pol.* 1307b19–23, and see 1296a32–35. This, for example, is what Cleomenes attempted at Athens in the last decade of the sixth century: see Rahe, *PC,* Chapter 2.

36. Athens promotes democracy: [Xen.] *Ath. Pol.* 1.14, 3.10–11; Arist. *Pol.* 1296a32–35, 1307b19–23. See Lys. 2.55–56; Isoc. 4.103–6, 12.68; Diod. 12.27.1–2; Xen. *Hell.* 3.4.7. Note Meiggs, *AE,* 112–16, and Robinson, *Democracy beyond Athens,* 137–40, 188–200.

37. Hegemonic regime preferences and civil wars: Thuc. 3.82.1. Note Arist. *Pol.* 1296a32–35, 1307b19–23.

38. Cimon's Alcmeonid wife: Plut. *Cim.* 4.10, 16.1. The identity of the Megacles in question is uncertain: see Wesley E. Thompson, "Euryptolemos," *TAPhA* 100 (1969): 583–86, and Davies, *APF* nos. 8429, IX–XII, and 9688, VIII. Aristocratic consolidation: Sally C. Humphreys, "Public and Private Interests in Classical Athens," *CJ* 73:2 (December 1977–January 1978): 97–104 (at 99–100), reprinted in Humphreys, *The Family, Women and Death: Comparative Studies* (London: Routledge and Kegan Paul, 1983), 22–32 (at 25–26). Cf. Stesimbrotos of Thasos *FGrH* 106 F6 and Plut. *Per.* 29.2 (which should be read alongside Arist. *Ath. Pol.* 26.1) with Alec Blamire, "Commentary," in Plutarch *Life of Kimon,* ed. and trans. Alec Blamire (London: Institute of Classical Studies, 1989), 163–65, and consider Robert D. Cromey, "The Mysterious Woman of Kleitor: Some Corrections to a Manuscript Once in Plutarch's Possession," *AJPh* 112:1 (Spring 1991): 87–101 (at 87–99). Note also Rhodes, *CAAP,* 324–28.

39. On Pindar in particular, see Henry Theodore Wade-Gery, "Thucydides the Son of Mele-sias: A Study of Periklean Policy," *JHS* 52:2 (1932): 205–27 (esp. 208–15), reprinted in Wade-Gery, *EGH,* 239–70 (esp. 243–52), with Forrest, "Themistokles and Argos," 222–23, 228–29, 232.

40. Aristeides' role: Arist. *Ath. Pol.* 41.2 (read in light of his depiction as a popular leader both at 23.2–24 and at Plut. *Arist.* 22.1). Cf., however, Plut. *Cim.* 10.8. Themistocles also: Arist. *Ath. Pol.* 25–27 with R. G. Lewis, "Themistokles and Ephialtes," *CQ* n. s. 47:2 (1997): 358–62. Even if the pairing of Themistocles and Ephialtes in Arist. *Ath. Pol.* 25 is a slip and the pairing should be Pericles and Ephialtes, the slip itself is suggestive. Note Plut. *Per.* 9.5, 10.7–8 with the subtle allusion in Xen. *Mem.* 3.5.19–21, and see Rhodes, *CAAP,* 311–12, and Podlecki, *PHC,* 46–54. It is also, I think, telling that Aristeides refrained from attacking his onetime rival when Cimon and his allies brought Themistocles to trial: Plut. *Arist.* 25.10. Cf., however, Samons, *PCH,* 82–83.

41. Lacedaemon without walls: Thuc. 1.10.2.

42. Epigraphic evidence for democracy at Elis: Lilian H. Jeffery, *The Local Scripts of Archaic Greece: A Study of the Origin of the Greek Alphabet and Its Development from the Eighth to the Fifth Centuries B.C.,* rev. ed. with a supplement by Alan W. Johnston (Oxford: Clarendon Press, 1990), 216–21 (esp. nos. 4–6), with James L. O'Neil, *The Origins and Development of Ancient Greek Democracy* (Lanham, MD: Rowman & Littlefield, 1995), 32–33, 38–39, and Robinson, *The First Democracies,* 108–11, and *Democracy beyond Athens,* 28–33. Elean empire: Strabo 8.3.30, 33; Sophie Minon, *Les Inscriptions éléennes dialectales (VIe–IIe siècle avant J.-C.)* (Geneva: Droz, 2007), I Nos. 5, 10, and 16; and *IG* I³ 83 = O&R no. 165 = Thuc. 5.47, with Joachim Ebert and Peter Siewert, "Eine archaische Bronzeurkunde aus Olympia mit Vorschriften für Ringkämpfer und Kampfrichter," in Ebert, *Agonismata: Kleine philologische Schriften zur Literatur, Geschichte und Kultur der Antike,* ed. Joachim Ebert, Rainer Jakobi, Wolfgang Luppe, and Michael Hillgriber (Stuttgart: Teubner, 1997), 200–236; James Roy, "The *Perioikoi* of Elis," in *The Polis as an Urban Centre and as a Political Community,* 282–320, and "The Nature and Extent of Elean Power in the Western Peloponnese," in *Forme sovrapoleiche e interpoleiche di organizzazione nel mondo greco antico,* ed. Mario Lombardo and Flavia Frisone (Galatina: Congedo Editore, 2008), 293–302; and James Capreedy, "A League within a League: The Preservation of the Elean Symmachy," *CW* 101:4 (Summer 2008): 485–503 (esp. 487–93). Synoecism and date: Leandros *FGrH* 492 F13, Diod. 11.54.1, Strabo 8.3.2, Paus. 5.4.3 with Mauro Moggi, *I Sinecismi interstatali greci I: Dalle Origini al 338 a. C.* (Pisa: Marlin, 1976), 157–66, and Nicholas F. Jones, *Public Organization in Ancient Greece: A Documentary Study* (Philadelphia: American Philosophical Society, 1987), 142–45. Majority of cities in what came to be called Triphylia seized and sacked: Hdt. 4.148.4 with Thomas Heine Nielsen, "Was Eutaia a *Polis*? A Note on Xenophon's Use of the Term *Polis* in the *Hellenika,*" in *Studies in the Ancient Greek Polis,* ed. Mogens Herman Hansen and Kurt Raaflaub (Stuttgart: Franz Steiner Verlag, 1995), 83–102 (at 88). The synoecism did not eventuate in the fortification of Elis at this time, however: Xen. *Hell.* 3.2.27. Whether the synoecism was but one aspect of a larger political reform is by no means clear. For a thorough discussion of the evidence and a full citation of the secondary literature, see James Roy, "The Synoikism of Elis," in *Even More Studies in the Ancient Greek Polis,* ed. Thomas Heine Nielsen (Stuttgart: Franz Steiner Verlag, 2002), 249–64.

43. Strabo on the synoecisms at Elis, Mantineia, and Tegea: 8.3.2 with Forrest, "Themistokles and Argos," 229, n. 8; Moggi, *I Sinecismi interstatali greci,* 131–56; and Jones, *Public Organization*

in Ancient Greece, 132–35, 139–42. Consider Paus. 8.45.1, where Caryae is listed among the Tegean demes, in light of Vitruvius' assertion (1.1.5) that the citizens of that *pólis* medized during the Persian Wars and were punished in the aftermath. Democracy at Mantineia in 421: Thuc. 5.29.1. Evidence for association between synoecism and democracy and between dioecism and oligarchy: Xen. *Hell.* 5.2.7, 6.5.3–5. Note also Isoc. 4.126, 8.100; Ephorus *FGrH* 70 F79; Polyb. 4.27.6, 38.2.11; Diod. 15.5.3–5, 12.1–2; Paus. 8.8.9, 9.14.4; Aristid. *Or.* 46.287 (Dindorf).

44. Mantineia's moderate democracy: Arist. *Pol.* 1318b6–27. Note Ael. *VH* 2.22. Whether this bears on the question of synoecism is not clear. Cf. Andrewes, "Sparta and Arcadia," 1–5; Forrest, "Themistokles and Argos," 221–41, and "Pausanias and Themistokles Again," 115–20; and Adshead, *Politics of the Archaic Peloponnese*, 86–103, whose reconstructions are attractive, with Wörrle, *Untersuchungen zur Verfassungsgeschichte von Argos im 5. Jahrhundert vor Christus*, 101–32 (esp. 120–22), and James L. O'Neil, "The Exile of Themistokles and Democracy in the Peloponnese," *CQ* n.s. 31:2 (1981): 335–46, who rightly judge them unproven, and see Robinson, *The First Democracies*, 113–14, and *Democracy beyond Athens*, 34–40. On the question of synoecism, note also Stephen and Hilary Hodkinson, "Mantineia and the Mantinike: Settlement and Society in a Greek Polis," *ABSA* 76 (1981): 239–96.

45. Chios as oligarchy: Thuc. 8.24.4. Samos also: 1.115.2–5. Mytilene as well: 3.27–28, 47.2–3. Later, after Oenophyta in 458, when the admirers of Themistocles were in charge at Athens, the Athenians cooperated with oligarchies in Boeotia; and, at some point, they did so with an oligarchy in Miletus: [Xen.] *Ath. Pol.* 3.11. It was easy, in retrospect, to exaggerate Athens' commitment to the propagation of democracy: cf. Lys. 2.55–56 and Isoc. 4.103–6, 12.68, with Arist. *Ath. Pol.* 24.2, and see *ATL*, III 149–54, and Roger Brock, "Did the Athenian Empire Promote Democracy?" in *Interpreting the Athenian Empire*, ed. John T. Ma, Nikolaos Papazarkadas, and Robert Parker (London: Duckworth, 2009), 149–66.

46. Cf. Forrest, "Themistocles at Argos," 221–32, and "Pausanias and Themistokles Again," 115–20 (esp. 119, n. 2), with Lewis, *OFPW*, 71–78 (at 73, n. 6), reprinted in Lewis, *SPGNEH*, 9–21 (at 12, n. 6), and see Piérart, "L'Attitude d'Argos à l'égard des autres cités d'Argolide," 327–40. Note also Tomlinson, *Argos and the Argolid*, 102–9.

47. Central importance of reconsolidation of the Argolid: Paus. 8.27.1 with Mauro Moggi, "I Sinecismi et le annessioni territoriali di Argo nel V secolo a. C.," *ASNP* 3rd ser. 4:4 (1974): 1249–63; Piérart, "L'Attitude d'Argos à l'égard des autres cités d'Argolide," 321–51; and Bearzot, "Argo nel V secolo," 106–22. As this makes clear, there was more at stake in this struggle than relative rank: cf., however, Lendon, *SoW*, 89–90.

48. Main thoroughfare: see Chapter 4, note 58, below.

49. Battle at Tegea with Argos and Tegea: Hdt. 9.33–35, Paus. 3.11.5–7 with Bearzot, "Argo nel V secolo," 114–18. Roads linking Laconia and Messenia: Giannēs A. Pikoulas, *Tò Hodikò Díktuo tēs Lakōnýkēs* (Athens: Ēoros, 2012), 110–36, 392–435, 456–59, 492–502, 562–64. Two kings responsible for the system of roads within the Spartan realm: Hdt. 6.57.4. For further discussion and a more extensive citation of the secondary literature, see Rahe, *SR*, Chapter 4 (with note 25).

50. Victory at Tegea over Argos and Tegea: Hdt. 9.33–35. Celebration of the Hellenes and the Athenians who fought at Tegea: Simonides F122–23 (Diehl). Simonides an associate of Themistocles: Plut. *Them.* 5.6–7, Cic. *Fin.* 2.32.104. Note Anthony J. Podlecki, "Simonides: 480," *Historia* 17:3 (July 1968): 257–75.

51. Date of Simonides' death: *Marmor Parium FGrH* 239 A 57.

52. With regard to the chronology suggested here, everything turns on the date of Pausanias' death. To the compelling argument articulated by Mary E. White, "Some Agiad Dates: Pausanias and His Sons," *JHS* 84 (1964): 140–52, concerning the likelihood that Pausanias was unmarried in the 480s and very early 470s and that he was still siring sons in the early 460s, I would add that, unless he had a wife with him when he was abroad (which seems unlikely), he had no opportunity to sire more than one legitimate child in the period stretching from the spring of 478 to his time of his recall from Colonae ca. 470. Cf. Frost, *PT*, 190–91, with James Allan Stewart Evans, "The Medism of Pausanias: Two Versions," *Antichthon* 22 (1988): 1–11 (at 7), reprinted with added material in Evans, *The Beginnings of History: Herodotus and the Persian Wars* (Toronto: University

of Toronto Press, 2006), 305–20 (at 313–14), who rightly asserts that White's argument "has never been refuted."

53. Pausanias' demise: Thuc. 1.131.2–135.1; Nep. *Paus.* 3.4–5.5; Diod. 11.44–45; Paus. 3.14.1, 17.7–9; Plut. *Mor.* 560f; Aristodemus *FGrH* 104 F8.2–4.

54. Scholarly speculation: Józef Wolski, "Pausanias et le problème de la politique Spartiate (années 480–470)," *Eos* 47 (1954–1955): 75–94; Adolf Lippold, "Pausanias von Sparta und die Perser," *RhM* 108:4 (1965): 320–41; Raphael Sealey, "The Origins of the Delian League," in *ASI*, 233–55 (at 248–49); Charles W. Fornara, "Some Aspects of the Career of Pausanias of Sparta," *Historia* 15:3 (August 1966): 257–71; Mabel Lang, "Scapegoat Pausanias," *CJ* 63:2 (November 1967): 79–85, reprinted in Lang, *Thucydidean Narrative and Discourse*, ed. Jeffrey S. Rusten and Richard Hamilton (Ann Arbor: University of Michigan Press, 2011), 37–47; Peter J. Rhodes, "Thucydides on Pausanias and Themistocles," *Historia* 19:4 (November 1970): 387–400; Alec Blamire, "Pausanias and Persia," *GRBS* 11:4 (Winter 1970): 295–305; George L. Cawkwell, "The Fall of Themistocles," in *Auckland Classical Essays Presented to E. M. Blaiklock*, ed. B. F. Harris (Oxford: Oxford University Press, 1970), 39–58, reprinted in Cawkwell, *CC*, 95–113; John F. Lazenby, "Pausanias, Son of Kleombrotos," *Hermes* 103:2 (1975): 235–51; Henry D. Westlake, "Thucydides on Pausanias and Themistocles—A Written Source?" *CQ* n.s. 27:1 (May 1977): 95–110, reprinted in Westlake, *Studies in Thucydides and Greek History* (Bristol: Bristol Classical Press, 1989), 1–18; Antony Andrewes, "Spartan Imperialism?" in *Imperialism in the Ancient World*, 91–102 (at 91–95); Andre S. Schieber, "Thucydides and Pausanias," *Athenaeum* 58 (1980): 396–405; Frost, *PT*, 193–99; Félix Bourriot, "Pausanias fils de Cleombrotos: Vainqueur de Platées," *L'Information Historique* 44 (1982): 1–16; Evans, "The Medism of Pausanias: Two Versions," 1–11, reprinted with added material in Evans, *The Beginnings of History*, 305–20; Badian, *Outbreak*, 52–54, reprinted in Badian, *FPP*, 130–32; Marr, *Commentary*, 136; and Victor Parker, "Pausanias the Spartiate as Depicted by Charon of Lampsacus and Herodotus," *Philologus* 149:1 (2005): 3–11.

55. Helot suppliants dragged from Taenarum: Thuc. 1.128.1 with Critias ap. Lib. *Or.* 25.63 and Borimir Jordan, "The Ceremony of the Helots in Thucydides IV, 80," *AC* 59 (1990): 37–69 (esp. 45–50).

56. Letters exchanged: Thuc. 1.128.7, 129.2–3.

57. See A. Ten Eyk Olmstead, "A Persian Letter in Thucydides," *American Journal of Semitic Languages and Literature* 49:2 (January 1933): 154–61.

58. Pseudepigraphical letters from Themistocles to Pausanias: [Them.] *Ep. Gr.* 2, 14.741–42, 754 (Hercher) = [Them.] *Ep.* 2, 14 (Doenges). Close friends (and presumably guest-friends): Diod. 11.54.3–4, which should be read in light of Gabriel Herman, *Ritualised Friendship and the Greek City* (Cambridge: Cambridge University Press, 1987), 148. Simonides praises Leonidas, Themistocles, and Pausanias but not Cimon: Podlecki, "Simonides: 480," 257–75.

59. Cimon and Alcmaeon denounce, Leobotes prosecutes Themistocles: consider Arist. *Ath. Pol.* 25.3; Diod. 11.54.2–6; Plut. *Arist.* 25.10, *Them.* 23, *Mor.* 605e, 805c; Hyp. Isoc. 7; and [Them.] *Ep. Gr.* 8.747 (Hercher) = [Them.] *Ep.* 8.1–2 (Doenges) in light of Hdt. 1.65, 7.204, and Peter J. Bicknell, "Leobotes Alkmeonos and Alkmeon Aristonymou," in Bicknell, *Studies in Athenian Politics and Genealogy* (Wiesbaden: Franz Steiner Verlag, 1972), 54–63 (esp. 58). Then, see John F. Barrett, "The Downfall of Themistocles," *GRBS* 18:4 (Winter 1977): 291–305, and "Alcmeon, the Enemy of Themistocles," *AW* 1 (1978): 67–69; and Frost, *PT*, 193–99, along with Edwin M. Carawan, "*Eisangelia* and *Euthyna*: The Trials of Miltiades, Themistocles, and Cimon," *GRBS* 28:2 (Summer 1987): 167–208 (esp. 190–91, 196–200). Cf. Marr, *Commentary*, 133–38, and Keaveney, *The Life and Journey of Athenian Statesman Themistocles*, 105–8, with Peter Green, "Commentary," in *DS*, 114–16, nn. 203–5.

60. Themistocles helps his friends: Plut. *Mor.* 807a–b. Ethos of *xenía*: Hdt. 7.237.2–3 with Herman, *Ritualised Friendship and the Greek City*, passim. Note also Lynette G. Mitchell, *Greeks Bearing Gifts: The Public Use of Private Relationships in the Greek World, 435–323 BC* (Cambridge: Cambridge University Press, 2002).

61. Incriminating correspondence: Thuc. 1.135.2, Diod. 11.54.2–55.8, Plut. *Them.* 23 (where the chronology is muddled), Aristodemus *FGrH* 104 F10.1. Themistocles' motive: Fornara/Samons, *ACP*, 126–27.

62. Themistocles' flight, its timing, his arrival in Anatolia, news of Xerxes' death: Charon of Lampsacus *FGrH* 262 F11, Thuc. 1.136.1–137.3, Nep. *Them.* 8.2–9.1, Diod. 11.55.4–56.4, Plut. *Them.* 24.1–26.1, Polyaen. *Strat.* 1.30.7, Aristodemus *FGrH* 104 F8.2–5 with Robert Flacelière, "Sur quelques points obscurs de la vie de Thémistocle," *REA* 55:1–2 (January–June 1953): 5–28; Philip Deane, *Thucydides' Dates, 465–431 B.C.* (Don Mills, Ontario: Longman Canada, 1972), 9–13; Forrest, "Pausanias and Themistokles Again," 115–20; Marcus P. Milton, "The Date of Thucydides' Synchronism of the Siege of Naxos with Themistokles' Flight," *Historia* 28:3 (3rd Quarter, 1979): 257–75; Ron K. Unz, "The Chronology of the Pentekontaetia," *CQ* n.s. 36:1 (1986): 68–85 (at 69–73); Victor Parker, "The Chronology of the Pentecontaetia from 465 to 456," *Athenaeum* 81 (1993): 129–47 (at 130–33); Marr, *Commentary*, 142–55; W. Kendrick Pritchett, "Thucydides' Pentekontaetia: 5. Naxos, Thasos, and Themistokles' Flight," in Pritchett, *Thucydides' Pentekontaetia and Other Essays* (Leiden: Brill, 1995), 81–94; Briant, *CA*, 563; Keaveney, *The Life and Journey of Athenian Statesman Themistocles*, 23–26, 114–16; and Green, "Commentary," 119–20, n. 213. Death of Hiero ca. 467: Diod. 11.38.7, 66.4. If I follow Flacelière, Forrest, Pritchett, Marr, and Briant, rather than Deane, Milton, Unz, Parker, Keaveney, and, I presume, Green in preferring the testimony of the best manuscript of Plutarch to that of the surviving manuscripts of Thucydides and in supposing that Themistocles slipped past the Athenians besieging Thasos, not Naxos, it is because I believe that what we can surmise concerning the chronology of this period requires it. The sequence of events in Thucydides is clear. The revolt of Naxos preceded the battle of Eurymedon, which came before the revolt of Thasos. The first of these three events began at some point after 476. Deane, Milton, Unz, and Parker to the contrary notwithstanding, it is not likely that these three events were bunched together in and after 466; and, Keaveney to the contrary notwithstanding, the revolt of Naxos is not likely to have continued for more than two or three years, if that. Eurymedon is likely to have taken place in 469, the year before Cimon and his fellow generals were asked to judge the tragic competition; and the beginning of the revolt at Thasos can be dated to 465, the year Xerxes is known to have died. Unless we are to suppose that it took a number of years for Themistocles to journey from Argos to Anatolia via Corcyra, the court of Admetus in Epirus, and Pydna in Macedon—as Marr and Green are inclined to suppose—this journey must be dated to 466 and 465, as Milton, Unz, Parker, Pritchett, and Keaveney point out. This chronology also fits what we can surmise from the investigations of White, "Some Agiad Dates," 140–52, as they pertain to the timing of Pausanias' return to Sparta from Byzantium and Colonae, the date of his death, and the subsequent discovery of his correspondence with Themistocles. The fact that, in the Aegean, especially in the summer, northerlies are far more common than southerlies does not rule out Themistocles' ship having encountered a sirocco on this particular occasion. Nor is there any compelling reason to suppose that he traveled in the summer rather than in the stormy months of winter, and, as I intimate in the text, nothing rules out the supposition that the merchant captain in question was making his way from Pydna in the direction of Asia Minor by way of one or more northern ports of call: cf. Frank J. Frost, "Thucydides i.137.2," *CR* n.s. 12:1 (March 1962): 15–16, and *PT*, 206–8, with White, "Some Agiad Dates," 148, n. 32, and see Pritchett, "Thucydides' Pentekontaetia: 5. Naxos, Thasos, and Themistokles' Flight," 55–92.

63. Themistocles in Aeolis: Plut. *Them.* 26.1–2. Cf. Thuc. 1.37.2 and Nep. *Them.* 8.7, who have him land at Ephesus. Themistocles cannot have contacted or journeyed to the Great King without the help of a satrap: Briant, *CA*, 563, is right to draw attention to the report in one of the pseudepigraphical letters attributed to Themistocles—[Them.] *Ep. Gr.* 20.760 (Hercher) = [Them.] *Ep.* 20.27–28 (Doenges)—that Artabazus (in whose satrapy Cumae and Aeolis more generally were located) was the intermediary and that he supplied the Athenian with a retinue. Themistocles accompanied to Susa by a Persian, sends letter ahead, takes time off to study Persian, then formally presents himself at court: Thuc. 1.137.3–138.2, Nep. *Them.* 9.1–10.1. Cf. the fanciful tale told by Ephorus, who has him make his way to Susa in the guise of a concubine and meet with Xerxes: Diod. 11.56.4–57.6, Plut. *Them.* 26.3–27.1 with Frost, *PT*, 213–14. Meeting with Artabanus: Phanias F26 (Wehrli) ap. Plut. *Them.* 27.2–8, read in light of Ctesias *FGrH* 688 F13.33–F14.34, and Diod. 11.69.1–5. Xerxes' firstborn son Darius an adolescent, Artaxerxes a child: Just. *Epit.* 3.1. Xerxes' uncle Artabanus: Hdt. 4.83, 7.10–18, 46.1–53.1, 8.54.1. Megabyzus' grandfather co-conspirator of Darius: 3.70. Father's reconquest of Babylon: 3.153–60. Megabyzus son-in-law of Xer-

xes: Ctesias *FGrH* 688 F13.26. Accompanies Xerxes as marshal on march into Greece: Hdt. 7.82, 121.3. Thwarts Artabanus' coup d'état: Ctesias *FGrH* 688 F14.33. Cf. Diod. 11.69.5–6, 71.1. Challenge mounted by Hystaspes: Ctesias *FGrH* 688 F14.34. Roxanes' introduction: Plut. *Them.* 29.1–2. Cf. Lewis, *SP,* 19, n. 96; Frost, *PT,* 214–15; and Marr, *Commentary,* 150, who believe that the Chiliarch Artabanus cannot have survived the assassination of Xerxes by more than a few days (as Diodorus' highly compressed account could be taken to imply), with Manetho *FGrH* 609 F2–3C, p. 50, who testifies that he ruled Persia for seven months, and with Ctesias *FGrH* 688 F14.33, which presupposes a considerable passage of time. Honor and reward: Thuc. 1.138.2, 4–5, Nep. *Them.* 10.1–4, Diod. 11.57.6–7, Plut. *Them.* 29.5–32.4.

64. Little assembly: Xen. *Hell.* 3.3.8 with Rahe, *SR,* Chapter 2, note 39.

Part II. Yokefellows No More

Epigraph: Ion of Chios F76 (Leurini) = *TrGF* 19 F63 = F107 (Blumenthal) ap. Sext. Emp. *Math.* 2.24.

1. Earthquake and aftershocks: Thuc. 1.101.2, 128.1, 2.27.2, 3.54.5, 4.56.2. Date: Paus. 4.24.5–6, Plut. *Cim.* 16.4. Cf. Diod. 11.63.1 and Schol. Ar. *Lys.* 1144, which date the earthquake and the attendant revolt to 469/8, with David M. Lewis, "Chronological Notes," in *CAH* V² 499–500, who makes sense of their error. Five houses left standing: Plut. *Cim.* 16.4–5, Cic. *De div.* 1.112, Pliny *NH* 2.191, Ael. *VH* 6.7, Polyaen. *Strat.* 1.41.3. Twenty thousand Lacedaemonians dead with more than half of all the Spartiates killed: Diod. 11.63.1–3, 15.66.4. Helot revolt: Thuc. 1.101.2, 2.27.2, 3.54.5, 4.56.2; Critias ap. Lib. *Or.* 25.63; Diod. 11.63.4–64.1; Plut. *Cim.* 16.6–7; Paus. 1.29.8, 3.11.8, 4.24.5–6. Battles and losses: Hdt. 9.33–35, 64.2. See also Plut. *Lyc.* 28.12. For the impact on Lacedaemon, see Ludwig Ziehen, "Das spartanische Bevölkerungsproblem," *Hermes* 68:2 (1933): 218–37; W. H. Porter, "The Antecedents of the Spartan Revolution of 243 B.C.," *Hermathena* 24:49 (1935): 1–15; and Timothy Doran, *Spartan Oliganthropia* (Leiden: Brill, 2018), passim (esp. 22–29). Cf. Paul Cartledge, "Seismicity in Spartan Society," *LCM* 1 (1976): 25–28, and *Sparta and Lakonia: A Regional History, 1300–362 B.C.* (London: Routledge & Kegan Paul, 1979), 221–22, with Mogens Herman Hansen, "Demographic Reflections on the Number of Athenian Citizens, 451–309 B.C.," *AJAH* 7 (1982): 172–89 (at 173).

2. See Chapter 4, below.

3. Mycenae at Thermopylae and Plataea: *ML* no. 27 with Hdt. 7.202, 9.28.4, 31.3; Diod. 11.65.2; Paus. 5.23.2, 10.20.2. Claim on Argive Heraeum: Diod. 11.65.2. Actual control: *SEG* XIII 246. In this connection, note Cleomenes' sacrifice at the Heraeum after the battle of Sepeia: Hdt. 6.81. Mycenaean rivalry with Cleonae (*IACP* no. 351) over Nemean Games: cf. Pind. *Nem.* 4.17, 10.42 and Paus. 2.15.2–3 with Diod. 11.65.2. Argives' preoccupation with and their conquest and destruction of Mycenae: Diod. 11.65; Strabo 8.6.19; Paus. 2.15.4, 16.5–6, 5.23.3, 7.25.5–6, 8.27.1. Cleonaeans and Tegeans present among the Argives' allies: Strabo 8.6.19. Tenea was much closer to Mycenae than was Tegea. But given the fact that the Argives had supported the Tegeans earlier at the battle of Tegea and that the reported Tegean presence at Mycenae makes sense as a matter of reciprocal obligation, I see no reason to follow Marcel Piérart, "Deux notes sur l'histoire de Mycènes (Ve, III/IIes)," in *Serta Leodiensia secunda* (Liège: Université de Liège, 1992), 377–87 (at 377–82), in emending *Tegeatōn* on the presumption that Strabo wrote *Teneatōn.* Cf. W. G. G. Forrest, "Themistokles and Argos," *CQ* n.s. 10:2 (November 1960): 221–41, at 230 (with n. 5).

4. Dipaea: Hdt. 9.33–35; Paus. 3.11.5–7, 8.8.6, 45.2.

5. Sons of the slain, struggle with Tiryns: Hdt. 6.83. See also Paus. 2.25.8. Argive reorientation ca. 460: Chapter 4, note 60, below.

6. All of the Arcadians, apart from the Mantineians, with Tegea at Dipaea: Hdt. 9.33–35; Paus. 3.11.7, 8.8.6, 45.2.

7. Location of Dipaea: Paus. 8.30.1 with Thomas Heine Nielsen, *Arkadia and Its Poleis in the Archaic and Classical Periods* (Göttingen: Vandenhoeck & Ruprecht, 2002), 553–54 and *IACP* no. 268. Location of Arcadian Orchomenos: *IACP* no. 286. Location of Phigaleia: *IACP* no. 292. Routes within Laconia: Giannēs A. Pikoulas, *Tò Hodikò Díktuo tēs Lakōnýkēs* (Athens: Ēoros, 2012), pas-

sim (esp. 54–97, 110–29, 450–59). Routes through and within Arcadia: William Loring, "Some Ancient Routes in the Peloponnese," *JHS* 15 (1895): 25–89 (esp. 75–77); Gomme, *HCT*, IV 32, and Yannis (Giannēs) A. Pikoulas, "The Road-Network of Arcadia," in *DAA*, 248–319 (esp. 258, 261–63, 272, 274–80, 293–96, 302). See also Giannēs A. Pikoulas, "Tò Hodikò díktuo tēs kentrikēs Arkadías," in *Praktikà toû 4. Diethnoûs Sinedríou Peloponnesiakōn Spoudōn* (Athens: Peloponnesiaka Supplement No. 19:2, 1992–93), 201–6, reprinted in Giannēs A. Pikoulas, *Arkadía: Sullogē meletōn* (Athens: Ēoros, 2002), 359–66. Material signs of Lacedaemonian hegemony in south-central Arcadia: Catherine Morgan, "Cultural Subzones in Early Iron Age and Archaic Arcadia," in *DAA*, 382–456 (esp. 400–406).

8. See Roderick T. Williams, *The Confederate Coinage of the Arcadians in the Fifth Century BCE* (New York: American Numismatic Society, 1965), with Colin M. Kraay, *Archaic and Classical Greek Coins* (London: Methuen, 1976), 97–98, who redates the issue to the period after the Persian Wars, and with David M. Lewis, "Mainland Greece, 479–451 B.C.," in *CAH* V² 105, who points to Thuc. 5.47.6 and argues that a confederacy had been formed. For doubts as to the existence of such a confederacy, see Thomas Heine Nielsen, "Was There an Arcadian Confederacy in the Fifth Century B.C.?" in *More Studies in the Ancient Greek Polis,* ed. Mogens Herman Hansen and Kurt Raaflaub (Stuttgart: Franz Steiner Verlag, 1996), 39–61, and *Arkadia and Its Poleis in the Archaic and Classical Periods,* 113–57. Note Maria Pretzler, "Arcadia: Ethnicity and Politics in the Fifth and Fourth Centuries BCE," in *The Politics of Ethnicity and the Crisis of the Peloponnesian League,* ed. Peter Funke and Nino Luraghi (Washington, DC: Center for Hellenic Studies, 2009), 86–109. For an overview of the Arcadians and their land, see Thomas Heine Nielsen, "The Concept of Arcadia—The People, Their Land, and Their Organisation"; Mary E. Voyatzis, "The Role of Temple Building in Consolidating Arkadian Communities"; Madeleine Jost, "Les Schémas de peuplement de l'Arcadie aux époques archaïque et classique"; James Roy, "The Economies of Arcadia"; and Catherine Morgan, "Cultural Subzones in Early Iron Age and Archaic Arkadia," in *DAA*, 16–79, 130–68, 192–247, 320–456. Standard three-obol daily allowance: Thuc. 5.47.6, Xen. *Hell.* 5.2.21.

9. One file deep: Isoc. 6.99.

Chapter 4. A Parting of the Ways

Epigraph: Winston S. Churchill, *My Early Life: A Roving Commission,* 1930 (Glasgow: William Collins Sons, 1959), 235.

1. Rents, landslides, collapsing buildings, fate of ephebes: Plut. *Cim.* 16.4–5. See Strabo 8.5.7, Cic. *Div.* 1.12, Plin. *NH* 2.191. Collapse of buildings, many pinned in the debris: Diod. 11.63.1–2. Women and young children especially vulnerable: Ludwig Ziehen, "Das spartanische Bevölkerungsproblem," *Hermes* 68:2 (1933): 218–37, and W. H. Porter, "The Antecedents of the Spartan Revolution of 243 B.C.," *Hermathena* 24:49 (1935): 1–15.

2. Fourth year after Archidamus' succession as king: Plut. *Cim.* 16.4 with Chapter 1, note 57, above; and David M. Lewis, "Chronological Notes," in *CAH* V² 499–500. Sounds alarm, rallies compatriots against the helots: Diod. 11.63.4–6, Plut. *Cim.* 16.6–7, Polyaen. *Strat.* 1.41.3.

3. Ion hails Archidamus, praises Lacedaemon: Ion of Chios F90 (Leurini) = F27 (West) = F27 (Blumenthal) ap. Ath. 11. 463a–c, 496c and Ion of Chios F76 (Leurini) = *TrGF* 19 F63 = F107 (Blumenthal) ap. Sext. Emp. *Math.* 2.24 with George L. Huxley, "Ion of Chios," *GRBS* 6:1 (1965): 29–46 (at 31–33). Ion resided at Athens in this period; had ample contact with Cimon; and may well be the source for all of the anecdotes concerning this period that appear in Plutarch's biography of the man. If this is the case, as seems highly likely, there is reason to suspect that Ion accompanied Cimon on his first expedition to Lacedaemon in the immediate aftermath of the earthquake and the helot revolt: note Ion of Chios F105–7 (Leurini) = *FGrH* 329 F12–14 ap. Plut. *Cim.* 5.3, 9.1–6, 16.8–10; then consider Ion of Chios F132 (Leurini) ap. Plut. *Cim.* 17.1; and see the secondary literature cited in Chapter 2, note 40, above.

4. Thirty-five thousand helots accompany Spartiates to Boeotia: Hdt. 9.10.1, Plut. *Arist.* 10.8. Cf. Nino Luraghi, "Der Erdbebenaufstand und die Entstehung der messenischen Identität," in *Gab es das griechische Wunder? Griechenland zwischen dem Ende des 6. und der Mitte des 5.*

Jahrhunderts v. Chr., ed. Dietrich Papanfuss and Volker M. Strocka (Mainz: Ph. von Zabern, 2001), 279–301, who underestimates the degree to which the helots of Messenia already thought of themselves as a single people and were inclined to rebellion, but who correctly draws attention to the likely impact on the generation that rebelled in 465/4 of their experience at Plataea in 479. Earthquake and revolt blamed on sacrilege at Taenarum: Thuc. 1.128.1, Critias ap. Lib. *Or.* 25.63.

5. Messenians and some of the *períoikoi* join the rebellion: Plut. *Cim.* 16.7. See Thuc. 1.101.2.

6. Tegean-Mantineian hostility: Thuc. 5.65.4.

7. Around three thousand Mantineian hoplites: Diod. 12.78.4, Lys. 34.7. Cf., however, Stephen and Hilary Hodkinson, "Mantineia and the Mantinike: Settlement and Society in a Greek Polis," *ABSA* 76 (1981): 239–96, and Björn Forsén, "Population and Political Strength of Some Southeastern Arkadian *Poleis*," in *Further Studies in the Ancient Greek Polis*, ed. Pernille Flensted-Jensen (Stuttgart: Franz Steiner Verlag, 2000), 35–55 (at 36–51), who doubt that the territory of Mantineia was sufficient to enable it to field an army of three thousand hoplites. They may underestimate the contribution of pastoralism to the carrying capacity of the Mantinike. After all, like the rest of Arcadia, it was proverbially "rich in flocks." I am also inclined to suspect that the poor in Mantineia were systematically trained and deployed as hoplites, which would help explain why so many of them found service abroad as mercenaries. Consider Ath. 4.154d in conjunction with James Roy, "The Economies of Arkadia," and Catherine Morgan, "Cultural Subzones in Early Iron Age and Archaic Arkadia," in *DAA*, 320–81 (esp. 331–32, 340–56), 382–456 (at 431–32). But it is also possible that Lysias and Diodorus took into account Mantineia's subject allies, as I suggest above.

8. Agesilaus on help from Mantineia: Xen. *Hell.* 5.2.3. If Agesilaus' older brother Agis adopted a similar posture, it would explain why the Agiad king Pleistoanax, not Agis, was sent to chastise the Mantineians in 421: Thuc. 5.33.

9. Gratitude for the help provided by Aegina: Thuc. 2.27.2, 4.56.2.

10. Aeginetan forces at Salamis: Hdt. 8.46.1. Prize for valor: 8.93.1, 122. Aeginetan forces at Mycale and Plataea: 8.131, 132.2, 9.28.6, 31.4. Aeginetans man more ships than any city other than Athens: Paus. 2.29.5.

11. Aeginetan troop transports: Hdt. 6.76, 92.1–2.

12. General appeal to allies: Diod. 11.64.2.

13. Geopolitical dynamics of northeastern Peloponnesus; religious, cultural, and economic opposition between Argos and Corinth: Katherine M. Adshead, *Politics of the Archaic Peloponnese: The Transition from Archaic to Classical Politics* (Aldershot: Avebury, 1986), 1–66. For the course of the main road as it stretches from Argos to Hysiae and on to Tegea further south, see note 58, below. For the road system in this region as a whole, see Giannēs A. Pikoulas, *Tò Hodikò Díktuo kaì Ámyna: Ápo tēn Kórintho stò Árgos kaì tēn Arkadía* (Athens: Ēoros, 1995). For a supplement to the picture provided therein, see Yannis A. Lolos, *Land of Sikyon: Archaeology and History of a Greek City-State* (Princeton, NJ: American School of Classical Studies, 2011), 93–179.

14. Early archaic Corinthian alliance with Lacedaemon: consider Paus. 4.11.1, 8, in light of W. G. Forrest, "Colonisation and the Rise of Delphi," *Historia* 6:2 (April 1957): 160–75 (esp. 162, 167–68, 172–73). Later Spartan overthrow of Cypselid tyranny: Plut. *Mor.* 859c–d. On this, cf., however, Salmon, *WC*, 67–70, 229–30, who is (I think, unduly) skeptical. Then, consider his discussion of Corinth's involvement in the Peloponnesian League: ibid. 240–52.

15. Corinthian-Argive rivalry: Adshead, *Politics of the Archaic Peloponnese*, 67–103, and Cinzia S. Bearzot, "Argo nel V secolo: Ambizioni egemoniche, crisi interne, condizionamenti esterni," in *Argo: Una Demcrazia diversa*, ed. Cinzia S. Bearzot and Franca Landucci Gattinoni (Milan: Vita e pensiero, 2006), 105–46 (esp. 106–22).

16. Aggressiveness of Corinth vis-à-vis Cleonae: Plut. *Cim.* 17.2 with Lewis, *OFPW*, 71–78, reprinted in Lewis, *SPGNEH*, 9–21; and Adshead, *Politics of the Archaic Peloponnese*, 67–85. Main thoroughfare and more difficult road: note 58, below; Adshead, *Politics of the Archaic Peloponnese*, 1–18; and Pikoulas, *Tò Hodikò Díktyo kaì Ámyna*, 31–74. Cleonae presides over the Nemean Games: Pind. *Nem.* 4.17, 10.42, with Malcolm F. McGregor, "Cleisthenes of Sicyon and the Pan-

hellenic Festivals," *TAPhA* 72 (1941): 266–87 (at 277–78). Corinthians usurp presidency: *Hyp. Schol.* Pind. *Nem.*, in *Scholia vetera in Pindari carmina*, ed. A. B. Drachmann (Amsterdam: Adolf M. Hakkert, 1964), III 3, 5. See Catherine Morgan, "Debating Patronage: The Cases of Argos and Corinth," in *Pindar's Poetry, Patrons, and Festivals: From Archaic Greece to the Roman Empire*, ed. Simon Hornblower and Catherine Morgan (Oxford: Oxford University Press, 2007), 213–63 (esp. 257–61).

17. Makeup of Corinthian alliance: consider Thuc. 1.105–6, 108.5, 111.2, 114.1, 115.1; Plut. *Per.* 19.2; Diod. 11.79.3 in light of Thuc.1.27.2–28.1, 5.53, and see *SEG* XXXI 369 with A. James Holladay, "Sparta's Role in the First Peloponnesian War," *JHS* 97 (1977): 54–63 (esp. 57–59 with n. 24), reprinted in Holladay, *AFC*, 105–17 (esp. 109–12 with n. 24); Lewis, *OFPW*, 71–78 (esp. 73–76 with n. 26), reprinted in Lewis, *SPGNEH*, 9–21 (esp. 12–17 with n. 26); Audrey Griffin, *Sikyon* (Oxford: Clarendon Press, 1982), 62; and Lolos, *Land of Sikyon*, 65–66. Main road: Adshead, *Politics of the Archaic Peloponnese*, 1–18, and the material cited in note 58, below. Cities once in Argive orbit: Chapter 3, note 28, above. Participants in the Hellenic League: Chapter 3, note 32, above. Surviving Tirynthians flee to Epidaurus and Hermione, then settle at Halieis: consider Strabo 8.6.11 in light of the material cited in note 62, below.

18. Cleonae's alliance with Argos against Mycenae in 465/4: Strabo 8.6.19, Diod. 11.65.2–3, Paus. 1.29.7.

19. Seizure of Perachora: Nicholas G. L. Hammond, "The Heraeum at Perachora and Corinthian Encroachment," *ABSA* 49 (1954): 93–102, and Ronald P. Legon, *Megara: The Political History of a Greek City-State to 336 B.C.* (Ithaca, NY: Cornell University Press, 1981), 59–70. Megarians, with Argive help, defeat Corinthians in late archaic period: consider Paus. 6.19.12–14 in light of Alastair H. Jackson, "Argos' Victory over Corinth," *ZPE* 132 (2000): 295–311. Renewed Corinthian pressure on Megara before 464: Plut. *Cim.* 17.2, Thuc. 1.103.4. At a less serious level, there may have been tension all along: Plut. *Mor.* 295b–c. For an overview, see *IACP* no. 225.

20. Pausanias' pledge to the Plataeans: Thuc. 2.71.2–4.

21. Arimnestus or Aeimnestus commands Plataeans at Marathon and Plataea: Paus. 9.4.1–2. Scouts out Pantassa ridge with Aristeides: Plut. *Arist.* 11.5–8. Plataean bearing this name present with the Spartans at the battle of Plataea: Hdt. 9.72.2. Brings down Mardonius: 9.64.2. It is, of course, conceivable that in 479 there were two men at the battle who bore the pertinent name—the one, a Spartiate; and the other, a Plataean—that they shared a name because they were hereditary guest-friends and that it was the Spartiate who killed Mardonius, as Gabriel Herman, "Epimenides and the Question of Omissions in Thucydides," *CQ* n.s. 39:1 (1989): 83–93 (at 92–93), suggests. But with William of Ockham I think it imprudent to multiply entities.

22. Arimnestus or Aeimnestus *próxenos* of the Lacedaemonians at Plataea: Thuc. 3.52.4 with George L. Huxley, "Two Notes on Herodotos," *GRBS* 4:1 (1963): 5–8 (at 5–7). One-third of the adult male Plataeans march to Lacedaemon's defense: Thuc. 3.54.8. Arimnestus or Aeimnestus and the three hundred killed in Messenia: Hdt. 9.64.2.

23. Help from Athens: Thuc. 1.102.1–2; Xen. *Hell.* 6.5.33; Diod. 11.64.2; Plut. *Cim.* 16.8–10; Paus. 1.29.8, 4.24.5–6; Just. *Epit.* 3.6.2.

24. Pericleidas' request: Ion of Chios F107 (Leurini) = *FGrH* 392 F14 ap. Plut. *Cim.* 16.8 with Ar. *Lys.* 1137–44. His status and his son's name: Thuc. 4.119.2 with Ste. Croix, *OPW*, 182, n. 52.

25. Ephialtes' argument against aiding Lacedaemon: Plut. *Cim.* 16.9. Unimpeachable honesty: Dem. 23.205; Arist. *Ath. Pol.* 25.1; Plut. *Cim.* 10.8; Ael. *VH* 2.43, 11.9, 13.39. Reason to suppose longtime ally of Themistocles: Chapter 3, note 40, above.

26. Cimon argues for aiding Lacedaemon: Ion of Chios F107 (Leurini) = *FGrH* 392 F14 ap. Plut. *Cim.* 16.9–10. Leads four thousand hoplites to Lacedaemon: Ar. *Lys.* 1143–44. *Proxenía* of Lacedaemon hereditary within the family of Callias: Xen. *Hell.* 6.3.4. Ion of Chios as friend and admirer of Cimon: Chapter 2, note 40, above.

27. Xerxes has bridges built to span the Strymon at Ennea Hodoi: Hdt. 7.24, 114.1. Extensive remains of ancient bridge, discovered by Dimitrios Lazaridis when he excavated Amphipolis, dates back to archaic period: Y. Maniatis et al., "Radiocarbon Dating of the Amphipolis Bridge in Northern Greece, Maintained and Functioned for 2500 Years," *Radiocarbon* 52:1 (2010): 41–63.

Histiaeus' fort: Hdt. 5.11.2, 23–24. Athens and allies send colony: Thuc. 1.100.3, 4.102.2. For the likely location of the settlement established at this time at Ennea Hodoi, see W. Kendrick Pritchett, "Thucydides' Pentekontaetia: 6. Drabeskos," in Pritchett, *Thucydides' Pentekontaetia and Other Essays* (Leiden: Brill, 1995), 94–122 (at 102–5).

28. Massacre at Drabeskos near the gold mines in the valley of Daton: consider Hdt. 9.75; Thuc. 1.100.3 (where, against the judgment of Gomme, *HCT*, I 296–97, and *ATL*, III 106–10, 258–59, I follow the textual reading of Lorenzo Valla, recently defended by Hornblower, *CT*, I 155–56); Diod. 11.70.5, 12.68.2; and Paus. 1.29.4–5 in light of Strabo 7 F33–36; and, for the location, see Pritchett, "Thucydides' Pentekontaetia: 6. Drabeskos," 102–21. To calculate the date of the disaster (465/4), one need only compare Thuc. 4.100.2–102.4 with Diod. 12.32.1 and 3 and Schol. Aesch. 2.31. The scholiast appears to have named Lysikrates as the archon in the year when the colony was destroyed where he should have mentioned Lysitheos, who was archon in 465/4: see *ATL*, III 176, n. 57, 179–80. Cf., however, Ernst Badian, "Toward a Chronology of the Pentecontaetia down to the Renewal of the Peace of Callias," *EMC* 32 n.s. 7:3 (1988): 289–320 (at 298–300), reprinted (with added material concerning the location of Drabeskos) in Badian, *FPP*, 73–107 (at 81–86), who thinks the scholiast correct, with Pritchett, "Thucydides' Pentekontaetia: 6. Drabeskos," 100–102. Manuscripts differ as to whether Isoc. 8.86 refers to a loss of ten thousand hoplites in the Deceleian War or to such a loss at Daton. Aristotle's observation: Arist. *Ath. Pol.* 26.1 with Rhodes, *CAAP*, 326–28. Commemoration of the dead: Paus. 1.29.4–5 with *IG* I³ 1144 and 1146, on which see Donald W. Bradeen, "The Casualty List of 464 B.C.," *Hesperia* 36:3 (July–September 1967): 321–28, and Pritchett, *GSAW*, IV 178–80. Institution of the practice of civic burial as an annual event: Paus. 1.29.4 as interpreted by Felix Jacoby, "*Patrios Nomos*: State Burial in Athens and the Public Cemetery at the Kerameikos," *JHS* 64 (1944): 37–66, reprinted in Jacoby, *Abhandlungen zur griechischen Geschichtschreibung*, ed. Herbert Bloch (Leiden: E. J. Brill, 1956), 260–315. In this connection, see Polly Low, "Commemoration of the War Dead in Classical Athens: Remembering Defeat and Victory," in *War, Democracy and Culture in Classical Athens*, ed. David M. Pritchard (Cambridge: Cambridge University Press, 2010), 341–58, and Nathan T. Arrington, *Ashes, Images, and Memories: The Presence of the War Dead in Fifth-Century Athens* (Oxford: Oxford University Press, 2014). The word *muríos*—literally "ten thousand"—can be and often is shorthand for a countless body of men: W. Kendrick Pritchett, "Thucydides' Campaign of Tanagra," in Pritchett, *Greek Archives, Cults, and Topography* (Amsterdam: J. C. Gieben, 1996), 149–72 (at 154–55).

29. See Nep. *Cim.* 2.2, where, in suggesting that Cimon founded Amphipolis, Nepos is presumably referring to the earlier colony established at Ennea Hodoi not long before 465/4.

30. Cimon active at this time in the Thracian Chersonnesus, at Thasos, and on the continent nearby: Plut. *Cim.* 14.1–2.

31. Envy directed at Cimon: Nep. *Cim.* 3.1. Miltiades and Themistocles as object of envy: Rahe, *PC*, Chapters 5 and 8. See also Aristodemus *FGrH* 104 F6.1. Cultural hegemony of Homer: Pl. *Resp.* 10.606e. Cf. Hdt. 2.53 with Hes. *Theog.* 108–15, and see Hdt. 1.131. See also Xenophanes *Vorsokr.*⁶ 21 B14–16 and Arist. *Pol.* 1252b24–27.

32. Scurrilous talk about Cimon: Eupolis F221 (PCG) ap. Plut. *Cim.* 15.3–4. Sexually voracious: 4.6–9. Political role played by Elpinike: 14.5, *Per.* 10.5. Note Ath. 13.589e-f.

33. Charge against Cimon: Plut. *Cim.* 14.3. Alexander as Athens' benefactor and *próxenos*: Chapter 2, note 16, above. Seizure of Strymon basin: consider Strabo 7 F11 in light of Hdt. 8.121.2 and [Dem.] 12.20–21 (which should be read with 23.200), and see Nicholas G. L. Hammond and Guy T. Griffith, *A History of Macedonia II: 550–336 B.C.* (Oxford: Clarendon Press, 1979), 98–104. Resources in Strymon basin: Chapter 1, note 44, above.

34. Importance of Pericles' background: Thomas R. Martin, *Pericles: A Biography in Context* (Cambridge: Cambridge University Press, 2016), 1–98. Significance of Pericles' service as *chorēgós* for Aeschylus' *Persians*: Chapter 2, note 20, above, with Samons, *PCH*, 66–68. Pericles' prosecution of Cimon: Arist. *Ath. Pol.* 27.1; Plut. *Cim.* 14.3–5, *Per.* 10.6, with Rhodes, *CAAP*, 335–36, and Edwin M. Carawan, "*Eisangelia* and *Euthyna*: The Trials of Miltiades, Themistocles, and Cimon," *GRBS* 28:2 (Summer 1987): 167–208 (esp. 190–91, 201–5). Alignment with Ephialtes: cf. Fornara/ Samons, *ACP*, 25–28, who treat the ancient sources with a measure of skepticism that seems to me

unjustified, with Podlecki, *PHC*, 46–54. On Pericles' caution in these circumstances, see Kagan, *Outbreak*, 62–67.

35. Cimon's defense and acquittal: Plut. *Cim.* 14.4, 15.1. Cf. Dem. 23.205, which is sometimes taken as evidence that Cimon was on this occasion fined: see, for example, Antony E. Raubitschek, "Theophrastos on Ostracism," *CM* 19 (1958): 73–109 (at 91, n. 7), reprinted in Raubitschek, *SH*, 81–107 (at 94, n. 7).

36. First, Dipaea; then, a victory over the Messenians at "the isthmus" or, if the passage requires emendation, as some suppose, "at Ithome": Hdt. 9.33–35. Second Lacedaemonian request for Athenian help: Plut. *Cim.* 17.3. The fact that Thucydides, Diodorus Siculus, and Pausanias mention only the Athenian expedition against Ithome reflects the abbreviated and narrowly focused character of their reports and does not tell against Plutarch's more elaborate account. Moreover, as George A. Papantoniou, "One or Two?" *AJPh* 72:2 (1951): 176–81, points out, the testimony of Ion of Chios, Aristophanes, and Critias, which Plutarch cites, refers to a time when Lacedaemon's very existence was at stake and not to the mopping-up operation later attempted at Ithome. Thucydides, Diodorus, and Pausanias are interested chiefly in the Lacedaemonians' failure to deliver on their promise to the Thasians and on Athens' ultimate breach with Sparta, which is why they focus narrowly on the earthquake and the expedition to Ithome and ignore the first of the two expeditions that Cimon led in support of Lacedaemon. See also Nicholas G. L. Hammond, "Studies in Greek Chronology of the Sixth and Fifth Centuries B.C.," *Historia* 4:4 (1955): 371–411 (at 376–79), and note Badian, "Toward a Chronology of the Pentecontaetia down to the Renewal of the Peace of Callias," 304–6, reprinted in Badian, *FPP*, 89–92. For a different view of Cimon's whereabouts after the defeat of the Thasian fleet and the investment of Thasos, see Victor Parker, "The Chronology of the Pentecontaetia from 465 to 456," *Athenaeum* 81 (1993): 129–47 (at 131–33), who reads more into Plutarch's use of the verb *exepoliórkēse* at *Cim.* 14.2 than is required.

37. Guerrilla war: Diod. 11.64.1.

38. The *aspís* and the phalanx: Rahe, *SR*, Chapter 3, where I cite the extensive secondary literature.

39. Spartans seek and receive Athenian help in siege of Ithome: Thuc. 1.102.1–2. Specialists—"select men"—sent: Paus. 1.29.8.

40. Artaxerxes' elevation and consolidation of power: Ctesias F13.33–F14.35; Diod. 11.69, 71.1–2; Plut. *Them.* 29.4–5, 31.3–5, *Art.* 4.1, *Mor.* 173d–e; Joseph. *AJ* 11.185 with Briant, *CA*, 569–73. Callias' embassy: Hdt. 7.151. The fact that the Argives were in Susa at the same time, asking whether the close friendship that they had established with Xerxes still remained firm (7.151 with Matt Waters, "Earth, Water, and Friendship with the King: Argos and Persia in the Mid-Fifth Century," in *Extraction and Control: Studies in Honor of Matthew W. Stolper*, ed. Michael Kozuh [Chicago: Oriental Institute, 2014], 331–36), strongly suggests that Callias' visit took place in the first year after Artaxerxes came to power, as diplomatic propriety will have dictated: cf. Fornara/Samons, *ACP*, 174–75, with Peter Green, "Commentary," in *DS*, 140–41, n. 273. Persian court and customary gifts: Ath. 6.229f.

41. Evidence Artaxerxes' policy at odds with that of Xerxes: Kamyar Abdi, "The Passing of the Throne from Xerxes to Artaxerxes I, or How an Archaeological Observation Can Be a Potential Contribution to Achaemenid Historiography," in *The World of Achaemenid Persia: History, Art and Society in Iran and the Ancient Near East*, ed. John Curtis and St. John Simpson (London: I. B. Tauris, 2010), 275–84. Callias fined: Dem. 19.273–75. I agree with Derek J. Mosley, "Callias' Fine," *Mnemosyne*, 4th ser. 26:1 (1973): 57–58, on the timing of and occasion for the imposition of a fine on Callias but not with regard to the date of the original agreement with Persia.

42. Surrender of Thasos: Thuc. 1.101.3. Spartan offer to Thasos: Thuc. 1.101.1–2. I see no reason to dismiss Thucydides' testimony in this regard. But there are those who think him—wrongly, in my opinion—an Athenian partisan apt to lie for the purpose of making his compatriots look good, and at least some of them think the notion that Lacedaemon was ready to side with Thasos implausible: see Chapter 3, note 15, above. Cf. Kagan, *Outbreak*, 61–62, and Ste. Croix, *OPW*, 178–80, who make neither error but do fail to properly consider when the news about Sparta's offer is likely to have come to light.

43. Ephialtic reform: consider Arist. *Ath. Pol.* 3.6, 8.4, 25, 35.2, 41.2, 43.4, 45.2–3, 47.1, 48.2–5, 49.5, 54.2, 55.2–4, *Pol.* 1274a7–8; Philochoros *FGrH* 326 F64; Plut. *Sol.* 19.2, *Cim.* 15.2–3, *Per.* 9.5, 10.7–8, *Mor.* 805d, 812d, in light of Rhodes, *CAAP,* 311–22; Martin Ostwald, *From Popular Sovereignty to the Sovereignty of Law* (Berkeley: University of California Press, 1986), 3–83, 179–81, "The Reform of the State by Cleisthenes," in *CAH* IV² 303–46 (esp. 329–32), and "The Areopagus in the *Athēnaiōn Politeía,*" in *Aristote et Athènes / Aristoteles and Athens,* ed. Marcel Piérart (Paris: de Boccard, 1993), 139–53; Carawan, "*Eisangelia* and *Euthyna,*" 167–208; George L. Cawkwell, "*NOMOPHYLAKIA* and the Areopagus," *JHS* 108 (1988): 1–12, reprinted in Cawkwell, *CC,* 114–33; Robert W. Wallace, *The Areopagos Council, to 307 B.C.* (Baltimore: Johns Hopkins University Press, 1989), passim (esp. 70–93); Tracey E. Rihll, "Democracy Denied: Why Ephialtes Attacked the Areiopagus," *JHS* 115 (1995): 87–98, which should be read in conjunction with Lindsay G. H. Hall, "Ephialtes, the Areopagus and the Thirty," *CQ* n.s. 40:2 (1990): 319–28; and Kurt A. Raaflaub, "The Breakthrough of *Dēmokratia* in Mid-Fifth-Century Athens," in *Origins of Democracy in Ancient Greece,* ed. Kurt A. Raaflaub, Josiah Ober, and Robert W. Wallace (Berkeley: University of California Press, 2007), 105–54. Note Xenophon's playful allusion confirming what the later sources have to say concerning the role played by Pericles: *Mem.* 3.5.19–21. For a far more thorough survey of the evidence, the secondary literature, and the issues in dispute than is appropriate here, see Podlecki, *PHC,* 48–53.

44. Spartans nervous, fear Athenian defection to the Messenians, send Cimon and his soldiers home: Thuc. 1.102.3; Diod. 11.64.2; Plut *Cim.* 17.3; Paus. 1.29.8–9, 4.24.6–7; Just. *Epit.* 3.6.3. I see no reason to question Thucydides' testimony—which, in context, makes perfect sense, as I have tried to show above—and I find it very hard to believe that, at a time when they were themselves facing a helot rebellion, the Spartans managed to get worked up about the Ephialtic reform at Athens. Cf. John R. Cole, "Cimon's Dismissal, Ephialtes' Revolution and the Peloponnesian Wars," *GRBS* 15:4 (1974): 369–85; Rhodes, *CAAP,* 311; Fornara/Samons, *ACP,* 127–29; and Samons, *PCH,* 78–81, with Philip Deane, *Thucydides' Dates, 465–431 B.C.* (Don Mills, Ontario: Longman Canada, 1972), 18–22. Critias' judgment of Cimon: Critias B52 (D–K) ap. Plut. *Cim.* 16.9. Cf. Lendon, *SoW,* esp. 51–55, who rejects Thucydides' testimony that the Lacedaemonians had offered help to Thasos and who traces the breach between Sparta and Athens that took place at this time solely to Athenian pique.

45. Cimon tries, fails to overturn Ephialtic reform: Plut. *Cim.* 15.3, 17.3. Note *Per.* 9.5.

46. Diplomatic revolution: Thuc. 1.102.4; Paus. 1.29.8–9, 4.24.7. Note Thuc. 2.22.3. Cimon ostracized: Pl. *Grg.* 516d, Nep. *Cim.* 3.1. Occasion for ostracism: Plut. *Cim.* 15.3, 17.3, *Per.* 9.5.

47. Alcibiades son of Cleinias resigns *proxenía:* Thuc. 5.43.2, 6.89.2. Ostracism: Lys. 14.39, Andoc. 4.34 with Eugene Vanderpool, "The Ostracism of the Elder Alkibiades," *Hesperia* 21:1 (January–March 1952): 1–8, and Stefan Brenne, *Ostrakismos und Prominenz in Athen: Attische Bürger des 5. Jhs. v. Chr. auf den Ostraka* (Vienna: A. Holzhausens, 2001), 95–97.

48. Strategic rivalry: Paul A. Rahe, "Athens and Sparta," in *Great Strategic Rivalries: From the Classical World to the Cold War,* ed. James Lacey (Oxford: Oxford University Press, 2016), 52–78. See also Karl Walling, "Thucydides on Policy, Strategy, and War Termination," *Naval War College Review* 66:4 (Autumn 2013): 47–85.

49. Athens' control of the passes over the Geraneia between Megara and Corinth was a considerable deterrent, as Thucydides (4.72.1) implies, but it was not as great a constraint as some think: cf. Ste. Croix, *OPW,* 190–96, with Holladay, "Sparta's Role in the First Peloponnesian War," 54–63, reprinted in Holladay, *AFC,* 105–17, and Lewis, *OFPW,* 71–78, reprinted in Lewis, *SPGNEH,* 9–21; then, cf. Salmon, *WC,* 420–21, with A. James Holladay, "Sparta and the First Peloponnesian War," *JHS* 105 (1985): 161–62, reprinted in Holladay, *AFC,* 119–22. Sparta's security environment nearer home the chief constraint: Fornara/ Samons, *ACP,* 129–35.

50. Euripides on Laconia: F1083 (Nauck) ap. Strabo 8.5.6. Laconia as Peloponnesian acropolis: Diod. 14.82.4.

51. Messenia: Euripides F1083 (Nauck) ap. Strabo 8.5.6.

52. Proverb: Strabo 8.6.20. Approaching and rounding Malea difficult and dangerous: Morton, *RPEAGS,* 81–85, 137–42.

53. Corinthian leader on Spartan weakness nearer home: Xen. *Hell.* 4.2.11–12.

54. Athenian descent on Halieis: Thuc. 1.105.1, Diod. 11.78.2. If Dobree and Wyse are correct in suggesting *Halieûsin* as an emendation to replace *Eleusîni* at Is. 5.42—as, I think, they are—the general in charge on this occasion will have been Dikaiogenes son of Menexenos. That Halieis lay in the territory of Hermione is affirmed by Ephorus *FGrH* 70 F56 ap. Stephanus of Byzantium s.v. *Halieîs* and suggested by Strabo 8.6.12 and makes excellent geographical sense. For the strategic importance of Halieis and a highly intelligent attempt to sort out its complex history with an eye to the geopolitics of the region wherein it lies, see Michael H. Jameson, Curtis N. Runnels, and Tjeerd H. van Andel, *A Greek Countryside: The Southern Argolid from Prehistory to the Present Day* (Stanford, CA: Stanford University Press, 1994), 57–85 (esp. 63–66, 69–85). Note also *IACP* no. 349. For a more detailed discussion of what can be gleaned from the literary evidence, the inscriptions, and the archaeology concerning Halieis as such, see Michael H. Jameson, "Excavations at Halieis, History of the Site, and Testimonia," forthcoming in Christina F. Dengate, James A. Dengate, Michael H. Jameson, David Reese, and Charles K. Williams II, *The Excavations at Halieis III:1: The Acropolis and Industrial Terrace,* which James Dengate kindly allowed me to see. The fortifications—both those of the archaic period and those of the classical period—are testimony to the town's strategic significance: see Marian H. McAllister, *The Excavations at Ancient Halieis I: The Fortifications and Adjacent Structures* (Bloomington: Indiana University Press, 2005), 1–84, and Michael H. Jameson, "Submerged Remains of the Town and Its Immediate Vicinity," in ibid. 85–97. In 430 and in 425, during the Archidamian War, the Athenians attacked Halieis once more: Thuc. 2.56.5, 4.45.2. In the aftermath, Halieis accepted an Athenian garrison: *IG* I³ 75, *SEG* X 80, XIV 8.

55. Duration of struggle for Tiryns: Hdt. 6.83. Ultimate Argive victory and destruction of Tiryns: Paus. 2.25.8, 5.23.3, 8.27.1.

56. If I make no mention of the fourth-century Argive inscription, posted by a religious confraternity, prescribing that a festival be celebrated on the seventeenth day of each month to commemorate an occasion in the past when Apollo aided the Argives in fending off a night attack led by a certain Pleistarchus, it is because it is now clear that the Pleistarchus in question was not the son of Leonidas, but was, instead, the brother of the Macedonian king Cassander: cf. R. Herzog, "Auf den Spuren der Telesilla," *Philologus* 71 (1912): 1–23 (esp. 6, 20–21, and pl. 1), with Wilhelm Vollgraff, *Le Sanctuaire d'Apollon pythéen à Argos* (Paris: Librairie philosophique J. Vrin, 1956), 79–84. Then, cf. E. David Francis and Michael Vickers, "Argive Oenoe," *AC* 54 (1985): 105–15 (at 109–10), with Marcel Piérart, "Note sur l'alliance entre Athènes et Argos au cours de la première guerre du Péloponnèse: À propos de Thucydide I 107–108," *MH* 44 (1987): 175–80.

57. Battle of Oenoe: Paus. 1.15.1, 10.10.3–4. Location: Paus. 2.25.1–3, 8.6.4–6 with W. Kendrick Pritchett, "The Routes over the Prinos and Klimax Passes," in *SAGT*, III 1–53 (esp. 2–12, 31–51)—as corrected in W. Kendrick Pritchett, "The 'Disputed' Sites of J. E. and F. E. Winter," in *SAGT*, VII 205–26 (at 222–26). In this connection, note Ludwig Ross, *Reisen und Reiserouten durch Griechenland* (Berlin: Reimer, 1841), 129, and see Giannēs A. Pikoulas, "Klīmax (Paus. viii 6,4)," *Horos* 8–9 (1990–91): 279–83, reprinted in Giannēs A. Pikoulas, *Arkadía: Sullogē meletōn* (Athens: Ēoros, 2002), 349–57, as well as Pikoulas, *Tò Hodikò Díktuo kaì Ámyna,* 104–11, 118–25, 288–97, and Yanis (Giannēs) A. Pikoulas, "The Road-Network of Arkadia," in *DAA*, 248–319 (esp. 258–61, 272, 274–80). The argument in favor of emending Pausanias' text and replacing Oeonoe with Orneai later articulated by Pritchett does not, in my opinion, survive the application of Ockham's razor: cf., however, W. Kendrick Pritchett, "The Alleged Battle of Oinoa," in Pritchett, *Essays in Greek History* (Amsterdam: J. C. Gieben, 1994), 1–25.

58. Wagon road stretching from Argos to Lerna, then Hysiae, and on to Tegea, Caryae, and Lacedaemon: Paus. 2.24.5–7, 8.6.4, 54.5–7 with W. Kendrick Pritchett, "The Road from Argos to Hysiai via Kenchreai," and "The Road from Tegea to Hysiai," in *SAGT*, III 54–101, and "The Tegea-Hysiai Roads," in *SAGT*, VI 107–11; and Giannēs A. Pikoulas, *Tò Hodikò Díktuo tês Lakōnýkēs* (Athens: Ēoros, 2012), 54–97. For overviews, in which the significance of transport by carts is highlighted, see Pritchett, "Ancient Greek Roads," in *SAGT*, III 143–96; Yannis (Giannēs) A. Pikoulas, "Traveling by Land in Ancient Greece," in *Travel, Geography and Culture in Ancient Greece,*

Egypt, and the Near East, ed. Colin E. P. Adams and James Roy (Oxford: Oxbow Books, 2007), 78–87; and Lolos, *Land of Sikyon,* 93–98, 176–79. Note also Yannis A. Lolos, "Greek Roads: A Commentary on the Ancient Terms," *Glotta* 79:1–4 (2003): 137–74. Road through Oenoe difficult and inconvenient but quite plausible as a route when the road through Tegea closed: cf. Antony Andrewes, "Could There Have Been a Battle at Oinoe?" in *Essays in Honour of C. E. Stevens on His Seventieth Birthday,* ed. Barbara M. Levick (Farnborough, Hants.: Gregg International, 1975), 9–15 (at 11–13), with Johan Henrik Schreiner, *Hellanikos, Thukydides and the Era of Kimon* (Aarhus: University of Aarhus Press, 1997), 30–33.

59. Cf. Lilian H. Jeffery, "The Battle of Oinoe in the Stoa Poikile: A Problem in Greek Art and History," *ABSA* 60 (1965): 41–57, who cites the earlier scholarship and has much of value to say concerning the battle and its larger context, with Meiggs, *AE,* 95–97, 469–72; Jan Bollansée, "The Battle of Oinoe in the Stoa Poikile: A Fake Jewel in the Fifth-Century Crown?" *AncSoc* 22 (1991): 91–126; and Robert D. Luginbill, "The Battle of Oinoe, the Painting in the Stoa Poikile, and Thucydides' Silence," *Historia* 63:3 (July 2014): 278–92, whose dating of Oenoe and whose narratives make better sense. Cf. Schreiner, *Hellanikos, Thukydides and the Era of Kimon,* 21–37, who— for no good reason—denies that Thucydides' chronology of the 460s and 450s leaves any time for Oenoe, and Jeremy G. Taylor, "Oinoe and the Painted Stoa: Ancient and Modern Misunderstandings?" *AJPh* 119:2 (Summer 1998): 223–43, who suggests that there were two battles of the same name that took place in different regions at different times.

60. Monuments at Argos and at Delphi, campaign of construction, Argive games: Paus. 2.20.5, 10.10.3–4 with Pierre Amandry, "Sur les Concours argiens," *Études Argiennes, BCH* Supp. 6:1 (1980): 211–53, and "Hydries argiennes," in *Essays in Honor of Dietrich von Bothmer,* ed. Andrew J. Clark, Jasper Gaunt, and Benedicte Gilman (Amsterdam: Allard Pierson, 2002), 29–32, as well as with Anne Pariente, "Le Monument argien des 'Sept contre Thèbes,'" and Jacques des Courtils, "L'Architecture et l'histoire d'Argos dans la première moitié du cinquième siècle av. J.-C.," in *Polydipsion Argos: Argos de la fin des palais mycéniens à la constitution de l'État classique,* ed. Marcel Piérart (Athens: École française d'Athènes, 1992), 195–225, 241–51, and Morgan, "Debating Patronage," 249–57, 261–63. For an overview, see Bearzot, "Argo nel V secolo," 105–46 (esp. 118–22). I doubt very much whether the conquest of Mycenae and Tiryns gave rise at this time to an Argive appropriation of their mythology, as Jonathan M. Hall, "How Argive Was the 'Argive' Heraion? The Political and Cultic Geography of the Argive Plain, 900–400 B.C.," *AJA* 99:4 (October 1995): 577–613, and *Ethnic Identity in Greek Antiquity* (Cambridge: Cambridge University Press, 1997), 57–110, and Barbara Kowalzig, *Singing for the Gods: Performances of Myth and Ritual in Archaic and Classical Greece* (Oxford: Oxford University Press, 2007), 161–78, contend. The sharp contrast that they draw between Argos, on the one hand, and Mycenae and Tiryns, on the other, has little in the way of foundation. Linguistically, if we are to judge by the inscriptions, the three communities in the Argeia were indistinguishable, and there is excellent reason to suppose that Argos was preeminent from very early on and that any cultural appropriation that took place within the Argeia took place in the archaic period: see Marcel Piérart, "Argos des origines au synœcisme du VIIIe siècle avant J.-C.," in *Argo: Una Democrazia diversa,* 3–26, and Matt Kõiv, "Cults, Myths and State Formation in Archaic Argos," in *When Gods Spoke: Researches and Reflections on Religious Phenomena and Artefacts,* ed. Peeter Espak, Märt Läänemets, and Vladimir Sazonov (Tartu: University of Tartu Press, 2015), 125–64 (esp. 126–35, 140–55).

61. As Pritchett, "The Routes over the Prinos and Klimax Passes," 49–51, points out, little weight can be assigned arguments from the silence of our sources regarding incidents of modest importance in a period about which these sources tell us next to nothing.

62. Spartiate Aneristus' seizure of Halieis, Tirynthians find refuge there: Hdt. 7.137.2 (where we are told that the Halieis in question was the one that the Tirynthians settled) with Ephorus *FGrH* 70 F56 ap. Stephanus of Byzantium s.v. *Halieîs* and Strabo 8.6.11, which should be read in accord with the emendations suggested by Wolfgang Aly and Francesco Sbordone, "Zum neuen Strabon Text," *PP* 5 (1950): 228–63 (at 245–46), and by Raoul Baladié in the *apparatus criticus* of Strabon, *Géographie Tome V (Livre VIII),* ed. Raoul Baladié (Paris: Budé, 1978), 167–68. The numismatic evidence and the archaeological excavations conducted by Michael H. Jameson and

others confirm the subsequent Tirynthian presence: note Ioannis N. Svoronos, "Hermíonιlos: Halíeιs Hoι Ek Tιrúnthos Kaì Tà Nomísmata Aútōn," *Journal international d'archéologie numismatique* 10 (1907): 5–34, and see Michael H. Jameson, "A Treasury of Athena in the Argolid (*IG*, 544)," in *Phoros: Tribute to Benjamin Dean Merritt*, ed. Donald W. Bradeen and Malcolm F. McGregor (Locust Valley, NY: J. J. Augustin, 1974), 67–75; Jameson, Runnels, and van Andel, *A Greek Countryside*, 77; James A. Dengate, "The Mint," and "The Coins: Provenances," in McAllister, *The Excavations at Ancient Halieis I: The Fortifications and Adjacent Structures*, 98–140, 154–57; and Jameson, "Excavations at Halieis, History of the Site, and Testimonia."

63. Timing of Aneristus' operation: cf. Jameson, Runnels, and van Andel, *A Greek Countryside*, 77, and Jameson, "Excavations at Halieis, History of the Site, and Testimonia," where the incident is dated to the period of the Thirty Years' Peace or the very beginning of the Peloponnesian War, with Meiggs, *AE*, 96–97, who prefers the earlier date, as do I.

64. Hermione (*IACP* no. 350) later aligned with Athens: *IG* I³ 31. Troezen also: Thuc. 1.115.2, Andoc. 3.3. Note Cleon's keen interest in the latter in 425: Thuc. 4.21.3. Neither mentioned among the cities defending Halieis in 459 against the Athenian assault: Chapter 5, note 6, below. There is no other context in which the operation mounted by Aneristus makes any sense. By 459, in any case, Halieis was in the hands of the Peloponnesians, and the Tirynthian refugees were presumably in residence there by that time.

Chapter 5. War in Two Theaters

Epigraph: Aesch. *Eum.* 976–87.

1. Megara and Salamis: Ronald P. Legon, *Megara: The Political History of a Greek City-State to 336 B.C.* (Ithaca: Cornell University Press, 1981), 122–40. Border dispute with Athens: Thuc. 1.139.2, Plut. *Per.* 30.2 with Legon, *Megara*, 202–3.

2. Athens' alliance with Megara: Thuc. 1.103.4, Diod. 11.79.1–2, read in light of Plut. *Cim.* 17.1–2.

3. Geraneia passes can be closed: Thuc. 4.72.1 read in light of 1.107.3. For a description of these passes, see Strabo 9.1.4 and Nicholas G. L. Hammond, "The Main Road from Boeotia to the Peloponnese through the Northern Megarid," *ABSA* 49 (1954): 103–122, reprinted as "The Main Road from Boeotia to the Peloponnese," in Hammond, *Studies in Greek History: A Companion Volume to a History of Greece to 322 B.C.* (Oxford: Clarendon Press, 1973), 417–46, with James Wiseman, *The Land of the Ancient Corinthians* (Göteborg: P. Åström, 1978), 17–27; Legon, *Megara*, 21–22, 33–37; and Arthur Muller, "Megarika XII: Mégare et son territoire: Routes et rues," *BCH* 108:1 (1984): 249–56.

4. Athens' alliance with Megara, building of Long Walls: Thuc. 1.103.4 with Legon, *Megara*, 181–90. Nisaea eight furlongs from Megara: Thuc. 4.66.3. Cf. Strabo 9.1.4. For its likely location, see Gomme, *HCT*, II 334–36, and Legon, *Megara*, 27–32. Note Hornblower, *CT*, I 105–6.

5. Violent hatred: Thuc. 1.103.4.

6. Battle at Halieis: Thuc. 1.105.1, Diod. 11.78.2. Sicyonians at Halieis as well: *SEG* XXXI 369 with A. James Holladay, "Sparta's Role in the First Peloponnesian War," *JHS* 97 (1977): 54–63 (at 57–59 with n. 24), reprinted in Holladay, *AFC*, 105–17 (at 109–12 with n. 24); Lewis, *OFPW*, 71–78 (at 73–76 with n. 26), reprinted in Lewis, *SPGNEH*, 9–21 (at 12–17 with n. 26); and Audrey Griffin, *Sikyon* (Oxford: Clarendon Press, 1982), 62. The same coalition was active against Athens in 446: Thuc. 1.114.1.

7. Naval battles off Cecryphalia and Aegina, Leocrates and the siege of Aegina: Thuc. 1.105.1–2, Lys. 2.48, Diod. 11.78.2–4. For a confused account, see Diod. 11.70.2–3. For the date, see David M. Lewis, "Chronological Notes," in *CAH* V² 500–501. Cf. Philip Deane, *Thucydides' Dates, 465–431 B.C.* (Don Mills, Ontario: Longman Canada, 1972), 31–45. Leocrates a general at Plataea: Plut. *Arist.* 20.1. Cf. Just. *Epit.* 3.6.6, who attributes to the Athenians a loss at sea against the Peloponnesians at about this time.

8. Artaxerxes' consolidation of power and military buildup: Diod. 11.71.1–2; Plut. *Them.* 29.4–5, 31.3–5; Joseph. *AJ* 11.185 with Briant, *CA*, 569–73. Note Plut. *Mor.* 173d–e, 565a.

9. Cypriot expedition and raids on Phoenicia: Thuc. 1.104.2 with *IG* I³ 1147 = *ML* no. 33 = *O&R* no. 109.

10. Libyan Inaros son of Psammetichus: Thuc. 1.104.1 with Jan Krzysztof Winnicki, "Der libysche Stamm der Bakaler im pharaonischen, persischen und ptolemäischen Ägypten," *AncSoc* 36 (2006): 135–42. Cf. Michel Chauveau, "Inaros, prince des rebelles," in *Res severa verum gaudium: Festschrift für Karl-Theodor Zauzich*, ed. Friedhelm Hoffman and Heinz-Josef Thissen (Leuven: Peeters, 2004), 39–46. Rebellion's initial success: Thuc. 1.104.1, Diod. 11.71.3 with Stephen Ruzicka, *Trouble in the West: Egypt and the Persian Empire, 525–332 BCE* (Oxford: Oxford University Press, 2012), 21–30. The papyrological evidence suggests that the Persians lost control of upper Egypt at some point tolerably soon after 2 January 464 and that they did not regain it for five to six years: Dan'el Kahn, "Inaros' Rebellion against Artaxerxes I and the Athenian Disaster in Egypt," *CQ* n.s. 58:2 (December 2008): 424–40 (at 428–31).

11. Inaros defeats Achaemenes at Papremis, Athens and her allies (notably, including Samos) defeat the satrap's fleet, take control of the river, and assist in the siege of the White Castle: Hdt. 3.12.4, 15.3, 7.7.1; Thuc. 1.104; *ML* no. 34 (with 1988 addendum = *IG* XII 6 I 279) = *O&R* no. 110; and Aristodemus *FGrH* 104 F11.3. For a somewhat different account, see Ctesias *FGrH* 688 F14.36; Diod. 11.71.3–6, 74.1–4, 13.25.2. See Ruzicka, *Trouble in the West*, 30–31. The fact that a Persian eunuch left a graffito at Wadi Hammamat in upper Egypt dated to the fifth year of Artaxerxes' reign (16 December 461–16 December 460) says a great deal about the man's loyalties, but it does not in and of itself demonstrate Persian control: cf. Kahn, "Inaros' Rebellion against Artaxerxes I and the Athenian Disaster in Egypt," 428–29.

12. Loss of upper Egypt: Kahn, "Inaros' Rebellion against Artaxerxes I and the Athenian Disaster in Egypt," 429–30. The fact that Egypt south of Memphis was under the control of Persia or of Persian sympathizers—Kahn to the contrary notwithstanding—proves nothing about the situation in lower Egypt: cf. ibid. 428–40. Nor does this evidence justify preferring the testimony of Ctesias or even that of Diodorus Siculus to that of Thucydides.

13. Peloponnesian hoplites dispatched to Aegina: Thuc. 1.105.3. Note Andoc. 3.6. Victories achieved by the young and older Athenians commanded by Myronides: Thuc. 1.105.3–106.2, Diod. 11.79.1–4, Lys. 2.48–53, Aristid. *Panath.* 155. The sterling qualities of Myronides as a general, service in high command at Plataea and elsewhere, see Thuc. 1.108.2–3, 111.1, 4.95.3; Ar. *Lys.* 801–4, *Eccl.* 303–6; Diod. 11.81.4–83.4; Plut. *Arist.* 10.10, 20.1, *Per.* 16.3, *Comp. Per. et Fab.* 1.2, *Mor.* 345c–d; Polyaen. *Strat.* 1.35.2.

14. Erechtheid casualty list for 459: *IG* I³ 1147 = *ML* no. 33 = *O&R* no. 109. Fragments from another such tribal list for this year survive: *SEG* XXIV 45. Size of Athens' population in 480: Hdt. 5.97.2. Note also 8.65.1, Ar. *Eccl.* 1132–33, Pl. *Symp.* 175e. To this number, one should perhaps add the four thousand cleruchs settled in 506 at Chalcis on Euboea: Hdt. 5.77.2, 6.100.1. Adult male population likely to have reached sixty thousand or more by 431 (a generation after the debacle in Egypt in 454): Mogens Herman Hansen, "A Note on the Growing Tendency to Underestimate the Population of Classical Athens" and "Athenian Population Losses 431–403 B.C. and the Number of Athenian Citizens in 431 B.C.," in Hansen, *Three Studies in Athenian Demography* (Copenhagen: Det Kongelige Danske Videnskabernes Selskab: Munksgaard, 1988), 7–28.

15. Cimon and the Long Walls: see Chapter 2, note 50, above.

16. Theban hegemony at an end, Boeotian League no threat: Diod. 11.81.2, Just. *Epit.* 3.6.10 with Robert J. Buck, *A History of Boeotia* (Edmonton: University of Alberta Press, 1979), 141–43, and Nancy H. Demand, *Thebes in the Fifth Century: Heracles Resurgent* (London: Routledge & Kegan Paul, 1982), 27–31. That the Boeotian League survived in some form seems clear: Moshe Amit, "The Boeotian Confederation during the Pentekontaetia," *RSA* 1 (1971): 49–64.

17. Athenians finish the Long Walls: Thuc. 1.108.3. Construction begun: Thuc. 1.107.1, Plut. *Per.* 13.7–8. Cf. John R. Ellis, "Thucydides I.105–108: The Long Walls and Their Significance," in *Ventures into Greek History*, ed. Ian Worthington (Oxford: Oxford University Press, 1994), 3–14, with W. Kendrick Pritchett, "Thucydides' Pentekontaetia: 7. Thucydides 1.107–108: Athenian Long Walls," in Pritchett, *Thucydides' Pentekontaetia and Other Essays* (Leiden: Brill, 1995), 122–29, and see David H. Conwell, *Connecting a City to the Sea: The History of the Athenian Long Walls* (Leiden:

Brill, 2008), 1–64, who cites the pertinent secondary literature and argues cogently with regard to the timetable.

18. Themistocles on the Peiraeus: Chapter 2, at note 14, above.

19. Purpose to make Athens an island: Thuc. 1.143.5, [Xen.] *Ath. Pol.* 2.14–16 with Conwell, *Connecting a City to the Sea,* 55–60. Foundations twelve feet thick: William Martin Leake, *The Topography of Athens with Some Remarks on Its Antiquities* (London: J. Rodwell, 1841), I 417–20.

20. Doris regarded as ancestral homeland: Thuc. 1.107.2, Diod. 11.79.4–6. Tetrapolis: Strabo 9.4.10, 10.4.6. Lacedaemon, Doris, and the Amphictyonic League: Simon Hornblower, "The Religious Dimension to the Peloponnesian War, or, What Thucydides Does Not Tell Us," *HSPh* 94 (1992): 169–97, reprinted with added material in Hornblower, *Thucydidean Themes* (Oxford: Oxford University Press, 2011), 25–53. Intensity of Lacedaemonian piety: Hdt. 5.63.2, 9.7.1. Note, however, Paus. 3.5.8–9.

21. Duration of helot revolt: Thuc. 1.103.1—confirmed by Ephorus: Diod. 11.64.4. The fact that Archidamus did not lead the expedition to Doris suggests that the reading of all of the Thucydides' manuscripts should be retained. See also David W. Reece, "The Date of the Fall of Ithome," *JHS* 82 (1962): 111–20 with R. A. McNeal, "Historical Methods and Thucydides 1.103.1," *Historia* 19:30 (July 1970): 306–25, and Deane, *Thucydides' Dates,* 23–30, who show that there are no philological grounds for emending the text. Cf., however, Pritchett, "Thucydides' Pentekontaetia: 3. Thucydides 1.103: Numeral," 24–61, who cannot bring himself to believe that at any time in his account of the Pentekontaetia Thucydides departed from strict chronological order. That Thucydides mentioned events in chronological order *insofar as this was possible* seems clear enough. That he chose not to do so on this particular occasion he makes clear, lest his reader be confused, by expressly indicating as much when he specifies the length of the revolt: Fornara/ Samons, *ACP,* 133–35. His overall purpose is to trace the growth of Athenian power. His discussion of the origins of the helot revolt is a digression made necessary because of its impact on Spartan-Athenian relations. He alludes to the end of the revolt in order to dispose of the matter and return to his main theme. See Deane, *Thucydides' Dates,* 18, 22–23; Ron K. Unz, "The Chronology of the Pentekontaetia," *CQ* n.s. 36:1 (1986): 68–85 (at 73–76); and Lewis, "Chronological Notes," 500.

22. Pleistoanax' guardian Nicomedes leads ten thousand Peloponnesians and fifteen hundred Lacedaemonians to defend Doris: Thuc. 1.107.2. See also Diod. 11.79.4–6, who rightly recognizes in Thucydides' phrase "the Lacedaemonians and the allies" the standard formula for Sparta's Peloponnesian alliance; cf. Thuc. 1.108.1 with 3.9.1, 4.119.1, and see Gomme, *HCT,* I 313–14. Nicomedes' patronymic disputed: Thuc. 1.107.2, Diod. 11.79.5. Ten thousand Lacedaemonians dispatched in 479 to Plataea: Hdt. 9.10–11. Likely predominance of *períoikoi* in Nicomedes' force: Paul A. Cartledge, *Sparta and Lakonia: A Regional History, 1300–362 BC* (London: Routledge & Kegan Paul, 1979), 227–28.

23. Available routes: Thuc. 1.107.3 (with 4.72.1). Route from Itea via Amphissa: W. Kendrick Pritchett, "Thucydides' Campaign of Tanagra," in Pritchett, *Greek Archives, Cults, and Topography* (Amsterdam: J. C. Gieben, 1996), 149–72 (at 159–62). Route from Crisa via Delphi: W. Kendrick Pritchett, "The Hypate-Kallion Route through Central Greece. 5. The Upper Kephisos—Delphi Route," in ibid. 207–12.

24. Nicomedes in Doris: Thuc. 1.107.2, Diod. 11.79.6.

25. Delphi: Plut. *Cim.* 17.4. Thucydides' Spartan informants: 5.26.5.

26. Impact on Lacedaemonians of oracle concerning suppliant at Ithome: Thuc. 1.103.2, Paus. 4.24.7. Later Phocian seizure of Delphi—and reoccupation with Athenian backing: Thuc. 1.112.5. On the struggle taking place in these years for control of the sanctuary, see Gerhard Zeilhofer, *Sparta, Delphoi und die Amphiktyonen im 5. Jahrhundert vor Christus* (Erlangen: Friedrich-Alexander-Universität, 1959), 36–45. See also Robert C. R. Parker, "Greek States and Greek Oracles," in *CRUX: Essays Presented to G. E. M. de Ste. Croix on His 75th Birthday,* ed. Paul Cartledge and F. D. Harvey, *HPTh* 6:1/2 (1985), 298–326 (esp. 325).

27. Nicomedes shores up the Thebans: Diod. 11.81.2–3, Just. *Epit.* 3.6.10 with Pl. *Menex.* 242a–b and Kagan, *Outbreak,* 85–94. Cf. Robert J. Buck, "The Athenian Domination of Boeotia," *CPh* 65:4 (October 1970): 217–27 (at 217–21), and *A History of Boeotia,* 143–47, and Fornara/

Samons, *ACP*, 135–37, who reject this testimony, with Demand, *Thebes in the Fifth Century*, 31–35, who suspects that, apart from the order of events, it is apt to be true, and with Johan Henrik Schreiner, *Hellanikos, Thukydides and the Era of Kimon* (Aarhus: University of Aarhus Press, 1997), 75–85, who prefers this testimony to that of Thucydides in all respects.

28. Spartan secretiveness: Thuc. 5.68.2. Tendency to say one thing and do another: Hdt. 9.54–55.

29. Athenian fleet in Corinthian Gulf: Thuc. 1.107.3, as interpreted by T. T. B. Ryder, "Thucydides and Athenian Strategy in the Early 450s: A Consensus of Mistranslations," *G&R* 25:2 (October 1978): 121–24. Size of fleet: Diod. 11.80.1.

30. Routes home likely to be obstructed: Thuc. 1.107.3 (with 4.72.1), Diod. 1.80.1–2.

31. Supposed assassination of Ephialtes: cf. Arist. *Ath. Pol.* 25.4 and Plut. *Per.* 10.7–8, who claim that Aristodikos of Tanagra was the assassin, with Antiphon 5.68 and Diod. 11.77.6, who deny that the murderer was ever identified or found, and Idomeneus of Lampsacus *FGrH* 338 F8, who fingered Pericles; then see David Stockton, "The Death of Ephialtes," *CQ* n.s. 32:1 (1982): 227–28, who questions whether an assassination even took place. There is certainly something strange about the tales later told—for, as Duane W. Roller, "Who Murdered Ephialtes?" *Historia* 38:3 (3rd Quarter 1989): 257–66, points out, although we can catalogue the names of a great many Tanagrans, we know of no one at Tanagra or, for that matter, in Boeotia more generally who ever bore the name Aristodikos. On Aeschylus' testimony and the likelihood that an assassination did take place, see Alan H. Sommerstein, "Sleeping Safe in Our Beds: Stasis, Assassination and the *Oresteia*," in *Literary Responses to Civil Discord*, ed. John H. Molyneux, Nottingham Classical Literature Studies (Nottingham: University of Nottingham, 1993), 1–17. I would regard Sommerstein's argument as dispositive were it not for what Roller, whose work Sommerstein does not mention, has to report.

32. Tale of Agamemnon, Clythemnestra, Aegisthus, and Orestes: Hom. *Od.* 1.26–47, 11.385–464, 24.1–204. That Aeschylus favored the Argive alliance is clear, and it is also evident that, in mentioning the Areopagus, he is commenting on the political reform championed by Ephialtes. Precisely where he stands with regard to the latter is, however, disputed: cf. Kenneth J. Dover, "The Political Aspect of Aeschylus' *Eumenides*," *JHS* 77 (1957): 230–37, with Eric R. Dodds, "Morals and Politics in the *Oresteia*," *PCPhS* 186, n.s. 6 (January 1960): 19–31, reprinted in Dodds, *The Ancient Concept of Progress and Other Essays on Greek Literature and Belief* (Oxford: Clarendon Press, 1973), 45–63; and see Anthony J. Podlecki, *The Political Background of Aeschylean Tragedy* (Ann Arbor: University of Michigan Press, 1966), 63–100, and John L. Marr, "Ephialtes the Moderate?" *G&R*, 2nd ser. 40 (1993): 11–19. Note also, however, Colin W. MacLeod, "Politics and the *Oresteia*," *JHS* 102 (1982): 124–44, reprinted in MacLeod, *Collected Essays* (Oxford: Clarendon Press, 1996), 20–40, and David M. Schaps, "Aeschylus' Politics and the Theme of the *Oresteia*," in *Nomodeiktes: Greek Studies in Honor of Martin Ostwald*, ed. Ralph M. Rosen and Joseph Farrell (Ann Arbor: University of Michigan Press, 1993), 505–15. If we knew more about domestic affairs at Athens in this period and about the arguments deployed for and against Ephialtes' reform, we would be better able to decipher the drift of Aeschylus' drama. Cf. Loren J. Samons II, "Aeschylus, the Alkmeonids, and the Reform of the Areopagos," *CJ* 94:3 (February–March 1999): 221–33, who may be right in arguing that the absolution of Orestes from pollution bears on the plight of Aeschylus' onetime *chorēgós* Pericles, whose mother belonged to a clan once considered accursed.

33. Athena's plea, choral prayer: Aesch. *Eum.* 858–66, 976–87. Athenian dissidents approach Nicomedes: Thuc. 1.107.4.

34. Strategic context explaining construction of Corinthian Long Walls in the 450s: Strabo 8.6.20–25 with Arthur W. Parsons, "The Long Walls to the Gulf," in Antoine Bon, Rhys Carpenter, and Arthur W. Parsons, *Corinth*: III:2: *The Defenses of Acrocorinth and the Lower Town* (Cambridge, MA: Harvard University Press, 1936), 84–125 (esp. 120–21), 282–96. Note also Salmon, *WC*, 180. Bitter Corinthian complaints: Thuc. 1.69.1.

35. Spartan aims from the outset quite likely more extensive than Thucydides reports: Ian M. Plant, "The Battle of Tanagra: A Spartan Initiative?" *Historia* 43:3 (3rd Quarter 1994): 259–74. Cf.

Joseph Roisman, "The Background of the Battle of Tanagra and Some Related Issues," *AC* 62:1 (1993): 69–85, and Pritchett, "Thucydides' Campaign of Tanagra," 149–72, who are correct in defending Thucydides' integrity but, I think, mistaken in supposing that the Athenian historian was right in trusting what his Spartan informants had to say three decades later about the purpose of the expedition.

36. Normal to reduce besieging force after circumvallation: Thuc. 1.65.2, 2.77.1–78.2, 4.133.4, 5.114. Battle of Tanagra: Thuc. 1.107.5–108.2 with Hdt. 9.33–35; Pl. *Menex.* 242a–b; Diod. 11.80; Plut. *Cim.* 17.4–7, *Per.* 10.1–3; Paus. 1.29.6–9; and Just. *Epit.* 3.6.10 as well as Paus. 5.10.4; *ML* no. 35 = *IG* I³ 1149 = *O&R* no. 111; *ML* no. 36 = *O&R* no. 112; *SEG* XVII 243 = *O&R* no. 117A; and *SEG* XXXIV 560 = *O&R* no. 117B. Cf. Aristodemus *FGrH* 104 F12.1. Some Boeotians fight alongside the Lacedaemonians at Tanagra: Pl. *Alc.* I 112c, Paus. 1.29.6, 9. The fact that Pausanias mentions Athenian cavalry losses in this context suggests the presence at Tanagra of Boeotian cavalry as well: see Glenn Richard Bugh, *The Horsemen of Athens* (Princeton, NJ: Princeton University Press, 1988), 43–47, with Pritchett, "Thucydides' Campaign of Tanagra. 1. Numbers," 157–58. Two-day battle: Diod. 11.80, Paus. 1.29.9. For the pertinent documents, see Duane W. Roller, *Tanagran Studies I. Sources and Documents on Tanagra in Boiotia* (Amsterdam: J. C. Gieben, 1989). Cf. David W. Reece, "The Battle of Tanagra," *JHS* 70 (1950): 75–76, and Pritchett, "Thucydides' Campaign of Tanagra. 1. Numbers," 154–59, who exaggerate the number of Boeotians present and presume that they were hoplites. That Tanagra had laid claim to hegemony within Boeotia is suggested by its coinage: Barbara Hughes Fowler, "Thucydides 1.107–108 and the Tanagran Federal Issues," *Phoenix* 11:4 (Winter 1957): 164–70. That the ruling order at Tanagra had gone over to Nicomedes' side or that he had succeeded in installing a regime friendly to the ambitions of Thebes we can infer from the harsh fate meted out to Tanagra by the Athenians two months later: Thuc. 108.2–3, Diod. 11.82.5. Import of Argive presence: Nikolaos Papazarkadas and Dimitris Sourlas, "The Funerary Monument for the Argives Who Fell at Tanagra (*IG* I³ 1149)," *Hesperia* 81:4 (October–December 2012): 585–617 (esp. 600–607). The fact that the siege of Aegina, which lasted nine months (Diod. 11.78.4), was still under way dictates that one assume that the battle of Tanagra took place the year following the initiation of that siege. If one thinks it inconceivable that the naval battles in the Saronic Gulf at Cecryphalia and Aegina could have taken place while the Athenians had a great fleet operating in Egypt, as Deane, *Thucydides' Dates,* 31–45, does, one will date the battle of Tanagra well after 458, as he also does: ibid. 46–62.

37. Spartan victory, strategic defeat: Pl. *Menex.* 242a–b.

38. Thucydides on Myronides' campaign: 1.108.2–3. Note Aristodemus *FGrH* 104 F12.2. The Locrian families mentioned by Thucydides may be the Hundred Houses that apparently made up the aristocratic ruling order of Opuntian Locris and that were expected to supply two maidens annually for a year of service in the temple of Athena at Ilium: consider Aen. Tact. 31.24 and Polyb. 12.5.7 in light of Walbank, *HCP,* I 334, and Arnaldo Momigliano, "The Locrian Maidens and the Date of Lycophron's *Alexandra,*" *CQ* 39:1/2 (January–April 1945): 49–53, and see James M. Redfield, *The Locrian Maidens: Love and Death in Greek Italy* (Princeton, NJ: Princeton University Press, 2003), 85–150.

39. Diodorus' confusion: 11.81.2–3 should be put before 11.80. Rhetorical hyperbole: Antony Andrewes, "Diodoros and Ephorus: One Source of Misunderstanding," in *The Craft of the Ancient Historian: Essays in Honor of Chester G. Starr,* ed. John W. Eadie and Josiah Ober (Lanham, MD: University Press of America, 1985), 189–97. I see no reason, however, to reject Diodorus' contention that Myronides fought two battles in Boeotia. His description of the second is not a doublet of his description of the first. Cf. Buck, "The Athenian Domination of Boeotia," 219–22, and *A History of Boeotia,* 144–48, who doubts the validity of Diodorus' testimony, with Demand, *Thebes in the Fifth Century,* 31–35.

40. Diodorus on Myronides' expedition subsequent to the battle at Tanagra against the Lacedaemonians: 11.81.4–82.4. One indicator of Theban morale in the aftermath is Pind. *Isthm.* 7. The walls of Tanagra were not soon rebuilt: Duane W. Roller, "The Date of the Walls of Tanagra," *Hesperia* 43:2 (April–June 1974): 260–63.

41. Diodorus on battle near Tanagra, on Oenophyta, Myronides' conquest of Opunitan Locris and Phocis, and his invasion of Thessaly: 11.83.1-4. Later date for Thessalian venture: Thuc. 1.111.1. Aristotle on Thebes: *Pol.* 1302b29-32 with Demand, *Thebes in the Fifth Century*, 34-35.

42. Conflicts within Boeotia weaken the Boeotians: Thuc. 3.62.4, 4.92.6. Pericles on the Boeotians: Arist. *Rh.* 1407a2-6. In this connection, see Buck, "The Athenian Domination of Boeotia," 221-23, and *A History of Boeotia*, 148-50.

43. Alliance with Amphictyonic League: *IG* I³ 9 = *O&R* no. 116. For the context, see Meiggs, *AE*, 175. 418-20, confirmed by Peter J. Rhodes, "After the Three-Bar 'Sigma' Controversy: The History of Athenian Imperialism Reassessed," *CQ* n.s. 58:2 (December 2008): 500-506. Cf. however, Georges Roux, *L'Amphictionie, Delphes et le temple d'Apollon au IVe siècle* (Lyon: Maison de l'Orient, 1979), 44-46, 239-40, who harbors doubts. Evidence Delphi restored to the Phocians: Thuc. 1.112.5.

44. Long Walls finished: Thuc. 1.108.3 with Conwell, *Connecting a City to the Sea*, 53-54. Aeginetans surrender: Thuc. 1.108.4 with *IG* I³ 1503 = *O&R* no. 113. Reason to suspect autonomy may have been guaranteed: Thuc. 1.67.2. Nine-month siege: Diod. 11.78.4.

45. Tanagra accorded central place in Thucydides' account of the *Pentekontaetia*: Terry E. Wick, "The Compositional Structure of Chapters 98-117 of Thucydides' Excursus on the Pentecontaetia (I, 89 ff.)," *AC* 51 (1982): 15-24, and Marcel Piérart, "Note sur l'alliance entre Athènes et Argos au cours de la première guerre du Péloponnèse: À propos de Thucydide I 107-108," *MH* 44:3 (1987): 175-80.

46. Trial for treason in absentia and condemnation: Thuc. 1.135.2-3, 138.6; Ar. *Eq.* 818-19; Pl. *Grg.* 516d; Idomeneus of Lampsacus *FGrH* 338 F1; Diod. 11.54.5, 55.4; Nep. *Them.* 8.3; Paus. 1.1.2 with Marr, *Commentary*, 134-35. Natural death at Magnesia: cf. Ar. *Eq.* 83-84 (with the scholia); Diod. 11.58.1-3; Plut. *Cim.* 18.5-7, *Them.* 31.3-32.5 with Thuc. 1.138.4-5, Nep. *Them.* 10.4, and Cic. *Brut.* 11.43; and see John L. Marr, "The Death of Themistocles," *G&R* 42:2 (October 1995): 159-67, and Marr, *Commentary*, 161-67. Recall of sons: Pl. *Meno* 93d; Paus. 1.1.2, 26.4. Tomb near large harbor in the Peiraeus: Paus. 1.1.2 with Paul W. Wallace, "The Tomb of Themistocles in the Piraeus," *Hesperia* 41:4 (October-December 1972): 451-62. Cf. Plut. *Them.* 32.5. See Frost, *PT*, 226-36.

47. Tolmides' circumnavigation of the Peloponnesus, recruitment of volunteers, and campaigns: Thuc. 1.108.5; Diod. 11.84.2-8; Paus. 1.27.5, 4.24.7; Polyaen. *Strat.* 3.3.1; Aristodemus *FGrH* 104 F15.1; Schol. Aeschin. 2.75 (Blass = 78 Dinsdorf) with Cartledge, *Sparta and Lakonia*, 228-29, and Lewis, "Chronological Notes," 501. With regard to the Spartan fleet, see Hdt. 8.43. On Gytheion, see Cic. *Off.* 111.11.49 and Strabo 8.5.2 with *IACP* no. 333. After reading Diod. 11.84.6 and Paus. 1.27.5 regarding the attack on Gytheion, cf. Caroline Falkner, "A Note on Sparta and Gytheum in the Fifth Century," *Historia* 43:4 (4th Quarter 1994): 495-501, with W. Kendrick Pritchett, "Diodoros' Pentekontaetia," in Pritchett, *Thucydides' Pentekontaetia and Other Essays*, 163-71 (at 167), who observes that Pausanias, who visited Gytheion and conversed with the locals (3.21.8), is apt to have known what he was talking about. Distance across Corinthian Gulf at mouth: Thuc. 2.86.3—corrected by Gomme, *HCT*, II 222. Zacynthus: *IACP* no. 141. Four *póleis* on Cephallenia: *IACP* nos. 125, 132, 135-36.

48. Tolmides settles Messenians at Naupactus (*IACP* no. 165): Thuc. 1.103.1-3. For the Ozolian Locrians at Naupactus, see *ML* no. 20. There is an inscription, discovered more than fifty years ago and recently published, that spells out the arrangements under which the two communities shared the *pólis*: *SEG* LI 642 = *O&R* no. 163 with E. Mastrokostas, "Archaiótetes kaì mnēmeîa Aitolías kaì Akarnanías," *AD* 19 B2 (1964): 294-300 (at 295), and Angelos P. Matthaiou and E. Mastrokostas, "Sunthḗkē Messeníōn kaì Naupaktíōn," *Horos* 14-16 (2000-2003): 433-54. See also Adolfo J. Domínguez Monedero, "Locrios y Mesenios: De su cohabitación en Naupacto a la fundación de Mesene: Una aproximación al estudio de la diáspora y el 'retorno' de los Mesenios," *Polis* 18 (2006): 39-73. Note also *ML* no. 13. Both groups of Naupactians appear to have been steadfastly loyal to Athens and hostile to Lacedaemon: no. 74 = *O&R* no. 164. Myronides' earlier seizure of hostages in Opuntian Locris may help explain the willingness of the Ozolian Locrians to welcome the Messenians: see Ernst Badian, "Athens, the Locrians, and Naupactus," *CQ* n.s. 40:2

(1990): 364–69, reprinted in Badian, *FPP,* 163–69. Cf., however, Pritchett, "Thucydides' Pentekontaetia: 4. Settlement at Naupaktos–7. The Ozolian Hostages of 1.108.3," 61–81.

49. Achaeans aligned with Athens: Thuc. 1.111.2 with John K. Anderson, "A Topographical and Historical Study of Achaea," *ABSA* 49 (1954): 72–92 (esp. 81–83). Note also *IACP,* 472–77.

50. Phormio at Naupactus in 429, interferes with maritime traffic in and out Corinth and the Gulf of Corinth: Thuc. 2.69.1. Athenian interest in blocking grain shipments from the west: 3.86.3–4. Athenians blockade Nisaea: 2.93.4, 3.51. Use of Chalcis and Molycreium: 1.108.5, 2.83.3, 84.4, 3.102.2. Location and strategic importance of the former: Strabo 9.4.8 and Polyb. 5.94.7–9 with *IACP* no. 145. Location of the latter: Strabo 10.2.4, 21 with *IACP* no. 150. With [Xen.] *Ath. Pol.* 2.11–13, cf. Henry D. Westlake, "Seaborne Raids in Periclean Strategy," *CQ* 39:3/4 (July–October 1945): 75–84 (at 77–78), reprinted in Westlake, *Essays on the Greek Historians and Greek History* (Manchester: Manchester University Press, 1969), 84–100 (at 88–89); Peter A. Brunt, "Spartan Policy and Strategy in the Archidamian War," *Phoenix* 19:4 (Winter 1965): 255–80 (at 271–72), reprinted in Brunt, *Studies in Greek History and Thought* (Oxford: Clarendon Press, 1993), 84–111 (at 102–4); and Ste. Croix, *OPW,* 216–17, who—misapplying the argument advanced by Arnold W. Gomme, "A Forgotten Factor of Greek Naval Strategy," *JHS* 53:1 (1933): 16–24, reprinted in Gomme, *Essays in Greek History and Literature* (Oxford: Basil Blackwell, 1937), 190–203—expressly deny that Phormio could have done what, Thucydides plainly asserts, he did. As David M. Lewis, "The Archidamian War," in *CAH* V² 370–432 (at 388), observes, when provided with a safe base from which to operate, triremes can without difficulty maintain a blockade. With regard to the obstacles facing galleys and merchant ships intent on running such a blockade, consider Morton, *RPEAGS,* 255–83. Given their aim, the difficulties that ancient sailing ships and merchant galleys had to overcome were greater than those faced by a blockading squadron. Although sailing ships could operate under cover of night on the open sea, it was highly risky for them to do so close to shore: James Beresford, *The Ancient Sailing Season* (Leiden: Brill, 2013), 204–9. Regarding the Corinthians' need for imported grain, note their resort to a convoy: Polyaen. *Strat.* 5.13.1 with Salmon, *WC,* 128–31 (esp. n. 11), 308.

51. Patras (*IACP* no. 239) and Achaean Rhium in 419: Thuc. 5.52.2 with Gomme and Andrewes, *HCT,* IV 69–71; Donald Kagan, *The Peace of Nicias and the Sicilian Expedition* (Ithaca, NY: Cornell University Press, 1981), 78–82; John F. Lazenby, *The Peloponnesian War: A Military Study* (London: Routledge, 2004), 111; and Hornblower, *CT,* III 139. There is evidence suggesting that the blockade instituted during the Archidamian war caused considerable grief: Simon Hornblower, *The Greek World, 479–323,* fourth edition (London: Routledge, 2011), 120.

52. Pointed warning to cities in the interior: Thuc. 1.120.2. Economic leverage exercised by the lord of the sea: [Xen.] *Ath. Pol.* 2.11–13. Cf. Kagan, *Outbreak,* 77–130, 205–316; Ste. Croix, *OPW,* 55–60, 66–88, 181, 186–87, 211–20; Lazenby, *The Peloponnesian War,* 16–30, 40–41, 44–48; and John R. Hale, *Lords of the Sea: The Epic Story of the Athenian Navy and the Birth of Democracy* (New York: Viking Penguin, 2009), 105–7, 154–70, who—though aware that, in the Corinthian Gulf, the Athenians had a capacity to interfere with commercial shipping as well as with naval activity—neglect to consider the possibility that the Athenians had mounted a blockade against Corinth in the 450s and, therefore, fail to ponder the manner in which the Corinthians' experience in that period is apt to have influenced their calculations in the late 430s. Note David M. Lewis, "Mainland Greece, 479–451," in *CAH* V² 96–120 (at 119), who touches on the possibility but does not pursue the matter, and who neglects to consider its potential as an explanation for the aggressive conduct of the Corinthians in the late 430s: cf. Lewis, "The Archidamian War," 370–80, with Rahe, *SSAW,* Chapters 1–2.

53. Abortive expedition against Pharsalus (*IACP* no. 413): Thuc. 1.111.1. Perhaps led by Myronides: Diod. 11.83.3–4 (who may, following Ephorus, have lumped together more than one discrete expedition). Pericles' expedition in the Corinthian Gulf, to Sicyon, and Acarnania; Tolmides preoccupied in Boeotia: Thuc. 1.111.2–3, Diod. 11.85, Plut. *Per.* 19.2–3. Pericles employs fifty triremes: Diod. 11.85. One hundred triremes: Plut. *Per.* 19.2–3. The Messenians at Naupactus may have attacked Oeniadae (*IACP* no. 130) a year or two before Pericles' expedition: Paus. 4.25. Cf., however, Klaus Freitag, "Oiniadai als Hafenstadt: Einige historisch-topographische Überlegungen,"

Klio 76 (1994): 212–38, and "Der Akarnanische Bund im 5. Jh. v. Chr.," in *Akarnanien: Eine Land-schaft im antiken Griechenland*, ed. Percy Berktold, Jürgen Schmid, and Christian Wacker (Würz-burg: Ergon Verlag, 1996), 75–86 (at 78–82).

54. Corinth on Athenians and Spartans: Thuc. 1.67.5–71.7 (esp. 70) with Clifford Orwin, *The Humanity of Thucydides* (Princeton, NJ: Princeton University Press, 1994), 41–43; Paula Debnar, *Speaking the Same Language: Speech and Audience in Thucydides' Spartan Debates* (Ann Arbor: University of Michigan Press, 2001), 30–47; and Seth N. Jaffe, *Thucydides on the Outbreak of War: Character and Contest* (Oxford: Oxford University Press, 2017), 62–76.

55. Athenians on their right to dominion: Thuc. 1.72–78 (esp. 73–77) with Orwin, *The Hu-manity of Thucydides*, 44–63; Debnar, *Speaking the Same Language*, 47–58; and Jaffe, *Thucydides on the Outbreak of War*, 76–101.

56. Necho's fortifications near Pelusium: Donald B. Redford, "New Light on Egypt's Stance towards Asia, 610–586 BCE," in *Rethinking the Foundations: Historiography in the Ancient World and in the Bible: Essays in Honour of John Van Seters*, ed. Stephen L. McKenzie and Thomas Römer (Berlin: Walter de Gruyter, 2000), 183–96 (esp. 185–86, 190–93). Egypt difficult to conquer: Dan'el Kahn and Oded Tammuz, "Egypt Is Difficult to Enter: Invading Egypt—A Game Plan (Seventh to Fourth Centuries BCE)," *Journal of the Society for the Study of Egyptian Antiquities* 36 (2009): 37–66. Age-old Egyptian strategy: Ruzicka, *Trouble in the West*, 4–13.

57. Megabazos' gold not persuasive: Thuc. 1.109.2–3, Diod. 11.74.5–6.

58. Two hundred triremes to Egypt: Thuc. 1.104.2, Diod. 11.74.3. Cf. 11.71.5, where Di-odorus mentions three hundred triremes, and 13.25.2, where a Syracusan reports that the Athe-nians lost three hundred triremes and their crews in Egypt.

59. Samian contribution: *ML* no. 34 (with 1988 addendum = *IG* XII 6 I 279) = *O&R* no. 110.

60. Manning the fleet: Moshe Amit, *Athens and the Sea: A Study in Athenian Sea-Power* (Brussels: Latomus, 1965), 30–49; Meiggs, *AE*, 439–41; and Borimir Jordan, *The Athenian Navy in the Classical Period: A Study of Athenian Naval Administration and Military Organization in the Fifth and Fourth Centuries B.C.* (Berkeley: University of California Press, 1975), 210–40.

61. Megabyzus to Egypt: Thuc. 1.109.3 with Hdt. 3.160.2. See Ruzicka, *Trouble in the West*, 31–33. Mainstay of Artaxerxes, eventually satrap of Syria: Ctesias *FGrH* 688 F14.34, 37–38. Note also F14.40–42.

62. Triremes lost in Egypt: Thuc. 1.109.4–110.3 read in light of 1.104.1–2 and 109.1, Aristo-demus *FGrH* 104 F11.4. Island Prosopitis: Hdt. 2.41.4–6, Strabo 17.1.20, Ptolemy *Geog.* 4.5.9 with Alan B. Lloyd, *Commentary on Herodotus, Book II, 1–98* (Leiden: E. J. Brill, 1976), 187. Island's carrying capacity in ancient and modern times: Hermann Kees, *Ancient Egypt: A Cultural Topog-raphy* (London: Faber and Faber, 1961), 184–89. Likely mode of defense: A. James Holladay, "The Hellenic Disaster in Egypt," *JHS* 109 (1989): 176–82 (at 176–78), reprinted in Holladay, *AFC*, 43–53 (at 44–47).

63. Destruction of relief expedition as well: Thuc. 1.110.4, Aristodemus *FGrH* 104 F11.4.

64. Two hundred triremes lost: Thuc. 1.109.4–110.3, read in light of 1.104.1–2 and 109.1; Isoc. 8.86; Ael. *VH* 5.10.

65. Scholarly incredulity: Henry D. Westlake, "Thucydides and the Athenian Disaster in Egypt," *CPh* 45:4 (October 1950): 209–16, reprinted in Westlake, *Essays on the Greek Historians and Greek History*, 61–73, where the earlier scholarly literature is cited; Pierre Salmon, *La Politique égyptienne d'Athènes (VIe et Ve siècles avant J.-C.)* (Brussels: Palais des académies, 1965), 90–192; Holladay, "The Hellenic Disaster in Egypt," 176–82, reprinted in Holladay, *AFC*, 43–53; Eric W. Robinson, "Thucydidean Sieges, Prosopitis, and the Hellenic Disaster in Egypt," *CA* 18:1 (April 1999): 132–52; Peter Green, "Appendix B," in *DS*, 242–43; and Kahn, "Inaros' Rebellion against Artaxerxes I and the Athenian Disaster in Egypt," 424–40.

66. See Joan M. Bigwood, "Ctesias' Account of the Revolt of Inarus," *Phoenix* 30:1 (Spring 1976): 1–25.

67. With regard to the Egyptian revolt, cf. Ctesias *FGrH* 688 F14.36–38 and Diodorus 11.75, 77.1–5 with Thuc. 1.110; then, see Diod. 13.25.2. Thucydides a child: Charles W. Fornara, "Thu-cydides' Birth Date," in *Nomodeiktes*, 71–80.

68. Pompeius Trogus' incredulity (Just. *Epit.* 3.6.6–7) is rooted in his belief that the Athenians, overstretched, lost a battle at sea against the Peloponnesians at a time when Thucydides (1.105–6), though he emphasizes that his compatriots were short of manpower, has them routing the Peloponnesians and Aeginetans at sea, initiating a siege of Aegina, and defeating the Corinthians on land. Thucydides' poignant choice of language: cf. 1.110.1, which should be read in light of Hornblower, *CT*, I 176, with Thuc. 7.87.6, and note Diod. 13.25.2. To their credit, Holladay, "The Hellenic Disaster in Egypt," 176–82, reprinted in Holladay, *AFC*, 43–53; and Robinson, "Thucydidean Sieges, Prosopitis, and the Hellenic Disaster," 132–52, recognize that the testimony of Diodorus and Ctesias on this question is worthless. Holladay underestimates the resources apt to have been available to the Athenians and exaggerates the number of triremes likely to have been available to Corinth, Aegina, and their allies at this time. Robinson errs solely in supposing that an island that could support more than a million people in modern times could not sustain forty to fifty thousand men in antiquity. Egyptian farms are known to have produced a large surplus. If Prosopitis could support numerous villages, as Herodotus (2.41.4–6) claims, it could surely support the Athenians bottled up there. See Jan M. Libourel, "The Athenian Disaster in Egypt," *AJPh* 92:4 (October 1971): 605–15; Meiggs, *AE*, 101–8, 473–76; and Samons, *PCH*, 107–8. Although David Blackman, "The Athenian Navy and Allied Naval Contributions in the Pentecontaetia," *GRBS* 10:3 (Fall 1969): 179–216, does not directly address the question raised by Pompeius Trogus, the argument advanced in his article suggests the likelihood that, in time of war, the Athenians made sure that they had a sufficient reserve.

Chapter 6. Back to Square One

Epigraph: Charles Louis de Secondat, baron de La Brède et de Montesquieu, *Considérations sur les causes de la grandeur des Romains et de leur décadence*, 1734, ed. Françoise Weil and Cecil Courtney, IX, in *Œuvres complètes de Montesquieu*, ed. Jean Ehrard and Catherine Volpilhac-Auger (Oxford: Voltaire Foundation, 1998–2008; Paris: Éditions Garnier Classiques, 2010–), II 154.

1. Amyrtaeus: Thuc. 1.110.2–3, 112.3; Plut. *Cim.* 18.1–19.2. Thannyras son of Inaros and Pausiris son of Amyrtaeus: Hdt. 2.140, 3.15. On the marshlands, see Briant, *CA*, 575–77.

2. Athenian encroachments in the eastern Mediterranean: Meiggs, *AE*, 102, 420–21. Note Ezra 7:7–8 and Nehemiah 2:1–8 with Robert J. Littman, "Dor and the Athenian Empire," *AJAH* 15:2 (1990): 155–76, and Christopher Ehrhardt, "Athens, Egypt, Phoenicia, c. 459–444 B.C.," *AJAH* 15:2 (1990): 177–96. Although there is no evidence to confirm their hypothesis, I find attractive the suggestion advanced by Littman, Ehrhardt, and John R. Hale, *Lords of the Sea: The Epic Story of the Athenian Navy and the Birth of Democracy* (New York: Viking Penguin, 2009), 102–3, that the Athenians, while involved in Egypt, seized Dorus on the Palestinian coast to use as a naval base.

3. Consider the mention of Ahriman at Plut. *Them.* 28.6 in light of Rahe, *PC*, Chapter 1.

4. Literary evidence treasury moved to Athens on an occasion, not long before 449, when Pericles was in charge and it was feared that the Persians might seize Delos: Diod. 12.38.2, Plut. *Per.* 12.1. Note Diod. 12.40.1, 54.3, 13.21.3; Isoc. 8.126, 15.234; Nep. *Arist.* 3.1. Note also Aristodemus *FGrH* 104 F7. Treasury in Athens by 454/3: Meiggs, *AE*, 109. See Samons, *EO*, 92–106. Contemplation of such a move not long before Eurymedon: Chapter 2, note 10, above. Cf. Just. *Epit.* 3.6.1–4 (which should be read in light of Diod. 11.64.3), who contends, implausibly, that it was the Spartan threat in 461 that occasioned the shift; and note Noel D. Robertson, "The True Nature of the 'Delian League,' 478–461 BC," *AJAH* 5:1–2 (1980): 64–96, 110–33 (at 112–19), and Peter Green, "Commentary," in *DS*, 130, n. 240, 139, n. 270, who point to Diod. 11.70 and 12.38.2 and speculate that discontent within the Delian League in the wake of the Thasian revolt and Athens' breach with Sparta occasioned the shift. If the treasury was shifted to Athens at Pericles' insistence in 454 as a consequence of a Persian resurgence in the wake of Athens' Egyptian catastrophe, as Plutarch and Diodorus claim, it makes no sense to date the Egyptian disaster to 457/6 and the Peace of Callias to 456/5, as Antony E. Raubitschek, "The Peace Policy of Pericles," *AJA* 70:1 (January 1966): 37–41, reprinted in Raubitschek, *SH*, 16–22, does.

5. The memory of this event may be reflected in a confused passage in Andocides—in which the orator attributes to Miltiades the arrangement of a truce with Sparta that was, we know, Cimon's work and also mentions a building campaign aimed at producing one hundred new triremes to replace those no longer seaworthy which had been used in the Persian Wars: 3.3–5.

6. Pericles and recall of Cimon: Plut. *Cim.* 17.8. Negotiations with Elpinike: *Per.* 10.5, *Mor.* 812f; Ath. 13.589e–f. Cf. Fornara/ Samons, *ACP,* 138–39, who refuse to believe that Pericles recalled Cimon and the two reached a modus vivendi.

7. Cimon and his friends at Tanagra: Plut. *Cim.* 17.4–7, *Per.* 10.1–3. Recall for the purpose of negotiating a truce and accomplishment of that in short order: *Cim.* 17.8–18.1, *Per.* 10.3–5, *Mor.* 812f; Nep. *Cim.* 3.3; Theopompus of Chios *FGrH* 115 F88. Andocides' confusion: 3.3. Likely timing of recall: cf. Antony E. Raubitschek, "Kimons Zurückberufung," *Historia* 3:3 (1955): 379–80, and "The Peace Policy of Pericles," 37–41, the latter reprinted in Raubitschek, *SH,* 16–22, and Ron K. Unz, "The Chronology of the Pentekontaetia," *CQ* n.s. 36:1 (1986): 68–85 (at 76–82), with Meiggs, *AE,* 422–23. I see no reason to doubt Plutarch's testimony, but cf. Rhodes, *CAAP,* 339; and Samons, *PCH,* 90–91.

8. Boeotian cities made to pay *phóros: IG* I³ 260.9.9 with Lewis, *OFPW,* 71–78 (at 77, n. 43), reprinted in Lewis, *SPGNEH,* 9–21 (at 20, n. 43), and "Mainland Greece, 479–451 B.C.," in *CAH* V² 116, n. 72. Regime disputes in Thebes and elsewhere in Boeotia a problem for Athens: Arist. *Pol.* 1302b29–32 with [Xen.] *Ath. Pol.* 3.10–11. Getting to the bottom of this is difficult: Robert J. Buck, "The Athenian Domination of Boeotia," *CPh* 65:4 (October 1970): 217–27 (esp. 221–25). Tolmides deals with troubles in Boeotia, installs cleruchies on Euboea and Naxos: consider Diod. 11.85.1, 88.3, in conjunction with Schol. Ar. *Aves* 556 and *Suda* s.v. *hieròs pólemos,* and see Paus. 1.27.5, 5.23.4 (where the rebellion on Euboea in 446 is referred to as the second such revolt); Plut. *Per.* 11.5, 19.1–2; Andoc. 3.3, 9. See also Plut. *Per.* 7.8, Ael. *VH* 6.1, Schol. Ar. *Nub.* 211. Andros (*IACP* no. 475) also a possibility: Plut. *Per.* 11.5. See Meiggs, *AE,* 120–25, and Peter J. Rhodes, "The Delian League to 449 B.C.," in *CAH,* V² 34–61 (at 54–61, esp. 59–60), on the reduction of the *phóros* assessment attendant on the installation of these cleruchies. In this connection, something can be gleaned from Johan Henrik Schreiner, *Hellanikos, Thukydides and the Era of Kimon* (Aarhus: University of Aarhus Press, 1997), 85–97. Troubles elsewhere in Delian League: Diod. 11.70.3–4 with what can be inferred from the absence of various cities from the so-called tribute lists for this time: see *ATL,* II 8–12 = *IG* I³ 259–63 with *ML* no. 39 = *O&R* no. 119 (where this material is published only in part) and the as-yet unpublished Ph.D. thesis of Bjørn Paarmann, "*Aparchai* and *Phoroi:* A New Commented Edition of the Athenian Tribute Quota Lists and Assessment Decrees," dissertation, University of Fribourg, 2007, II 14–23 (with III 3–23), which is slated to appear in revised form as a *Hesperia* supplement; and consider Meiggs, *AE,* 109–26. Persian meddling at Erythrae: *ML* no. 40 = *IG* I³ 14 = *O&R* no. 121 with Meiggs, *AE,* 421–22.

9. Five-year truce: Thuc. 1.112.1. Diodorus (11.86.1), who is no doubt following Ephorus, is confused about the date—perhaps because he supposes that Cimon was recalled immediately after the battle of Tanagra: see note 7, above, and its context.

10. Lacedaemon's motive for making truce: Lewis, *SP,* 62–63.

11. Argive peace with Sparta: Thuc. 5.14.4, 28.2. Note, in this connection, Thuc. 2.9.2, Diod. 12.42.3–4.

12. Cleandridas at Tegea: Polyaen. *Strat.* 2.10.3. Later stature of Cleandridas: note 46, in context, below. Tegea's dogged loyalty thereafter: Thuc. 5.32.3–4, 57, 61–64 (with 4.134, 5.65.4); Diod. 12.79.3. That loyalty's oligarchical roots: Xen. *Hell.* 6.5.6–9, Diod. 15.59.1–4. See Christian Callmer, *Studien zur Geschichte Arkadiens bis zur Grundzug des arkadischen Bundes* (Lund: A.-B. Gleerup, 1943), 86, and Thomas Heine Nielsen, *Arkadia and Its Poleis in the Archaic and Classical Periods* (Göttingen: Vandenhoeck & Ruprecht, 2002), 342–43, 394–96.

13. Cypriot expedition: Thuc. 1.112.2–4; Diod. 12.3.1–4.6; Nep. *Cim.* 3.4; Plut. *Cim.* 18.1–19.2 (with Phanodemos *FGrH* 325 F23), *Per.* 10.4–5; Aristid. *Panath.* 151f; *Suda* s.v. *Kímōn.* Epigram: Diod. 11.62.3 (where the reference to Cyprus shows that the battle in question was not the one fought at Eurymedon, as Diodorus supposes, but the struggle that took place nearly two decades thereafter at Cypriot Salamis): see note 19, below. Cf. Isoc. 8.86 and Ael. *VH* 5.10, who claim that

the Athenians and their allies lost in the battle at sea 150 triremes—a number that would have rendered their victory a crippling defeat. There is no real evidence to support the notion that Cimon led an expedition to Cyprus in 461 (rather than in 451) and that Diodorus' narrative refers to it. Cf., however, John Barns, "Cimon and the First Athenian Expedition to Cyprus," *Historia* 2:2 (1953): 163–76, who cites much of the earlier secondary literature, and see the sensible remarks of Meiggs, *AE*, 124–28. In this connection, note also Eduard Meyer, "Die Schlacht am Eurymedon und Kimons cyprischer Feldzug," in Meyer, *Forschungen zur alten Geschichte* (Halle: Max Niemeyer, 1892–99), II 1–25 (esp. 7–25).

14. Various aims imputed to Cimon: Plut. *Cim.* 18.1, 6; S. Thomas Parker, "The Objectives and Strategy of Cimon's Expedition to Cyprus," *AJPh* 97:1 (Spring 1976): 30–38; and Green, "Commentary," in *DS*, 184–86, nn. 24 and 27.

15. Negotiation of peace with Artaxerxes: Diod. 12.4.4 (with 9.10.5 and 15.28). Callias as Athenian interlocutor: Diod. 12.4.4, Paus. 1.8.2, Aristodemus *FGrH* 104 F13, *Suda* s.v. *Kallías*. Terms of agreement:, Diod. 12.4.4–6; Isoc. 4.118–20, 7.80, 12.59; Dem. 19.273; Lycurg. *In Leocr.* 73; Plut. *Cim.* 13.4; Ael. Arist. *Panath.* 153; Aristodemus *FGrH* 104 F13; *Suda* s.v. *Kímōn.* Timetable: Meiggs, *AE*, 124–55, 456–57, 515–18. Cf. David M. Lewis, "Chronological Notes," in *CAH* V² 501–2. Note, in this connection, Tonio Hölscher, "Penelope für Persepolis, oder wie man einen Kriege gegen den Erzfeind beendet," *JDAI* 126 (2011): 33–76.

16. Cf. John O. Hyland, *Persian Interventions: The Achaemenid Empire, Athens and Sparta, 450–386 BCE* (Baltimore: Johns Hopkins University Press, 2018), 15–34, who labors assiduously to recharacterize Artaxerxes' reluctant acceptance of defeat and his acknowledgment of the limits to his capacity to project power in the Mediterranean as a positive decision predicated on a rational, cost-benefit calculation of the likelihood that the Persian exchequer would benefit from a regime of arms control, with Stephen Ruzicka, *Trouble in the West: Egypt and the Persian Empire, 525–332 BCE* (Oxford: Oxford University Press, 2012), 33–34. If the great-grandson of Cyrus and grandson of Darius abandoned Persia's policy of aggression in the Mediterranean, it was surely not to save money. It was because Achaemenid Persia had suffered successive, devastating military defeats at Salamis, Plataea, Mycale, Eurymedon, and Cypriot Salamis and because Artaxerxes himself had lost heart. The strategy pioneered by Darius and pursued by Xerxes had failed too often to be sustained. Occasional breaches of terms, covert warfare in Anatolia, maintenance of cold peace, nonetheless: Samuel K. Eddy, "The Cold War between Athens and Persia, c. 448–412 B.C.," *CPh* 68:4 (October 1973): 241–58; Peter Thonemann, "Lycia, Athens and Amorges," in *Interpreting the Athenian Empire*, ed. John T. Ma, Nikolaos Papazarkadas, and Robert Parker (London: Duckworth, 2009), 167–94 (esp. 173–94); and Hyland, *Persian Interventions*, 34–45.

17. Polemical references: Isoc. 4.118–20, 7.80, 12.59; Dem. 19.273; Lycurg. *In Leocr.* 72–73. Note also the reference to the Great King's giving up something that belonged to him in Lys. 2.56–57. Theopompus' argument and its defects: consider *FGrH* 115 F153–54, where Darius and not Artaxerxes is mentioned as the pertinent Persian ruler, in light of Gomme, *HCT*, I 331–35, and Angelos P. Matthaiou, "Attic Public Inscriptions of the Fifth Century BC in Ionic Script," in *Greek History and Epigraphy: Essays in Honour of P. J. Rhodes*, ed. Lynette Mitchell and Lene Rubinstein (Swansea: Classical Press of Wales, 2009), 201–12. A few scholars, nonetheless, side with Theopompus: Chapter 3, note 6, above. Most do not: Chapter 3, note 4, above.

18. Mytilenian reference to Athens' abandonment of war: Thuc. 3.10.2–4. Persians excluded from Ionia, fleet barred from the Aegean: 8.56.4. Evidence hinting at prior limitations on the Great King's freedom of action in Anatolia: 8.58.2. Ionian cities unwalled: 3.33.2 with Teleclides F42 (Kock) ap. Plut. *Per.* 16.2, who treats Pericles as the arbiter in this particular. See Hornblower, *CT*, I 179–81.

19. Dedication: Paus. 10.15.4–5; Plut. *Nic.* 13.5, *Mor.* 397f, 724b. Epigram: Diod. 11.62.3, *Anth. Pal.* 7.296, Aristid. *Or.* 46.156, 49.380 (Dindorf) = 28.64 (Keil); Schol. Ael. Aristid. *Or.* 3.209 (Dindorf) with John H. Molyneux, *Simonides: A Historical Study* (Wauconda, IL: Bochazy-Carducci, 1992), 291–300. Cf. Henry Theodore Wade-Gery, "Classical Epigrams and Epitaphs: A Study of the Kimonian Age," *JHS* 53:1 (1933): 71–104 (at 83–87), who thinks that the first four lines refer to Eurymedon and the rest to Cypriot Salamis, with Meyer, "Die Schlacht am Eurymedon und

Kimons cyprischer Feldzug," 9–25; Gomme, *HCT,* I 288–89 (esp. n. 1); Page, *FGE,* 264–68; and Ernst Badian, "The Peace of Callias: Appendix," in Badian, *FPP,* 61–72 (at 64–66), who argue persuasively that the two quatrains are inseparable and that the epigram in its entirety refers to the battle of Cypriot Salamis. Cf., however, Pétros J. Stylianou, "The Untenability of Peace with Persia in the 460s B.C.," *Meletai kai Upomnemata* 2 (1988): 339–71 (at 353–58), and Hornblower, *CT,* I 153–54, who link the epigram solely with Eurymedon.

20. In the 450s, Pericles one among many: Podlecki, *PHC,* 55–76. Thucydides son of Melesias a kinsman by marriage of Cimon: Arist. *Ath. Pol.* 28.2, Plut. *Per.* 11.1 with Rhodes, *CAAP,* 349–51.

21. Archonship opened to *zeugítai:* Arist. *Ath. Pol.* 26.2. *Terminus ante quem:* Diod. 11.81.1 with *CAAP,* 329–31. Juridical definition of *hippeîs* and *zeugítai* in terms of function in war: Geoffrey Ernest Maurice de Ste. Croix, "The Solonian Census Classes and the Qualifications for Cavalry and Hoplite Service," in Ste. Croix, *Athenian Democratic Origins and Other Essays,* ed. David Harvey and Robert Parker (New York: Oxford University Press, 2005), 5–72. Jury pay: Arist. *Ath. Pol.* 27.3–4, *Pol.* 1274a8–10; Pl. *Grg.* 515e; Plut. *Per.* 9.1–3; Aristid. *Or.* 46.192 (Dindorf) with *CAAP,* 338–40; Minor M. Markle, "Jury Pay and Assembly Pay," in *CRUX: Essays Presented to G. E. M. de Ste. Croix on His 75th Birthday,* ed. Paul Cartledge and F. D. Harvey, *HPTh* 6:1/2 (1985), 265–97; Stadter, *CPP,* 117; and Stephan Podes, "The Introduction of Jury Pay by Pericles: Some Mainly Chronological Considerations," *Athenaeum* 82 (1994): 95–110. Rate: Ar. *Eq.* 797–800, Schol. Ar. *Vesp.* 88 (where 300 should be emended to 3); Arist. *Ath. Pol.* 62.2. Pay for infantrymen, cavalrymen, guards (and, of course, naval personnel): Plut. *Per.* 11.4, 12.3–5 with Thuc. 3.17.4; [Xen.] *Ath. Pol.* 1.13; Arist. *Ath. Pol.* 24.3, 27.2. Pericles responsible for military pay: Ulpian on Dem. 13 (p. 222 Dindorf = p. 167 Dilts). See Pritchett, *GSAW,* I 7–14; *CAAP,* 303–6; and Stadter, *CPP,* 117–18. Salaried city: Plut. *Per.* 12.4 (with 11.4). Note Ar. *Vesp.* 655–724, Thuc. 6.24.3, [Xen.] *Ath. Pol.* 1.13. For the extent in the fifth century, see Arist. *Ath. Pol.* 24.3 with *CAAP,* 300–309. Note also Arist. *Ath. Pol.* 62.2 with *CAAP,* 691–95.

22. Citizenship law: Arist. *Ath. Pol.* 26.4, Philochorus *FGrH* 328 F119, Plut. *Per.* 37.3–4 with *CAAP,* 331–35, and Stadter, *CPP,* 333–35. Note also Ar. *Aves* 1649–52; Ael. *VH* 6.10, 13.24, F68. Excessive demographic growth is not likely to have been a pressing concern so soon after the losses Athens suffered in Egypt: cf. Cynthia B. Patterson, *Pericles' Citizenship Law of 451–450 BC* (Salem, NH: Ayer, 1981), with Samons, *PCH,* 88–90, 107–8. Massive influx of metics, shortage of Athenian men, need to boost Athenian morale: Josine H. Blok, "Perikles' Citizenship Law: A New Perspective," *Historia* 58:2 (2009): 141–70. For another view, see Alan L. Boegehold, "Perikles' Citizenship Law of 451/0 B.C.," in *Athenian Identity and Civic Ideology,* ed. Alan L. Boegehold and Adele C. Scafuro (Baltimore: Johns Hopkins University Press, 1994), 57–66.

23. Evidence for mass migration to Attica's towns: Ar. *Eq.* 813–15 with Aksel Damsgaard-Madsen, "Attic Funeral Inscriptions—Their Use as Historical Sources and Some Preliminary Results," in *Studies in Ancient History and Numismatics Presented to Rudi Thomsen,* ed. Aksel Damsgaard-Madsen et al. (Aarhus: Aarhus University Press, 1988), 55–68, and Mogens Herman Hansen et al., "The Demography of Attic Demes: The Evidence of the Sepulchral Inscriptions," *ARID* 19 (1990): 25–44. Verdict of nameless Athenian critic: [Xen.] *Ath. Pol.* 1.2–3. Political preeminence of the poor in a salaried democracy: Arist. *Pol.* 1292b41–1293a9. Increased importance of manufacturing and trade: Peter Acton, *Poiesis: Manufacturing in Classical Athens* (Oxford: Oxford University Press, 2014), which should be taken with a grain of salt. Regime change: cf. Robert W. Wallace, "Revolutions and a New Order in Solonian Athens and Archaic Greece," and Josiah Ober, "'I Besieged That Man': Democracy's Revolutionary Start," in *Origins of Democracy in Classical Greece,* ed. Kurt A. Raaflaub, Josiah Ober, and Robert W. Wallace (Berkeley: University of California Press, 2007), 49–104, who argue, respectively, that Solon and those in his generation and Cleisthenes and those in his were the true founders of Athens' democracy, with Kurt A. Raaflaub, "The Breakthrough of *Dēmokratia* in Mid-Fifth-Century Athens," in ibid. 105–54, who (rightly in my opinion) dates the transformation to the time of Ephialtes and Pericles and emphasizes the degree to which the rule of what its opponents with some justice would call the *nautikòs óchlos* distinguished the Athenian regime that emerged at this point not only from its less fully demo-

cratic predecessors at Athens but also from the populist polities elsewhere in Hellas, and then cf. Paola Ceccarelli, "Sans Thalassocratie, pas de démocratie? Le Rapport entre thalassocratie et démocratie à Athènes dans la discussion du Ve et IVe siècle av. J.-C.," *Historia* 42:4 (4th Quarter 1993): 444–70, with Fornara/ Samons, *ACP,* 58–75; David M. Pritchard, "From Hoplite Republic to Thetic Democracy," *AH* 24 (1994): 111–40; and Edmund M. Burke, "The Habit of Subsidization in Classical Athens: Toward a Thetic Ideology," *C&M* 56 (2005): 5–47 (esp. 5–30). In this connection, see Rhodes, *CAAP,* 315–19, and Martha C. Taylor, *Thucydides, Pericles, and the Idea of Athens in the Peloponnesian War* (Cambridge: Cambridge University Press, 2010), esp. 7–134. Salaries central to regime and its foreign policy: Samons, *PCH,* 85–88, 99–100.

24. Potential leaders: Plut. *Per.* 16.3, *Comp. Per. et Fab.* 1.2. Note Plut. *Mor.* 345c–d.

25. Drift toward a common currency: Thomas Figueira, *The Power of Money: Coinage and Politics in the Athenian Empire* (Philadelphia: University of Pennsylvania Press, 1998), 21–197.

26. Invitation to Panhellenic congress, Spartans reject: Plut. *Per.* 17.1–4 with Stadter, *CPP,* 201–8. On the so-called Oath of Plataea, see Rahe, *PC,* Chapter 8 (esp. note 61), with Meiggs, *AE,* 504–7; Johannes S. Boersma, *Athenian Building Policy from 561/0 to 405/4 B.C.* (Groningen: Wolters-Noordhof, 1970), 43–44; and Stadter, *CPP,* 205. Plataeans pledge to tend graves: Thuc. 3.58.4–5. Festival of the Eleutheria at Plataea: consider Plut. *Arist.* 21.1–6, who was especially knowledgeable about matters Boeotian, in conjunction with Strabo 9.2.31 and Paus. 9.2.6, and see Antony E. Raubitschek, "The Covenant of Plataea," *TAPhA* 91 (1960): 178–83, reprinted in Raubitschek, *SH,* 11–15, and Meiggs, *AE,* 507–8. Note Christian Habicht, "Falsche Urkunde zur Geschichte Athens im Zeitalter der Perserkriege," *Hermes* 89:1 (1961): 1–35, who contends that many of the documents of the fourth and later centuries pertinent to fifth-century events were forged, and cf. Ida Calabi, *Ricerche sui rapporti fra le poleis* (Florence: Nuova Italia, 1953), 67–78; Robin Seager, "The Congress Decree: Some Doubts and a Hypothesis," *Historia* 18:2 (April 1969): 129–41; A. Brian Bosworth, "The Congress Decree: Another Hypothesis," *Historia* 20:5/6 (4th Quarter 1971): 600–616; and Adrian Tronson, "The History and Mythology of 'Pericles' Panhellenic Congress' in Plutarch's Life of Pericles 17," *EMC* 44, n.s. 19:3 (2000): 359–93, who harbor doubts regarding the authenticity of the so-called Congress Decree, with Henry Theodore Wade-Gery, "The Question of Tribute in 449–448 B.C.," *Hesperia* 14:3 (July–September 1945): 212–29; *ATL,* III 279–80; Kagan, *Outbreak,* 109–16; Meiggs, *AE,* 512–15; Jack M. Balcer, "Separatism and Anti-Separatism in the Athenian Empire (478–433 B.C.)," *Historia* 23:1 (1st Quarter 1974): 21–39 (at 27–35); Shalom Perlman, "Panhellenism, the Polis and Imperialism," *Historia* 25:1 (1st Quarter 1976): 1–30 (esp. 6–13); Guy T. Griffith, "A Note on Plutarch *Pericles* 17," *Historia* 27:1 (1st Quarter 1978): 218–19; Brian R. MacDonald, "The Authenticity of the Congress Decree," *Historia* 31:1 (1st Quarter 1982): 120–23; Stadter, *CPP,* 202–3; Edmund F. Bloedow, "'Olympian' Thoughts: Plutarch on Pericles' Congress Decree," *OAth* 21 (1996): 7–12; George L. Cawkwell, "The Peace Between Athens and Persia," *Phoenix* 51:2 (Summer 1997): 115–30 (at 126–29), reprinted in Cawkwell, *CC,* 151–69 (at 165–68); and Jonathan M. Hall, "Eleusis, the Oath of Plataia, and the Peace of Kallias," in Hall, *Artifact and Artifice: Classical Archaeology and the Ancient Historian* (Chicago: University of Chicago Press, 2014), 55–76, who do not. Cf. John Walsh, "The Authenticity and the Dates of the Peace of Callias and the Congress Decree," *Chiron* 11 (1981): 31–63 (esp. 49–63), who argues for the decree's authenticity but dates it to the late 460s; and Raubitschek, "The Peace Policy of Pericles," 37–41, reprinted in Raubitschek, *SH,* 16–22, who does the same and dates it to the 450s.

27. For an admirably clear and succinct description of the records kept on stone for the years 454/3 through 440/39 (*ATL,* II 8–21 = *IG* I³ 269–72 = Paarmann, "*Aparchai* and *Phoroi,*" II 14–44 [with III 3–60]) and the evidence pertaining to the missing year, see Peter J. Rhodes, *A History of the Classical Greek World, 478–323 BC* (Malden, MA: Blackwell Publishing, 2006), 48–50.

28. Building program: *IG* I³ 436 with Thuc. 2.13.3; Diod. 12.38.2, 40.2; Cic. *Off.* 2.17.60; and Plut. *Per.* 12–14 with Stadter, *CPP,* 145–87. See Boersma, *Athenian Building Policy from 561/0 to 405/4 B.C.,* 65–81; Heiner Knell, *Perikleische Baukunst* (Darmstadt: Wissenschaftliche Buchgesellschaft, 1979); and Antonio Corso, *Monumenti Periclei: Saggio critico sulla attività edilizia di Pericle* (Venice: Istituto veneto di scienze, lettere ed arti, 1986). Cost: Alec Blamire, "Athenian Finance, 454–404 B.C.," *Hesperia* 70:1 (January–March 2001), 99–126 (at 99–101). For the date,

see *IG* I³ 449. Cf. the ingenious reconstruction of the evidence proposed by Henry Theodore Wade-Gery, "Thucydides the Son of Meslesias," *JHS* 52:2 (1932): 205–27 (at 222–23), reprinted in Wade-Gery, *EGH*, 239–70 (at 262–64); elaborated in *ATL*, III 326–32; and defended in one very important particular in Henry Theodore Wade-Gery and Benjamin D. Meritt, "Athenian Resources in 449 and 431 B.C.," *Hesperia* 26:3 (July–September 1957): 163–97 (at 163–88), with the intelligent criticism articulated by Kagan, *Outbreak*, 115; Ste. Croix, *OPW*, 311–12; Lisa Kallet-Marx, "Did the Tribute Fund the Parthenon?" *CA* 8:2 (October 1989): 252–66; Adalberto Giovannini, "Le Parthenon, le Trésor d'Athéna et le tribut des alliés," *Historia* 39:2 (1990): 129–48, reprinted in an English translation by Giselle Glassman as "The Parthenon, the Treasury of Athena and the Tribute of the Allies," in *The Athenian Empire*, ed. Polly Low (Edinburgh: Edinburgh University Press, 2008), 164–84, and "La Participation des alliés au financement du Parthénon: 'Aparchè' ou tribut?" *Historia* 46:2 (2nd Quarter 1997): 145–57; and Spencer A. Pope, "Financing and Design: The Development of the Parthenon Program and the Parthenon Building Accounts," in *Miscellanea Mediterranea*, ed. R. Ross Holloway, Archaeologia Transatlantica 18 (Providence, RI: Center for Old World Archaeology and Art, Brown University Press, 2000), 61–69; then, see David M. Lewis, "The Thirty Years' Peace," in *CAH* V² 121–46 (at 125–26). With Lewis and Loren J. Samons II, "Athenian Finance and the Treasury of Athena," *Historia* 42:2 (1993): 129–38, and *EO*, 25–83, 107–64, and in contrast with Kallet-Marx, Giovannini, and Pope, I am inclined to regard *IG* I³ 363, which records the expenditures for the expedition against Samos in 441/0, as a strong indication that the treasury of Athena—which is known to have paid for that expedition (and for the most part to have funded the building program)—had absorbed a substantial sum from the reserves of the Delian League treasury; and, although I recognize that, in the debates reported in Plut. *Per.* 12, Pericles' opponents had frequent resort to hyperbole, I cannot imagine such a debate taking place if the funds to be employed for the building program from the contributions made by the allies were as insubstantial as these three scholars seem to think. This suggests that Wade-Gery and Meritt may have been at least partially correct in their restoration and interpretation of the so-called Papyrus Decree (Strasbourg Papyrus Graeca 84: Anonymous Argentinensis). The five thousand talents of silver contributed by the allies in accord with the assessment of Aristeides mentioned therein may well have been set aside for the construction of the Propylaea and the Parthenon, which are referenced in the same document. There can be no doubt that the decree was introduced by Pericles, and the argument that Wade-Gery makes regarding the archon date is more plausible than Kallet-Marx is willing to acknowledge. For cautious assessments, see Kagan, *Outbreak*, 115–16 (with 382); Meiggs, *AE*, 155 (with 515–18); Stadter, *CPP*, 146–47; and Podlecki, *PHC*, 167–68. Cf., however, Ste. Croix, *OPW*, 310–11; Fornara/ Samons, *ACP*, 93–96 (which should be read with 176–78); and Samons, *EO*, 139–50.

29. Debate over the use of Delian League funds for the building program, ostracism of son of Melesias: Plut. *Per.* 11–14 (esp. 12 and 14), confirmed in one particular by *IG* I³ 49, with Stadter, *CPP*, 145–87; Podlecki, *PHC*, 86–87; and Samons *PCH*, 91–102. Exploitation of allies a source of embarrassment: note Xen. *Vect.* 1.1, and see Lisa Kallet, "Accounting for Culture in Fifth-Century Athens," in *Democracy, Empire, and the Arts in Fifth-Century* Athens, ed. Deborah Boedeker and Kurt A. Raaflaub (Cambridge, MA: Harvard University Press, 1998), 43–58. Reliability of Plutarch's account, Ion of Chios likely source for report of the debate: cf. William S. Ferguson, "The Historical Value of the Twelfth Chapter of Plutarch's Life of Pericles," *TAPA* 35 (1904): 5–20; Frank J. Frost, "Pericles, Thucydides, the son of Melesias, and Athenian Politics before the War," *Historia* 13:4 (October 1964): 385–99 (esp. 385–92), reprinted in Frost, *Politics and the Athenians: Essays on Athenian History and Historiography* (Toronto: Edgar Kent Publishers, 2005), 278–97 (esp. 278–88); Antony Andrewes, "The Opposition to Perikles," *JHS* 98 (1978): 1–8 (esp. 1–4); and Walter Ameling, "Plutarch, *Perikles* 12–14," *Historia* 34:1 (1st Quarter 1985): 47–63, with Anton Powell, "Athens' Pretty Face: Anti-Feminine Rhetoric and Fifth-Century Controversy over the Parthenon," in *The Greek World*, ed. Anton Powell (London: Routledge, 1995), 245–70. On the date of the ostracism, cf. Peter Krentz, "The Ostracism of Thoukydides, son of Melesias," *Historia* 33:4 (4th Quarter 1984): 499–504, who thinks that it took place ca. 437, with David J. Phillips, "Men Named Thoukydides and the General of 440/39 BC (*Thuc.* 1.117.2)," *Historia* 40:4 (1991): 385–95. In the

late 430s, when Pericles and his sons proposed to pay for the construction of a new springhouse, the assembly thanked them for their generosity, then voted public money to cover the expense: *IG* I³ 49. Incredulity regarding economic analysis: cf. Frost, "Pericles, Thucydides Son of Melesias, and Athenian Politics before the War," 385–99, reprinted in Frost, *Politics and the Athenians*, 278–97; Peter A. Brunt, "Free Labor and Public Works at Rome," *JRS* 70 (1980): 81–100; and Geoffrey Ernest Maurice de Ste. Croix, *The Class Struggle in the Ancient Greek World: From the Archaic Age to the Arab Conquests* (London: Duckworth, 1981), 188–97, who cannot believe that anyone in the fifth century could have conceived of economic relations in this fashion, with Stadter, *CPP,* 153–54, and Lewis, "The Thirty Years' Peace," 139–40. We know that fiscal expertise on a considerable scale was expected of the politically ambitious: Rahe, *SSAW,* Part II, preface. There is no reason why they could not also have developed an awareness of what economic stimulation could accomplish: the fruits were there to be observed in and around the dockyards of Athens. For the materials employed in the building program and the scale and scope of the effort involved, see Manolis Korres, *From Pentelicon to the Parthenon* (Athens: Melissa, 1995).

30. Pericles' propagation of a politicized eros: Thuc. 2.43.1–4.

31. Parthenon: Jerome J. Pollitt, "Art: Archaic to Classical," and Richard E. Wycherley, "Rebuilding in Athens and Attica," in *CAH* V² 171–83, 206–22 (esp. 176–78, 215–17). Legend of Erechtheus' daughter the subject of Ionic frieze: Joan Breton Connelly, *The Parthenon Enigma: A New Understanding of the West's Most Iconic Building and the People Who Made It* (New York: Alfred A. Knopf, 2014), 118–209, 229–36.

32. Pericles and Pheidias: Plut. *Per.* 13 with Stadter, *CPP,* 163–83. Program of pediments and Doric frieze: Connelly, *The Parthenon Enigma,* 76–118 (esp. 95–118), 201–2.

33. Architectural spectacle leads to overestimation of Athens' power: Thuc. 1.10.2.

34. Pericles' exhortations: Thuc. 2.64.3–5. Athenian self-regard: Jon Hesk, *Deception and Democracy in Classical Athens* (Cambridge: Cambridge University Press, 2000); Ryan K. Balot, *Greed and Injustice in Classical Athens* (Princeton, NJ: Princeton University Press, 2001); and Matthew R. Christ, *The Bad Citizen in Classical Athens* (Cambridge: Cambridge University Press, 2006), and *The Limits of Altruism in Democratic Athens* (Cambridge: Cambridge University Press, 2012).

35. Lacedaemon's power apt to be underestimated: Thuc. 1.10.2.

36. Tolmides in Boeotia and on Euboea and Naxos: note 8, above. Cleruchies of this sort were often—and for good reason—deeply resented by the local citizens who were reduced to the status of leaseholders or hirelings: Rachel Zelnick-Abramovitz, "Settlers and Dispossessed in the Athenian Empire," *Mnemosyne,* 4th series, 57:3 (2004): 325–45, and Alfonso Moreno, "'The Attic Neighbour': The Cleruchy in the Athenian Empire," in *Interpreting the Athenian Empire,* 211–21.

37. Duel over Delphi: Thuc. 1.112.5, Plut. *Per.* 21. Cf. Philochorus *FGrH* 328 F34b, who claims that there was a three-year interval before Athens put the Phocians back in charge, and see Gomme, *HCT,* I 337–38, and Hornblower, *CT,* I 181–83. Note also Schol. Ar. *Aves* 556—from which we have Theopompus of Chios *FGrH* 115 F156 and Eratosthenes 241 F38 as well as the Philochorus fragment referenced above—and *Suda* s.v. *hieròs pólemos.* See also Aristodemus *FGrH* 104 F14.1.

38. Pericles' caution: Plut. *Per.* 18.2–3, *Comp. Per. et Fab.* 3.3. Depicted as opponent of land empire: Ste. Croix, *OPW,* 315–17. Boeotian Orchomenos: *IACP* no. 213. Chaeronea: *IACP* no. 201.

39. Chaeronea recovered, defeat near Coronea, evacuation of Boeotia: Thuc. 1.113 (with the scholia), 3.62.4, 4.92.6; Diod. 12.6 (where there is confusion concerning the order of events); Plut. *Per.* 18.2–3, *Comp. Per. et Fab.* 3.3; Aristodemus *FGrH* 104 F14.2. Significance of defeat: Xen. *Mem.* 3.5.4. The precise location of the battle site or, at least, its proper denomination is disputed: cf. Thuc. 1.113.2, 4.92.6 with Xen. *Mem.* 3.5.4 and Paus. 1.27.5. Note Plut. *Ages.* 19.2 with Paus. 9.34.1. No one doubts, however, its rough location. Name of Theban commander: Plut. *Ages.* 19.2. Role of Orchomenizers: Hellanicus *FGrH* 4 F81, Theopompus of Chios *FGrH* 115 F407, Aristophanes of Boeotia *FGrH* 379 F3. Death of Cleinias: Pl. *Alc.* I 112c. Grave: Paus. 1.29.14. Thebans later claim victory as their own: Thuc. 3.62.4. Xenophon concurs: *Mem.* 3.5.4. Note also Thuc. 4.92.6. Cf. Jakob A. O. Larsen, "Orchomenus and the Formation of the Boeotian Confederacy in 447 B.C.," *CPh* 55:1 (January 1960): 9–18, and Buck, "The Athenian Domination of Boeotia," 223–27,

who attribute the victory in the main to the citizens of Orchomenos, with Clifford J. Dull, "Thucydides 1.113 and the Leadership of Orchomenus," *CPh* 72:4 (October 1977): 305–14, who demonstrates the likelihood that exiles from Thebes played a predominant role; and with Robert J. Buck, *A History of Boeotia* (Edmonton: University of Alberta Press, 1979), 150–52, and Nancy Demand, *Thebes in the Fifth Century: Heracles Resurgent* (London: Routledge & Kegan Paul, 1982), 35–40, who concur.

40. Epitaph for the fallen blames loss on local divinity: *SEG* X 410. Statue of Tolmides and seer: Paus. 1.27.5. Theft of war: David Whitehead, "*Klope polemou:* 'Theft' in Ancient Greek Warfare," *C&M* 39 (1988): 43–53.

41. As Buck, "The Athenian Domination of Boeotia," 224–26, and *A History of Boeotia*, 152–62, insists, the neutrality of the Boeotians is a necessary presumption.

42. Revolt of Chalcis (*IACP* no. 365), Eretria (*IACP* no. 370), Histiaea (*IACP* no. 372), and Carystus on the island of Euboea and of Megara, Pleistoanax invades Attica: Thuc. 1.114.1–2. Note also Aristodemus *FGrH* 104 F15.2. The Euboean revolt appears to have taken place in 446 after the *phóros* owed by the cities on the island was delivered to Athens: Gomme, *HCT*, I 340.

43. Athenians respond to revolt by invading Megarid, defeating the Megarians: Diod. 12.5.2. Pythion rescues Andocides and his men: *ML* no. 51 = *IG* I³ 1353 = *O&R* no. 130. See Gomme, *HCT*, I 340–41 and Davies, *APF* no. 828, V.

44. Thucydides on Pleistoanax' withdrawal, Pericles' reconquest of Euboea, the Thirty Years' Peace: 1.114.2–115.1. Note 4.21.3.

45. Details added by Diodorus (12.5.2, 7.1) and Andocides (3.6). See also Aeschin. 2.174, Plut. *Mor.* 834b (with Ruhnken's supplement). Callias a Spartan *próxenos:* Xen. *Hell.* 6.3.4. I do not believe Diodorus' chronology defensible: cf., however, Schreiner, *Hellanikos, Thukydides and the Era of Kimon,* 97–101.

46. Pleistoanax' invasion, Pericles' response: Plutarch (*Per.* 22–23) adds further details. Note *Mor.* 402a, and see Stadter, *CPP,* 225–32. On the age of Pleistoanax at this time, see Mary E. White, "Some Agiad Dates: Pausanias and His Sons," *JHS* 84 (1964): 140–52 (esp. 140–41). Cleandridas an ephor: *Suidas* s.v. *éphoros.* With regard to the bribery of Pleistoanax and Cleandridas, their exile, and Pericles' justification of the expenditure, see also Thuc. 2.21.1, 5.16.3; Ephorus *FGrH* 70 F193; Plut. *Nic.* 28.4; Diod. 13.106.10; Antiochus *FGrH* 555 F 11–12; Polyaen. *Strat.* 2.10.1–2, 4–5; Schol. Ar. *Nub.* 858–59, *Suda* s.v. *déon.* On the grounds for the fury directed at the Spartan king and his advisor, see Lendon, *SoW,* 79–82. Additional evidence for reconquest of Euboea and settlement of affairs on the island: Rahe, *SSAW,* Chapter 1.

47. Puzzle: Gomme, *HCT,* II 76. Cf. Ste. Croix, *OPW,* 196–200, who assumes what none of the sources tells us—that the army which Pericles brought back from Euboea to Attica was at this time safely housed in the city of Athens.

48. Athenians caught in a bind: Thuc. 4.21.3. Euboea Pericles' principal concern: Ste. Croix, *OPW,* 198–99.

49. For this suggestion, see M. Phillipides, "King Pleistoanax and the Spartan Invasion of Attica in 446 B.C.," *AW* 11 (1985): 33–41.

50. Terms apt to have been discussed by Pleistoanax and Pericles: Meiggs, *AE,* 181–82.

51. Chilon's influence: Rahe, *SR,* Chapter 4, to which I would now add Critias F7 (DK). Spartan moderation: consider Thuc. 8.24.4 in light of 8.40.2, and see Rahe, *SR,* Chapters 1 and 2.

Epilogue. A Fragile Truce

Epigraph: Adam Ferguson, *An Essay on the History of Civil Society, 1767* I.ix, ed. Duncan Forbes (Edinburgh: Edinburgh University Press, 1966), 59.

1. Terms of the extended truce: Thuc. 1.35.2, 40, 44.1, 45.3, 67.2–4, 78.4, 85.2, 140.2, 141.1, 144.2, 145, 7.18; Diod. 12.7; Paus. 5.23.4. That the guarantee of autonomy did not extend to members of the Delian League other than Aegina is clear from Thuc. 1.144.2. Cf. Badian, *Outbreak,* 60–67, reprinted in Badian, *FPP,* 137–42, and Cawkwell, *TPW,* 23, 129, n. 11, 133, n. 1, with Tim

Rood, *Thucydides: Narrative and Explanation* (Oxford: Oxford University Press, 1998), 216–19. That a guarantee for Aegina in particular is not unthinkable is evident from Thuc. 5.18.5. Cf., however, Thomas J. Figueira, "Autonomoi kata tas spondas (Thucydides 1.27.2)," *BICS* 37 (1990): 63–88, reprinted in Figueira, *Excursions in Epichoric History: Aiginetan Essays* (Lanham, MD: Rowman & Littlefield, 1993), 255–92, who doubts the Aeginetan claim. One must suppose Thucydides a shameless liar, as I do not, if one is to discount his explicit testimony (1.78.4, 85.2, 140.2, 141.1, 144.2, 145, 7.18.2–3) that there was an arbitration clause: cf. Badian, *Outbreak,* 67–70, reprinted in Badian, *FPP,* 142–44. In general, see Meiggs, *AE,* 182–85, and David M. Lewis, "The Thirty Years' Peace," in *CAH* V² 136–37, who rightly emphasizes the agreement's temporary character as a truce. Cf. Kagan, *Outbreak,* 128–30, who thinks otherwise, with Paul A. Rahe, "The Peace of Nicias," in *The Making of Peace,* ed. Williamson Murray and James Lacey (Cambridge: Cambridge University Press, 2009), 31–69 (esp. 31–59), and "Athens and Sparta," in *Great Strategic Rivalries: From the Classical World to the Cold War,* ed. James Lacey (Oxford: Oxford University Press, 2016), 52–78 (esp. 62–73), as well as Karl Walling, "Thucydides on Policy, Strategy, and War Termination," *Naval War College Review* 66:4 (Autumn 2013): 47–85 (esp. 48–49).

2. Dream of lasting peace: Immanuel Kant, "Zum ewigen Frieden: Ein philosophischer Entwurf," (1796), in Kant, *Werke in Zehn Bänden,* ed. Wilhelm Weischedel (Darmstadt: Wissenschaftliche Buchgesellschaft, 1971), IX 193–251.

3. Homer the educator of Hellas: Pl. *Resp.* 10.606e. Primacy of war: *Leg.* 1.626a.

4. Theft of war: note Thuc. 4.21.3, and consider Lendon, *SoW,* 78–82, in light of Chapter 6, note 40, in context, above.

5. Corinthian impression: Thuc. 1.70.

6. Significance of the growth in Athenian power: Thuc. 1.23.5–6, 33.2, 88, 118.2–3. Two wars a single conflict: Dion. Hal. *Thuc.* 10–12.

Author's Note and Acknowledgments

This book, intended as the second volume in a series dedicated to the study of Sparta and her conduct of diplomacy and war from the late archaic period down to the second battle of Mantineia, has—like the series' prelude, *The Spartan Regime: Its Character, Its Origins,* and its immediate predecessor in the series proper, *The Grand Strategy of Classical Sparta: The Persian Challenge*—been a long time in gestation, and I have incurred many debts along the way. I was first introduced to ancient history by Donald Kagan when I was a freshman at Cornell University in the spring of 1968. The following year, I took a seminar he taught on the ancient Greek city and another seminar on Plato's *Republic* taught by Allan Bloom. After graduating from Yale University in 1971, I read *Litterae Humaniores* at Wadham College, Oxford, on a Rhodes Scholarship. It was there that my ancient history tutor W. G. G. Forrest first piqued my interest in Lacedaemon.

I returned to Yale University in 1974 for graduate study. There, three years later, I completed a dissertation under the direction of Donald Kagan entitled *Lysander and the Spartan Settlement, 407–403 B.C.* In the aftermath, I profited from the comments and suggestions of Antony Andrewes, who was one of my readers, and my interest in Achaemenid Persia, which was already considerable, was increased when David M. Lewis sent me the page proofs of his as yet unpublished *Sparta and Persia.* It was my intention at that time to turn my thesis into a book focused on Sparta, Athens, and Persia, and I carved out of it an article on the selection of ephors at Sparta and penned another in which

I discussed the makeup of the Achaemenid Persian army at the time of Cunaxa, the tactics the Persians customarily employed, and the relative strength of Greek hoplites faced with such a challenge. But the book I had in mind I did not write.

Instead, with encouragement from Bernard Knox during the year in which I was a Junior Fellow at the Center for Hellenic Studies, I got sidetracked. I wrote one 1,200-page work entitled *Republics Ancient and Modern: Classical Republicanism and the American Revolution;* then, three shorter monographs— one on Machiavelli and English republicanism, another on the political philosophy of Montesquieu, and a third on modern republicanism in the thought of Montesquieu, Rousseau, and Tocqueville. In the intervening years, I ordinarily taught a lecture course on ancient Greek history in the fall and a seminar on some aspect of that subject in the spring, and I frequently gave thought to Lacedaemon, to questions of diplomacy and war, and to the work I had once done with George Forrest and Don Kagan. This book, like its companions, is a belated acknowledgment of what I owe them both.

I have also profited from the labors of John S. Morrison, John F. Coates, N. Boris Rankov, Alec Tilley, and the others in Britain, in Greece, and elsewhere who, in the 1980s and 1990s, contributed to designing, building, launching, and to rowing and sailing in sea trials a reconstructed trireme that they named the *Olympias.* If we now have a better sense of trireme warfare than scholars did in the past, it is because of the labors and ingenuity of the practitioners of what has come to be called "experimental archaeology" who devised this project and lent a hand.

I would also like to record my debt to Patrick Leigh Fermor. Long ago, when Peter Green learned that I was interested in the manner in which the rugged terrain in certain parts of Messenia might have facilitated banditry and resistance on the part of Lacedaemon's helots, he suggested that I contact Paddy, who had learned a thing or two about this sort of resistance while serving on Crete during the Second World War. In the summer of 1983, I followed up on this recommendation. Our meeting over a somewhat liquid lunch at Paddy's home in Kardamyli paved the way for a series of visits, often lasting a week or more, that took place at irregular intervals over the twenty-three years following that memorable repast. On nearly every occasion, our conversations returned to ancient Sparta; and in 1992, when *Republics Ancient and Modern* appeared, Paddy wrote a generous appraisal of it for the *Spectator.*

A draft of this volume was produced while I was a W. Glenn Campbell and Rita Ricardo-Campbell National Fellow at the Hoover Institution on the campus of Stanford University, where I received added assistance from the Earhart Foundation, These were invaluable opportunities, and I am grateful for the support I received.

Parts of this book were rewritten in years in which I was teaching history at Hillsdale College. I am grateful to the Charles O. Lee and Louise K. Lee Foundation, which supported the chair I held and still hold at the college; to the trustees of the college and to its president, Larry Arnn; and to my colleagues and students there, who were always supportive. I owe a special debt to Dan Knoch, the director of the Hillsdale College library; to Maurine McCourry, who arranged for the purchase of books; and to Pam Ryan, who handled interlibrary loan. Librarians are the unsung heroes of the academic world, and no one knows better than I how much we scholars owe them.

The fact that I was able to finish this book and its predecessor I owe to Dr. Marston Linehan, Dr. Peter Pinto, Dr. Piyush Kumar Agarwal, and the staff at the Clinical Center of the National Institutes of Health in Bethesda, Maryland—where in the summer of 2012 I was treated for prostate cancer and for complications attendant on surgery and in and after 2016 I was treated for bladder cancer. Had Dr. Pinto not devised a new method for diagnosing prostate cancer, had he not done my surgery with great precision, and had he and his colleagues not found a way to eliminate the lymphocele that bedeviled me in the aftermath, and had Dr. Agarwal not scraped out the cancer growing in my bladder, I would not now be in a position to write these words.

Throughout the period in which this book was written, my four children were patient, and they and my wife kept me sane. From time to time, they brought me back to the contemporary world from classical antiquity, where, at least in my imagination, I may sometimes have seemed more at home than in the here and now.

Index

Abdera in Thrace, Abderites, 90

Abydos in the Hellespont, Abydians, 74

Acarnania on the Ionian Sea, Acarnanians, 178, 191, 208–9, 217

Achaea in the Peloponnesus, Achaeans, 175–76, 178, 193, 208–9, 217, 223, 227

Adams, John Quincy, 7

Adeimantus son of Ocytus of Corinth, 27

Admetus, king of the Molossians, 110

Adriatic, 25–26, 176

Aegean Sea, 3, 14, 17–18, 20, 24–25, 34, 40, 42, 48, 59–60, 63, 73, 79, 83–86, 98–99, 128, 155, 169, 176, 182, 188–89, 194, 197, 201, 208, 217, 221, 228

Aegina in the Saronic Gulf, Aeginetans, 9, 20, 23–28, 63–64, 94, 98–99, 122, 127–31, 134, 154–55, 159, 162–63, 168, 170, 173–74, 185, 189, 192–93, 209, 229

    aid to Sparta during helot revolt, 127–28, 131, 134

    besieged 459/8 by Athens, 155, 159, 162–63, 168–70

    Peloponnesians support with 300 hoplites, 159, 162–63

    episodic war with Athens prior to Persian Wars, 24–25, 28, 128

    loss in 459 to Athens in great fleet action, 155, 159, 163, 185, 189

    made nervous by growth in Athenian power during Persian Wars, 24–25, 128

    relations with Argos change after Sepeia, 98–99, 130

    surrender to Athens on terms: deprived of arms, subject to *phóros*, 174, 193, 209

    tacitly conceded to Athens in Thirty Years' Peace, 229

Aeimnestus of Plataea in relation to Sparta, 131–32

Aelian (Claudius Aelianus), rhetorician, 126, 184–85

Aeolis in and off the coast of Anatolia, Aeolians, 14, 72, 112

Aeschylus, author of *The Persians* and *The Oresteia*, relations with Themistocles, Pericles, and Ephialtes, 65, 82, 101, 137, 152, 166–68

Agesilaus son of Archidamus, fourth-century Eurypontid king, 127

Ahura Mazda, 86–87, 188, 199, 231

Akkad, Akkadians, 58

Alcibiades son of Cleinias, and Sparta, 66, 109, 133, 144–45, 219

Aleion, plain of, 73

Aleuad clan from of Larissa in Thessaly, 49–50

Alexander I, king of Macedon, 7, 62, 110, 137

    conflict with Athens over upper Strymon basin, 137

Amasis, pharaoh in Egypt, 157

Ambracia near the Ionian Sea, Ambraciots, 208

Amestris, wife of Xerxes, 58

Amphictyonic League, 11, 37, 45, 61, 64, 163–65, 173

    Theban membership, 11